WRITING SEMINARS
IN THE CONTENT AREA

WRITING SEMINARS IN THE CONTENT AREA

IN SEARCH OF HEMINGWAY, SALINGER, AND STEINBECK

BROOKE WORKMAN
West High School, Iowa City

National Council of Teachers of English
1111 Kenyon Road, Urbana, Illinois 61801

Grateful acknowledgment is made for permission to reprint the following material. "A Telephone Call to Mary Hemingway" by Brooke Workman, which first appeared in *Today's Education,* September–October 1976. Reprinted by permission of the National Education Association. "Air Line" by Ernest Hemingway. Copyright © 1979 by the Ernest Hemingway Foundation. Reprinted by permission of the Ernest Hemingway Foundation. "On the Blue Water: A Gulf Stream Letter" by Ernest Hemingway. Copyright 1936 by Esquire, Inc.; renewed © 1964 by Mary Hemingway. Reprinted by permission. "*Catcher* Comes of Age" by Adam Moss. Reprinted from *Esquire* (December 1981). Copyright © 1981 by Esquire Publishing Inc. Used by permission.

Part I of this book, In Search of Ernest Hemingway, though slightly revised and updated herein, appeared previously as *In Search of Ernest Hemingway: A Model for Teaching a Literature Seminar* (Urbana, Ill.: NCTE, 1979).

Book Design: Tom Kovacs

NCTE Stock Number 58862

Library of Congress Cataloging in Publication Data

Workman, Brooke, 1933–
    Writing seminars in the content area.

    Includes bibliographies.
    1. American fiction—20th century—Study and
teaching.   2. Hemingway, Ernest, 1899–1961—Study and
teaching.   3. Salinger, J. D. (Jerome David),
1919-   —Study and teaching.   4. Steinbeck, John,
1902–1968—Study and teaching.   I. Title.
PS44.W67   1983   813'.5'071273   82-23966
ISBN 0-8141-5886-2

CONTENTS

LIST OF HANDOUTS

ACKNOWLEDGMENTS

I would like to thank all those Iowa City West High School students whose enthusiasm and hard work made successful seminars over the years possible, especially those juniors and seniors who contributed papers to this book: David Barker, Eugene Barth, Emily Buss, Mark Champe, Pat Chong, John Corrigan, Debbie Fedge, Amy Freeman, Cathy Freeman, Jennifer Gardner, Dan Goldberg, Janet Holm, Louise Milkman, Paul Milkman, Seth Meisel, Melody Myers, Anne Nusser, Greg Pope, Janice Weiner.

PREFACE

Last January three of my former students, all from my 1980 seminar on J.D. Salinger, stopped me in the hall of West High School and asked if they could audit the spring seminar on Ernest Hemingway. One of the seniors, Cathy Freeman, said, "We asked the counselor if we could take one of your seminars again, but he said all three sections are closed. And there's a waiting list. So we wondered if we could audit."

Audit! Do they really want to write seven papers in twelve weeks again, I thought. Don't they realize that they also must read a book of short stories, three novels, a book of choice, one hundred pages of biography or autobiography? For no credit? I reminded them of these facts. "Cathy," I said, "it really doesn't matter what author you study. It's the process that counts. And you have already gone through that process."

Cathy just smiled. "I know," she said. "But we like the process."

How could I argue with that? I like the process too, a dynamic process which came from my search for a new way to teach both literature and writing—a search which led to my NCTE publication, *In Search of Ernest Hemingway*.

My discovery of this process began in 1957, my first year of teaching. I had a captive audience at West High School in Waterloo, Iowa. American literature was required for all juniors. So I took those summer-fresh students from the delights of their jobs and swimming pools and started them with the colonial writers. As we moved forward in our chronological survey, I noticed that my classes were beginning to behave like tourists who had just completed a fifteen day tour of fifteen European countries. They were confused. Despite the required course guidebook, I tried a number of experiments with everything from choral reading to literary anecdotes to liven up the class. I transformed the formula, book report paper into creative topics—telegrams to the Pulitzer Prize committee or student film scripts of novels. Many of these ideas seemed to work, especially when students received recognition by reading their papers aloud or having them posted on the bulletin board.

Yet, literature was literature. And writing seemed peripheral, not part of any dynamic process. I was still correcting all the papers, still carrying the load on the teaching of writing.

In 1959, at Munich American High School in West Germany, I continued with captive audiences. But there was a difference: we had no required guidebook. So I revised the agonies of chronology and began with the more familiar twentieth century; then I related present to past. We also had in-depth studies of novels with the familiar term paper as a requirement. But by 1962 I began to experiment with what I called "Making Friends with an Author"; it was here that I made an exciting breakthrough in relating literature to writing.

Inspired by my own in-depth reading of authors like Thomas Wolfe, I asked my college prep American literature class to select one author and then read at least five works by that author in preparation for a single position paper. I also asked them to read at least 100 pages of biography or autobiography to relate the writer to his or her fiction. To my delight, I found my students—after they had recovered from the shock of this ambitious assignment—telling me that this was the most rewarding experience of their school year. Even later, after I returned to graduate school, I still heard from those students who did not forget that in-depth study with the likes of Willa Cather, John Steinbeck, Pearl Buck, Ernest Hemingway, and even Henry James.

In 1968, I began teaching at West High School in Iowa City. Now everything was elective. American literature survey had been reduced to a semester—though later to two trimesters. With the proliferation of electives, ones that often overlapped, I became concerned with fragmentation, with the problems of tightening already tightened literary material in my survey course. Then I remembered that experiment in Munich with the in-depth paper. I thought: Why not develop a class that works together in studying one author? Why not develop a seminar where students can share the territory of in-depth study—the chronological discovery of an author's basic style and themes, the relishing of characters and quotable quotes, the sense of how biography relates to fiction, the joy of expertise, the value of seeing a good book and a bad book by the same author?

It seemed to me that I had a process. Through reading and writing and discussion, we would make contact with a good writer. This dynamic process could provide an opening wedge to all of American literature, the dream of all English teachers, certainly of mine. Perhaps microcosm could become macrocosm.

The Hawthorne effect of that first seminar on Scott Fitzgerald has long since ended. After years of study of Hemingway, Steinbeck, Saroyan, Salinger—all student choices, the seminar is almost institutionalized at West High School. Four sections from a junior/senior total of around 600 have signed up for this year. And sometimes I wonder why this demanding course is so popular, especially when one considers the course description in the student handbook: "American literature seminar requires that every student write and type seven position papers, each three to five pages in length."

When students begin the seminar, they learn that the writing requirement is only part of a total process, a process that builds upon itself. For the first paper, they begin the process by reading short stories aloud in class. We pool ideas about style and theme; we discuss the concept of a single position which must be clear. Students are shown models of position papers written by students in previous seminars. And after they have read the assigned short story for written analysis, they are given suggested topics for their papers—which they are free to reject.

Then comes the most dynamic element of the seminar—Defense Day. Two papers are chosen for photocopying so that the entire seminar can prepare to evaluate them, first overnight and then for an entire class period. Every student is guaranteed that he or she will be evaluated twice on Defense Days. Peer grading, of course, has its tensions, and we have used both teacher-directed evaluation (though the teacher does not grade) and anonymous evaluation with a written vehicle. The procedure, however, is the same:

1. The student reads the paper aloud.
2. The instructor asks individual students to state the paper's position. The seminar arrives at what it feels is the position, if they can find one, often referring to specific lines in the beginning or ending of the paper.
3. The writer is asked if he or she agrees with the class.
4. The writer is asked to describe how the position is organized and supported.
5. The seminar has open discussion on organization and support. The writer responds to questions.
6. The seminar goes page by page discussing mechanics.
7. The seminar suggests a grade for the paper, beginning with the first student who stated the position. Each student explains his or her grade.
8. The instructor writes the consensus grade on the paper. Or collects and tabulates the grade from written evaluations which are then given to the writer.
9. The instructor returns all position papers to the seminar at the end of the Defense Day or the last Defense Day, if more than one is scheduled.

After the first Defense Day, the students understand the basic process—reading aloud, discussion, prewriting interaction with specific goals and suggestions, Defense Day. They also know that the required readings for position papers will be longer, and they know that their work will be reinforced by the study of maps dealing with the geography of the novels, by guest speakers and telephone interviews with people knowledgeable of the author, by Anecdote Day stories about the writer, and by audiovisual materials. A demanding course.

Why then do our students take this course? Why would Cathy and her friends opt for auditing? My best guesses are these:

1. This is no survey, no mini-fragmentation. This is the real, the total thing. This is Ernest Miller Hemingway, rebellious teenager, off to war and Paris, bullfights and fishing, son-father-husband (four times), simple, complex, creator of Nick Adams, Jake Barnes, Lady Brett Ashley, Frederic Henry and Catherine Barkley, Santiago, Pulitzer and Nobel Prize winner. This is John Ernst Steinbeck, big-eared child, shy Californian always in search of his Arthurian dream, student of protest and biology, phalanx and teleology, Okies and Danny, Lennie, and Johnny Bear. And this is Jerome David Salinger, silent now on his Cornish, New Hampshire hill, dropout and Zen, Holden and the Glass family, Franny and Zooey, Buddy and Seymour, all those italicized words, all that sharp wit turned outward and then inward, unpublished since 1965, and why?

2. This course sharpens the skills. You read the author. You discuss the author's writing. Then you reread and write, rewrite, and then your classmates read and discuss your writing. And you get advice from everyone—from your teacher, from your classmates, and even from the author. Try repetition, says Hemingway. Stop when things are going good, says Steinbeck. Write intriguing or outrageous titles, says Salinger. You and they dissect prose and punctuation, adjectives and adverbs, vocabulary and nuance, even titles and dedications. And the payoff becomes obvious, especially when the students take a whack at parody.

3. Finally there is the total process of everyone working together. With a good deal of both teacher and peer recognition, there comes an emerging sense of community, of mutual discovery. And the process produces a product, something to be proud of: seven position papers. There is the impact of books and stories shared and digested; the students feel that they know something well, that they have gone in deep with a recognized author. The material sticks, the process has an effect, and the student has made a friend—or an enemy.

The American literature seminar is probably the most demanding *writing* course that I have ever taught. Surprisingly enough, my students, who often groan about writing assignments in my survey course, do not refer to the seminar as a writing course. They call it the Hemingway course or the Salinger course—or whatever author we have chosen. I like that. I like the idea that writing is not a thing by itself but instead a method of *thinking* about something else, something very human. Perhaps, this is ultimately what Cathy meant when she said, "We like the process."

INTRODUCTION

CHOICES

This handbook offers many choices. It is premised on the belief that American English teachers need choices in their search for a vital method for teaching both literature and writing. It is the product of over twenty years of teaching American literature and over seven years of experience with in-depth seminars at West High School in Iowa City, Iowa. Its design is intended to be flexible to meet the needs of different schools, teachers, and students.

Let's consider the choices.

1. The handbook offers three semester designs for discovering three famous American writers, Ernest Hemingway, J.D. Salinger, and John Steinbeck. Each section includes a schedule, lesson plans, material for reproduction and distribution, and serviceable bibliographies. For those of us who have never quite recovered from reading books like *A Farewell to Arms, Of Mice and Men,* or *The Catcher in the Rye,* there is the delightful dilemma of selecting Hemingway, Salinger, or Steinbeck.

2. While the time schedules cover ninety class periods for eighteen weeks, the design can be easily adapted to trimesters or even quarters by choosing to eliminate certain readings or in-class activities.

3. The basic activities of the courses are aimed at students who are interested in literature and self-improvement, but the instructor can structure the readings, writing, and such concerns as literary criticism so that they will appeal to gifted students. And while schedules are designed for teachers who have no special expertise or graduate study with these three authors, those who do have such experience can expand upon the suggested materials.

4. The handbook describes a seminar format with considerable interaction during classroom discussions, on the Defense Day evaluations of the seven required position papers, and the instruction of specific writing goals for each paper. But again the students and instructor have considerable flexibility to allow for variety and interruptions—assemblies, special events, snow days—which are part of a school's normal life. Instructors are encouraged to use resource persons, telephone interviews, an eighth paper, and formal testing. The number of Defense Days can be varied; there need not be just two for each paper. The sequence of writing skills is only suggested, not absolute.

5. Experience has shown that a successful seminar in terms of interaction and time for evaluating papers is between fifteen and twenty students. This is especially important if a student is to be evaluated at least twice by the class on Defense Days. But if such class sizes are impossible, the instructor may wish to grade six of the seven position papers, allowing only one Defense Day for each student.

6. Even evaluation should involve choice. While the handbook suggests oral student evaluation on Defense Days, it also contains a written vehicle for anonymous evaluation. Normally, Defense Days have delightful interaction and suspense, but sometimes peer evaluation can prove to be a burden for careful, thoughtful grading. However, a good seminar is marked by a cooperative spirit.

7. For the instructors who cannot or do not wish to have such in-depth seminars, the

handbook is a valuable teaching aid for individual works by the authors and useful as well for biographical and bibliographical suggestions. I have used the position paper/Defense Day system with my humanities classes with considerable success, even with only one or two papers. The handbook offers many choices for teachers who are looking for ideas.

THE SEMINAR METHOD

The seminar is a process. First of all, the literary content is essentially discovered in chronological order so that students can see each writer's emerging style and themes. The choices of works for the seven papers are intentional: they are either recognized major works or those which initiate key ideas of Hemingway, Salinger, and Steinbeck. After the first four writings are analyzed in-depth, there is a shift to biography or author profile—a natural point where students can respond to their evolving interest in the writer as a human being, as well as their discovery of how fiction and biography are related. Then the course returns to literature and summation.

But the design is more than literature and biography. It reveals an intense writing process. This process begins immediately during the orientation period, the time for getting acquainted. Since at least twenty-eight papers will be evaluated by the students in this course, it is essential to establish rapport and to foster the critical skills for objective grading. The first assignment in each section is a short story; its brevity allows time not only for oral reading of additional stories but also for discussion of what makes a position paper and what is expected in a Defense Day. As the seminar moves into longer works and the profile, there will also be time for review and instruction of selected writing skills. The impact is accumulative. Reading and discussing the author's writing, reading and discussing student's writing whether it be for Defense Day or for instructor evaluation, discussing and practicing writing skills—all these form a dynamic writing process.

It also should be noted that each section of the design has its own process. The process involves variety and yet consistency. First there is the assignment and background notes, then a time for reading, followed by suggestions for positions, and finally some focus on the required skill, as well as time for in-class writing. Some sections offer additional variety through oral readings, audio-visual presentations, use of resource persons, Anecdote Days, and follow-up discussions of Defense Day.

No instructor should suffer from boredom in this course. Nor should there be any serious concern about the work load. The design builds in a number of reading and writing days—times when a teacher can read and review, hold conferences, correct papers. Then, too, the Defense Day evaluations can be seen as a bonus time. The instructional load of the seminar should not be any more burdensome than, for example, a literature survey course.

DEFENSE DAY: BACKGROUNDS

This course design suggests seven typed papers, three-to-five pages in length. Each paper is defined as a "position paper" because students are asked to limit their analysis to a single focus. This position is to be organized, supported by concrete detail, and mechanically sound. Since the readings are largely chronological, students are encouraged to build upon their papers in successive assignments. There are also sequential writing goals, ranging from concern with proofreading and clarity to the more complex skills of documentation and synthesis. A model student paper, which can be used before or after Defense Day, is provided for each of the seven assignments.

Obviously, Defense Day is a time for tension. For the student facing a peer audience, there are the questions that all writers must face: Will they understand my position? Is my position supported by concrete detail? Is it mechanically sound—at least sound enough to satisfy my readers? Will I be able to respond to their questions and criticism? What will be their final assessment? And if the class load allows more than one Defense Day for a student, there is the natural concern that the second paper be as good as, if not better than, the first.

But Defense Day should be rewarding. It should offer a dramatic focus for each assignment. It should not be Destruction Day. Since everyone comes up for Defense Day, everyone both evaluates and is evaluated. Thus, the spirit of Defense Day should be one of cooperation. After the initial shock of surprise when receiving the copies of the position papers the day before each Defense Day, the students must understand that their job is to work together to become better students of literature and better writers. They will learn from each other, as well as from the instructor. With each Defense Day, students will acquire more experience in discussing and implementing the criteria of good writing. Indeed, the goal of each Defense Day and of the entire writing design becomes obvious: The Next Paper. The process should give each student a better understanding of his or her own writing. The search for Ernest Hemingway or J.D. Salinger or John Steinbeck inevitably leads home.

As the preface suggests, Defense Day procedure is managed by the instructor. It is the instructor's job to establish and maintain the spirit of cooperation, as well as to control the time segments so that all major goals are accomplished and each defender is given equal time. The instructor also has a choice of oral or written evaluation by the students. Experience has shown the oral method to be highly successful for open discussion and seminar rapport, but it is possible that the group dynamics of some seminars will dictate the written and anonymous grading. Whatever the choice, the instructor must not be actively involved in the grading— only in helping the class arrive at consensus. Otherwise, the students will become suspicious that their opinions are secondary.

DEFENSE DAY: PROCEDURE

1. Defense Day begins with calm and some humor. The total experience should be supportive for future writers and defenders, as well as for the defenders for the day. While you need not select the best papers for each Defense Day, your choices should be generally strong papers. Conflicting viewpoints, if equally well written, can be very stimulating for the discussions. But it is advisable to hold off the weaker writers so that they can profit from the instruction and their peers.

2. While students should have brought their copies of the papers for evaluation, as well as the works under discussion for possible reference, the teacher should have classroom copies of both for those who have forgotten them. Advance distribution usually generates interest and prior student annotation of the position papers, but the instructor is advised to both read and annotate the papers to stimulate any lagging discussion. (However, you must be careful not to dominate any Defense Day!)

3. Ask each student to begin the Defense Day segment allotted to them by reading his or her paper aloud. This provides a number of benefits: a calming effect, a review or even a first reading for some students, proofreading, a final annotating, and a chance to hear each writer's inflections and stresses.

4. Without comment, the instructor asks a member of the class to state the writer's position. (If the written evaluation form is used, the students should be asked to write the position. Then the instructor can ask a student to read his or her position sentence.) The instructor should then repeat the student's response and ask if that is what he or she has said. This technique is important since many students may wish to alter their wording; many students think better aloud than they do silently.

5. Then ask other students if they agree with the first student. This may involve some classroom management to achieve consensus wording, though usually there is general agreement—or an awareness that the position is not clear to many students. The instructor may wish to ask students if they see the position in particular lines, such as in the introduction or conclusion. This can be an important discovery for future writers.

6. Next ask the writer if the class or any individual student has stated his or her position. Ask if there is any line in the paper that was intentionally written as a position statement. By now, the writer and class have discussed the standard of *clarity*. While the writer should be encouraged to reflect on his or her position and to clarify that position to those who found it un-

clear, the instructor and the class must be alert to the difference between the paper's clarity and clarity that comes from ideas and support which are not in the paper.

7. The second criterion is *organization and support*. The writer should be asked to describe the basic outline of the paper (Introduction, Body, Conclusion); the procedure for developing a single focus; and the concrete use of plot, characters, and direct quotation to support generalizations. The instructor should encourage the class to comment on the logic of the organization, as well as the selection of supporting detail. Reference can be made to the handout, "Defense Day: Criteria for Grading Position Papers," in dealing with essential questions about the second criterion. Focus should be made on the impact of the title, the relationship of introduction to conclusion, and the importance of direct support for convincing the reader.

8. At this point, there may be some disagreement with the position. Here again is an important point of responsibility for the instructor. While the class should be encouraged to air opinions about the position and the writer should respond to these opinions, there should be a reminder that good writers have often had their critics. If the position is well defended, why do some members of the seminar continue to disagree with it? The seminar should also be reminded that the follow-up discussion day will provide time for pursuing other positions, including those of major critics.

9. *Mechanics*. Now the seminar goes page by page discussing proofreading errors and mechanical problems that range from obvious errors in spelling, capitalization, and usage to concerns that students often identify as style—wordiness, awkward sentences, word choice that is imprecise or repetitive, slang and colloquialisms. This may be a time for brief comments about writing in the first person, paragraphing, transitions, inappropriate tone, insensitivity to nuance. While this critical examination

should not be an exercise in nitpicking, seminar members and especially the instructor should make clear that mechanical errors distract from the paper's content. The clarity of a position is heavily dependent on the writer's skill with mechanics.

10. Begin the grading process by asking the student who first suggested the writer's position—and thus first posed the problem of clarity—to grade the paper, based on the three criteria of *clarity, organization and support,* and *mechanics*. While pluses or minuses are allowed, this triad should allow only one grade. Then move to other students for grades and justifications. Almost always a consensus will emerge, though peer grading is difficult for classroom friends (and enemies) who wish to be objective. While you may feel that the grades for Defense Days are sometimes too high, this should not be seen as a diminution of "standards," for the total learning experience of Defense Day is more important than any single grade. My experience with seven years of Defense Days has confirmed my faith in the method. However, if oral grading creates problems with the supportive spirit of the seminar, the instructor should consider using the written form and arriving at consensus grades after the period ends. Be sure to return all papers, those for Defense Day and those corrected by the instructor, at the end of the final Defense Day. Remind students to bring these papers to the next class period follow-up discussion.

SEQUENCE OF WRITING SKILLS

While the papers and discussions build upon themselves, the instructor may wish to emphasize a sequence of writing skills. This handbook suggests the following developmental sequence for the seven position papers; its schedule has specific suggestions and activities for review and instruction.

Paper I

1. Following directions is important for the initial paper: 3–5 pages, typed manuscript form.

2. The idea of a single clear position is essential for the first paper. Handouts on the position paper idea, as well as a student model, are available for students.

3. The Salinger seminar discusses the prewriting process during this section.

Paper II

1. Emphasize the use of concrete examples. Ask students to use at least one direct quotation from the novel to document and to give "flavor" to the material.

2. Stress introduction and conclusions. What the reader reads first and last is essential in the psychology of writing.

3. The Steinbeck seminar will discuss the prewriting process during this section.

Paper III

1. Stress transitions between sentences and paragraphs. Does the paper flow logically? Do the connectives help to unify it? Does the organization serve to clarify the single position? Does the introduction suggest the body of the paper? Does the position find its final definition in the conclusion?

2. Encourage students to work on sentence variety. Are the sentences appealing—not all simple or compound, not all beginning with subject-verb patterns. Students will work with various sentence-combining patterns to prepare for this paper.

3. Urge students to purchase a paperback copy of *Roget's Thesaurus.* They will be instructed on its use with a class copy.

Paper IV

1. Since students are by now sensitive to Defense Day discussions of varying writing styles, it is time for an open period review and instruction on specific concerns: for example, use of "I" in a formal paper; the function of special punctuation—colons, semicolons, dashes, elipses; selecting titles.

2. While sentence variety was a goal of Paper III, there could be further explorations: (1) repetition, such as repeating a line or using the same beginning for two sentences in a row; (2) variation, such as using a tight, short sentence to follow a long one—to catch the eye, to summarize, to punctuate.

3. Students should know the meaning and effect of standard Latin writing abbreviations: *etc., e.g., i.e.*

Paper V

1. Encourage students to use both biographical and literary material in formulating a profile position paper.

2. Discuss plagiarism and the need for footnotes and bibliography. Using a style sheet, review correct forms. Discuss how to edit a direct quotation, how to build a smooth transition from the text to the direct quotation, when to single space direct quotations and when to incorporate them into the double-spaced text.

3. Be sure to stress careful documentation: the use of *sic* when the original source is in error; the differing editions and copyrights of the same titles; the difference between style sheet form and that listed in the *Reader's Guide to Periodical Literature;* the gap between what is common knowledge and what is technical material.

Paper VI

1. The Steinbeck seminar offers a choice of readings for this paper, not just the in-common work. This requires a clear plot summary and precise character description since many Defense Day evaluators will not have read the work under consideration.

2. Both sections encourage students to relate previous in-common readings to the assigned work for this paper. Comparison and contrast techniques are discussed, especially since they are valuable for college-bound students.

3. Insist on careful proofreading and a minimum of mechanical errors.

Paper VII

1. Encourage students to use ideas from their previous papers and those of other students since one choice of this assignment is a synthesis position paper.

2. Review the satirical technique of parody, another choice for the final paper. Use of student models in the handbook is effective. Note that parodies can be made of parts or the entirety of an author's work. They also can be Salinger's or Steinbeck's exaggerated style imposed on a simple format, such as a children's story like "Goldilocks and the Three Bears" or on another famous American writer, for example, how Salinger would write a Poe story.

3. Since the final assignment is of an oral nature, students should be encouraged to read their papers aloud to themselves until they are satisfied, not only with their reading, but also with their writing—especially word choice and cadence.

I. IN SEARCH
OF ERNEST HEMINGWAY

ORIENTATION TO THE SEMINAR
DAYS 1–2

DAY 1: GETTING ACQUAINTED WITH THE COURSE AND EACH OTHER

Goals

1. To acquaint students with the nature of the seminar and to introduce them to its method and content.
2. To help students get to know each other.

Materials

1. Handout 1: Seminar in American Literature.
2. Handout 2: Tentative Schedule.
3. After you have taught the seminar, use evaluations from former students (see Day 90) to interest beginning students.

Procedure

1. Use Handout 1 as a brief introduction to the idea of an in-depth seminar.
2. Using Handout 2 as a guide, offer an overview of the course, noting particularly how writing and reading activities are correlated. Point out the variety in the course, the value of studying an author in depth, the fact that the course offers an opportunity to improve writing skills as well as opportunities for individual exploration and group discussion.
3. Stress that you genuinely want to know the students and to have them know each other. Everyone will be working together in the course.
4. Pair off students who do not know each other or who know each other only slightly. Find a partner for yourself. Ask each student to interview his or her partner without taking notes, asking questions that each partner would like answered—family, job,

favorite food, sports, music, travel, plans for the future.
5. After five or ten minutes, ask each student to introduce his or her partner to the seminar by summarizing the answers to the interview questions. Now the class has taken its first step toward becoming a genuine seminar. These introductions may lead to friendships, and they will certainly help to establish the understanding and cooperation needed in later discussions, especially the evaluations on Defense Day.

Additional Suggestion

A classroom bulletin board on Ernest Hemingway helps to develop interest: photographs, magazine clippings, a sample position paper (one from this handbook or from a previous seminar), maps (Illinois, Michigan, Florida, Idaho, France, Italy, Cuba, Spain). Perhaps some students have visited the geographical settings of Hemingway's life and literature and have materials to contribute to an evolving bulletin board.

DAY 2: INTRODUCING HEMINGWAY AND THE POSITION PAPER

Goals

1. To preview Hemingway's life and work.
2. To introduce the Position Paper.

Materials

1. Handout 3: The Hemingway Chronology. You may also refer to the materials on Hemingway's life and times and his family in Appendix B.
2. Handout 4: The Position Paper.

Procedure

1. Referring to Handout 3: The Hemingway Chronology, discuss the idea that the seminar will be one of discovery, of learning how Hemingway's ideas and writing developed. The first of the seven position papers focuses on the Nick Adams stories of the 1920s. In particular, the paper will formulate a position about "Indian Camp," an early short story that was written in Paris after World War I and appeared in a small book, *In Our Time*.

2. Note that Hemingway's life carried him from his boyhood home in Oak Park, a suburb of Chicago, to a summer home near Petoskey in upper Michigan, the setting for "Indian Camp." The family enjoyed the change of scenery and fishing (a life-long enthusiasm of the author), and Dr. Hemingway carried on his medical practice there by treating the local Ojibway Indians. Go on to observe that Hemingway moved out into the world after he graduated from high school: a cub reporter in Kansas City, World War I service in Italy, newspaper work in Toronto, expatriate life in Paris in the 1920s, trips throughout his life to Spain, Key West, Africa, Cuba, and Ketchum, Idaho.

3. Distribute Handout 4: The Position Paper and discuss the nature of a position paper. Stress the requirements of length and format (typed, double-spaced, one side, unlined paper) since clear, complete copies must be distributed for Defense Day. At this point, do not dwell on evaluation procedures since a positive attitude toward writing does not begin with apprehension about grades. Remind students that typing is required by most college teachers and that it is wise to improve their typing now. Tell them that you will provide position papers written by high school juniors and seniors for them to examine; assure them that they will be given considerable class time for reading and writing. Useful background material and even suggestions for topics will be given as specific papers are assigned.

Additional Suggestions

1. Some students may already have read books by or about Hemingway. Encourage them to share their initial impressions.

2. Use Peter Buckley's *Ernest* for photographic account of Hemingway's early years (see Bibliography).

HANDOUT 1
SEMINAR IN AMERICAN LITERATURE

Have you ever read an author in depth? If you have, you probably made a number of discoveries:

1. You became acquainted with the writer, his or her basic themes and style.

2. You felt the deliciousness of expertise which includes a sense of chronology, favorite characters, a knowledge of major and minor works, a delight in quotable lines.

3. It was as if the writer became your friend. You may have wanted to learn more about the person, his or her life. You may even have hungered to find other writings or eagerly awaited new books to be published.

So the seminar will go in depth, while the survey course that you just took has skimmed the surface. And as a small group, you will share your discoveries with the seminar–in discussion, in your papers, on Defense Day, informally.

One thing must be kept in focus: This seminar is not concerned with making you an expert on one author (though you may be). Our concern is with the *process* of studying any author. In fact, this is really a Basic Skills (sound familiar?) course: Reading, Writing, Speaking, and Listening.

Reading: Your reading will involve three novels, seventeen short stories, a hundred or so pages of autobiography or biography. You also will read at least twenty-eight position papers.

Writing: You will write seven position papers–three to five typed (skill) pages. You will be studying other people's writing; the seminar will discuss good writing.

Speaking: You will defend two of your position papers before the seminar. You will also be reading aloud and discussing what you have read–short stories, position papers.

Listening: You will have to listen carefully because Defense Day requires that everyone listen carefully to what is said and read. You will be involved in Defense Day grading.

HANDOUT 2
TENTATIVE SCHEDULE FOR SEMINAR IN AMERICAN LITERATURE:
ERNEST HEMINGWAY

Orientation to the Seminar

Day 1.   Getting acquainted with the course and each other
Day 2.   Introducing Hemingway and the Position Paper

Paper I: "Indian Camp" (1925)

Day 3.   Reading aloud and discussion of "Up in Michigan" (1923) and "The
            Doctor and the Doctor's Wife" (1925)
            ASSIGNMENT: Position Paper on "Indian Camp"
            Due: _____
Day 4.   Reading aloud and discussion of "The End of Something" (1925)
Day 5.   Reading aloud and discussion of "Three Day Blow" (1925)
Day 6.   Suggestions for Position Paper on "Indian Camp" and in-class writing
Day 7.   Reading aloud and discussion of "Ten Indians" (1927)
Day 8.   In-class writing
Day 9.   Reading aloud and discussion of "The Battler" (1925)
            Position paper on "Indian Camp" due
Day 10.   Film: *My Old Man* (story published 1923)

Paper II: *The Sun Also Rises* (1926)

Day 11.   Introduction to *The Sun Also Rises;* begin reading
            ASSIGNMENT: Position Paper on *The Sun Also Rises*
            Due: _____
Day 12.   Reading
Day 13.   Discussion: Life in Paris in the 1920s
Day 14.   Reading
Day 15.   Reading
Day 16.   Reading and/or distribution of Defense Day papers
Day 17.   Defense Day: "Indian Camp"
Day 18.   Follow-up discussion: students and critics
Day 19.   Film: *Hemingway's Spain: "The Sun Also Rises"*
Day 20.   Reading
Day 21.   Suggestions for Position Paper on *The Sun Also Rises* and reading or
            writing
Day 22.   Film: *Hemingway's Spain: "Death in the Afternoon"*
Day 23.   Reading aloud and discussion of "The Big Two-Hearted River" (1925)
Day 24.   Reading aloud and discussion of "The Big Two-Hearted River"
Day 25.   In-class writing and proofreading
Day 26.   Reading aloud and discussion of "In Another Country" (1927)
            Position paper on *The Sun Also Rises* due

Paper III: *A Farewell to Arms* **(1929)**

Day 27.   Introduction to *A Farewell to Arms;* begin reading
ASSIGNMENT: Position Paper on *A Farewell to Arms*
Due: _____

Day 28.   Reading

Day 29.   Reading

Day 30.   Reading aloud and discussion of "Now I Lay Me" (1927) and "A Very Short Story" (1927)

Day 31.   Suggestions for Position Paper on *A Farewell to Arms* and in-class reading

Day 32.   Discussion: World War I and Hemingway, Dr. Hemingway's suicide, Key West

Day 33.   Reading; distribution of papers for Defense Day

Day 34.   Defense Day: *The Sun Also Rises*

Day 35.   Follow-up discussion: students and critics

Day 36.   Reading

Day 37.   Reading aloud and discussion of "Soldier's Home" (1925)

Day 38.   Reading

Day 39.   Reading and writing

Day 40.   Writing

Day 41.   Writing and proofreading

Day 42.   Reading aloud and discussion of "Fathers and Sons" (1933)
Position Paper on *A Farewell to Arms* due

Paper IV: A Profile of Ernest Hemingway

Day 43.   Review of the Hemingway biography and introduction to Profile Paper
ASSIGNMENT: Profile Paper developed from 100 pages of reading in Hemingway's biographers
Due: _____

Day 44.   Film: *Hemingway*

Day 45.   Reading and research for Anecdote Day

Day 46.   Reading and research for Anecdote Day

Day 47.   Anecdote Day

Day 48.   Anecdote Day

Day 49.   Reading; distribution of papers for Defense Day

Day 50.   Defense Day: *A Farewell to Arms*

Day 51.   Follow-up discussion: students and critics

Day 52.   Reading aloud and discussion of "A Clean Well-Lighted Place" (1933)

Day 53.   Reading

Day 54.   Reading, research, and writing

Day 55.   Writing

Day 56.   Writing and proofreading

Day 57. Reading aloud and discussion of "A Day's Wait" (1933) and "The Old Man at the Bridge" (1938)
Profile Paper on Ernest Hemingway due

Paper V: Your Choice

Day 58. Consideration of reading choices for Paper V
ASSIGNMENT: Position Paper on Hemingway work of student's choice
Due: _____

Day 59. Reading

Day 60. Reading

Day 61. Reading

Day 62. Reading; distribution of papers for Defense Day

Day 63. Defense Day: Profile Paper

Day 64. Defense Day: Profile Paper

Day 65. Follow-up discussion: students and critics

Day 66. Reading and writing

Day 67. Writing

Day 68. Writing and proofreading

Day 69. Reading aloud and discussion of "On the Blue Water" (1936)
Your Choice Paper due

Paper VI: *The Old Man and the Sea* (1952)

Day 70. Introduction to *The Old Man and the Sea;* begin reading
ASSIGNMENT: Position Paper on *The Old Man and the Sea*
Due: _____

Day 71. Reading

Day 72. Discussion: Hemingway and the Nobel Prize

Day 73. Suggestions for Position Paper on *The Old Man and the Sea* and reading

Day 74. Reading, writing, and distribution of papers for Defense Day

Day 75. Defense Day: Your Choice Papers

Day 76. Follow-up discussion: students and critics

Day 77. Writing

Day 78. Writing and proofreading

Day 79. Previewing the Summation Paper
Position Paper on *The Old Man and the Sea* due

Paper VII: The Summing Up

Day 80. Reading, re-reading, research, and writing
ASSIGNMENT: Summation Paper and/or a Humorous Paper on Hemingway and his work
Due: _____

Day 81. Writing

Day 82. Writing and distribution of papers for Defense Day

Day 83. Defense Day: *The Old Man and the Sea*

Day 84. Follow-up discussion: students and critics

Day 85. Writing and proofreading

Day 86. Reading aloud of final papers

Day 87. Reading aloud of final papers

Day 88. Reading aloud by instructor

Day 89. Final discussion

Day 90. Evaluation of seminar

HANDOUT 3
THE HEMINGWAY CHRONOLOGY

1899	Born in Oak Park, Illinois, the second of six children of Dr. Clarence Hemingway and Grace Hall Hemingway.
1917	Graduates from Oak Park High School. Rejected by U.S. Army because of eye injury from boxing. Works as cub reporter for the Kansas City *Star*.
1918	Goes to Italy as Red Cross ambulance driver. Legs severely injured by mortar fragments and heavy machine gun fire near Fossalta di Piave at midnight, July 8, 1918, two weeks before his nineteenth birthday.
1920–1924	Reporter and foreign correspondent for the Toronto *Star* and *Star Weekly*.
1921	Marries Hadley Richardson. Leaves for Europe.
1923	*Three Stories and Ten Poems* published in Paris; volume includes "Up in Michigan," "Out of Season," and "My Old Man."
1924	*in our time*, with thirty-six pages of miniatures, published in Paris.
1925	*In Our Time*, U.S. edition, published by Boni & Liveright. Fourteen short stories, plus the miniatures of the Paris edition, which are used as interchapters.
1926	*The Torrents of Spring*, published by Charles Scribner's Sons, New York publisher of all his subsequent books. *The Sun Also Rises* is published in October.
1927	Divorces Hadley Richardson. Marries Pauline Pfeiffer. Publication of *Men Without Women*, fourteen short stories, ten of which had appeared in magazines.
1928–1938	Lives in Key West, Florida. Suicide of his father (1928).
1929	*A Farewell to Arms*, Hemingway's first commercial success: 80,000 copies sold in four months.
1932	*Death in the Afternoon*, a nonfiction book about bullfighting.
1933	*Winner Take Nothing*, fourteen short stories. Publishes first of thirty-one articles and stories to appear in *Esquire* during the next six years.
1935	*Green Hills of Africa*, a nonfiction book about hunting.
1936–1937	Writes, speaks, raises money for the Loyalists in the Spanish Civil War.
1937	Covers the Spanish Civil War for the North American Newspaper Alliance. *To Have and Have Not*, three interconnected stories, two of which had been published separately.
1938	*The Fifth Column and the First Forty-Nine Stories*, which contains a play, short stories from previous collections, and seven short stories previously published in magazines.
1940	*For Whom the Bell Tolls*, his best-selling novel. Divorced by Pauline Pfeiffer. Marries Martha Gellhorn.

1942   *Men at War,* a collection of war stories and accounts with an introduction by Hemingway.

1943–1945   Covers the European theater of war as a newspaper and magazine correspondent.

1944   Divorced by Martha Gellhorn. Marries Mary Welsh.

1945–1959   Lives in Cuba at the Finca.

1950   *Across the River and into the Trees,* a much criticized novel.

1951   Death of Grace Hemingway, his mother.

1952   *The Old Man and the Sea,* first published in *Life* magazine. Awarded Pulitzer Prize.

1954   Wins the Nobel Prize, cited for "forceful and style-making mastery of the art of modern narration."

1959   Buys hunting lodge near Ketchum, Idaho.

1961   Death on July 2 of self-inflicted gunshot wounds; buried near Ketchum.

1964   *A Moveable Feast,* Paris essays and reminiscences.

1970   *Islands in the Stream,* an unfinished sea novel begun in the fall of 1950.

HANDOUT 4
THE POSITION PAPER

1. The position paper is just that: you adopt a single position about what you have read, a narrowed focus that can be developed by using concrete examples from the reading or from supplements to the reading. The position is *your* position.

2. The position paper must be three to five typed pages. The papers must be typed because at least two papers will be chosen from each assignment, reproduced, and evaluated during Defense Day by members of the seminar.

3. The possibilities for positions are nearly unlimited. You may want to develop an important quotation from a work, an important symbol, a character or a comparison of two characters, the author's style, his or her ideas about love, death, maturity, society, nature, money. You may wish to explore the author's use of names, choice of title, brand of humor. Suggestions for positions will be given with each assignment.

4. The paper must be your best writing. It will always be read by the instructor. At least two of your papers will be discussed and evaluated by the entire seminar.

5. Do not use the title of the work for your paper. Instead, your title should suggest or reflect your position.

6. Present your position logically and support it with concrete material—quotations and examples from what you have read as well as your own observations about life and literature. Don't neglect the plot or ignore the names of the characters, yet assume that your reader is your seminar classmate, who is also familiar with the work.

7. Writing good papers is hard work. It requires a clear outline. Your paper needs sharp first and last sentences, transitions between solidly developed paragraphs, varied sentences—not all beginning with pronouns, not all simple or compound constructions. It requires your sharpest and most mature language. Good writing is correct writing: don't lose your reader by failing to proofread. Read your paper aloud before typing the final draft. Finally, a good paper uses psychology: work hard on introductions and conclusions —the first and last things that the reader reads.

8. Do not rely on critics. While there will be student position papers for you to examine, take your own position.

9. Do not be afraid to adopt a position that seems "way out," fanciful, outrageous. If you have a strong position, one that may be challenged in the seminar discussion, just be sure that you have the material to defend it.

10. The writing of seven position papers is a cumulative experience. Each paper builds upon its predecessors, so do not hesitate to refer to previous papers or ideas—yours or those of other classmates. Through your own writing and by studying the works of other students, you will make discoveries about your reading and writing. New ideas will come to you. You will become aware of your style as you consider the writing of others. And, while each paper will not necessarily be better than the last, your final production will speak for itself. You will be impressed!

PAPER I: "INDIAN CAMP"
DAYS 3–10

DAYS 3–5: READING THREE NICK ADAMS STORIES ALOUD

Goals

1. To introduce the Nick Adams stories by reading aloud and discussing on Day 3 "Up in Michigan" (1923) and "The Doctor and the Doctor's Wife" (1925); on Day 4 "The End of Something" (1925); and on Day 5 "The Three Day Blow" (1925).
2. To provide a background for an independent reading of "Indian Camp" (1925) and for writing the first Position Paper.

Materials

1. *The Short Stories of Ernest Hemingway,* which includes all of the short stories for Days 3–5.
2. *In Our Time,* which includes all but "Up in Michigan."

Assignment

1. Read "Indian Camp" and write a three-to-five-page Position Paper on that story.
2. Insert the DUE date for this paper on the Schedule. In addition, note the date of the first Defense Day and explain to students that copies of the position papers chosen for defense on that day will be given out on Day 16.

Procedure

1. Remind students that Hemingway's first published writings were about a young boy named Nick Adams, who, like Hemingway, went up to Michigan in the summer with his family. Suggest that the boy's name has been seen as symbolic, though you may not at this point want to deal with "Nick" (evildevil) and "Adams" (Adam of the Garden of Eden). Nevertheless, the Michigan landscape provided the setting for the awakening of a young innocent, a common theme in literature.

2. Read "Up in Michigan" aloud for immediate reaction. If you are uncertain about handling the sexual encounter between Jim and Liz, which may suggest certain parallels in the relationship between Nick and Marjorie, substitute an oral reading of "The Doctor and the Doctor's Wife," which appears after "Indian Camp" in *In Our Time.* Divide the story into sections of two or three paragraphs. Ask individual students to read a section aloud to the seminar; then summarize what they have read, observing whatever comes to mind about plot development, style, sentence length, dialogue, word choice, characters, names, the title, and the relationship of the story to Hemingway's life. Comment particularly on the relationship between Hemingway and his parents, the doctor-hunter father and the cultured Grace Hemingway who was not above using "illness" to get her way. It was his mother who insisted Ernest play the cello; it was his father who gave him his first gun.

3. As students read aloud these three stories on three consecutive days, they should begin to see the autobiographical nature of Hemingway's work, his emerging style, his use of the opening to mold the story, his ideas about what a boy learns. (What has Nick learned about his parents and himself in "The Doctor and the Doctor's Wife"? Why does Nick reject Marjorie yet accept the responsibility for hurting her? How does Nick's view of life differ from Bill's in "The Three Day Blow"?) A question for you: Do the stu-

dents relate readily to these stories? If not, what can you do to help them "connect"? A final question for the class: Suggest for each story at least one position that might be established in a three-to-five-page paper.

DAY 6: CHOOSING AND LIMITING TOPICS FOR POSITION PAPER I

Goals

1. To discuss appropriate topics for Position Paper I.
2. To demonstrate how to narrow a topic.

Materials

1. Handout 5: Suggestions for Position Paper I.
2. Handout 6: Student Model for Paper I.

Procedure

1. By now students have read "Indian Camp" and are beginning to understand Hemingway's early life and writing. Do not, however, discuss this story until *after* the position papers are handed in; but the concept of a position paper is probably incomplete and further clarification in class is needed.
2. Before suggesting suitable topics and how to narrow them, you may want to provide more background for the students. Useful sources:
   a. "Life" in Arthur Waldhorn's *A Reader's Guide to Ernest Hemingway,* pp. 6–10.
   b. "The High School Years" in Marcelline Hemingway Sanford's *At the Hemingways: A Family Portrait,* pp. 122–46.
   c. "The Michigan Years" and "Indian Camp" in Constance Cappel Montgomery's *Hemingway in Michigan,* pp. 11–18, 57–64.
   d. Carlos Baker, *Ernest Hemingway: A Life Story,* p. 160.
3. Distribute Handout 5 and discuss these suggestions for position papers on "Indian Camp." Since one of the suggestions deals with Hemingway's Code, his concept of "grace under pressure" in a world where ultimately one always loses, you will want to take time to develop this concept more fully. The idea of the Hemingway Hero facing a

hostile world with grace and courage will bear fruit throughout the seminar.
4. You may wish to use the model paper for "Indian Camp" at this point. You might post it on the bulletin board for student reference or make multiple copies for individual study. Note particularly the instructor's comments which follow the student paper.
5. If time remains, students should attempt to define individual positions, review the short story, and begin writing.

DAYS 7–10: COMPLETING PAPER I, READING, AND VIEWING A FILM

Goals

1. To provide in-class writing time for the completion of Paper I.
2. To read and discuss two additional Nick Adams stories: "Ten Indians" (1927), "The Battler" (1925), or "The Killers" (1927).
3. To view a film version of "My Old Man" (1923).

Materials

1. *The Short Stories of Ernest Hemingway.*
2. Film: *My Old Man* (27 min., color), Encyclopaedia Britannica Educational Corporation. Note: a brief follow-up discussion by critics accompanies this excellent dramatization of the story.

Procedure

1. Days 7 and 8 should be used for in-class writing. Proofreading, a concept that must be developed throughout the semester, can be handled briefly on Day 9 before the papers are collected.
2. "Ten Indians," another initiation story set in Michigan, can be used for oral reading and discussion since it suggests that Nick is beginning to mature but still has the protective shell of "Indian Camp" that keeps his heart from being broken.
3. Paper I is due on Day 9 (Day 10 if you wish to allow more time). Allow time for a final proofreading before collecting the papers. Students may then read aloud a final Nick

Adams story. In either "The Battler" or "The Killers," an older, more independent Nick now encounters evil in new forms.

4. Choose the papers for Defense Day as soon as possible and make multiple copies. Review the Defense Day procedures in the introduction in preparation for this discussion/evaluation period. The schedule allows time for you to grade the remaining papers before Defense Day (Day 17).

5. *My Old Man* is a superior film, beautifully acted with excellent timing. It retains the Hemingway ending that defies the formula story of mass media. Although the central character is named Joe, he is still Nick Adams, now abroad, finding life "funny" and puzzling. Students react immediately and intensely to the painful ending where the boy tries to find the truth in a world where "when they get started they don't leave a guy nothing." Suggestions for discussion: (a) List the names of the characters on the board and write a description of each. (b) Ask students what they know that Joe doesn't—about his father, about the prostitute. (c) Ask them about the title, its shades of meaning. Why did his father "betray" the gamblers, the bad guys? (d) What is Hemingway saying about life, about fathers and sons, about love (that pat on the knee on the train), about growing up? (e) Note that as in "Indian Camp" and "Ten Indians" no mother is present. Why does Hemingway leave the mother out?

HANDOUT 5
SUGGESTIONS FOR PAPER I: "INDIAN CAMP" (1925)

1. Consider the central character, the young Nick Adams. What is his function in the story? Why did Hemingway give him that name rather than Joe Smith or Archibald Beauchamp?

2. Note the title. The story is not called "Doctor and Son" but "Indian Camp." Why?

3. The story involves two groups: the whites on one side of the lake and the Indians on the other. What could this mean?

4. What is the function of Uncle George?

5. How do you see Nick's father—the wise scientist, the all-knowing father, the defeated man?

6. Hemingway believed in "grace under pressure," in living with reality in a world of pain, of good and bad luck. Who shows "grace under pressure" in this story?

7. Note Hemingway's style. Does any one aspect impress you? Why does he write in such short sentences? Why has he omitted the usual adverbs or other descriptions after the word "said"? Why does he use the variant name forms "Nick" and "Nickie," "Dad" and "Daddy"?

8. Use a key line or passage, such as the last two paragraphs, as the central idea for a position paper.

9. What is the meaning of the husband's suicide in the story?

10. Should the story have been longer? Should it, for example, have ended with the boy and his father returning home and discussing what had happened with Nick's mother?

11. Critic Arthur Waldhorn says that the Nick Adams stories are about "the terror of learning to live with the terrible." Is that what this story is about?

12. Hemingway was nearly killed in Italy during World War I. The theme of death haunted him for a lifetime. What does this story say about death?

HANDOUT 6
STUDENT MODEL FOR PAPER I

DIVIDED WE FALL

by Mark Champe

In his story "Indian Camp," Ernest Hemingway depicts the complex
social interactions of the whites and Indians in Upper Michigan without
seeming to take a definite stand. The segregation of the two groups is
apparent from the beginning. To get to the Indians, the doctor and his
son have to cross a bay. This suggests that the white and Indian settle-
ments are far enough apart by land to make the boat trip practical. By
separating them with water, Hemingway creates a much more vivid impression
of the division than if he had put the Indian camp "just down the road" or
on "the other side of town." The water acts as a social barrier as well
as a geographical one. This is not to say that the barrier prevents a
free flow of people between the two communities but rather that it consti-
tutes a social fencing of the Indians by reducing their status. Those who
are caged in are helpless; their status is automatically reduced by living
in the camp and they cannot raise it while living there, but neither can
they expect to go anywhere else and be accepted. They are far down the
ladder.

Their physical separation as a group makes them more visible and less
likely to be treated well by the majority. Throughout history, whenever
one group of people is set off from the rest, either by its own choice or
against it, social tensions between the two groups develop. The group in
the majority likes having the minority in one place so they can be watched

1

2

easily and kept in line. Having them together also would eliminate the
guilt feelings some members of the group might have about the mistreatment
of the smaller group and would make their presence less difficult to
accept. Any such feelings of guilt could be rationalized away by telling
oneself that those in the minority are quite content with their own kind.
This situation creates the impression of social balance, although the
underlying requirements for producing it have a great potential for dis-
sonance. When Uncle George gives cigars to the two Indians, it seems to
be a friendly act. It is more of a reward for being "good boys" than a
show of courtesy, more like giving a sugar cube to a horse than offering
someone a cigar.

The effect of separation and consequent pseudo-balance is the steady
dehumanizing and demoralizing of the minority. For this to work properly,
the oppressors must be very careful to bring about their injustices as
slowly as one would create a tolerance to poison, gradually increasing the
dosage. The thing most counter-productive to the oppressor's cause is to
aggravate the people enough to incite rebellion and possibly revolution.
The United States today still might be a subservient colony of Great
Britain had King George been more judicious with his levying of taxes.
Fortunately for all of the would-be oppressed, this type of tyrannical
equilibrium is very hard to attain because of the fairly strong human will.

The Upper Michigan example, however, comes quite close to this
perfectly balanced imbalance. The stability of the system comes from the
fact that the Indians don't seem to be on the verge of revolution, but
rather they have arrived at a state in which their desperation is so great
that they are completely insensitive to further action against them. When
Uncle George is bitten in the arm by the Indian woman, he yells, "Damn
squaw bitch!" Another Indian in the room just laughs at this, seemingly

3

not at all offended. This is a good example of what effective oppression does to people. If the Indians had had any pride at all left, the least response would have been a grim silence after the remark.

Another indication of the oppression is the decay of group solidarity. Had the Indian settlement existed before the white man came, the difficult birth would be everyone's concern and everyone's pain. The birth of a baby, especially a boy, was a very important event and if it was not going well the whole community would be empathetic. Instead, these Indians try as hard as they can to get out of range of the mother's cries. Only an old woman, who may remember the pain of her own childbirth, helps at all. The Indians still may have enough compassion to send for the doctor, but that is about as far as it goes.

What gives meaning to the story is the way Hemingway presents the two sides of the struggle. He never condemns either the whites nor the Indians for being the cause or the maintainers of the problem. Some bad and good points about each group are given, and the reader is left to decide who is right. Hemingway doesn't preach by making the doctor evil and the Indians good. The doctor is just a man who has found his own way of dealing with what he feels is an unchangeable reality, and the Indians are far from being saints. By examining the issues in the story, the reader can better understand the extent to which racism is a problem and why it probably will be around for some time to come.

Instructor's Comments

1. Strengths. This is a good first paper. The six paragraphs work
   together to define a clear and strongly personal position. More

4

sensitive than Hemingway's first readers were to civil rights, this student theorizes about social barriers and defines how Hemingway artistically defines racism in terms of the geography, plot, and language of this story. He relates literature to life.

2. <u>Weaknesses</u>. While the position is clear, the paper suffers from lack of extension. While the theorizing is more than adequate, un-developed lines such as "Some bad and good points about each group are given" suggest that more specific details could be given to support the position.

PAPER II: *THE SUN ALSO RISES* DAYS 11–26

DAYS 11–12: BEGINNING A HEMINGWAY NOVEL

Goals

1. To orient students to *The Sun Also Rises* (1926).
2. To begin reading the novel in class.

Materials

Class set of *The Sun Also Rises* or *Three Novels: The Sun Also Rises, A Farewell to Arms, The Old Man and the Sea.*

Assignment

Note the DUE date of Paper II on the Schedule.

Procedure

1. Remind students that the first Defense Day will be coming up in about five days. Copies of the papers for defense will be handed out the day prior to Defense Day. All papers will be returned at the end of Defense Day.
2. Ask students to review The Hemingway Chronology (Handout 3), noting that Hemingway has shifted to writing novels. *Torrents of Spring,* a minor work, was a parody of novelist Sherwood Anderson—a rather nasty publishing event since Anderson had befriended young Ernest, who was still an unknown. More can be said about this on Day 13. Pass out copies of *The Sun Also Rises* and help students to identify the names in the dedication (Hadley, the first wife; John or "Bumby," the first son).
3. *The Sun Also Rises* is a portrait of wounded people living in Paris, much as the wounded Hemingway did after serving as an ambulance driver on the northern Italian front in World War I. This book may seem slow to students ("Nothing really happens!"), but remind them that it shocked and intrigued the new generation of Americans who emerged from the high-blown idealism of the war. The style captures the mood of life in Paris. Ask students to note the biblical source (Ecclesiastes) of the title as well as the quote by Gertrude Stein, then living in Paris.
4. Before students begin reading, tell them that some students of Hemingway believe that the central character, Jake Barnes, is just Nick Adams, abroad and wounded.
5. Use the rest of Day 11 and all of Day 12 for in-class reading.

Additional Suggestions

1. Brief reference to maps of Paris, France, and Spain may be made at this point, as well as to books containing photographs of Hemingway at this time.
2. You may wish to use Hemingway's *A Moveable Feast,* pp. 11–31, to introduce Gertrude Stein ("Miss Stein Instructs") and to note Hemingway's scorn of the Lost Generation label ("Une Generation Perdue").

DAY 13: LEARNING ABOUT PARIS IN THE 1920s

Goal

To provide biographical, literary, and historical background for *The Sun Also Rises.*

Materials

Hemingway lived in Paris from 1921 to 1927, and numerous background accounts of the Paris expatriates are available. The following are readily obtainable and are suggested for background discussion and reading:

1. "Life" in Arthur Waldhorn's *A Reader's Guide to Ernest Hemingway*, pp. 10–14.
2. "Hemingway in Paris" in Malcolm Cowley's *A Second Flowering: Works and Days of the Lost Generation*, pp. 48–73.
3. Carlos Baker, *Ernest Hemingway*, pp. 153–55. A useful account of the background of the plot and title of *The Sun Also Rises*.

Procedure

1. Using maps, readings, and photographs, describe the excitement of Paris in the 1920s where life was inexpensive and culturally exciting for writers, painters, musicians (from Gertrude Stein to Picasso to George Gershwin)—a marked contrast to the more puritanical, Prohibition America. Paris was discovered by World War I soldiers, young Americans fed up with the slogans of the past. Expatriate writers especially gathered at Stein's salon to look at her collection of paintings, to discuss art and writing, to be free of Oak Park conventions. In Paris, Hemingway met a number of writers who influenced him: Ezra Pound, James Joyce, Sherwood Anderson, Stein, F. Scott Fitzgerald—the last three later getting rough treatment from Hemingway through parody, Anderson in *The Torrents of Spring* as a romantic primitivist, Stein in *A Moveable Feast* as a lesbian, Fitzgerald in *The Snows of Kilimanjaro* as a drunk.
2. For Hemingway, Paris meant writing as a reporter (note Cabelese in the Cowley chapter), living with Hadley and Bumby, losing his manuscripts (see the account in Baker, *Ernest Hemingway*, pp. 102–3), boxing, going to Sylvia Beach's book store (Shakespeare and Company), visiting the race track, traveling south to the bullfights in Pamplona and Madrid. Real people emerged as characters: Lady Duff Twysden as Lady Brett Ashley, Harold Loeb as Robert Cohn. In Paris, Ernest met Pauline Pfeiffer, and his first marriage fell apart.
3. Use maps to locate scenes in the novel as well as to identify important literary locations—the Left Bank, the Stein apartment at 27 rue de Fleurus, Notre Dame.

Additional Suggestion

Slides or resource persons (students if possible) can bring Paris alive. Even school-made slides from books on Paris and Hemingway can enliven the discussion and help students to visualize the locale of the novel.

DAYS 14–16: READING *THE SUN ALSO RISES* AND PREPARING FOR DEFENSE DAY

Goals

1. To provide time for students to continue reading *The Sun Also Rises*.
2. To prepare students for the first Defense Day.

Materials

1. Copies of the position papers on "Indian Camp" that you have chosen for the first Defense Day.
2. Handout 7: Defense Day: Criteria for Grading Position Papers.

Procedure

1. Two full days, 14 and 15, will give students time to read a good portion of this medium-length novel. Hopefully, the previous discussion of life in Paris will motivate this reading.
2. On Day 16, hand out copies of the papers you have chosen for discussion on Day 17, the first Defense Day.
3. Give each student a copy of Handout 7: Defense Day: Criteria for Grading Position Papers. This handout can be instructive for the oral grading after each paper has been evaluated by the seminar. (Prior to class, review the discussion of how to conduct a successful Defense Day in the introduction.) Students can use this handout during Day 18 as they read and annotate their copies of these papers so that they will be able to remember their initial reactions.
4. Some instructors may wish to develop a system of anonymous grading, using this handout with each Defense Day paper.
5. Encourage students to annotate their copies of these papers so that they will be able to remember their initial reactions to content and mechanics. Remind them that Defense

Day is not Destruction Day. It is a time to learn about the positions of others, to clarify what is not clear, to agree and disagree, to study organization and supporting evidence, to work on mechanics, and to defend what one has written. The word "criticism" implies two responsibilities, for critics try to understand what a writer has written as well as to react to the writing.

6. Students whose papers have been chosen for Defense Day should prepare to read them aloud.

DAYS 17–18: PARTICIPATING IN DEFENSE DAY AND FOLLOW-UP

Goals

1. To conduct a first Defense Day that will provide a useful model for the remaining six.
2. To provide a follow-up that offers other students the opportunity to express their positions.
3. To help students examine the position of critics.

Materials

1. Extra copies of the position papers for students who may have lost or forgotten them.
2. Prior to class, review the discussion of how to conduct a successful Defense Day in the introduction, The Seminar Method. Write the three criteria for evaluating papers on the board: Clarity of Position; Organization and Support; Mechanics.
3. The corrected copies of the remaining position papers ready to give out at the end of the period.

Procedure

1. It is important that you choose good models for the first Defense Day and that you allot the discussion time equally. Remember, the students, not you, are to do the evaluating. Too much direction on your part will destroy the spirit of Defense Day; instead, encourage discussion, restate or clarify student positions, work for a balanced discussion (call on everyone, ask students who suggest grades to justify their choices), and conclude the defenses with positive summation. Always the goal is the next paper.

4. Return the other position papers at the end of the period without comment. The next class period will be given over to these papers.
5. Follow-up, Day 18, will allow others in the class to state their positions. There are a number of options for this day:
   a. Review the positions taken by the papers defended on the previous day. You may have taken notes on the positions of the remaining students and can, therefore, call on students who have similar or contrasting positions. Or each student can be called upon to state his or her position. Or you may ask other students to read all or selected portions of their papers—again, excellent models but ones not chosen for Defense Day.
   b. You may wish to discuss the successes (and failures) of the first Defense Day. Clear the air. Ask students how Defense Days can be improved. If some students argue that the grading was too high or too low, ask them to formulate a fair standard, taking into consideration the pressures of such close examination. Remind them that learning to write is more than just a letter grade.
   c. You may wish to read aloud a critic's evaluation of the Nick Adams stories or of "Indian Camp." Suggestions: (1) pages 27–33 of "Initiation Experiences" in Joseph DeFalco's *The Hero in Hemingway's Short Stories;* (2) "In Our Time: A Review" by D. H. Lawrence, pages 93–94, or portions of Philip Young's "Adventures of Nick Adams," pages 95–111, both in *Hemingway: A Collection of Critical Essays,* edited by Robert P. Weeks.

DAYS 19–22: SETTING THE SCENE FOR *THE SUN ALSO RISES* AND CHOOSING TOPICS FOR PAPER II

Goals

1. To provide background for and insight into the novel through films.
2. To suggest topics for Paper II.

Materials

1. Films: (a) *Hemingway's Spain: "The Sun Also Rises,"* McGraw-Hill/ABC, 1969 (17 min., color); (b) *Hemingway's Spain: "Death in the Afternoon,"* McGraw-Hill/ABC, 1969 (15 min., color).
2. Handout 8: Suggestions for Paper II.
3. Handout 9: Student Model for Paper II.

Procedure

1. The two films on Hemingway's Spain can be shown on whatever days they are available. Both are very fine films picturing the landscape of Spain, the setting of the novel, and bullfighting. Rod Steiger and Jason Robards narrate, using Hemingway's own words. The first film sets the scene of the novel; the second uses material from the 1932 nonfiction book on bullfighting but is excellent background for *The Sun Also Rises* since bullfighting is so important to its theme.
2. Time to complete the novel may be provided in class if necessary.
3. Handout 8 may be used in identifying positions for the second paper. The student paper for this assignment may be posted on the bulletin board for individual reference or copies made for distribution and discussion.

DAYS 23–24: READING ALOUD ANOTHER HEMINGWAY STORY

Goals

1. To read out loud "The Big Two-Hearted River" (1925) and to relate its theme to *The Sun Also Rises.*
2. To discuss Hemingway's style through "The Big Two-Hearted River."

Materials

Class copies of *The Short Stories of Ernest Hemingway.*

Procedure

1. Remind students that Hemingway took Nick Adams through a series of initiation experiences. Then, in 1925, he wrote "The Big

Two-Hearted River," one of his most famous stories. The story tells of a wounded man who returns to Upper Michigan after World War I. The man is Nick Adams, not Nicky Adams. Nick is like the land he visits—burned out—and is looking for peace and quiet. Hemingway himself returned home to Oak Park a hero with medals, but then he too went back to his childhood summer home to recuperate and write. The story ties itself to *The Sun Also Rises* in many ways—the wound, fishing, the search for oneself. It is famous for its style.
2. Ask students to read the story aloud by paragraphs, your role being to piece together the plot, comment on the style, encourage student reactions. The story is unforgettable and will influence students throughout the course (see Handout 21). Take the full two days.
3. You may want to read the account in Joseph DeFalco, *The Hero in Hemingway's Short Stories,* pp. 144–51.

DAYS 25–26: COMPLETING PAPER II AND READING A BACKGROUND STORY FOR *A FAREWELL TO ARMS*

Goals

1. To complete the writing and proofreading of Paper II.
2. To read "In Another Country" (1927) in preparation for *A Farewell to Arms.*

Materials

Copies of *The Short Stories of Ernest Hemingway.*

Procedure

1. Day 25 should be given over to writing and proofreading. Since students saw that proofreading errors detracted from the papers read on the first Defense Day, they will now be more concerned about careful proofreading.
2. Remind students that Paper II is due at the beginning of the period on Day 26. On that day the class should read aloud, without comments, "In Another Country," the genesis for *A Farewell to Arms,* Hemingway's

next novel and the reading assignment on which Paper III will be based.

3. You may wish to preface the reading with Carlos Baker, *Ernest Hemingway,* p. 190, an account of how this story led to the novel. Again, refer to the map of Italy.

4. Immediately select the papers for the second Defense Day and have them reproduced. In-class time for grading the other papers is provided while the class goes on to read *A Farewell to Arms.*

HANDOUT 7
DEFENSE DAY: CRITERIA FOR GRADING POSITION PAPERS

____ **Clarity of Position**

1. Does the paper pursue *one* position?
2. Can you state this position? If so, write it below:

_____

_____

_____

____ **Organization and Support**

1. Is the position clear because it is logical?
2. Is it clear because it is supported by concrete material, such as direct references and quotations?
3. Is it clear because it pursues an obvious, even minor, position? Consider if the position is complex or original?
4. Is the position supported by the proper language, for example, a humorous position uses humorous images and words?
5. Is there coherence in the paper: transitions between sentences and paragraphs to enhance the organization?
6. Are the introduction and conclusion effective in clarifying the position?
7. Does the paper suffer from irrelevancies or over-emphasis of a minor point?

____ **Mechanics**

1. Do many proofreading errors detract from the paper's position?
2. Are there over ten basic mechanical errors—spelling, punctuation, capitalization, fragments, run-on sentences, usage, misplaced modifiers, parallel structure, words often confused, pronoun forms, verb forms?
3. Is the paper smooth reading? What about awkward sentences, imprecise or redundant word choice?

_____ Grade

USE THIS SHEET AS YOU EXAMINE EACH POSITION PAPER.

HANDOUT 8
SUGGESTIONS FOR PAPER II: *THE SUN ALSO RISES* **(1926)**

1. Examine the quotations from Gertrude Stein and the Bible. Can one of these be developed? Perhaps you should do more background reading on Stein and the passages from Ecclesiastes.

2. The first words of the novel are "Robert Cohn." What is his function in the book? Should he be truly despised or is he the other side of Jake Barnes?

3. Is Hemingway a racist? Are his remarks about Jews and blacks evidence of prejudice?

4. Hemingway uses the word "funny" a good deal. What does this word mean in the book?

5. Consider Jake Barnes. Is he a hero, a man with "grace under pressure"? Or is he pathetic, an emasculated man?

6. Why is so much of the book about bullfighting and the fiesta?

7. Hemingway once said, "A writer's job is to tell the truth." What truth is he telling in this story?

8. Is this novel a love story? Why can't Brett and Jake fall in love and get married like characters do in romantic novels?

9. Why does Hemingway use the first-person narration in this novel?

10. What does Paris mean in this story? A beautiful, exciting city? A different city at night compared to the day?

11. Is Jake Barnes just Nick Adams grown up?

12. Hemingway is said to have a Code: a man must try to impose meaning where none seems possible, he must have courage and not quit, he must have discipline and control his death, he must behave with dignity. Is the Code in this novel?

13. Use a key line, such as the last one of the novel, for a paper.

14. What is the meaning of religion in this novel?

15. Some scholars say this is a topical novel, one about the 1920s and expatriates. If so, what does it say about them?

HANDOUT 9
STUDENT MODEL FOR PAPER II

THINGS THAT GO BUMP IN THE NIGHT

by Pat Chong

At night people find themselves, perhaps for the only time in their lives, alone, completely alone. The normal distractions of the day have gone home, to bed, or off the air, and all the reassuring objects of reality are hidden or rendered indistinct by the darkness. In the dark a person is left to confront himself, and he must do it honestly. The characters in The Sun Also Rises continually try, with varying degrees of success, to avoid facing themselves. Their primary methods of escape are drinking and being with their friends for most, or all, of the night. Still, none of them can totally avoid the effect of the night.

As Jake Barnes is the narrator of the story he is able to give a more detailed account of what influence the night has on him. At the start of the book it is night, and Jake is sitting in a cafe, then picks up a prostitute, attends a party, meets Brett, and then goes home. When he is with the prostitute, he tells her he is "sick," referring to his war wound. Later, while in the taxi with Brett he tells her, "What happened to me is supposed to be funny." Both times he refers to his wound; he does so in a matter-of-fact tone, seemingly jaded to the changes it has brought to his life. When alone in his apartment, he starts thinking about "the old grievance." In the dark Jake candidly examines his emotions:

> I try and play it along and just not make trouble for
> people . . . The Catholic Church had an awfully good way
> of handling all that . . . Not to think about it. Oh, it

1

2

was swell advice. Try and take it sometime. Try and take
it.

Jake acknowledges the power the night has over him. He says, "It is
awfully easy to be hard-boiled about everything in the daytime, but at
night it is a different thing." Jake repeats this philosophy later in
the book; then he says he did not sleep without a light on for six months.
He uses the past tense in the sentence to signify the fact that he is no
longer scared of the new perspective of life that the dark allows him to
see. As he is not as afraid anymore, he does not rely on alcohol to help
him avoid the effect of the night. He does stay up and observe his
friends trying to escape by drinking and being with other people.

The night plays a significant role in Brett's life. Initially, she
tries to avoid the night, but at the end of the book she also learns of
the importance of the night. In the beginning, Brett is able to show her
love to Jake only during the night, and even then she tries to avoid
expressing it. The first night Brett gets extremely drunk and allows a
count to pick her up; then she goes to see Jake, in the middle of the
night, leaving the Count in the car waiting for her. To Jake she says,
"Just wanted to see you. Damn silly idea. Want to get dressed and come
down?" This statement reveals the battle that is going on inside her.
One side is fighting the night's effect on her; the other side is giving
in and telling him she wants to be with him.

A similar situation occurs the next evening when Jake, the Count,
and Brett dine together. She again becomes drunk. She offers to send
the Count away so they can be alone. Then later she tells Jake not to
kiss her and she will not see him again. Subsequently, she delays her
next encounter with Jake for three days by passing out on the train.
When she does meet up with him, she tries, once more, to avoid the night's

3

effect on her. She drinks and keeps her mind occupied with Mike Campbell and Pedro Romero. She is more successful this time as she fancies herself in love with Pedro. She confesses this to Jake while they take a nocturnal stroll. When she leaves Pedro, Brett shows her new understanding of how it is necessary to examine oneself carefully to be happy. During the meal she shares with Jake, she tells him not to get drunk, that it is not necessary. This reveals her new maturity since getting drunk was once her main way of combatting the dark. The final proof of her new awareness is in the last scene of the book. Brett rests against Jake in a taxi and says, "Oh, Jake, . . . we could have had such a damned good time together." This is said when it is "very hot and bright" outside, when daylight is at its strongest and Brett can openly admit her love. It is interesting to note that Brett and Jake at the start of the novel are in a cab at night where Brett asks Jake to kiss her and draws as far away as possible. At the end of The Sun Also Rises she knows the value of honestly facing up to herself. Brett will not fear the night again.

A symbolic incident involving Brett's growing awareness of the importance of the night occurs during her infatuation with Pedro. After a bullfight Pedro is awarded the ears of the bull, and he, in turn, gives them to Brett. She wraps them in Jake's handkerchief and places them, with several cigarette stubs, "far back" into her bed-table. The bed-table represents the night, and so everything she puts in it must be truthful. The stubs placed with the ears and handkerchief indicate that Jake and Pedro (in general, all men) are a vice to Brett, a fact estab-lished in the course of the book. Wrapping the ears with Jake's hand-kerchief shows Brett's desire to have both men in her life. That act also defines their separate roles. The ears are evidence of Pedro's skill in the arena, a major part of his allure, and so represent something

4

special and unique, yet also transitory. The handkerchief signifies Jake's role as a father figure, a protector. He is someone Brett always can go to for help. The symbolism is repeated in the novel. When Brett forces Pedro to leave, for the sake of his career, she turns to Jake for comfort.

Bill, a lesser character in the book, has a revealing discussion with Jake. While walking, they pass a taxidermist shop. Bill asks Jake if he wants a stuffed dog. Jake declines. Bill persists, saying, "[They] mean everything in the world to you after you bought it. Simple exchange of values. You give them money. They give you a stuffed dog." Bill expresses a certain cynicism. A dog symbolizes loyalty, friendship, trust, and blind love. Unfortunately, all these qualities are negated by the dog being stuffed. There is only the facade of these virtues. There is the suggestion that he has had a "stuffed dog" revealed to him, when he says they mean everything to the person who buys them. By bringing in money he degrades the value of the qualities a dog is supposed to possess. Later, he paraphrases a well known proverb: "Road to hell paved with unbought stuffed dogs." He equates stuffed dogs with good intentions. People's intentions, though seemingly good, really have no genuine inspiration. Finally, Bill confesses to have always loved stuffed animals. Again, this points to the fact that someone close to him may have been revealed as false. The nighttime brings Bill to the realization of human falsity, though alcohol helps him live with this understanding.

Mike appears to be the person most affected by the night. Three different times during the night he becomes drunk and attacks Cohn. The final time occurs in the evening of a foggy day. Mike, whom Jake describes as a "bad drunk," drinks to distort the view of life that night presents to him. His needling of Cohn, and to a lesser degree Pedro, shows that

5

at night Mike sees himself in a totally honest light, hating himself
because he always is bankrupt and cannot hold on to Brett. The alcohol
serves as an infuriator, an incentive to turn to other, weaker people,
and attack them to alleviate his self-hatred. Robert Cohn's fighting
back and knocking out Mike can be seen as Cohn's attempt to re-establish
some of his own ego. Mike and even Cohn use drinking as a safety valve
for releasing inner steam. Unlike the "good drunks," Bill and Brett,
they use the same tactics but fail because drinking for them is not an
escape mechanism.

All the characters in The Sun Also Rises to some extent try to avoid
facing themselves honestly. They reveal something of their character by
their method of escape, by their self-awareness in the night. Perhaps
when they hear things that go bump in the night, they are not so afraid
of their ghosts. They see that it is themselves knocking in their brains,
wanting to be recognized. Perhaps it is the fear of things that go bump
in the night that has driven them to escape into the world of alcohol, the
world of distorted images.

Instructor's Comments

1. Strengths. What a marvelous title! Not only has the author used it
    to suggest the paper's position but also to tie together the intro-
    duction, the conclusion, and all the concrete examples--the quotations,
    the four central characters--in her effort to defend a personal
    position. She has a sense of poetry, revealing to her classmates
    how a basic symbol was exploited in the novel and relating it as well
    to our own lives.

6

2. <u>Weaknesses</u>. While the paper may be flawed by wordiness, even by
    jerky sentences that do not always flow with each other, this first
    paper about a novel is ambitious and runs a full five pages. The
    reader cannot help but be sensitive to that ambition. You might point
    out the undocumented claim of the last paragraph that "all the charac-
    ters" avoid themselves, but you should also help the seminar to
    appreciate the larger success of this paper.

PAPER III: *A FAREWELL TO ARMS*
DAYS 27–42

DAY 27: BEGINNING TO READ
HEMINGWAY'S MOST SUCCESSFUL NOVEL

Goals

1. To orient students to *A Farewell to Arms* (1929).
2. To provide in-class time to begin the novel.

Materials

Class copies of *A Farewell to Arms* or *Three Novels: The Sun Also Rises, A Farewell to Arms, The Old Man and the Sea.*

Assignment

1. Ask students to note the DUE date for the third paper on the Schedule, Day 42.
2. Remind students that Defense Day for Paper II *(The Sun Also Rises)* will be Day 34. Copies of the papers chosen for defense will be handed out on Day 33.

Procedure

1. Ask students to review The Hemingway Chronology (Handout 3), noting that the next book for consideration is the very successful *A Farewell to Arms*. At this time, Hemingway is re-examining his life and experiencing personal trauma. His first marriage has broken up, he has remarried and moved from Paris to Key West, Florida, where he will live for the next ten years. While he works on *A Farewell to Arms,* his father commits suicide back in Oak Park. The novel becomes a commercial success, establishing Hemingway's reputation as a writer of unusual style and a man sensitive to the agonies of war. Note the dedication to Gustavus A. Pfeiffer, the wealthy Arkansas uncle of his second wife, Pauline Pfeiffer, and a man who became a good friend, one of the first of the wealthy Pfeiffer clan to approve of Ernest.

2. Point out that the novel's title comes from a poem by the English writer George Peele (1558?–1597). Read the poem (see the *Oxford Book of Verse*) or post it on the bulletin board.

3. Explain that, although *A Farewell to Arms* is longer than *The Sun Also Rises,* its commercial success is partly explained by the fact that it has more of a plot and a greater sense of movement than the first novel. It has humor, memorable lines (turn, for example, to page 249 of the 1929 Scribner edition and note the lines beginning with "If people bring so much courage. . . ."), and strong symbols—such as the weather. Its title is a two-edged sword, referring to both love and war.

4. Ask students to begin reading the novel during the remainder of the class period.

DAYS 28–31: CONTINUING TO READ
A FAREWELL TO ARMS, SHARING
RELATED HEMINGWAY SHORT STORIES,
AND CHOOSING TOPICS FOR PAPER III

Goals

1. To provide in-class time for reading *A Farewell to Arms.*
2. To read aloud two related war stories— "Now I Lay Me" and "A Very Short Story" —both written in 1927.
3. To suggest topics for Paper III.

Materials

1. Class copies of *A Farewell to Arms.*
2. *The Short Stories of Ernest Hemingway.*

3. Handout 10: Suggestions for Paper III.
4. Handout 11: Student Model for Paper III.

Procedure

1. Use Days 28–29 for in-class reading of *A Farewell to Arms.*
2. Day 30 can be used for the oral reading of the two war stories ("Now I Lay Me" and "A Very Short Story") set in Italy that can be seen as background stories for the novel. Again, suggest how these stories remind us of Nick Adams growing up. DeFalco's *The Hero in Hemingway's Short Stories,* pp. 110–14, 162–63, is useful in preparing for the discussion.
3. During Day 31 suggest positions for Paper III, using Handout 10 as a point of departure. You may also wish to introduce the student model (Handout 11) at this point.

DAY 32: DISCUSSING WORLD WAR I AND THE HEMINGWAY BIOGRAPHY OF THIS PERIOD

Goals

1. To provide historical background for *A Farewell to Arms.*
2. To relate elements of the Hemingway biography to the novel.

Materials

A number of materials are useful for discussing World War I and Hemingway—maps, films, records, filmstrips. The following books are very useful:

1. "The Other War" in Malcolm Cowley's *A Second Flowering: Works and Days of the Lost Generation,* pp. 3–18, especially for literary background of the period.
2. Arthur Waldhorn's *A Reader's Guide to Ernest Hemingway,* pp. 14–16.
3. Leicester Hemingway's *My Brother, Ernest Hemingway,* pp. 97–100, on Hemingway in Key West and his father's death.
4. "It Was Great Fun" in James McLendon's *Papa: Hemingway in Key West, 1928–1940,* pp. 47–57, for backgrounds of the novel and the author's life at that time.
5. Carlos Baker's *Ernest Hemingway: A Life Story,* pp. 44–52, for a discussion of Hem-

ingway's wound, his hospitalization, and his brief love affair with the prototype of Catherine Barkley—a nurse named Agnes von Kurowsky.

Procedure

1. Stress the fact that *A Farewell to Arms* is highly autobiographical; refer to Hemingway's own war wounds, his recuperation in Milan, his awful awareness that war was not like the stuff of the romantic novels that he had been raised on or jingoistic slogans (see Cowley, *A Second Flowering*), and his own love affair. In addition, the facts of Hemingway's life have their own death-in-life (the end of the love affair, the later dissolution of his first marriage, the death of his father by suicide, and even his wife Pauline's caesarian—note also "Indian Camp").
2. The novel is in microcosm the story of many young men and women who felt betrayed by the rhetoric of war when confronted by its realities. They, like Hemingway, were anxious to go "over there," wear fancy uniforms, and win medals. Other literary figures—Cummings, John Dos Passos, William Faulkner—eagerly enlisted in foreign organizations after the war began in 1914 and before the U.S. entered in 1917. They were the ones who later stayed in Paris and became part of the so-called Lost Generation.
3. Students will find much that is fascinating: Hemingway's awful wounds, his love affair, his return to Oak Park High School as a hero, his break with his parents after he goes up to Michigan to heal his psychic wounds ("The Big Two-Hearted River"). More can be said about this break on Day 37 when "Soldier's Home" is read out loud in class. Certainly the death of his father by suicide will spark discussion as to whether this event is related to Hemingway's own suicide.

DAYS 33–35: PREPARING FOR AND PARTICIPATING IN DEFENSE DAY AND THE FOLLOW-UP DISCUSSION

Goals

1. To provide additional in-class time for reading *A Farewell to Arms.*

2. To conduct a Defense Day and follow-up that offer students an opportunity to express and defend their positions.
3. To encourage students to look ahead to the third paper, accepting again the challenge of how best to present a well-documented position.

Materials

1. Copies of the papers you have chosen for Defense Day.
2. Corrected papers on *The Sun Also Rises* to return at the end of Defense Day.

Procedure

1. Day 33 is set aside for reading, though some students may use the class time to examine the position papers to be discussed during Defense Day.
2. Begin Day 34 by reviewing the Defense Day procedures, although the seminar should now be familiar with the system. Be sure to return all position papers on *The Sun Also Rises* at the end of the period.
3. During the follow-up discussion (Day 35), you might ask other students to read their papers for class comment, discuss the student paper (Handout 11), or present the viewpoint of a critic, e.g., "The Death of Love in *The Sun Also Rises*" by Mark Spilka in *Hemingway: A Collection of Critical Essays,* edited by Robert P. Weeks, pp. 127-38.

DAYS 36-42: COMPLETING THE NOVEL, DISCUSSING RELATED STORIES, AND WRITING PAPER III

Goals

1. To complete *A Farewell to Arms.*
2. To read and discuss in class two related stories, "Soldier's Home" (1925) and "Fathers and Sons" (1933).
3. To provide class time to write and revise Paper III.

Materials

Copies of *The Short Stories of Ernest Hemingway.*

Procedure

1. Days 36-38 should provide enough time to complete the novel and to read aloud "Soldier's Home." The story suggests Hemingway's state of mind as he returned home to Oak Park (though the young man is Krebs and he returns to Oklahoma) and correlates well with *A Farewell to Arms.* The piece is a marvelous artifact of the 1920s and may also be used to discuss Hemingway's emerging style (especially the idea of repetitions taught him by Gertrude Stein). The story also suggests Hemingway's break with his parents that took place in Michigan. You may wish to supplement this discussion with material from Constance Cappel Montgomery's *Hemingway in Michigan,* pp. 172-82, or Carlos Baker's *Ernest Hemingway,* pp. 56-74.
2. Days 39-41 should be used for writing, revising, and proofreading the third paper.
3. Use Day 42 to read out loud "Fathers and Sons," a story which makes an interesting transition between the war novel and the grown-up Nick Adams, now an author (with a son—Bumby) who is reflecting on his father's suicide—all materials related to Hemingway's own life. This last of the Nick Adams stories brings that part of Hemingway's writing career to an end. It is also a very moving story of a mature Hemingway, no longer so resentful of his parents (as in "Soldier's Home") and now aware of his own mortality, of being a father as well as a son. The prose is more mature as well, not so experimental, though there is the familiar Hemingway description of nature, the sharp dialogue, the repeat of earlier Nick Adams plots, and an awareness of life that high school students understand (cf. "My Old Man"): life must be learned; not everything can be taught, especially intense experiences such as Nick's childhood sexual encounter.
4. Collect the third Position Paper on Day 42. Select the papers for the next Defense Day and have them reproduced.

Additional Suggestion

The film version of "Soldier's Home" (see Bibliography) can be excellent for comparison with the actual short story.

HANDOUT 10
SUGGESTIONS FOR PAPER III: *A FAREWELL TO ARMS* (1929)

1. Consider the title. Does it have more than one meaning? Use the poem, too.
2. Is this a war novel, a romantic novel, or what?
3. The weather seems to play an important role in this novel. What do the various types of weather mean, especially the rain?
4. Is Lieutenant Henry another Code Hero? Are his flight from the war and his seeming coldness at the end of the novel symptoms of a Hero gone wrong?
5. What is the function of Rinaldi in the novel?
6. Is Catherine a rounded character or a stick figure? Does Hemingway understand women?
7. Does Hemingway have a sense of humor in this novel? If so, what kind of humor does he use?
8. Try a contrast paper: Jake Barnes and Lieutenant Frederic Henry.
9. What is the function of the first-person narration?
10. This might be the time to do some research. Is this novel more biography than fiction?
11. Why did Hemingway kill off Catherine Barkley in childbirth? Does anyone remember Thornton Wilder's *Our Town*?
12. What is the truth in this novel? Look at page 249 again, especially the line: "The world breaks every one and afterward many are strong at the broken places."
13. What about religion in this novel? Why does Henry pray?
14. What is the function of food in the novel?
15. While Hemingway was revising his first draft of this novel, his father committed suicide. Can you tie these two events together?

HANDOUT 11
STUDENT MODEL FOR PAPER III

ADOLESCENCE TO ADULTHOOD

by Melody Myers

Ernest Hemingway's characters are strong individuals, but he was inclined to build his characters with similar dispositions and reactions. Nick Adams of "Indian Camp" and Frederic Henry of A Farewell to Arms endured a similar situation and reacted to it as if they were the same person. Instead of the innocent onlooker that was Nick, Henry became painfully involved and a sufferer of life. They shared the same responses, but a change can be detected from Nick the boy to Henry the man. The difference between the two is that Henry represents a matured Nick Adams.

Nick's first unpleasant exposure to the Indian camp was to observe a screaming Indian woman who had been in labor for two days but was still unable to give birth to her child. The purpose of his father's trip to the camp was to deliver the child. The doctor examined the woman and concluded that a Caesarian section must be performed to give relief to the mother and child. Nick's primary concern was the woman's screaming. He even inquired if his father could stop her agony of pain.

> "Oh, Daddy, can't you give her something to make her stop screaming?" asked Nick.
> "No. I haven't any anaesthetic," his father said.

Henry also was confronted with a woman in childbirth. The woman was his lover, Catherine. The situation was more personal and emotional than Nick's, yet concern was shared by both. When complications occurred and Catherine began screaming, Henry tried to comfort her by giving her gas. Henry said, "I'll make it [the gas] work. I'll turn it all the way."

1

2

Like Nick, Henry wanted to relieve the pain of childbirth. Yet the possibility that too much gas could result in death worried Henry. Catherine's apparent suffering finally took priority over death.

In "Indian Camp," Nick had the opportunity to watch his father perform a Caesarian operation. Even though Nick held the basin for his father during the procedure, he preferred not to watch. In fact, after Dr. Adams invited Nick to observe him as he put in the stitches, Nick did not watch. "His curiosity had been gone for a long time." Apparently Nick had his fill of childbirth. He had already endured more than what he had anticipated.

Catherine's doctor also decided that a Caesarian section was the easiest and safest way to relieve both the mother and child. Henry was given the same chance to observe a Caesarian operation as had Nick.

> "You can go in the other door and sit up there," a nurse
> said to me [Henry]. There were benches behind a rail that
> looked down . . . at Catherine. The mask was over her face
> and she was quiet now. They wheeled the stretcher forward.
> I turned away and walked down the hall.

Henry also passed up the chance of medical observation. His sense of responsibility and guilt were too much for him. As much as he hated to face the truth, he knew that Catherine was paying the consequences for loving him. He hated it all, but later he returned to the operating room to watch the doctors sew up the incision. Henry thought, "I do not think I could have watched them cut, but I watched the wound closed into a high welted ridge with quick skillful-looking stitches like a cobbler's, and was glad." Henry, unlike Nick, enjoyed watching the final part of the operation. The completion of the surgery proved the first step of Catherine's recovery. The final stitches seemed to verify the ending of a traumatic ordeal. Now that the baby had been delivered, it was only logical that Catherine's recuperation would follow.

3

On the trip home from the Indian camp, Nick and his father discussed the pain of childbirth, suicide, the difference between male and female suicides, and death itself. Too early in life, Nick had seen too much suffering. This had been Nick's initiation to pain, to the violence of birth and death. The story concluded, "In the early morning on the lake sitting in the stern of the boat with his father rowing, he felt quite sure he would never die." After experiencing the unpleasantness of birth and death, Nick refused to accept them as part of reality. In returning home he concluded that he would never die. Childish? Perhaps. But that was what he believed. By rejecting the pain he had seen and felt, Nick thought he could avoid death forever. He was trying to cope with life, the burden of adulthood. He had shouldered more than what he was ready to carry. At one time or another, a young man may think he shall never die. It is easier for a young man to stand by and watch, for he is not yet painfully involved; he is not a sufferer, only an onlooker. Rather than swallow the truth about childbirth and death, Nick Adams justified them to suit himself.

Lt. Henry found himself confronted with the violence of birth and death, too. Facing reality did not come easy for Henry either. He realized the seriousness of Catherine's operation, but the possibility of her death was unacceptable.

> Yes, but what if she should die? She won't die. She's just having a bad time. . . . Afterward we'd say what a bad time and Catherine would say it wasn't really so bad. But what if she should die? . . . She can't die. Yes, but what if she should die? She can't, I tell you. Don't be a fool. . . . It's just nature giving her <u>hell</u>.

Henry had his doubts as to whether or not Catherine would live, but he loved her and he tried to avoid the likelihood of her death. Henry's reaction was human. Nobody wants loved ones to die. Rather than confronting the alternatives of what could happen, Henry justifies Catherine's

4

complications as "nature giving her hell." He felt that Catherine's suffering would end when "nature" decided to let her go from the grip of hell. He implied it was only a matter of time before Catherine would be relieved from her agony of pain. His justification gave him the hope he needed.

In "Indian Camp," Dr. Adams tells Nick, fathers "are usually the worst sufferers in these little affairs [childbirth]." Frederic Henry was the father of Catherine's child; he had suffered. Henry was numb from death, not from fears for himself--like Nick Adams, but from the loss of his lover. Henry had seen death in war, but it had never touched him the way this single death would for the rest of his life.

As a boy, Nick Adams had a hard time accepting reality. He could not look at life objectively because he had not lived life. Henry also tried to take life in stride, but obstacles got in his way. Henry has experienced war, death, love. He had lived life. Therefore, accepting life's consequences was easier for him as an adult than it was for Nick as an adolescent. Nevertheless, Henry was not untouched by life's misfortunes because memories would be with him forever. His pain was real and lasting. Instead of avoiding the facts of life as Nick Adams has done, Frederic Henry had confronted reality fact to face and accepted it for what it was.

Instructor's Comments

1. <u>Strengths</u>. This student tackled a difficult writing problem, comparing two characters from different works. She is sensitive to balance, to concrete documentation, and to the development of her position about the different perceptions of a boy and a man. Beneath the prose is her understanding of Hemingway's maturing concept

5

of life and death. I also think she is reflecting about her own maturity. In this writing design, she has obviously worked on organizational structure, if not on ways to integrate direct quotations into the text.

2. <u>Weaknesses</u>. While considerable effort was given to structure and the use of concrete illustration, this paper can be seen as somewhat flawed by its lack of sentence variety, a writing goal for Paper III. Many of the paragraphs are stitched together with simple and compound sentences, often beginning with a character's name or a pronoun.

PAPER IV: A PROFILE OF ERNEST HEMINGWAY DAYS 43–57

DAY 43: REVIEWING THE HEMINGWAY BIOGRAPHY AND INTRODUCING THE PROFILE PAPER

Goals

1. To review the Hemingway biography in broad outline.
2. To orient students to Paper IV, a profile of Ernest Hemingway.

Materials

1. Assemble a class library of biographical and autobiographical materials (see Bibliography).
2. Handout 12: Suggestions for Paper IV.
3. Handouts 13 and 14: Student Models for Paper IV.

Assignment

1. Ask students to note the DUE date for Paper IV on the Schedule, Day 57.
2. Paper IV should be based on at least one hundred pages of reading from nonfictional materials about or by Hemingway. The one hundred pages may be taken from a single source or from several sources. A bibliography and footnotes are required.

Procedure

1. In explaining the assignment, remind students that they may use the fictional writings of Hemingway previously read in class but that this material may not be counted toward the one hundred pages of reading required for the Profile Paper.
2. Distribute copies of the model papers for this assignment for subsequent discussion by the class.
3. Before considering ideas for the Profile Paper, review The Hemingway Chronology and place the following outline on the board:

   I. The Early Years, 1899–1921. Growing up in Oak Park (family, high school), summers in Michigan, Kansas City *Star* reporter, ambulance driver in Italy in World War I, reporter for the Toronto *Star,* marriage to Hadley.

   II. The Paris Years, 1921–1927. Foreign correspondent, life among the expatriates (Stein, Pound, Fitzgerald, Anderson, Joyce), literary success, birth of Bumby, bullfighting, divorce and remarriage (Pauline Pfeiffer).

   III. The Key West Period, 1927–1940. Interest in deep sea fishing, purchase of the *Pilar,* birth of Patrick and Gregory, Africa and big game hunting, father's suicide, literary support of Loyalists in Spanish Civil War, divorce by Pauline and marriage to Martha Gellhorn, move to Finca Vigia near Havana.

   IV. The World War II Period, 1940–1945. Sub chaser in Caribbean, war correspondent, "liberator" of Paris, divorce from Martha and marriage to Mary Welsh.

   V. The Cuban Period, 1945–1960. Critical attack on *Across the River and into the Trees,* death of mother, publication of *The Old Man and the Sea* in *Life,* Nobel Prize, purchase of Ketchum, Idaho, hunting lodge, work on memoirs.

   VI. Ketchum, Idaho, and the End. Beginning of breakdown, hospitalization in Rochester, Minnesota, death from self-inflicted gunshot wound.

4. Distribute Handout 12 (Suggestions for Paper IV) for previewing now and for reference later.

5. Encourage students to examine the class collection of Hemingway materials and to seek out materials in libraries. You may wish to distribute copies of portions of the Bibliography.

Additional Suggestions

1. You may wish to use the filmstrip-tape *Ernest Hemingway* in The American Experience in Literature: Five Modern Novelists, available from the Encyclopaedia Britannica Educational Corporation. See the Bibliography for this and other filmstrip/record-cassette suggestions.
2. The seminar may wish to contact resource persons through, for example, the Bell Telephone leased phone system (see Appendix A). Those who knew Hemingway or know much about him, such as college English professors, may be willing to be interviewed by seminar members.

DAYS 44–48: LOCATING AND SHARING A HEMINGWAY ANECDOTE WITH THE CLASS

Goals

1. To help students locate interesting biographical information about Hemingway.
2. To provide a range of anecdotal material that will help students choose a biographical focus for Paper IV.

Materials

1. Class library, supplemented by student research.
2. Film: *Hemingway*, McGraw-Hill (54 min., b/w).
3. Seven Anecdotes from the Hemingway Biography (Appendix C).

Assignment

1. Ask each student to find one concrete anecdote about Ernest Hemingway to share with the class. (See the seven anecdotes in Appendix C.)
2. Anecdote days (47–48) should help to trigger a position. A single anecdote may be used by a given student as the basis for a profile paper or several anecdotes along a similar line may suggest a tactic. Encourage students to use each other's anecdotes and to share source materials.

Procedure

1. Show the excellent documentary film on Hemingway's life on Day 44. If the film is not available, you might use the filmstrip-tape suggested for Day 43 or a slide show made from photographs on Hemingway's life prepared by your school's A-V department.
2. On Day 45, announce the anecdote assignment. While some students may be capable of independent research, others may require a more directed approach. The following suggestions will simplify the assignment and help to ensure that all students find interesting "slice-of-life" anecdotes. A retelling of the first seven anecdotes is included in Appendix C.
   a. Boxing in Paris: Carlos Baker, *Ernest Hemingway: A Life Story*, pp. 22–23; Morley Callaghan, *That Summer in Paris*, pp. 97–100, 118–22.
   b. A childhood accident: Leicester Hemingway, *My Brother*, pp. 19–22.
   c. Hadley loses manuscripts: Carlos Baker, *Ernest Hemingway: A Life Story*, pp. 102–3.
   d. Key West, at Sloppy Joe's, fishing: Leicester Hemingway, *My Brother*, p. 164; McLendon, *Papa*, pp. 152–53.
   e. Punches poet Wallace Stevens: McLendon, *Papa*, pp. 55–57.
   f. African air crashes: Carlos Baker, *Ernest Hemingway: A Life Story*, pp. 518–22.
   g. Suicide attempts: Leicester Hemingway, *My Brother*, p. 256; Carlos Baker, *Ernest Hemingway: A Life Story*, pp. 199, 554–64; A. E. Hotchner, *Papa Hemingway: A Personal Memoir*, pp. 264–304.
   h. Average workday, Sloppy Joe's: McLendon, *Papa*, pp. 145–48.
   i. Fitzgerald referees a Hemingway boxing match: Callaghan, *That Summer in Paris*, pp. 209–13.

j. Ernest wants father's suicide gun: Leicester Hemingway, *My Brother,* pp. 98–100.

k. Hemingway discovers new writing technique: Carlos Baker, *Ernest Hemingway: A Life Story,* pp. 525–29.

l. Hotchner's last talk with Ernest: Hotchner, *Papa Hemingway,* pp. 296–300.

m. Mary and Ernest Hemingway meet, fight: Mary Hemingway, *How It Was,* pp. 121–31.

n. Winning the Nobel Prize: Carlos Baker, *Ernest Hemingway: A Life Story,* pp. 525–29. (Note: here the student or instructor may wish to use the record or tape *Ernest Hemingway Reading,* available from Caedmon, which includes his reading of his Nobel Address.)

3. Share and discuss the anecdotes on Days 47–48. You may wish to bring an anecdote to share, too. Remind students that the research reading for Anecdote Day should help to locate material for Paper IV; the shared anecdotes should also provide a pool of biographical information for the class to draw upon in writing the Profile Paper.

DAYS 49–51: PREPARING FOR AND PARTICIPATING IN DEFENSE DAY AND FOLLOW-UP

Goal

To help students refine their understanding of how a position becomes warranted through clear argumentation and adequate documentation.

Materials

1. Copies of the papers you have chosen for Defense Day.
2. Corrected papers on *A Farewell to Arms* to return at the end of Defense Day.

Procedure

1. Use Day 49 for research reading for Paper IV or for the study of the position papers to be used on Defense Day.

2. Follow the Defense Day procedures outlined earlier. Return all papers at the end of the period.

3. Use the follow-up day to discuss the papers of other students, to evaluate the student models (Handouts 13 and 14), or to consider a critic's point of view, e.g., "Loser Take Nothing" by Philip Young in *20th Century Interpretations of "A Farewell to Arms,"* edited by Jay Gellens, pp. 28–32.

DAY 52: LEARNING ABOUT "NADA" THROUGH READING ANOTHER HEMINGWAY STORY

Goals

1. To read out loud "A Clean Well-Lighted Place" (1933) and to relate its theme to other Hemingway works and to the Hemingway biography.
2. To discuss the concept of *Nada,* an important term in Hemingway criticism.

Materials

Copies of *The Short Stories of Ernest Hemingway.*

Procedure

1. At this point, introduce the concept of *Nada* through "A Clean Well-Lighted Place." This idea will appear in the biographical and critical reading being done by students for Paper IV and will add a new dimension to their understanding of Hemingway's Code Heroes.

2. Read the story aloud, asking students to take turns reading and reacting. The relatively negligible plot deals with Hemingway's poetic vision of despair—perhaps darkest in this story—of people trying to find meaning in a world where none is possible. The story reminds us that the lights go out for everyone, and thus the parody of the Lord's Prayer. Yet all people "need a light for the night." (See pages 27–29 in Waldhorn's *A Reader's Guide to Ernest Hemingway.*)

3. Use the remaining time for research reading for Paper IV.

DAYS 53–57: COMPLETING PAPER IV AND READING TWO MORE HEMINGWAY STORIES

Goals

1. To give students time in class to write, revise, and proofread the Profile Paper.
2. To read out loud "A Day's Wait" (1933) and "The Old Man at the Bridge" (1938).

Materials

Class copies of *The Short Stories of Ernest Hemingway*.

Procedure

1. Day 53 is the final reading and research day for Paper IV. On Day 54 students begin work on rough drafts of the Profile Paper, completing revisions and proofreading on Days 55 and 56.
2. The Profile Position Paper is due on Day 57. You may wish to schedule two Defense Days so that all students will have defended at least one paper before Paper VII, the Summation Paper. At this point, inform the class that something *different* will be done on Defense Day for the last paper. Do not, however, discuss Paper VII at this time. The number of papers you select for the fifth and sixth Defense Days will, of course, depend upon the number of students in your seminar.
3. After collecting the profile papers, read aloud two very short stories. "A Day's Wait" is an amusing story about a boy who thinks he is dying but isn't. The story has biographical overtones: in 1932, the Hemingways were in Arkansas visiting Pauline's relatives when Bumby came down with the flu and a temperature of 102. In this story, the boy's sudden maturity and then retreat back to childhood are of special interest. "The Old Man at the Bridge," set on an Easter Sunday during the Spanish Civil War, not only suggests Hemingway's personal involvement in that struggle, but also lends itself to a discussion of his theme and style—the irony of a man with no hope on a dry, desolate day compared to Christ's Easter, the use of animals (who have instinct), the awfulness of innocence caught up in human evil, the symbol of the bridge, the central character without a name.
4. Select and reproduce papers for the coming Defense Day.

HANDOUT 12
SUGGESTIONS FOR PAPER IV: THE PROFILE PAPER

1. Can any one of the readings define a narrowed theme? For example, is Morley Callaghan's observation about Hemingway and boxing related to what you have read?

2. Try to synthesize Hemingway the man into a single word. What would it be? Then expand upon how Hemingway meets the definition of that word.

3. Who taught Hemingway? Can you name three teachers? How did they mold him?

4. Hemingway had four wives. Were they at all alike? Why would a boy from a proper Oak Park, Illinois, background lead such an unconventional life?

5. Is there a key event in Hemingway's early life that did a great deal to shape him, for example, his World War I injury?

6. Is Hemingway a male chauvinist?

7. Do the early writing and biography suggest that Hemingway would later commit suicide? Was his suicide consistent with his Code and his writing?

8. Hemingway loved boxing, fishing, hunting, the out-of-doors. Why?

9. Can you find a Hemingway quotation that seems to define him and his writing?

10. Was Hemingway a disciplined writer? If so, how would you define and illustrate his "discipline"?

11. Would you like to have been a friend or relative of this famous man and writer?

12. Ernest Hemingway seemed entranced with bullfighting. Why?

13. Relate Hemingway to Nick, Jake, and Frederic. Are they his mouthpieces?

14. Do some research on a friend that Hemingway later rebuffed (Gertrude Stein, F. Scott Fitzgerald, Sherwood Anderson). How do you explain the break?

15. Was Hemingway an American or a citizen of the world, a kind of man without a country? What values did he hold?

HANDOUT 13
STUDENT MODEL FOR PAPER IV

THE ROMANCE AND TREACHERY OF HEMINGWAY'S EGO

by Dan Goldberg

Celebrity status in America has traditionally been reserved for performers and athletes. Occasionally, political or social registers may spawn such superstars, but only one author has ever attained such prestige: Ernest Hemingway. Hemingway is the only American writer of modern times whose fame has exceeded his literary accomplishments. He is the most biographed, talked about, romanticized author in our literary heritage.

Hemingway's own energies were responsible for making him such a newsworthy item. He was in constant motion, in public view, whirling from one romantic stage to another. Everything he did was bigger than life. For the press, he was a perpetual drama, always good for a scoop. After Hem's death, Hemingway constituted the walls of a fort: Hemingway had given the power to believe that he could still shout down the corridors of a hospital, live next to the breath of the beast, accept his portion of dread each day. Yet the greatest living romantic was also mortal.

The motivating force in Hemingway's life, that which made him so romantic, was his own insatiable ego. He continuously sought ways to assert his masculine independence. There was never a time when he was not battling to prove himself. Most of the battles were waged from within, for he rarely had trouble obtaining the respect of his peers.

Hemingway's reputation as a double-crosser was a result of such self-liberating impulses. Whenever he felt a benefactor edging in, a

1

2

friend expecting thanks, he pulled the rug from beneath them. Sherwood Anderson was a classic example of this kind of treatment. He had championed Hemingway's work and even helped the younger author to obtain a publisher. The two men had been friends for a number of years when Ernest decided to do his number on him. Hemingway devoted an entire book, The Torrents of Spring, to satirizing Anderson. He even had the gall to send it to Anderson's own publisher. This came at a time when Anderson was a hot item and considered to be Ernest's mentor. Ernest hated this. It withered his sense of independence. And that is why he attempted to mangle Anderson's reputation and dissociate himself from any previous connection he had with the author of Winesburg, Ohio.

The Torrents of Spring was not an entirely undeserved attack. There are some indications that Anderson was taking credit for some of Hemingway's style. That kind of thing was just enough to tousle Ernest's pride and ignite his paranoic ego. He always wanted to give the impression that everything he had was self-acquired, particularly his writing. Anderson was hurt by Hemingway's over-reaction, but he might have had some of it coming to him.

Gertrude Stein had a similar relationship with Hemingway, and she too got hers in the end. In his early years in Paris in the 1920s, Ernest spent a good deal of time in Stein's apartment, enjoying her company and art collection. They had a close relationship professionally as well as socially. He often consulted her about his work and greatly respected her advice. Yet, when she began to close in on Hemingway, the ax fell upon her also. There was method in this attack. Stein was a powerful personality and demanded a certain amount of conformity from her friends, yet Hemingway's rebellion seems particularly cruel. Much later, in A Moveable Feast, he went so far as to insinuate that she was a lesbian. Ironically, this attack was published long after she died.

3

Hemingway always resorted to dramatic measures to cut his imagined apron strings. He violated Stein's friendship with many personal barbs that deliberately cut deep. In retrospect, his attack seems to have come almost spontaneously. One moment he was congenial and then suddenly he turned ferocious, a type of behavior that repeated itself many times throughout Ernest's life, especially after he had lived in one place for a stretch of time. When he wasn't free to roam, he thirsted for a collision.

While writing, Hemingway also seemed to be battling. Once he had attained a degree of success, he often went to war with his critics. From the time of For Whom the Bell Tolls (1940) to the appearance of The Old Man and the Sea (1952), every piece he published had a challenge to go with it. He loved to rage over reviews, for it gave him a chance to prove himself over and over. He all but declared himself king of contemporary American literature and glorified in his fights with pretenders to the throne.

The Hemingway legend is packed with stories of fist fights and bloodied noses. The image of himself in constant combat was food for his ego. He could obtain no final victory, for such an event would leave him with nothing to do. For Ernest, writing--as life itself--was an endless marathon. Yet a person had to continue as if a finish was in sight. "They can't yank novelists like they can pitchers," Hemingway would stutter. "A novelist has to go the full nine, even if it kills him" (Ross, 1962, p. 18). Even if it kills him. In Ernest's case, it had to kill him. Otherwise he would not have gone the full nine. Pride dictates that there is always another battle to be won. There was never a final victorious battle in his own ego war. One conquest merely led to the next. He said,

4

> It is sort of fun to be fifty and feel you are going to
> defend the title again. . . . I won it in the twenties and
> defended it in the thirties and the forties, and I don't
> mind at all defending it in the fifties. (Ross, 1962, p.
> 28)

Hemingway put his pride on the line with every new book. He devoured every triumph and never acknowledged defeat. In his own mind, every novel was a prize fight, a championship, standing proof that he still could pack a knockout punch. When he lost that punch, it was over for him. An ego of his size could not reconcile the fatigues of turning sixty. He felt his body going bad and his words drying up. There were no more titles to defend. Therein lies the reason for his suicide.

Ernest's last few months were spent in misery. He was in and out of the Mayo Clinic for mental and physical examinations. Doctors perforated his brain with electric shocks, mechanical stimulants to exercise his titanic depression. Or maybe they were futile attempts to poke air holes in his suffocating ego.

The outdoor world, which had tantalized Hemingway practically since his birth, now turned gray on him. What good were the beauties of nature if there was no way to describe them? The words wouldn't "come any more," and he grew thinner and weaker and more depressed.

There was no way for a man of Hemingway's beliefs to grow old gracefully. In Hemingway's vernacular, the day you could no longer write was the day you died. There was no "old" in the Hemingway ego system. When he created, he was forever young; when he could no longer fight the battle, he was done. There was no middle ground. He set about single-mindedly to kill himself.

It could be said that he died of strangulation, murdered by his own pride. He had always carried his own ego like a beast upon his back. When it was well fed, it was docile; as it grew hungry, it was murderous.

5

His majestic pride gave him the desire to create. It had been glossy and glowed like the sun before the public. But the sun also must set, says Ecclesiastes, Hemingway's only bible, and his unsatisfied ego took back its gift.

After such a richly dramatic life, his death was painstakingly simple. He put two bullets in his head and that was all. Death was the very end; he had always made that clear. There was no need for romance afterward. And there are not chronicles of utter grief at Ernest's funeral. Those that understood him knew there was no reason for it. When the end came, he had done all he could do. He had splurged lifelong on pleasures that took their physical toll. His soul had been wrung for all the lessons it could give the world, so there was no more left there either. Despite his sovereign ego, Hemingway was a mortal man. He had reached his limitations.

Bibliography

Baker, Carlos. Ernest Hemingway: A Life Story. New York: Scribner's, 1969.

Keats, John. You Might As Well Live: The Life and Times of Dorothy Parker. New York: Simon and Schuster, 1970.

Mellow, James. Charmed Circle: Gertrude Stein and Company. New York: Praeger, 1974.

Ross, Lillian. "How Do You Like It Now, Gentlemen?" in Hemingway, edited by Robert P. Weeks. Englewood Cliffs, N.J.: Prentice-Hall, 1962.

Instructor's Comments

1. Strengths. This is a strong position paper, one that is not interested in a balanced profile. The student has been to Roget and back; he is well read, he knows how to use language and anecdote. This paper will

6

stimulate any seminar and may irritate some instructors ("she too got hers in the end"). It brings to flesh the cold facts of most high school reference books.

2. <u>Weaknesses</u>. The startling generalizations ("There was no middle ground") and the dramatic prose ("his suffocating ego") often seem more personal than documented. While the bibliography is there, the footnotes are missing. Perhaps the paper would have been more convincing if one situation, such as his relationship with Sherwood Anderson, had been exploited in depth.

HANDOUT 14
STUDENT MODEL FOR PAPER IV

THE ULTIMATE QUESTION

by Amy Freeman

> He was a man of prowess and did not want to live without
> it: writing prowess, physical prowess, sexual prowess,
> drinking and eating prowess. . . . But if he could only be
> made to adjust to a life where these prowesses were not
> so all important. . . .
>
> A. E. Hotchner, 1961

But he would not adjust. During his last days at Ketchum, Idaho, and
Rochester, Minnesota, Ernest Hemingway finally completed the ideas which
his characters had implied throughout his works. Through the action and
the feelings that he exhibited during this time, he composed his final
plot: a plot which answered the essential question of whether a man can
control his entire life, or whether destiny eventually will take command.

Hemingway's famous concepts about how people should live were frequently expressed in his writing, but in each case these ideas were not
really complete. His well-established Code of "Grace Under Pressure" and
the necessity of accepting death were never quite adequate because they
did not designate any course of action by which one could extend control
over life into the control of death.

One of the earliest illustrations of this deficiency in his ideas
occurred in the short story "Indian Camp." In this story, Nick Adams
accompanied his father on a trip to an Indian village where Dr. Adams
planned to help an Indian woman with a difficult childbirth. The woman,
who had been in labor for two days, was very distraught and could have
died. As Nick became aware of his inability to control the situation, he

1

2

became very uneasy though he didn't take any action. The woman's cries heightened his anxiety about his uselessness until he begged, "Oh, Daddy, can't you give her something to make her stop screaming?" Nick's obvious apprehension over the fact that he could not control this aspect of his life is interesting when one finds that Hemingway did not present any solution to the problem.

In the novel, A Farewell to Arms, Frederic Henry encountered a similar situation. At the end of the book, as Catherine was dying, Frederic realized that destiny had taken control of his life; he could not control whether Catherine lived or died. Confused, upset by this actuality, he argued with himself,

> So now they got her in the end. You never got away with
> anything. Get away hell! It would have been the same if
> we had been married fifty times. And what if she should
> die? She won't die. People don't die in childbirth
> nowadays. That was what all husbands thought. Yes, but
> what if she should die? She won't die. She's just having
> a bad time. The initial labor is usually protracted. She's
> only having a bad time. Afterward we'd say what a bad time
> and Catherine would say it wasn't really so bad. But what
> if she should die? She can't, I tell you. Don't be a fool.
> It's just a bad time. It's just nature giving her hell.
> (Hemingway, 1969, p. 320)

It was at this point that Hemingway began to develop his final plot: A man cannot rely on fate, but he must try to control his life and his death. Frederic's actions immediately became more animated, and he even found some comfort in regulating Catherine's anesthetic. Although he knew that the gas would not actually prolong Catherine's life, it was his first attempt to control death--the beginning of Hemingway's final plot.

Near the end of his life, Hemingway repeated the idea that one should control as much of one's life as possible. In referring to his friend Antonio, who was considering retiring from bullfighting, he felt good that the bullfighter could make his own decision:

3

> No one can advise you on something as delicate as your own
> machinery. But . . . when you're the champ, it's better
> to step down on the best day you've had than to wait until
> it's leaving you and everyone notices. (Hotchner, 1966,
> p. 262)

By retiring, Antonio would be controlling his life, rather than waiting
until something forced him to quit. The author's repetition of this idea
was significant because he would soon face the ultimate test: Could this
control over one's life be applied to one's death, or would fate have the
final control?

The conclusion to Ernest Hemingway's final plot was composed when he
was forced to resolve his own loss of control over his life. The desperation which he felt over this loss was apparent in his conversations with
his friend, A. E. Hotchner. In his biography, Papa Hemingway, Hotchner
referred to his talks with the author, to one of Hemingway's outbursts
that foreshadowed his suicide:

> Hotch, if I can't exist on my own terms, then existence
> is impossible. Do you understand? That is how I've
> lived, and that is how I must live--or not live. (Hotch-
> ner, 1966, p. 328)

Hotchner suggested that Hemingway retire, but this failed to comfort the
despair over his loss of control. Hotchner realized the problem:

> . . . unlike your baseball player and your prize fighter
> and your matador, how does a writer retire? No one ac-
> cepts that his legs are shot or the whiplash gone from his
> reflexes. Everywhere he goes, he hears the same goddamn
> question--What are you working on? (Hotchner, 1966, p.
> 298)

With the belief that he wouldn't be allowed to retire and his personal conviction that he could no longer write, Hemingway felt that his
opportunities for action were quickly diminishing. He felt that his
control over his life was slipping. He then asked,

> What does a man care about? Staying healthy. Working
> good. Eating and drinking with his friends. Enjoying
> himself in bed. I haven't any of them. Do you understand,
> goddamn it? None of them. (Hotchner, 1966, pp. 299-300)

4

Ernest Hemingway no longer possessed the ability to enjoy life. His
marked loss of control over what he could and could not do left him very
little reason to continue. A broken man who knew it, he refused to forget
his personal Code: "a man can be defeated, but not destroyed." He would
not resign the ultimate control to destiny, so on July 2, 1961, Ernest
Hemingway completed his final plot. By taking his own life, he committed
the final act of control. He determined his own death, resolving at last
the question which had puzzled him throughout his life: How much of man's
life can he control?

Bibliography

Baker, Carlos. _Ernest Hemingway_. New York: Scribner's, 1969.
Hemingway, Ernest. _A Farewell to Arms_. New York: Scribner's, 1969.
Hemingway, Mary Welsh. _How It Was_. New York: Alfred A. Knopf, 1976.
Hotchner, A. E. _Papa Hemingway_. New York: Random House, 1966.

Instructor's Comments

1. _Strengths_. This paper uses an interesting technique that can be a
   useful model to students: a direct quotation beneath the title which
   triggers the first paragraph as well as the entire position. The
   writer also was sensitive to two of the writing goals of this
   assignment--weaving together biography and fiction and experimenting
   with direct quotations--including footnoting them. And finally, she
   has a strong profile position from title to final sentence, one that
   should intrigue her readers since Hemingway's fiction is so autobiographical.

5

2. <u>Weaknesses</u>. Long quotations, such as the one from <u>A Farewell to
    Arms</u>, can dilute the impact of a position. More editing and indirect
    quoting might have been more successful. Perhaps even more biographi-
    cal documentation of the agonies of Hemingway's final days, such as
    his long list of physical problems, might have been exploited in
    describing the "final plot."

PAPER V: PAPER OF CHOICE
DAYS 58–69

DAY 58: CONSIDERING READING CHOICES FOR PAPER V

Goals

1. To suggest topics for Paper V, the paper of choice.
2. To note writing problems special to this paper.

Materials

1. Copies of *The Short Stories of Ernest Hemingway*.
2. Handout 15: Suggestions for Paper V.
3. Handout 16: Student Model for Paper V.

Assignment

1. Ask students to note the DUE date for the fifth paper on the Schedule, Day 69.
2. Remind students that the defenses of Paper IV (the Profile Paper) will begin on Day 63.

Procedure

1. This time students may select any book or long story that has not been studied in class. Assess the time remaining in the semester and consider the interests and reading skills of individual students in suggesting whether a student should read another book or a long story for this assignment. Briefly review the materials, giving plot summaries. Suggestions:

   Books

   The Torrents of Spring (1926). A minor work and a parody of Sherwood Anderson.

   Death in the Afternoon (1932). Hemingway's nonfictional study of the art and tragedy of bullfighting.

   Green Hills of Africa (1935). Hunting with Hemingway in Africa.

   To Have and Have Not (1937). In a three-part novel, a Key West fishing boat captain finds adventure smuggling Chinese, Cuban revolutionaries, and bootleg liquor.

   For Whom the Bell Tolls (1940). A major work in which an American goes to the Spanish Civil War to aid the Loyalists in blowing up a bridge and discovers the spirit of humanity.

   Across the River and into the Trees (1950). The critics attacked this novel of a fifty-five-year-old American army colonel who goes to Venice during the last three days of his life.

   A Moveable Feast (1964). A posthumous memoir in which Hemingway remembers Paris, his people, and the 1920s, when life was young.

   Islands in the Stream (1970). Posthumous sea novel.

   Stories

   "The Undefeated" (1925). The story of an aging bullfighter who refuses to quit.

   "Fifty Grand" (1927). The story of a champion boxer who bets against himself.

   "The Gambler, the Nun, and the Radio" (1933). The story of people's adjustments to the world as seen by the hospitalized Mr. Frazer.

   "The Snows of Kilimanjaro" (1936). The story of a dying American in Africa who reflects upon death and a misused life.

   "The Short Happy Life of Francis Macomber" (1936). A hunting safari in Africa becomes a drama of Macomber's search for honor and manhood.

2. Distribute and discuss Handout 15: Suggestions for Paper V.
3. Stress that this paper should be especially clear about the basic plot and characters since most readers will not have read the material.
4. You may distribute Handout 16: Student Model for Paper V now or reserve it for discussion later.

DAYS 59–62: READING HEMINGWAY MATERIAL OF CHOICE AND PREPARING FOR DEFENSE DAY

Goals

1. To provide time for students to read the Hemingway material of choice.
2. To prepare for Defense Day on Paper IV.

Materials

1. *The Short Stories of Ernest Hemingway.*
2. Copies of the profile papers chosen for Defense Day.

Procedure

1. Days 59–62 give students time to read the book or story of their choice and the instructor time to correct the profile papers.
2. On Day 62, hand out the profile papers to be used during Defense Day. If you will require more than one Defense Day, decide which students will be responsible for defenses on each day. Do not return the corrected papers until all defenses are complete.

DAYS 63–65: PARTICIPATING IN DEFENSE DAY AND FOLLOW-UP

Goals

1. To allow students to defend the position taken in the Hemingway Profile Paper.
2. To consider autobiographical insights of major Hemingway critics.

Materials

1. Again, extra copies of the papers for defense may be needed.
2. Corrected papers to be returned when the defenses have been completed.

Procedure

1. More than one Defense Day may be necessary if all students are to have defended at least one Position Paper before the seventh paper. The Profile Paper is a likely time for scheduling consecutive days of discussion because it provides interesting new information and builds toward the Summation Paper.
2. Day 65 is follow-up, and you again have the options of discussing the papers of other students, the student model papers (Handouts 13 and 14), or the observations of literary critics. Suggestions for the latter include (1) Malcolm Cowley's profile, "A Portrait of Mister Papa," in *Life* (10 January 1949), which was revised and appeared in *Ernest Hemingway: The Man and His Work,* edited by John K. M. McCaffery, pp. 34–56; and (2) Philip Young's "The Man and His Legend" in *Ernest Hemingway: A Reconsideration,* pp. 147–52, 170–71.

DAYS 66–69: COMPLETING PAPER V AND LOOKING TOWARD PAPER VI

Goals

1. To provide time to complete the writing, revision, and proofreading of Paper V.
2. To introduce Paper VI.

Procedure

1. Use Days 66–68 for in-class time to write and proofread Paper V, which is due on Day 69.
2. Collect the papers of choice and, as soon as possible, choose those that will be used during Defense Day.

3. Remind students that Paper VI will focus on a short work, one that appeared in an issue of *Life* magazine. Yet, *The Old Man and the Sea* is a major work, one that was instrumental in Hemingway's winning the Nobel Prize. Many students may have already read it or seen the film on television. It is an immensely readable book, a popular short novel that students will like. It is a fish story —and much more.

4. Like all Hemingway novels, *The Old Man and the Sea* has its origins in the author's life, although it is not so autobiographical as some. The story does come from Hemingway's life in Key West, from his love of fishing and the sea, from his years in Cuba. To suggest its early origins, read aloud Hemingway's April 1936 *Esquire* article "On the Blue Water: A Gulf Stream Letter" (see Appendix D).

HANDOUT 15
SUGGESTIONS FOR PAPER V: PAPER OF CHOICE

Books

1. *The Torrents of Spring* (1926)
   a. Carlos Baker sees this parody-satire as Hemingway's first public announcement that he was on his own. Expand on this idea.
   b. What are the hazards of parody such as this? Should Hemingway have written this book?

2. *Death in the Afternoon* (1932)
   a. Why was Hemingway so drawn to the bullfight?
   b. Deal with this book in terms of Hemingway's concept of the Hero—a man of action and an artist.

3. *Green Hills of Africa* (1935)
   a. Expand on Hemingway's affection for Mark Twain's *Huckleberry Finn.*
   b. Hemingway wrote in the introduction that he attempted to write "an absolutely true book." What is truth in this book?

4. *To Have and Have Not* (1937)
   a. Consider Harry Morgan as an American with his roots in American values, a nineteenth-century man destroyed in the twentieth.
   b. Deal with the two parts of the title.

5. *For Whom the Bell Tolls* (1940)
   a. How does this novel differ from previous works?
   b. What is the significance of Maria?
   c. Deal with a symbol, e.g., Donne's sermon *(Devotions XII),* the bridge, the airplanes.

6. *Across the River and into the Trees* (1950)
   a. Review the background of the title and explain its choice for this post-World War II novel.
   b. Analyze wind as symbol in the novel.

7. *A Moveable Feast* (1964)
   a. How does Hemingway treat his fellow writers?
   b. Deal with the title in terms of the total impact of the book.

8. *Islands in the Stream* (1970)
   a. Consider the book in terms of Hemingway's suicide.
   b. This sea novel was written during the same time as *The Old Man and the Sea.* Why didn't Hemingway release it then? Some critics said that it needs revision. Do you agree?

Stories

1. "The Undefeated" (1925)
   a. Can this story be seen as more than a bullfighting story? Does it say something about the young and the old today?
   b. The title seems to relate to the Code. How?

2. "Fifty Grand" (1927)
    a. One critic says that this story is a portrait of an individual who exemplifies the theme of the "adjusted" man. What does that mean?
    b. This is a story of irony. What is the essential irony?

3. "The Gambler, the Nun, and the Radio" (1933)
    a. How do all three parts of the title relate to the theme of the story?
    b. What is the meaning of the setting, the hospital?

4. "The Snows of Kilimanjaro" (1936)
    a. Expand on a symbol, e.g., the leopard, Harry's death by gangrene.
    b. Why would Hemingway say that this story was "about as good as any" of his writings? (See Carlos Baker, *Hemingway: The Writer as Artist,* p. 191)

5. "The Short Happy Life of Francis Macomber" (1936)
    a. Analyze why Macomber's wife shot him.
    b. Examine the title. What does the word "happy" mean?

HANDOUT 16
STUDENT MODEL FOR PAPER V

ONE'S RESPONSIBILITY TO HUMANITY

by Emily Buss

"For what are we living?" This is one of the most serious questions

that plagues our minds throughout our lives. Many believe we ought to

live to serve a god. Others feel we should live merely to gratify our own

selfish wants. In For Whom the Bell Tolls, Ernest Hemingway picks a third

alternative. He writes that each one of us must live for the good of

every human being. His belief in an individual's responsibility to the

whole is expressed in the passage by John Donne from which Hemingway took

his title.

> No man is an Island, intire of it selfe; every man is
> a peace of the Continent, a part of the maine; if a Clod
> bee washed away by the Sea, Europe is the lesse, as well
> as if a Promontorie were, as well as if a Mannor of they
> friens or of thine owne were; any mans death diminishes me,
> because I am involved in Mankinde; And therefore never send
> to know for whom the bell tolls; It tolls for thee.

Hemingway expresses this idea of one's responsibility to Mankind through

several of his characters, particularly the central character, Robert

Jordan.

For Whom the Bell Tolls is the story of a young American professor,

Robert Jordan, who is a dynamiter for the Republicans in the Spanish

Civil War. Jordan is assigned to blow up a bridge held by the Fascists

as a part of a Republican offensive. For three days, he lives behind

enemy lines with the guerilla band which will help him destroy the bridge.

Hemingway's entire novel takes place during these three days. While in

1

2

the mountains, Jordan falls in love with Maria, a young girl once held as
a Fascist prisoner. In addition, Jordan must deal with the cowardice and
mutiny of Pablo, the fallen leader of the peasant band; the strong-minded
and even bitter nature of Pilar, Pablo's wife; and the gradual crumbling
of his support for the attack. At the end of the story, Jordan success-
fully blows up the bridge. Several of the guerilla band are killed, but
Pablo, Pilar, and Maria escape unharmed. Robert Jordan does not go with
them for his badly wounded leg virtually immobilizes him. In his last
moments of life, despite his unbearable pain, Jordan prepares to shoot a
Fascist officer. In the short time he spends in the mountains, Jordan
learns a great deal about life. "I wish there was some way to pass on
what I've learned, though," he said. "Christ, I was learning fast there
at the end" (Hemingway, 1940, p. 467).

Hemingway first expresses his idea that every person is obligated to
a cause greater than himself through Jordan's thoughts about his father
and grandfather. Jordan's grandfather was involved in a great deal of
warfare which required a vast amount of courage. Such courage, Jordan
feels, could only come from a concern for humanity rather than for oneself.
Like his grandfather, Jordan is making great sacrifices and risking his
own life for a cause he believes in: the liberty of the Spanish people.
His father, on the other hand, committed suicide. To Jordan, such an act
seems cowardly and selfish.

> [Jordan] realized that if there was such a thing as [a
> hereafter] both he and his grandfather would be acutely
> embarrassed by the presence of his father. Anyone has a
> right to [commit suicide, he thought]. . . . But it isn't
> a good thing to do. I understand it, but I do not approve
> of it. . . . You have to be awfully occupied with yourself
> to do a thing like that. (Hemingway, 1940, p. 338)

As the time of his attack draws near and his tension mounts, Jordan's
bitterness towards those who avoid war because of selfish fears increases.

3

> Durriti [a Republican military leader] was good and his
> own people shot him. . . . Shot him because he wanted them
> to attack. . . . The cowardly swine. (Hemingway, 1940, p.
> 370)

Robert Jordan feels a similar disgust toward Pablo when Pablo runs

away from the camp the night before the offensive. Throughout the story

Pablo shows a great dislike for Jordan and his mission, for he realizes

the destruction of the bridge will force his gang from the security of

their mountain home. Already a coward, Pablo loathes Robert Jordan who

brings great danger to his band. As the attack on the bridge becomes

imminent, Pablo perceives the virtual impossibility of Jordan's mission.

In a selfish attempt to protect himself and ruin the mission he detests,

Pablo sneaks from the camp with some of Jordan's equipment. This self-

centered act throws Jordan into a rage.

> Muck the whole treachery ridden country. Muck their
> [the Spanish leaders'] egotism and their selfishness and
> their egotism and their conceit and their treachery. . . .
> God muck Pablo. Pablo is all of them. (Hemingway, 1940,
> pp. 369-370)

The morning following Pablo's mutiny, he returns. He returns because he,

too, is learning that each man owes his life service to mankind. Pablo

realizes it is not enough to follow one's selfish desires, and upon his

return he confesses to Pilar, "Having done such a thing [deserting his

fellow men] there is a loneliness that cannot be borne" (Hemingway,

1940, p. 390).

Hemingway's belief that each individual must contribute to a larger

community is revealed to a lesser extent by other characters. Andres,

a member of Pablo's gang whom Jordan sends with an emergency message to

Republican headquarters, realizes that all he possesses only has worth if

it is given away. Reflecting sadly on his life, Andres discovers he is

worthless to himself.

4

> You have four grenades in your pocket, but they are only
> good to throw away. You have a carbine on your back but it
> is only good to give away bullets. You have a message to
> give away. . . . Everything you have is to give. (Hemingway,
> 1940, p. 368)

Like Robert Jordan, Maria expresses a desire to forget her selfish inter-

ests and take her place in the group. As the gang prepares to leave the

mountains towards the end of the novel, Maria refuses to take a safer

position in the line of retreating horses as Jordan tells her to. "'Nay,'

she told him. . . . 'I go in the order that I am to go'" (Hemingway, 1940,

p. 458).

The best expression of Hemingway's belief that one must cast aside

selfish ideas to serve mankind is found in the last pages of For Whom the

Bell Tolls, when Robert Jordan realizes he is about to die. Jordan is

left alone with a badly fractured femur, not far from the enemy which is

unable to advance because of the destroyed bridge. Fully aware that his

death is near, he thinks not of himself, but of the cause and the people

to whom he has devoted his life.

> I [Jordan] hate to leave [life] very much and I hope
> I have done some good in it. I have tried to with what
> talent I had. (Hemingway, 1940, p. 467)

In his last moments of life, he is still able to struggle for the freedom

of the Spanish people. As the enemy begins to detour around the useless

bridge, it enters Jordan's firing range. He wants above all things to be

useful up to the last minutes of his life. "You better get fixed around

some way where you will be useful instead of leaning against this tree

like a tramp," he thinks. (466) However, the pain caused by Jordan's leg

wound is almost unbearable, and he is continuously tempted to kill himself

to escape his agony. As his life draws to a close, Jordan refuses to

gratify his selfish wants as long as he is still able to serve the

Spanish people.

5

> No, it isn't [all right to kill yourself]. Because
> there is something you can do yet. . . . If you wait and
> hold [the enemy] even a little while or just get the
> officer that may make all the difference. (Hemingway,
> 1940, p. 470)

It would be unfair not to mention that Hemingway later committed

suicide. This suicide clearly does not coincide with the ideas he ex-

pressed in his novel, For Whom the Bell Tolls. In considering this point

one must realize that Ernest Hemingway probably was attempting to describe

an ideal human trait which he wished to attain, not a trait that he believed

he had already attained. Through the attitudes of his characters, Hemingway

reveals his own ideas on how our lives should be lived. In For Whom the

Bell Tolls, he tells us to live for one another and not for ourselves.

Bibliography

Hemingway, Ernest. For Whom the Bell Tolls. New York: Scribner's, 1940.

Instructor's Comments

1. Strengths. This paper is especially successful in the clear description of plot and character, a major goal of the assignment since many
   students may not have read the novel. Her logical focus on Robert
   Jordan, her organization of the supporting characters, her use of
   concrete detail--all those document her title and her position.

2. Weaknesses. The conclusion raises issues that might best be left
   alone. While Hemingway's suicide is an interesting aside, the writer
   might have been more successful in keeping her reader on target by
   either referring to material read earlier by the seminar or by
   restatement.

PAPER IV: *THE OLD MAN AND THE SEA*
DAYS 70–79

DAYS 70–71: READING *THE OLD MAN AND THE SEA*

Goal

To provide class time to read *The Old Man and the Sea* (1952).

Materials

Copies of *The Old Man and the Sea* or *Three Novels: The Sun Also Rises, A Farewell to Arms, The Old Man and the Sea.*

Assignment

Ask students to note on the Schedule the DUE date of Paper VI, Day 79.

Procedure

1. Begin by reviewing briefly the earlier discussion of the *Esquire* article "On the Blue Water."
2. Remind students that *The Old Man and the Sea,* first published in *Life* magazine, won the 1953 Pulitzer Prize and was instrumental in Hemingway's winning the 1954 Nobel Prize. More will be said about this on Day 72.
3. Ask students to note the dedication: "To Charlie Scribner and to Max Perkins." Scribner, of course, was Hemingway's longtime friend and publisher. Maxwell Perkins was Hemingway's Scribner editor and friend, one of the most famous editors in American literature; he was especially noted for his work with Thomas Wolfe.
4. Most students will be able to complete the novel during these two days.

Additional Suggestion

If the budget allows, order the 1958 Warner Brothers production of *The Old Man and the Sea* starring Spencer Tracy as Santiago. The film is especially interesting since Hemingway watched the filmmaking and later called it a waste of time.

DAY 72: DISCUSSING HEMINGWAY AND THE NOBEL AND PULITZER PRIZES

Goal

To provide background information on Hemingway's winning of the Nobel and Pulitzer Prizes.

Materials

1. Texts of the Nobel Prize Citation and Nobel Prize Speech (included at the end of the outline for Day 72).
2. You may wish to use two references: (a) W. J. Stuckey's *The Pulitzer Prize Novels,* pp. 165–70; (b) *American Winners of the Nobel Literary Prize,* edited by Warren G. French and Walter E. Kidd, specifically the chapter "Ernest Hemingway" by Ken Moritz, pp. 158–92.

Procedure

1. After the criticism of his 1950 novel *Across the River and into the Trees,* Hemingway wrote *The Old Man and the Sea,* which restored his reputation. The 1952 novel had been brewing for a long time. (Here you might wish to read chapter 4, "The Boy and the Sea," in *Hemingway and Jake* by Vernon

"Jake" Klimo and Will Oursler, pp. 35–38.) The novel won Hemingway the 1953 Pulitzer Prize and was instrumental in his being chosen in 1954 as the sixth American writer ever to win the Nobel Prize.

2. At this point, review the two prizes.

    a. *The Pulitzer Prize.* When Joseph Pulitzer died in 1911, he left a fortune of nearly $19 million amassed through his development of sensational journalism; owner of the St. Louis *Post-Dispatch* and the New York *World,* he nevertheless felt his work to have integrity. So in 1903 he convinced Columbia University to enhance the field of journalism by establishing a school of journalism—and he gave $1 million for the project. Then, he was persuaded to use half of another million-dollar gift for his pet project: annual cash prizes for journalism and letters. Thus the Pulitzer Prizes were established. An advisory board was placed in charge of the $1000 prizes, including the category of the best novel: "Annually, for the American novel published during the year which shall best present the wholesome atmosphere of American life and the highest standard of American manners and manhood, $1000" (Stuckey, *The Pulitzer Prize Novels,* p. 6). The prizes for novels began in 1917.

    Through the years, the advisory board wrestled with the problem of the standards for choosing a winner, especially the problem of "wholesome" since many famous novels, such as *The Sun Also Rises,* challenged American life. The wording was changed and expanded, though the concern for "moral" standards led to rejection of Hemingway's early novels: physical love outside marriage in *A Farewell to Arms* disturbed the judges; the rather explicit sex of *For Whom the Bell Tolls* was distasteful to the honorary chairman of the advisory board, though the other members voted for the novel. But in 1953 *The Old Man and the Sea* was found to be sufficiently wholesome to pass the test.

    b. *The Nobel Prize.* The Nobel Prize for Literature was one of five international awards established in the 1895 will of Swedish industrialist Alfred Nobel, the inventor of dynamite. The prize "to the person who shall have produced in the field of Literature the most distinguished work of an idealistic tendency" (French and Kidd, eds., *American Winners of the Nobel Literary Prize,* p. 6) is directed by the Nobel Foundation; the annual award includes a large cash gift (from the accrued interest of Nobel's original gift), a gold medal, and a diploma bearing the winner's name and field of achievement. Like the Pulitzer Board, the Nobel judges may decide not to give an award for a particular year.

    The first awards were given in 1901, but no American writer received one until 1930. Hemingway became the sixth winner on the American list, which has since increased to nine: Sinclair Lewis, 1930; Eugene O'Neill, 1936; Pearl Buck, 1938; T. S. Eliot (then a British citizen), 1948; William Faulkner, 1949; Hemingway, 1954; John Steinbeck, 1962; Saul Bellow, 1976; Isaac Bashevis Singer, 1978.

3. Present the texts of the Nobel Prize Citation and Nobel Prize Speech (see below). Play again the Caedmon record/tape, *Ernest Hemingway Reading,* that includes Hemingway reading his Nobel Address.

4. Background stories on Hemingway's Nobel Prize may have been covered during Anecdote Day; nevertheless, review is advisable. See Carlos Baker's *Ernest Hemingway: A Life Story,* "The Bounty of Sweden," pp. 525–29. Hemingway was unable to make the trip to Stockholm for the award largely because the fifty-five-year-old author was on the mend from an airplane crash in Uganda. He had suffered a ruptured kidney, a cracked skull, two compressed and one cracked vertebra, and serious burns.

5. It is interesting to discuss awards at this point, since many writers both want them and fear them. Fame, recognition, sudden popularity can be time-consuming, distracting from one's work, the kiss of death. Writers like John Steinbeck believed that little good material was written by Nobel

winners after they received their awards. Some writers were even driven to suicide after winning the Pulitzer (see Leggett, *Ross and Tom: Two American Tragedies*). The period might conclude with a discussion: Why does a writer write? Why did Hemingway write?

Nobel Prize Citation

Hemingway's Nobel Citation reads as follows:

> For his powerful, style-forming mastery of the art of modern narration, as most recently evinced in *The Old Man and the Sea*.
>
> Swedish Academy

At the December 10 ceremony, Anders Oesterling, permanent secretary of the Swedish Academy, expanded upon the citation:

> . . . Hemingway's earlier writings display brutal, cynical and callous signs which may be considered at variance with the Nobel Prize requirements for a work of ideal tendencies. But on the other hand, he also possesses a heroic pathos which forms the basic element of his awareness of life, a manly love of danger and adventure, with a natural admiration of every individual who fights the good fight in a world of reality overshadowed by violence and death. . . . [The central theme of courage can be seen in] the bearing of one who is put to the test and who steels himself to meet the cold cruelty of existence without by so doing repudiating the great and generous moments. . . . [He is] one of the great writers of our time, one of those who, honestly and undauntedly, reproduces the genuine features of the hard countenance of the age. . . . [French and Kidd, eds., *American Winners*, pp. 158-59.]

The Nobel Prize Speech

In 1954 Ernest Hemingway was awarded the Nobel Prize for Literature, an award that carried a $35,000 check, a gold medal (which he later presented to the Virgin of Cobre, Cuba's national saint, and kept in the shrine of Our Lady at Santiago de Cuba), and the opportunity to make a speech in Stockholm. Since he felt that giving the spech would interrupt his work, invade his privacy, and produce distasteful publicity—and because he was still recuperating from his African airplane crashes—he sent along a speech with the American Ambassador to Sweden, John Cabot, who accepted the prize on Hemingway's behalf:

> Members of the Swedish Academy, Ladies and Gentlemen: Having no facility for speechmaking nor any domination of rhetoric, I wish to thank the administrators of the generosity of Alfred Nobel for this prize. No writer who knows the great writers who did not receive the prize can accept it other than with humility. There is no need to list these writers. Everyone here may make his own list according to his knowledge and his conscience. It would be impossible for me to ask the Ambassador of my country to read a speech in which a writer said all of the things which are in his heart. Things may not be immediately discernible in what a man writes, and in this sometimes he is fortunate; but eventually they are quite clear and by these and the degree of alchemy that he possesses he will endure or be forgotten. Writing, at its best, is a lonely life. Organizations for writers palliate the writer's loneliness but I doubt if they improve his writing. He grows in public stature as he sheds his loneliness and often his work deteriorates. For he does his work alone and if he is a good writer he must face eternity, or the lack of it, each day. For a true writer each book should be a new beginning where he tries again for something that is beyond attainment. He should always try for something that has never been done or that others have tried and failed. Then sometimes, with great luck, he will succeed. How simple the writing of literature would be if it were only necessary to write in another way what has been well written. It is because we have had such great writers in the past that a writer is driven far out past where he can go, out to where no one can help him. I have spoken too long for a writer. A writer should write what he has to say and not speak it. Again I thank you. [Horst Frenz, ed., *Nobel Lectures: Literature, 1901-1967*, pp. 501-02.]

DAYS 73-76: CHOOSING A TOPIC FOR PAPER VI AND PARTICIPATING IN DEFENSE DAY AND FOLLOW-UP

Goals

1. To suggest topics for Paper VI.
2. To complete the Defense Day and follow-up discussion of the Papers of Choice.

Materials

1. Handout 17: Suggestions for Paper VI.
2. Handout 18: Student Model for Paper VI.
3. Copies of papers for Defense Day on Paper V.
4. Corrected papers to distribute at the end of Defense Day.

Procedure

1. Distribute Handout 17 on Day 73 and discuss positions for papers on *The Old Man and the Sea*. Handout 18 may also be discussed at this time.
2. Distribute the papers to be considered on Defense Day on Day 74. The day may be given over to studying these papers or to beginning the drafts of Paper VI.
3. Defense Day is held on Day 75, following the procedure outlined in the introduction. Return all corrected papers at the end of the hour.
4. For the follow-up discussion on Day 76, you may use the papers of other students, the Student Model (Handout 18), or the discussion of a critic such as Richard Hovey's essay "*The Snows of Kilimanjaro:* The Triumph of Death," in *Hemingway: The Inward Terrain,* pp. 127–31.

DAYS 77–79: COMPLETING PAPER VI AND LOOKING TOWARD THE FINAL PAPER

Goals

1. To provide time to complete Paper VI.
2. To orient students to the final paper.

Procedure

1. Days 77 and 78 should be given over to writing and proofreading Paper VI.

2. On Day 79, collect the papers. As soon as possible, select and reproduce the papers to be used in the final Defense Day discussions.
3. Orient students to the final paper by suggesting that it offers a number of alternatives:
   a. If time allows, you may wish to assign two papers—a serious summation of Ernest Hemingway and his work and a parody assignment.
   b. If time is short and spirits weary, you may wish to be more flexible. Students may elect to write either a serious or a humorous paper. Even the length may be shortened to three pages.
   c. Another possibility that has worked very well: agree to give a grade of A to any final paper that is read aloud to the seminar. These presentations may take two or three days, but they release final tensions. There is, then, no Defense Day for Paper VII; instead, there is a chance for creativity and an opportunity to summarize. In addition, everyone is justifiably rewarded for having cooperated throughout the course. Note: still require that Paper VII be typed.
4. Refer to Handout 3: The Hemingway Chronology for a last time, noting Hemingway's death and the posthumous publications. You may also wish to refer to Hemingway's funeral. An interesting account is found in Leicester Hemingway, *My Brother,* pp. 11–13.

HANDOUT 17
SUGGESTIONS FOR PAPER VI: *THE OLD MAN AND THE SEA* (1952)

1. Why was this novel so important in Hemingway's winning the Nobel Prize?
2. Is the Old Man just an old man or does he represent something else? Try to define him as a symbol.
3. What is the function of the boy Manolin?
4. Some see this novel as a parable. Review the meaning of "parable" and try to define your position in this way.
5. Take a key line, such as the last one in the book, and try to mold your position around that line.
6. Joe DiMaggio is mentioned in the novel more than once. Could this lead to a position?
7. This novel also won the Pulitzer Prize. Do some research on the prize and the historical period. Why do you think the book won the award during the Cold War?
8. Contrast or compare this novel with another story, such as "The Big Two-Hearted River" or the *Esquire* article "On the Blue Water."
9. Explain how this later work is an *extension* of earlier Nick Adams stories, such as "The Big Two-Hearted River."
10. Is Santiago a Code Hero? Can he be contrasted with another Hemingway character?
11. Does this novel suggest a religious comparison? Is it a Christian story?
12. Can this novel be seen in terms of biography, of an aging and wounded author beset by adversity, by critics?
13. One critic said that the book is related to the "American Dream." Can you accept this? What does this mean?
14. Examine the style. Does it relate to the theme?
15. Consider the ending. Is this story tragic or basically triumphant?

HANDOUT 18
STUDENT MODEL FOR PAPER VI

DETERMINATION AND FAITH

by Anne Nusser

In Ernest Hemingway's 1952 novel, The Old Man and the Sea, self-
determination and faith were the two forces which drove the old fisherman
Santiago to be an achiever. He was an achiever in the sense that his
goals were personal rather than materialistic. His success was in believ-
ing in himself and having the strength to hold up his head and be proud of
himself even when society labeled him as a "failure" and "defeated." This
strong belief was one which he carried with him and used to help him
survive.

Hemingway first suggests this belief in self-determination in his
description of Santiago. He described the old man as having skin which
was blotched from many years of fishing in the sun: "His hands had deep-
creased scars from handling heavy fish on the cords. But none of these
scars were fresh. They were as old as erosions in a fishless desert."
This description reveals a man who had lived a hard life. The scars
showed the many hardships that he had gone through and that he had been
able to survive these hard times. The words "fishless desert" emphasized
the fact that Santiago had been labeled a "failure" by other fishermen.
Even though his body appeared defeated, his spirit was not. It was his
eyes which showed his inner self. They were "cheerful and undefeated."
This was the true spirit by which the old man lived.

1

2

Santiago was an old fisherman who had an unlucky streak in fishing.
It had been eighty-four days since he had his last catch. Everyone in
the village except the boy Manolin believed that he was an unlucky person;
they thought of him as an outcast. Despite this public opinion, he was
never defeated. He believed that he would catch fish again. This is
stated early in the book when he and Manolin were talking about the lack
of faith that Manolin's father had in the old man.

> "He hasn't much faith."
> "No," the old man said. "But we have. Haven't we?"

This reaffirmation of faith only showed this man's determination. He
would wait any length of time to again catch fish.

It was when Santiago was struggling with the marlin that he again
showed his determination and courage. While fighting, he encountered
several problems which would have defeated most fishermen, but he held
strong so that he could remain victorious. After the fish had dragged
him out to sea, his back, which was anchoring the lines, became stiff and
sore. To try and counteract this feeling, Santiago talked himself into
feeling comfortable. He wanted to catch this fish, and he was not willing
to let his body be a factor against him.

After his back pains, his right hand became cut by the line when the
fish lurched forward. He was not happy that his hand was hurt so early
in the struggle. However, he did not let it bother him because he did not
want to give the marlin any clues that he had been injured. A short time
later, his left hand became cramped. He tried to massage it to get it to
open, but it would not relax. He decided to leave it alone and let the
sun's warmth heal it. Santiago knew that this hand had been through much
abuse and that was why it had become cramped. He also felt sure that if
he needed it in an emergency he could open it: "I will open it, cost
whatever it costs." With two injured hands many men would have given up.

3

But with all of the old man's determination, he knew that he could count
on his inner strength to help him heal his hands if they were needed in
a crisis.

Struggling with the fish caused Santiago to become fatigued. He
knew he had to sleep, but through the art of positive thinking he convinced
his body that it was not necessary. He received his strength from thoughts.
The first was about his hero, Joe DiMaggio. He knew that in baseball this
man had both youth and strength on his side. That is what Santiago needed
now, and he drew those two strengths into his body by thinking about them.
The other thought was of his youth. He had arm-wrestled a Black man for
one day, and finally he drew up all his strength and smashed his opponent's
arm to the table. For this he received the title "El Champéon." He enjoyed
this feeling; he wanted to be triumphant again. He knew that he could have
the title again if he caught this fish. This gave him more incentive to
battle his fatigue. The relief he received was only temporary. Finally,
it came to the point where he knew that he must sleep a little. He went
to sleep and dreamt about the qualities that he would need to beat the
fish. He dreamt of strength, youth, and happiness. Through these dreams,
he was able to fill his psychological reservoir which had been emptied.
When he awoke, he again was ready to fight the fish.

The marlin finally tired, and Santiago was able to kill him. The
struggle consisted of gains and losses on both sides. However, it was the
old man who was triumphant over the fish. Santiago now was faced with the
return trip home. Even though he had just overcome one struggle, he knew
there would be others. This next battle was with the sharks. At first,
just a few came and he was able to kill them, but he knew that soon they
would come in packs. The sharks would try to defeat him. To this he
said, "I am still an old man. But I am not unarmed." With incredible

4

determination, Santiago fought the sharks all night. The sharks, however, were the victors.

When he arrived on shore at last, he went to his shack to sleep. And when he awoke, he saw the boy Manolin. Then he and Manolin discussed what had happened.

> "They beat me, Manolin," he said. "They truly beat me."
> "He didn't beat you. Not the fish."
> "No. Truly. It was afterwards."

Although Santiago seemed to feel defeated at first, he realized that he had won two victories. The first was over the fish, and the other was for himself. He knew that he had fought well to win the fish, and he proved to himself that he still had the strength to do it. This gave him new courage to try again. He was so determined that he and Manolin began to make plans to fish again when the old man had rested.

Santiago had many things going against him from the start. He was old, his body was not that strong anymore, and few people had faith in him. Although he did not have the physical attributes to prove to the village that he was not a failure, he had his self-determination and faith to prove to the people that he was not defeated. This belief in himself helped him survive. Eventually, it helped him prove to the village that he was successful.

Instructor's Comments

1. <u>Strengths</u>. This paper reveals a strong outline, keen observation to develop each paragraph, and a language which matches the personality and emotion of Santiago. It builds convincingly toward its logical conclusion. It is a sound position since it defines the triumphant quality of the novel. Her use of repetitions, key words, compound

5

sentences with semicolons to tighten the line are all interesting

aspects in terms of the writing goal for Paper VI--to try new writing

techniques.

2. <u>Weaknesses</u>. There is some trouble with position words--"determination,"

"self-determination," "faith," "courage." Perhaps a sharper title

could have come from Hemingway's own words in the novel. Then, too,

even more use of direct quotation would strengthen the position of the

paper and reflect the tone of the novel.

PAPER VII: THE SUMMING UP
DAYS 80–90

DAYS 80–82: BEGINNING THE FINAL PAPER AND PREPARING FOR DEFENSE DAY

Goals

1. To help students select a topic for Paper VII.
2. To provide in-class time to begin writing the final paper.
3. To prepare for Defense Day.

Materials

1. Handout 19: Suggestions for Paper VII, Summing Up.
2. Handout 20: Suggestions for Paper VII, Parody.
3. Handouts 21 and 22: Student Models for Paper VII.
4. Copies of Paper VI (*The Old Man and the Sea*) to be used on Day 82, Defense Day.

Assignment

Ask students to insert the DUE date for Paper VII on the Schedule.

Procedure

1. Define the writing assignment, using Handouts 19 and 20 as a point of departure. Encourage students to review materials in the class library and to re-read their previous papers in preparation for Paper VII. If time allows, you may wish to assign both a summation paper and a humorous paper.
2. The model papers may be distributed and discussed on Day 80 or 81. The remainder of the time should be given over to in-class writing.
3. Hand out on Day 82 copies of the papers to be defended. Students may study these papers in class or continue to work on Paper VII.

DAYS 83–84: PARTICIPATING IN DEFENSE DAY AND FOLLOW-UP

Goal

To complete the Defense Day and follow-up discussion.

Materials

Extra copies of the final position papers for students who have forgotten them.

Procedure

1. Follow the established procedures for Defense Day. Return all papers at the end of the period on Day 83.
2. The final follow-up (Day 84) can be spent discussing other papers, the student models, or the insights of a well-known critic such as Carlos Baker in "The Boy and the Lions," *20th Century Interpretations of "The Old Man and the Sea,"* edited by Katherine T. Jobes, pp. 27–33.

DAYS 85–87: COMPLETING THE FINAL PAPER AND SHARING IT IN CLASS

Goals

1. To provide in-class time to complete Paper VII.
2. To encourage students to share their final paper with the class and to respond to the papers of fellow students.
3. To offer a final scholarly evaluation of Hemingway.

Procedure

1. Day 85 should be given over to the completion of Paper VII.
2. Days 86–87 can be set aside for all students to read aloud their final papers. If you elect to cut off the final pressure by granting a uniform grade of A on Paper VII, the experience will be even more enjoyable, and more students may elect a humorous approach. Although these readings do not constitute a Defense Day, the class should attempt to respond to each paper—and so should the instructor.

Additional Suggestion

You may wish to read a final critical evaluation of Ernest Hemingway. Suggestions: "The Art of Evasion" by Leon Edel (pp. 169–71) or "Hemingway: A Defense" by Philip Young (pp. 171–73) in *Hemingway: A Collection of Critical Essays,* edited by Robert P. Weeks.

DAYS 88–89: ENDING THE SEMINAR WITH A SMILE

Goals

1. To share "take-offs" on Hemingway.
2. To end the seminar in high spirits.

Materials

1. "For Whom the Gong Sounds" by Cornelia Otis Skinner in *American Literature in Parody,* edited by R. P. Falk, pp. 241–44.
2. "The Kilimanjaro Device" by Ray Bradbury in *I Sing the Body Electric,* pp. 3–14.
3. "Across the Street and into the Grill" by E. B. White in *An E. B. White Reader,* edited

by William W. Watt and Robert Bradford, pp. 215–218 (New York: Harper and Row, 1966).

Procedure

1. The class will enjoy hearing either or both of the parodies listed above (Day 88).
2. On Day 89 you may wish to ask seminar members to give their final impressions of the course, what they feel they have learned; or the class may elect to have a kind of fun day, such as a Twenty-Questions Day or a Charades Day based on Hemingway plots and characters. One of my seminars even planned a Hemingway party, and each student dressed as a character from one of the stories or novels. Some instructors may wish to use this day for a final examination.

DAY 90: EVALUATING THE SEMINAR

Goals

1. To encourage students to evaluate the seminar.
2. To share your own evaluation of the course with students.

Materials

Handout: Seminar Evaluation (see Appendix E).

Procedure

1. Without comment, ask the students to complete the evaluation anonymously. Collect the evaluations.
2. You may wish to offer some final summary comments and personal reactions to the course. Comments on grades may be in order.

HANDOUT 19
SUGGESTIONS FOR PAPER VII: SUMMING UP

1. Did Hemingway deserve the Nobel Prize?
2. Were his works consistent in theme, in character, in style? Does his writing have a Code? Characterize Ernest Hemingway's world.
3. How did Hemingway treat nature?
4. Was Hemingway an American writer, even though most of his works are not set in America?
5. How does Hemingway treat women in his writing?
6. Is he a classic writer, one that is not bound to topical material, one that will survive in the next hundred years?
7. Which work was your favorite?
8. Develop a theory about Hemingway's style. What was his basic style?
9. While Ernest Hemingway was obviously not religious in the conventional meaning of the word (attending church, an active church member), was he "religious"?
10. Was Hemingway a poetic novelist?
11. Consider his titles. Can you develop a theory about his choices?
12. Some critics feel that Hemingway has little, if anything, to say—few ideas. Do you agree?
13. Examine his Nobel Acceptance Speech. Can this lead to a position?
14. Did Ernest Hemingway have a "death wish"?
15. What is the meaning of "love" in his writings?

HANDOUT 20
SUGGESTIONS FOR PAPER VII: PARODY

1. Try a parody of a work by Hemingway. Take a short story or passage from a novel and distort the famous Hemingway style.

2. Try a parody of Hemingway by taking a simple plot and writing it in the famous Hemingway style. For example, take a children's story such as "Little Red Riding Hood."

3. Write a "recently discovered" work of Ernest Hemingway.

4. Write an imaginary interview with Hemingway.

5. Develop a series of letters between Hemingway and a member of this class.

6. Write a newspaper article about a professor who has found an astonishing piece of information that reveals a new side of Hemingway (for example, he really hated to fish).

7. Develop an overblown Hollywood film (much like the film version of "The Killers") about a Nick Adams story, including a cast of contemporary actors from film or TV.

8. Write the first draft of Hemingway's Nobel Prize address which he threw away because Mary didn't like it.

9. Write a personal essay on the agonies this class experienced while studying Ernest Hemingway.

10. Write a personal essay on "Ten Steps to the Understanding and Enjoyment of Ernest Hemingway"—a kind of Robert Benchley approach.

HANDOUT 21
STUDENT MODEL FOR PAPER VII: SUMMING UP

HEMINGWAY: A SENSITIVITY TO LIFE

by Greg Pope

Ernest Hemingway was known as a tough, masculine, crisp, objective writer. He was all of these, yet he was more. Hemingway was a writer of great sensitivity. He was deeply moved by the things he saw in life, more so than most people. Life touched his sensitive mind, and he, in turn, portrayed what he felt.

Considering his background, one is not surprised that Hemingway had a sensitive mind. His mother, Grace, was a highly cultured woman who early taught him to appreciate the fine arts:

> She wanted her children to enjoy life. To her this meant above all an awareness of the arts. She saw from the first that they all had music lessons. As soon as they were old enough, she bought them tickets for symphony concerts, operatic performances, and the better plays that came to Chicago, and they were encouraged quite early to acquaint themselves with the paintings and drawings at the Chicago Art Institute. Her own deep-dyed belief in creativity made her long to develop the talents of her children to the highest possible level. (Baker, 1969, p. 9)

Ernest's father also contributed to his young son's perceptive awareness of the world. Dr. Hemingway took his family on trips to sylvan northern Michigan where Ernest developed a love for nature that is evident in his writing. His initiation into the darker side of life during this time deeply affected him, a boy with a sensitive mind.

As Ernest grew into manhood, he became a writer with a crisp, fresh style that conveyed the sense impressions of a sensitive mind; his words, as Ford Madox Ford exclaimed, "strike you, each one, as if they were

1

2

pebbles fetched fresh from a brook" (Hemingway, 1953, p. xiv). This was
a writer who perused the paintings of Cezanne and saw in watercolor what
he was attempting to paint in words.

What were the things in life that touched his delicate mind, that
this mind put into words?

First, a profound sensitivity to nature pervades Hemingway's work.
His description of a noble, grand nature is moving:

> We passed through a town and stopped in front of the posada
> and the driver took on several packages. Then we started
> on again, and outside the town the road commenced to mount.
> We were going through farming country with rocky hills that
> sloped down into the fields. The grain-fields went up the
> hillsides. Now as we went higher there was a wind blowing
> the grain. The road was white and dusty, and the dust rose
> under the wheels and hung in the air behind us. The road
> climbed up into the hills and left the rich grain-fields
> below. Now there were only patches of grain on the bare
> hillsides and on each side of the watercourses. . . . Up
> there the country was quite barren and the hills were rocky
> and hard-baked clay furrowed by the rain. (Hemingway, 1926,
> p. 105)

These lines from The Sun Also Rises make the eternal earth the hero of the
novel. In another Hemingway novel, A Farewell to Arms, there is also
beautiful description of nature and weather which form an important total
effect. In virtually all his works, Hemingway describes man in terms of
nature, sometimes struggling violently against its powerful forces. In
his last major work, The Old Man and the Sea, he writes clearly of man and
nature, together and yet in conflict. Santiago and the marlin are
"brothers," yet one must die. The beautiful description is there:

> The clouds over the land now rose like mountains and the
> coast was only a long green line with the gray blue hills
> behind it. The water was a dark blue now, so dark that it
> was almost purple. As he looked down into it he saw the
> red sifting of the plankton in the dark water and the
> strange light they made now . . . nothing showed on the
> surface of the water but some patches of yellow, sun-
> bleached Sargasso weed and the purple, formalized, iri-
> descent, gelatinous bladder of a Portuguese man-of-war
> floating close beside the boat. It turned on its side

3

and then righted itself. It floated cheerfully as a bubble
with its long deadly purple filaments trailing a yard behind
in the water. (Hemingway, 1952, p. 35)

Of course, Hemingway was concerned with man as well as with nature.
Not surprisingly, his sensitive mind saw and portrayed suffering as a
major component of the human condition. There is physical suffering in
his work. The childbirth pains of the woman in "Indian Camp" are an
example from his early work. A Farewell to Arms is dominated by the
suffering of men in war, of Frederic Henry who receives a terrible leg
wound, of women like Catherine Barkley who dies painfully in childbirth.
In The Old Man and the Sea, Santiago undergoes physical torture, an agony
that Hemingway compares to a crucifixion.

Psychological suffering can be even more painful than physical suffering. Hemingway's work is permeated with the suffering of mind as well as
body. In "Indian Camp," the psyche of young, innocent Nick Adams is
shocked by the brutal events he witnesses. The Sun Also Rises is a novel
of people wounded psychologically by World War I, people who lead hedon-
istic lives to cover their deep melancholia. Especially poignant is the
suffering of Jake Barnes and Brett Ashley, who live lives dominated by
frustrated love. Frederic Henry of A Farewell to Arms is nearly crushed
by the strain of war and the death of Catherine; Santiago calls upon all
his mental strength to conquer the marlin.

Perhaps Hemingway's fictional world was so filled with suffering
because his own life was one of pain. Literary biographer Philip Young
chronicles Ernest's wounds:

> His skull was fractured at least once; he sustained at
> least a dozen brain concussions . . . he was in three bad
> automobile accidents . . . in the African jungle he was
> in two airplane accidents in the space of two days, during
> which time he suffered severe internal injuries. . . . In
> warfare he was shot through nine parts of the body. . . .
> (Young, 1965, pp. 25-26)

4

Hemingway saw man in an adverse world, replete with suffering, one in which man could not win.

But through this world of agony, Hemingway did find some redeeming factors in life. Man can be great in the way he reacts to a world of suffering. If a man has courage and endurance, then he is noble and dignified. The life of Jake Barnes in The Sun Also Rises is a frustrated, circular one, but he refuses to wallow in self-pity. Similarly, Frederic Henry has virtually everything he values taken away from him, but he does not crack. But it is in The Old Man and the Sea that Hemingway's view of man's nobility is best developed. Santiago, in his pursuit of the marlin and his defeat by the sharks, remains unbeaten, strong in a world of suffering. He acts in accordance with his maxims: "a man can be destroyed, but not beaten" and "a man is not made for defeat." Santiago is the epitome of man's tragic heroism.

In addition, Hemingway's highly developed aesthetic sense saw man's relationships with fellow human beings as beautiful and delicate. At times during "Indian Camp" Dr. Adams is insensitive to his son Nick, but at the end of the story, as Dr. Adams rows Nick across the lake, there also is a strong and trusting bond between father and son. In The Sun Also Rises, Jake Barnes and Bill Gorton enjoy a deep, personal relationship. In A Farewell to Arms, Rinaldi and Henry, Catherine and Henry, share mutual ties of great warmth and love; these relationships are among the few positive aspects of life in the novel. In The Old Man and the Sea, Santiago and the boy Manolin are two human beings very close to each other. Yes, the world is a tough place, but human love and interdependence soften the blow.

Thus, Hemingway was a man and writer of refined and delicate sensibilities under a tough outer veneer. He was shocked by the terrible

5

violence and suffering in the world. (Perhaps it was so shocking to him that he was fascinated by it, "the fascination with the abomination.") His sensitive mind saw the beautiful and the noble in life as well as the brutality and the agony. He was touched by the beauty and dignity of nature. He was impressed by man's potential of courage in an adverse universe. He saw warm human relationships as desirable. Ernest Hemingway was a sensitive man who lived in the Twentieth Century and portrayed life as he saw it, uncompromisingly.

Bibliography

Baker, Carlos. Ernest Hemingway: A Life Story. New York: Scribner's, 1969.

Hemingway, Ernest. The Old Man and the Sea. New York: Scribner's, 1952.

Hemingway, Ernest. The Sun Also Rises. New York: Scribner's, 1926.

Hemingway, Ernest. The Hemingway Reader. Edited by Charles Poore. New York: Scribner's, 1953.

Young, Philip. Ernest Hemingway. Rev. ed. Minneapolis: University of Minnesota Press, 1965.

Instructor's Comments

This summation paper is a lesson in synthesis. Appreciative, it weaves biography, research, the common seminar readings, sharp (if rather lengthy) direct quotations, and personal reflection together. The writer remembers--words, themes, characters. He reveals the total experience of the course, his sensitivity to literature, to the man and writer Ernest Hemingway. His title, his introduction, his paragraphs and prose and punctuation, his conclusion are all gratifying results of the seminar.

HANDOUT 22
STUDENT MODEL FOR PAPER VII: PARODY

THE MIDDLE OF SOMETHING
(A Nick Adams story)

by Louise Milkman

Up in Michigan Nick, his mother, and his father had a cabin. By the
cabin was a lake. Across the lake were Indians. There was grass around
the lake. There was also a stream. In the stream were fish. Some of the
fish were trout. The fact that some of the fish were trout is irrelevant,
but a reader may wonder what kind of fish some of the fish were and not
knowing would upset the reader and he would be upset and feel ignorant and
wonder what kind of fish was in the stream, the stream which he didn't
even know the name of but which was, by the way, the Big Two-Kidneyed
River, and the reader would lose his self-respect and know that the world
breaks everyone and afterward many are strong in the broken places and
besides, man is not made for defeat. So Nick was always very happy and
satisfied to fish or do anything well. This was the case one morning.

One morning, it was morning. The sun rose. This did not surprise
Nick because the sun often behaved that way in the morning. Nick was
used to such things. The three boys ate breakfast. They often ate
breakfast in the morning as the sun rose. They sat there eating and the
sun would rise. This usually occurred in the morning. Except when Nick
had seen an Indian cut his throat the night before and he couldn't eat.

There were three boys: Nick, his friend Bill, and his other friend,
Bill. All Nick's friends were named Bill except one who was named Wemedge.
Nick was eating oatmeal. He ate oatmeal every morning as the sun rose

1

2

(which it often did in the morning). The oatmeal was in a bowl which had oatmeal in it. It was good oatmeal. Nick reflected on the various oat-meals he had had and he knew good oatmeal when he saw it. Or tasted it. There was oatmeal and there was oatmeal. Nick knew that. Nick had a spoon with which he ate the oatmeal. He used this spoon every morning as the sun rose. He put the spoon in the bowl. It went in the oatmeal. It was obviously a Code Spoon since it could maintain grace under oatmeal. However, as Nick knew, this spoon could never compete with bullfighters. He pictured the spoon fighting a bull. It was funny. He laughed. He laughed and laughed. Did he laugh. What is funnier than a spoon in a bull ring chasing a bull. He shared his humor with Bill and Bill. He couldn't share it with Wemedge because Wemedge was not there. Bill laughed. So did Bill.

"That's one for the medical journal, George," said Nick.

But he began to be hungry. He could not remember a time when he had been so hungry. He lifted the spoon out of the bowl which had oatmeal in it. Keeping the oatmeal in the spoon, he drew the spoon towards his mouth. He kept the round part level so he would not drop the oatmeal. This took deep concentration on Nick's part and he sweated into the oatmeal. But Nick did not mind salty oatmeal. Using all the muscles of his right hand Nick carefully lifted the spoon which had oatmeal in it up to his mouth. Thus, he had transferred the oatmeal from the bowl to his mouth. Nick was very proud. It reminded him of black grasshoppers.

"Speaking of black grasshoppers," Nick said, "I saw a brown cockroach today. Boy, was he brown."

"Yes, I know what you mean," Bill said, "I saw a cockroach and it was so brown."

"There's nothing like brown cockroaches," said Bill.

3

"Except black grasshoppers," Nick said. Bill got angry. He said, "You just don't appreciate true brownness when you see it."

"Oh, boy," Nick exclaimed. Every once in a while Nick felt like exclaiming, "Oh, boy."

Bill went on talking to Bill. "Bill," Bill said to Bill, "You oughta see those brown cockroaches. They're quite brown and when there are a lot of them they look very brown."

Bill said, "Well, if we are going to brag, I knocked a whole bunch of ants off a log into a fire once."

"No," Bill said, "that was Frederic Henry."

"Oh," said Bill. Wemedge didn't comment. He couldn't because he wasn't there.

Nick wanted action. He threw some sweaty oatmeal at Bill. Bill said, "I'll kill you."

But in the early morning, sitting there by his oatmeal with his father in the next room, Nick felt quite sure he would never die.

Instructor's Comments

This student writer had fun and wants to share it with the seminar. After six papers and a great deal of seminar interaction, she is ready for parody. Her eye and ear have caught the Hemingway style--the plots, the characters, the repetitions, the length of line, the dialogue, the simple sentences with few adjectives or adverbs. By twisting a title and combining a few plots and characters, as well as adding a dash of absurdity and a heavy Hemingway theme, she has also completed the seminar. Was her parody built out of criticism? Was it a chance at last to attack and yet be praised for her skill? Or was it an exercise in creative skill? Her success as a parody writer leaves those questions unanswered.

APPENDIXES

APPENDIXES

APPENDIX A
A TELEPHONE CALL
TO MARY HEMINGWAY

Tuesday, April 29, 1975, 8:30 a.m. C.S.T.

It was a Big Day for the first period American litera-ture seminar at West High School in Iowa City, Iowa. Mary Hemingway had agreed to a telephone interview from her apartment in New York City.

What's so exciting about a telephone interview? Well, let's go back a month, to early March, when my twelve juniors and seniors had already written their papers on the Nick Adams stories and *The Sun Also Rises*. After two students had completed their oral defenses of their position papers on the latter novel, Stoney—a bright eager junior—said, "I wonder what Ernest Hemingway was *really* like. I mean, after we finish *A Farewell to Arms* we have to write a paper on both the writer and the man. The stuff I've been reading in Carlos Baker's biography is good but . . . "

Connie nodded in agreement. "Wouldn't it be neat if we could talk to somebody that knew him?" she said.

I thought for a moment as the rest of the class said something about taking an extended field trip to Oak Park, Key West, Ketchum—and Cuba, if Castro were willing.

"Well, let's see . . . we have some money in the audio-visual budget for telephone calls," I said. "I've never tried that."

The class laughed. "Not that much money," said Dan.

"Wait a minute," I said. "I'm referring to the tele-phone kit our school has leased from Ma Bell. It's a two-way thing where the whole class can both talk and listen. We have the kit up in the A-V Center."

"Great!" shouted Dan. "Let's call someone. But who?"

"How about Mary Hemingway?" said Stoney. "You know, his wife. The last one. She has all the rights to his books and everything. Ernest used to call her 'Miss Mary.'"

"Hey, Stoney, you have been reading ahead," said Dan.

So we did. Or rather, I told the class that I had better write Mrs. Hemingway a letter to see if she would agree. On second thought, the class began to expect the worst. Someone famous talking to a high school class in *Iowa!* Indeed! But I wrote anyway, and in less than a week, Mary Hemingway sent back my letter in the self-addressed envelope. At the bottom, she wrote, "OK." But "may

the questions be specific." She noted her private phone number and suggested the best time and days of the week for an interview.

When I told the seminar about the good news, a kind of frenzy broke out. "I don't believe it. Gosh, now that we can really do it, what are we going to ask?" said Stoney.

"It was your idea in the first place," said Connie.

"We had better know something about Mrs. Heming-way," said Dan.

"We had better know something about Hemingway!" shouted Jeremy, who had just written a paper entitled "Grace Under Pressure."

We laid the groundwork for the interview. We decided to hold off the paper on *A Farewell to Arms;* we would go into biographical material about the Nobel Prize win-ner. With this study and the interview, the next paper on the writer would be especially meaningful. So we built up a class library of Hemingway biography, as well as articles by and about Mary Hemingway. In fact, the next day we studied a capsule biography on Mrs. Hem-ingway which appeared in our library issue of *Current Biography*.

It was soon obvious that Mary Hemingway was more than just the wife of an author. A noted World War II correspondent, she had met Ernest in London in 1944; he had proposed to her in a week. Ten years after their marriage and two years after the Nobel Prize, Ernest himself described his wife's many talents:

> Miss Mary is durable. She is also brave, charming, witty, exciting to look at, a pleasure to be with and a good wife. She is also an excellent fisherman, a fair wing shot, a strong swimmer, a really good cook, a good judge of wine, an excellent gardener, an ama-teur astronomer, a student of art, political economy, Swahili, French and Italian and can run a boat or a household in Spanish. She can also sing well. . . .

Finally, each student planned one question to ask Mary Hemingway; we also added some consensus class questions. And when we were finished, about a week before the interview, we mailed her our questions as well as a reminder of the time and date—especially the time since we were on Central Standard Time. My assessment of our questions: she would need about six hours to answer them. Maybe more. Yet we had a half-hour of budgeted telephone time.

But we were ready. So we thought.

The day of the interview was a comedy of frenzy, errors, and delight. Obviously untrained in the science of interview, we hooked up the telephone kit in the office conference room. Nervous—we called one student's home three times to make sure the phone was working. About the only intelligent planning was a last-minute discussion of whether we should tape the interview. Somebody screamed something about Watergate. Another said he had checked with the A-V director who said we would need a beeper as well as written permission from Mrs. Hemingway. So no tape recording.

In desperation, wanting to have some record, some expert note-taking, we asked a school secretary to take shorthand notes. Later, we discovered that she had been so flustered by the obvious excitement and tension in the conference room that she did not get one sentence on paper!

Aside from this, the interview went perfectly. Everybody asked a question; everybody spoke to "Miss Mary." Each student was absolutely satisfied with her responses —always to the point, never ducking an issue, complete with anecdotes, kind, and so very alive and intelligent. During the interview, I looked across the room with delight as everybody seemed to be nodding and smiling and taking notes.

When our half-hour was up, everybody shouted—oh, so unsophisticated but oh, so natural—"Goodbye! Goodbye . . . and thanks!"

The next day we pooled our notes, our memories.

"She *really* answered my question about how she felt when she and Ernest were in those two airplane crashes in Africa," said Marzia.

"What did she say?" groaned Dan, who had missed the interview because of the flu.

"She said, 'Try it sometime. And you'll know,'" laughed Marzia.

"Did anybody ask my question about what Ernest's routine was down in Cuba and whether she ever talked with him about his writing when he was working?" said Dan.

"I did," said Will. "She said he was at work fairly steady, usually from seven to twelve in the morning. She said he didn't talk much about his writing even though she typed the manuscript of *The Old Man and the Sea.* But she did say that she had told him she hoped he wouldn't kill off the Old Man at the end."

Then Greg, a serious National Merit winner, began to review what Mary had said about literary criticism. "She said she wasn't a critic, but she did say she had a fondness for *The Sun Also Rises* because it seemed like a vital and true book about the special craziness of Paris in the 1920s. And she loved the way Ernest had dealt with the beautiful scenery of Spain—and the bullfights in Pamplona."

"Hey, Greg, don't forget that Mary said that picking her favorite book is like asking a mother which of her seven children she likes best," said Stoney.

"Right," said Greg. "I guess you could sum up the whole point about literary criticism by saying that she felt Hemingway was largely unconcerned about critics. He didn't write to prove himself—certainly not with *The Old Man and the Sea.* He was a writer who wrote about what interested him."

During our discussion, we began to piece together the rest of the interview into a kind of *U.S. News and World Report* format:

Cheryl: "Why do you think many Communist countries like Ernest's writings?"

M. H.: "I'm not sure. But the Russians compare him to Shakespeare. Though we see the royalties piling up in Russia, we can't take any money out. Of course, they never liked *For Whom the Bell Tolls.*"

Stoney: "What were Ernest's political and racial views?"

M. H.: "Ernest was apolitical. He lived much of his life outside the United States. As for prejudices, he had none. Our friends included Orientals and blacks. For example, one of our good friends was a black boxer who used to live in our home in Cuba."

Charles: "Where did Ernest get his ideas for the so-called 'Code Hero,' the man who could endure the hardships of life?"

M. H.: "I think he lived the life of the Code Hero because he believed in grace under pressure, in courage. Those important values were taught to him by his Victorian background back in Oak Park, Illinois."

Connie: "I read that one of the most important assets that a woman friend of Ernest Hemingway can have is *durability.* What were some of the things about him that made this true?"

M. H. (laughing): "Oh, that was something I had said as kind of a joke. We had been down in Peru doing some fishing under pretty rugged circumstances. The weather and the ocean were rough. I had said something about how you had to be 'durable' to go fishing with Ernest. Later, he repeated that line."

Janie: "What were Ernest's personal tastes in such things as favorite writers, clothing, food, automobiles, and movies?"

M. H.: "Ernest had lots of favorite writers—oh, Tolstoi, Twain, Balzac, and Shakespeare's *King Lear.* He wasn't much on clothing, though he was sensitive to texture. That's something that's not been noted about him. He especially loved texture in food, especially Chinese food. And he loved spicey food, too . . . he loved convertibles, always had one. He saw few movies, though I do remember how much he liked *Around the World in 80 Days*."

Class: "Are you planning to release any more of his unpublished writing?"

M. H.: "Maybe. But it *must* always be up to his best standards. Nothing must be added. We still are considering "Dangerous Summer" and a long amorphous book called "Garden of Eden."

As we sat there, transcribing our notes and heading into the next Hemingway paper, a kind of euphoria settled over the room. A special kind of confidence—though admittedly bolstered by only a brief and fragmentary telephone call—prevailed. But it was a telephone call to remember for the rest of your life.

APPENDIX B
THE LIFE AND TIMES
OF ERNEST HEMINGWAY

Ernest Hemingway	The Times
THE EARLY YEARS, 1899–1919	
1899	
Hemingway born on July 21 in Oak Park, Illinois, second of six children of Dr. Clarence and Grace Hall Hemingway.	U.S. population: 75,994,575. McKinley administration (1897–1901). Taft (1909–1913). Model T mass produced (1909).
1914–1918	
Summers at Windemere in Northern Michigan.	World War I (1914–18). Wilson administration (1913–1921). Panama Canal opens.
1917	
Graduation from Oak Park High School. Reporter for Kansas City *Star*. Rejected by U.S. Army for bad eye.	U.S. in World War I. Caporetto campaigns begin in Italy.
1918	
Red Cross ambulance driver in Italy. Wounded near Fossalta di Piave, July 8. Love affair with Agnes von Kurowsky.	Armistice, November 1918, ending World War I. Wilson's Fourteen Points.
1919	
In Petoskey, Michigan, the "Big Two-Hearted River" country, writing.	Treaty of Versailles. Sherwood Anderson, *Winesburg, Ohio*. Volstead Prohibition Act.
THE PARIS PERIOD, 1920–1927	
1920–1924	
Reporter for Toronto *Star* and *Star Weekly*. Life in Paris. Meets Gertrude Stein. Marriage to Hadley (1921). John ("Bumby") born (1923).	F. Scott Fitzgerald, *This Side of Paradise* (1920). The Roaring 20s. Harding administration (1921–1923). Sacco and Vanzetti trial (1921).
1921–1924	
Foreign correspondent for Toronto papers. First war correspondence, Graeco-Turkish War (1922).	Graeco-Turkish War (1921–1922). James Joyce, *Ulysses* (1922). T. S. Eliot, *The Waste Land* (1922).
1923	
Three Stories and Ten Poems, Paris. Contains "Up in Michigan," "Out of Season," "My Old Man."	U.S. population over 105 million. Coolidge administration (1923–1929). Teapot Dome Scandal (1923–1924).
1924	
in our time, Paris, thirty-two pages. Contains "Indian Camp."	

1925

In Our Time, first Hemingway book published in U.S., Boni & Liveright publishers. Adds fourteen short stories to the miniatures, now interchapters, of *in our time*.

Fitzgerald, *The Great Gatsby*. Anderson, *Dark Laughter*. Scopes "Monkey" trial.

1926

Torrents of Spring, parody of Anderson's *Dark Laughter*. *The Sun Also Rises* (British title: *Fiesta*).

Transatlantic wireless telephone. Byrd flies over North Pole.

1927

Men Without Women, fourteen short stories (ten of which had appeared in magazines). Divorce from Hadley, marriage to Pauline Pfeiffer.

Charles Lindbergh flies from New York to Paris in *Spirit of St. Louis*.

KEY WEST PERIOD, 1927–1940

1928

Birth of son Patrick. Moves to Key West, Florida. Father commits suicide in Oak Park.

Talking movies, first Mickey Mouse cartoon.

1929

A Farewell to Arms, first commercial success: 80,000 copies sold in four months.

Stock market crash. William Faulkner, *The Sound and the Fury*. Hoover administration (1929–1933).

1931

Birth of son Gregory.

1932

Death in the Afternoon, nonfiction work on bullfighting.

U.S. population over 122 million. Ford's 20 millionth car. FDR elected (1933–1945).

1933

Winner Take Nothing, fourteen short stories. Writes for *Esquire*, first of thirty-one articles for magazine over next six years.

Depression. FDR's CCC, TVA, NRA, AAA. Hitler, German Chancellor.

1934

Purchases *Pilar*, thirty-eight-foot cruiser, fishing.

Mao's Long March in China.

1935

Green Hills of Africa, nonfiction work about big-game hunting.

Italy invades Ethiopia. WPA. Regular transpacific air service.

1936

Writes, speaks, raises money for Loyalists in Spanish Civil War.

Spanish Civil War, Franco vs. Loyalists.

1937

In Spain covering civil war for Northern American Newspaper Alliance. Film work on *The Spanish Earth*. *To Have and Have Not*, three interconnected stories, two of which had been published separately.

CIO sitdown strike. Japan invades China.

1938

The Fifth Column and the First Forty-Nine Stories. Contains a play, stories from previous collections, and seven stories previously published in magazines.

Thornton Wilder, *Our Town.* Pearl Buck wins Nobel Prize. Hitler and Chamberlain meet at Munich Conference.

1939

Ernest and Pauline separate. Ernest moves to Finca Vigia estate, fifteen miles from Havana, Cuba.

World War II begins; Germany attacks Poland. John Steinbeck, *The Grapes of Wrath.*

THE WAR PERIOD, 1940–1945

1940

For Whom the Bell Tolls, his best-selling novel. Divorced by Pauline; marries Martha Gellhorn.

U.S. population 131 million. New York World's Fair closes. Nazi bombing of Britain.

1941

Goes to China as war correspondent.

December 7, Japanese bomb Pearl Harbor. U.S. enters World War II.

1942

Pilar patrols Caribbean for U-boats. *Men at War,* collection of war stories and accounts.

U.S. Air Force bombs Europe, naval battles in Pacific.

1943–1945

Covers European Theater of war as newspaper and magazine correspondent. Divorced by Martha Gellhorn (1944). Marries Mary Welsh.

D-Day, V-E, V-J Days. Atomic Age begins. U.N. Charter. Death of FDR. Truman administration (1945–1952).

THE CUBAN PERIOD, 1945–1960

1948–1949

Interviewed by Malcolm Cowley. Allows first biographical study for *Life.*

Norman Mailer, *The Naked and the Dead* (1948). Berlin Airlift (1948).

1950

Across the River and into the Trees, much criticized novel.

Korean War begins. McCarthy era.

1951

Death of Hemingway's mother.

J. D. Salinger, *Catcher in the Rye.*

1952

The Old Man and the Sea, first published in *Life.* Pulitzer Prize.

Ralph Ellison, *Invisible Man.* Eisenhower administration (1952-60).

1954

Nobel Prize for Literature. Cited for "forceful and style-making mastery of the art of modern narration." Injured in two airplane crashes in Africa.

Supreme Court rules racial segregation unconstitutional.

1956

Filming of *The Old Man and the Sea* as Hemingway observes.

Israeli-Egyptian War.

1957–1958

Works on Paris memoirs.

1959

Buys hunting lodge near Ketchum, Idaho.

Cuban Revolution and rise of Fidel Castro.

KETCHUM, IDAHO, 1960–1961, AND POSTHUMOUS

1960–1961

Onset of breakdown. Hospitalization in Rochester, Minnesota, at Mayo Clinic (1960). Begins a bullfighting story, "The Dangerous Summer."

First jet passenger service. Kennedy administration (1960–63).

1961

Death on July 2 of self-inflicted gunshot wounds.

Alan Shepard's suborbital space flight.

1964

A Moveable Feast—Paris memoirs.

1967

By-Line: Ernest Hemingway—selected news writings.

1970

Islands in the Stream.

THE HEMINGWAY FAMILY

Ernest Miller Hemingway

Born July 21, 1899, in Oak Park, Illinois, the second oldest child of Clarence and Grace Hemingway. Died July 2, 1961, in Ketchum, Idaho, of self-inflicted gunshot wounds.

Grandparents

Anson T. Hemingway
Adelaide Edmonds Hemingway
Ernest Miller Hall
Caroline Hancock Hall

Parents

Dr. Clarence Edmonds Hemingway: died of self-inflicted gunshot wounds in 1928 in Oak Park, Illinois.
Grace Hall Hemingway: died in 1951 at the age of seventy-nine in Memphis, Tennessee.

Brother and Sisters

Marcelline (born 1898)
Ursula (born 1902)
Madelaine "Sunny" (born 1904)
Carol (born 1911)
Leicester (born 1915)

Wives and Children

Hadley Richardson (marriage: 1921–1927)
　Son: John "Bumby" (born 1923)
Pauline Pfeiffer (marriage: 1927–1940)
　Sons: Patrick (born 1928)
　　　　Gregory (born 1931)
Martha Gellhorn (marriage: 1940–1944)
Mary Welsh (marriage: 1944–1961)

APPENDIX C
ANECDOTES FROM
THE HEMINGWAY BIOGRAPHY

The following seven anecdotes are included in this handbook to initiate the profile discussion. For those students and teachers who have difficulty locating reference materials in their school or community, these anecdotes are offered as models, resources, alternates for a large group discussion, or whatever seems most useful.

ANECDOTE 1

Ernest Hemingway liked boxing. Though his father had taught him to enjoy outdoor sports such as hunting and fishing, Ernest began to box when he was in high school. When the coast was clear, he and his friends would engage in vigorous one-round bouts in his family's Oak Park, Illinois, music room where he was supposed to be practicing on his cello. Even though his father had a horror of physical violence, Ernest would take boxing lessons at a Chicago gym.

Later in the 1920s, Hemingway would continue boxing workouts in Paris. One of his most memorable matches was with Morley Callaghan, another American expatriate author.

Ernest and Morley would go the American Club. At first, Callaghan was plenty worried, being only five eight and overweight, plus being aware of the story that Ernest had flattened the French middleweight champion. Ernest became frustrated with Morley's poor style, but Callaghan gained confidence with each punch.

One dark cloudy morning, Callaghan caught Ernest with a solid left to the mouth. Hemingway's mouth began to bleed. Then Ernest caught another punch, which made him furious at the sight of his own blood. He spat in Callaghan's face and on his shirt. Shocked, Callaghan stopped fighting. They stared at each other. Then Ernest said, "That's what bullfighters do when they're wounded. It's a way of showing contempt." Then Hemingway smiled, was friendly and sweet again. Callaghan always wondered about that match. Was it all pure theater? [Source: Carlos Baker, *Ernest Hemingway: A Life Story,* pp. 22-23; Morley Callaghan, *That Summer in Paris,* pp. 97-100, 118-22.]

ANECDOTE 2

Ernest Hemingway was accident-prone all his life. While amateur psychologists might call it part of his death wish, others remember how bravely he bore with these accidents, his "grace under pressure." One of his earliest accidents was remembered by his younger brother Leicester.

In the summer, the Hemingway family would leave their Oak Park home and go to northern Michigan near Walloon Lake, the setting of Ernest's "Up in Michigan" stories. They had a cottage where Dr. Hemingway would relax. The entire family loved the woods and the fishing. The children had errands too, Ernest's being a daily milk run to the Bacon farm about a half mile away. On one of these errands to bring home milk, Ernest had a bad accident.

One morning as he ran off to get the milk, carrying a short stick, he stumbled near a ravine and fell forward. The stick was driven into the back of his throat into both tonsils. Blood gushed forth as he rushed back to the cottage for treatment. As his father stanched the blood, Ernest remained stoic though his mother was horrified. The throat remained tender for some time, and his father told him to whistle whenever he felt like crying. Leicester later remembered that he saw a photograph of Ernest at an Italian hospital recuperating from numerous mortar wounds: Ernest was whistling through clenched teeth. [Source: Leicester Hemingway, *My Brother,* pp. 19-22.]

ANECDOTE 3

Ernest covered the 1922 Lausanne Peace Conference in Switzerland while his wife Hadley nursed a cold in Paris. While at the conference, he kept pleading that she fly down and join him. Finally, Hadley agreed to come by train, rushed down to the station, and made a journey that biographer Carlos Baker called "so horrible for Ernest that neither of them was ever able to forget it."

Hadley had decided to take all of Ernest's manuscripts in a separate small valise so that he could get on with his writing during the Christmas holiday. Except for two stories, "Up in Michigan" and "My Old Man," she brought all the fiction and poetry that she could find.

When Hadley left their Paris apartment, she took a taxi to the Gare de Lyon and there secured a porter to carry the luggage to the train compartment. Somehow the valise with the manuscripts disappeared as she boarded to travel south. The trip was one of horror.

When she arrived, Ernest listened to her tale of woe amidst a vale of tears. He later wrote how he rushed back to Paris in hopes that the carbons had been left behind. But they had been in the valise too. [Source: Carlos Baker, *Ernest Hemingway: A Life Story*, pp. 102-3.]

ANECDOTE 4

In the mid-1930s, Ernest Hemingway was living in Key West, Florida, with his second wife Pauline. Besides writing, Ernest would hang around Sloppy Joe's Bar or take his Mob fishing for marlin with his thirty-eight-footer, the diesel-powered *Pilar*. People began to call him "Papa," and a kind of myth was built around him.

At least two good stories came from this period.

The first was at Sloppy Joe's where one of his drinking companions named George Brooks, a local attorney, enjoyed making Hemingway miserable. Brooks's favorite trick was with homosexuals who came in the bar in search for sailors. One day he told a young man that Hemingway was "as queer as a three dollar bill." Then he said, "Just go up to him and give him a big kiss and tell him you love him." When the young man did, Ernest turned white as a ghost, then spat and knocked the guy cold with a right punch. Turning to George Brooks, he said, "I know you're behind this you conniving son-of-a-bitch, I know it." George denied it, innocently insisting the poor devil was a genuine fan of the great Ernest Hemingway.

The second story is a fish story. One April Sunday in 1935, Papa was trolling the Gulf Stream on the way to Bimini. He sighted a large green turtle, and he and two companions then got simultaneous strikes. Ernest pulled his line first, a large shark. Holding the shark in position alongside with the gaff in his left hand and his Colt in the right, Hemingway began to pump bullets into the shark's head. Suddenly the gaff broke and Hemingway found himself with legs all covered with blood. Somehow, he had managed to shoot himself in both legs! "Dammit," he told his brother who theorized the damage came from the ricochet, "That's one for the books." [Source: Leicester Hemingway, *My Brother*, p. 164; James McLendon, *Papa*, pp. 152-53.]

ANECDOTE 5

When Ernest Hemingway's temper was roused, he was inclined to punch out his adversary. Around Easter of 1936, the poet Wallace Stevens had the misfortune of arousing the Oak Park boxer-author.

Stevens, a portly Hartford insurance executive and some twenty years Hemingway's senior, had the myopia to make negative remarks about Hemingway at a Key West cocktail party to Hemingway's sister Sunny. She had just completed the arduous task of typing *A Farewell to Arms* for her brother and then had to come to

Ernest's defense as Stevens pressed the criticism. Stevens's remark that she had little literary insight sent her home near tears.

When Sunny told Ernest, he rushed out of his house and drove to the party. The genteel members of the soiree were horrified to discover Ernest calling Stevens outside and then proceeding to break the poet's jaw with a vicious left hook. After that Ernest went into what he called "hiding from the law," while Stevens lay in pain at the local Marine Hospital, receiving nourishment through a straw in his wired jaw.

Later, Hemingway felt bad about the matter, partly because he knew that he was open to a case of assault and battery. But Stevens had kept quiet and when he was released, he showed up at Hemingway's South Street front door—and again announced his displeasure with Hemingway's prose though he did apologize for insulting Sunny. Ernest was impressed with the spunk of the "little squirt" and invited Stevens in for a drink. The matter ended there, kept from public attention. [Source: James McLendon, *Papa*, pp. 55-57.]

ANECDOTE 6

There is an old literary chestnut about "the reports of my death being grossly exaggerated." Such was the case with Ernest Hemingway in January of 1954.

Hemingway and his wife Mary had gone to Africa for a safari and a vacation. On January 21, they climbed into Roy Marsh's Cessna 180 at the West Nairobi airport for a trip to the Belgian Congo. The first day's flight was uneventful though nostalgic as Ernest pointed out the old 1933 campsite where his former wife Pauline had killed a lion. That night they stayed at Bukava. The next day was much the same with Mary taking lots of photographs of African wildlife. But on the third day, near Murchison Falls, a flight of ibis suddenly crossed the path of the plane.

Hemingway's friend Marsh dived to avoid the ibis, struck an abandoned telephone wire, crunched to a landing about three miles from the falls. Though Mary suffered initial shock and Ernest a sprained right shoulder, no one was badly hurt. But they didn't receive any response to their "Mayday" pleas.

Luckily, they spotted a large white boat on a nearby river. They caught a ride (and had to pay the fare) to Lake Albert and Butiaba. There a bush pilot named Reggie Cartwright took them to the local airport for a trip to Entebbe. As the plane taxied across the badly plowed field, it suddenly burst into flames as it attempted to rise. Ernest smashed his way through the jammed cabin door as Mary managed to escape through the port side. Mary had a damaged knee, Ernest a bleeding scalp. A local policeman rescued them and took them fifty miles to Masindi to the Railway Hotel. The next day a doctor arrived, and they were transported a hundred miles away to the Lake Victorian Hotel.

The next morning the whole place was buzzing with the press who had learned of the first wreck and announced to the world that Ernest Hemingway was dead. Mary cabled her parents while Ernest began to recuperate from a collapsed intestine, kidney trouble, an aching backbone, and a head like an egg. Roy Marsh got a Cessna to take Hemingway to Nairobi.

Only nine days had passed, but Hemingway had experienced two air crashes, multiple injuries. Ernest read the host of premature obituaries with what Mary called "immortal zest." He also wondered how many people had welcomed the news of his "death." [Source: Carlos Baker, *Ernest Hemingway: A Life Story,* pp. 518-22.]

ANECDOTE 7

When Ernest Hemingway was found dead on July 2, 1961, at his Ketchum, Idaho, lodge, some people insisted that he had died from an accident. They said that the "incredible accident" was caused while Ernest was cleaning his favorite shotgun. Few people think such things today.

Ernest's ideas about death go back as early as 1918 when he wrote his parents from Italy where he had been badly wounded. He wrote them that death was a very simple thing because he had seen it and knew. As a young man, he feared the time when his body was old, worn out, when his illusions might be shattered. Close readers of his works from *A Farewell to Arms* to *To Have and Have Not* trace these early ideas about death. They also point out that Hemingway's father committed suicide with a gun.

The events just before his suicide belie that death was accidental. For over a year, the strain of poor health took its toll. He began to worry about money, about his telephones being bugged by the federal government, about going crazy, about his blood pressure. In December of 1960, he was admitted to the Rochester, Minnesota, Mayo Clinic and given eleven treatments with electric shock. After he left the Clinic, he became even less communicative, and by April of 1961, Mary saw that a great sadness had come over him: he couldn't write. One morning at Ketchum she found him in his bathrobe holding his shotgun.

Then events began to mount: (1) Just before he was to return to Rochester, a friend wrestled his loaded shotgun from him as he held it to his throat. (2) At a refueling stop at the Rapid City airport, he went looking for a gun in the hangar. (3) At Rapid City, he tried to walk into the propeller of another plane. (4) At Rochester, he promised his doctor not to commit suicide. And then in June, he convinced the doctors that he was fit to go back to Ketchum.

Mary Hemingway knew that a mistake had been made in letting him go back to Ketchum, but when they reached the lodge on Friday, June 30, she hoped for the best. On Sunday morning, she found him dead with a double-barreled Boss shotgun that he used for pigeon hunting. [Source: Leicester Hemingway, *My Brother,* p. 256; Carlos Baker, *Ernest Hemingway: A Life Story,* pp. 199, 554-64; A. E. Hotchner, *Papa Hemingway: A Personal Memoir,* pp. 264-304.]

APPENDIX D
ON THE BLUE WATER:
A GULF STREAM LETTER

Ernest Hemingway

Certainly there is no hunting like the hunting of man and those who have hunted armed men long enough and liked it, never really care for anything else thereafter. You will meet them doing various things with resolve, but their interest rarely holds because after the other thing ordinary life is as flat as the taste of wine when the taste buds have been burned off your tongue. Wine, when your tongue has been burned clean with lye and water, feels like puddle water in your mouth, while mustard feels like axle-grease, and you can smell crisp, fried bacon, but when you taste it, there is only a feeling of crinkly lard.

You can learn about this matter of the tongue by coming into the kitchen of a villa on the Riviera late at night and taking a drink from what should be a bottle of Evian water and which turns out to be *Eau de Javel,* a concentrated lye product used for cleaning sinks. The taste buds on your tongue, if burned off by *Eau de Javel,* will begin to function again after about a week. At what rate other things regenerate one does not know, since you lose track of friends and the things one could learn in a week were mostly learned a long time ago.

The other night I was talking with a good friend to whom all hunting is dull except elephant hunting. To him there is no sport in anything unless there is great danger and, if the danger is not enough, he will increase it for his own satisfaction. A hunting companion of his had told me how this friend was not satisfied with the risks of ordinary elephant hunting but would, if possible, have the elephants driven, or turned, so he could take them head-on, so it was a choice of killing them with the difficult frontal shot as they came, trumpeting, with their ears spread, or having them run over him. This is to elephant hunting what the German cult of suicide climbing is to ordinary mountaineering, and I suppose it is, in a way, an attempt to approximate the old hunting of the armed man who is hunting you.

This friend was speaking of elephant hunting and urging me to hunt elephant, as he said that once you took it up no other hunting would mean anything to you. I was arguing that I enjoyed all hunting and shooting, any sort I could get, and had no desire to wipe this capacity for enjoyment out with the *Eau de Javel* of the old elephant coming straight at you with his trunk up and his ears spread.

"Of course you like that big fishing too," he said rather sadly. "Frankly, I can't see where the excitement is in that."

"You'd think it was marvelous if the fish shot at you with Tommy guns or jumped back and forth through the cockpit with swords on the ends of their noses."

"Don't be silly," he said. "But frankly I don't see where the thrill is."

"Look at so and so," I said. "He's an elephant hunter and this last year he's gone fishing for big fish and he's goofy about it. He must get a kick out of it or he wouldn't do it."

"Yes," my friend said. "There must be something about it but I can't see it. Tell me where you get a thrill out of it."

"I'll try to write it in a piece sometime," I told him.

"I wish you would," he said. "Because you people are sensible on other subjects. Moderately sensible I mean."

"I'll write it."

In the first place, the Gulf Stream and the other great ocean currents are the last wild country there is left. Once you are out of sight of land and of the other boats you are more alone than you can ever be hunting and the sea is the same as it has been since before men ever went on it in boats. In a season fishing you will see it oily flat as the becalmed galleons saw it while they drifted to the westward; white-capped with a fresh breeze as they saw it running with the trades; and in high, rolling blue hills the tops blowing off them like snow as they were punished by it, so that sometimes you will see three great hills of water with your fish jumping from the top of the farthest one and if you tried to make a turn to go with him without picking your chance, one of those breaking crests would roar down in on you with a thousand tons of water and you would hunt no more elephants, Richard, my lad.

There is no danger from the fish, but anyone who goes on the sea the year around in a small power boat does not seek danger. You may be absolutely sure that in a year you will have it without seeking, so you try always to avoid it all you can.

Because the Gulf Stream is an unexploited country, only the very fringe of it ever being fished, and then only at a dozen places in thousands of miles of current, no one knows what fish live in it, or how great size they reach or what age, or even what kinds of fish and animals live in it at different depths. When you are drifting, out of sight of land, fishing four lines, sixty, eighty, one hundred and one hundred fifty fathoms down, in water that is seven hundred fathoms deep you never know what may take the small tuna that you use for bait, and every time the line starts to run off the reel, slowly first, then with a scream of the click as the rod bends and you feel it double and the huge weight of the friction of the line rushing through that depth of water while you pump and reel, pump and reel, pump and reel, trying to get the belly out of the line before the fish jumps, there is always a thrill that needs no danger to make it real. It may be a marlin that will jump high and clear off to your right and then go off in a series of leaps, throwing a splash like a speedboat in a sea as you shout for the boat to turn with him watching the line melting off the reel before the boat can get around. Or it may be a broadbill that will show wagging his great broadsword. Or it may be some fish that you will never see at all that will head straight out to the northwest like a submerged submarine and never show and at the end of five hours the angler has a straightened-out hook. There is always a feeling of excitement when a fish takes hold when you are drifting deep.

In hunting you know what you are after and the top you can get is an elephant. But who can say what you will hook sometime when drifting in a hundred and fifty fathoms in the Gulf Stream? There are probably marlin and swordfish to which the fish we have seen caught are pygmies; and every time a fish takes the bait drifting you have a feeling perhaps you are hooked to one of these.

Carlos, our Cuban mate, who is fifty-three years old and has been fishing for marlin since he went in the bow of a skiff with his father when he was seven, was fishing drifting deep one time when he hooked a white marlin. The fish jumped twice and then sounded and when he sounded suddenly Carlos felt a great weight and he could not hold the line which went out and down and down irresistibly until the fish had taken out over a hundred

and fifty fathoms. Carlos says it felt as heavy and solid as though he were hooked to the bottom of the sea. Then suddenly the strain was loosened but he could feel the weight of his original fish and pulled it up stone dead. Some toothless fish like a swordfish or marlin had closed his jaws across the middle of the eighty pound white marlin and squeezed it and held it so that every bit of the insides of the fish had been crushed out while the huge fish moved off with the eighty-pound fish in its mouth. Finally it let go. What size of a fish would that be? I thought it might be a giant squid but Carlos said there were no sucker marks on the fish and that it showed plainly the shape of the marlin's mouth where he had crushed it.

Another time an old man fishing alone in a skiff out of Cabañas hooked a great marlin that, on the heavy sashcord handline, pulled the skiff far out to sea. Two days later the old man was picked up by fishermen sixty miles to the eastward, the head and forward part of the marlin lashed alongside. What was left of the fish, less than half, weighed eight hundred pounds. The old man had stayed with him a day, a night, a day and another night while the fish swam deep and pulled the boat. When he had come up the old man had pulled the boat up on him and harpooned him. Lashed alongside the sharks had hit him and the old man had fought them out alone in the Gulf Stream in a skiff, clubbing them, stabbing at them, lunging at them with an oar until he was exhausted and the sharks had eaten all that they could hold. He was crying on the boat when the fishermen picked him up, half crazy from his loss, and the sharks were still circling the boat.

But what is the excitement in catching them from a launch? It comes from the fact that they are strange and wild things of unbelievable speed and power and a beauty, in the water and leaping, that is indescribable, which you would never see if you did not fish for them, and to which you are suddenly harnessed so that you feel their speed, their force and their savage power as intimately as if you were riding a bucking horse. For half an hour, an hour, or five hours, you are fastened to the fish as much as he is fastened to you and you tame him and break him the way a wild horse is broken and finally lead him to the boat. For pride and because the fish is worth plenty of money in the Havana market, you gaff him at the boat and bring him onboard, but the having him in the boat isn't the excitement; it is while you are fighting him that is the fun.

If the fish is hooked in the bony part of the mouth I am sure the hook hurts him no more than the harness hurts the angler. A large fish when he is hooked often does not feel the hook at all and will swim toward the boat, unconcerned, to take another bait. At other times he will swim away deep, completely unconscious of the hook, and it is when he feels himself held and pressure exerted to turn him, that he knows something is wrong and starts to make his fight. Unless he is hooked where it hurts he makes his fight not against the pain of the hook, but against being captured and if, when he is out of sight, you figure what he is doing, in what direction he is pulling when deep down, and why, you can convince him and bring him to the boat by the same system you break a wild horse. It is not necessary to kill him, or even completely exhaust him to bring him to the boat.

To kill a fish that fights deep you pull against the direction he wants to go until he is worn out and dies. It takes hours and when the fish dies the sharks are liable to get him before the angler can raise him to the top. To catch such a fish quickly you figure by trying to hold him absolutely, which direction he is working (a sounding fish is going in the direction the line slants in the water when you have put enough pressure on the drag so the line would break if you held it any tighter); then get ahead of him on that direction and he can be brought to the boat without killing him. You do not tow him or pull him with the motor boat; you use the engine to shift your position just as you would walk up or down stream with a salmon. A fish is caught most surely from a small boat such as a dory since the angler can shut down on his drag and simply let the fish pull the boat. Towing the boat will kill him in time. But the most satisfaction is to dominate and convince the fish and bring him intact in everything but spirit to the boat as rapidly as possible.

"Very instructive," says the friend. "But where does the thrill come in?"

The thrill comes when you are standing at the wheel drinking a cold bottle of beer and watching the outriggers jump the baits so they look like small live tuna leaping along and then behind one you see a long dark shadow wing up and then a big spear thrust out followed by an eye and head and dorsal fin and the tuna jumps with the wave and he's missed it.

"Marlin," Carlos yells from the top of the house and stamps his feet up and down, the signal that a fish is raised. He swarms down to the wheel and you go back to where the rod rests in its socket and there comes the shadow again, fast as the shadow of a plane moving over the water, and the spear, head, fin and shoulders smash out of water and you hear the click the closepin makes as the line pulls out and the long bight of line whishes through the water as the fish turns and as you hold the rod, you feel it double and the butt kicks you in the belly as you come back hard and feel his weight, as you strike him again and again, and again.

Then the heavy rod arc-ing out toward the fish, and the reel in a band-saw zinging scream, the marlin leaps clear and long, silver in the sun long, round as a hogshead and banded with lavender stripes and, when he goes into the water, it throws a column of spray like a shell lighting.

Then he comes out again, and the spray roars, and

again, then the line feels slack and out he bursts headed across and in, then jumps wildly twice more seeming to hang high and stiff in the air before falling to throw the column of water and you can see the hook in the corner of his jaw.

Then in a series of jumps like a greyhound he heads to the northwest and standing up, you follow him in the boat, the line taut as a banjo string and little drops coming from it until you finally get the belly of it clear of that friction against the water and have a straight pull out toward the fish.

And all the time Carlos is shouting, "Oh, God the bread of my children! Oh look at the bread of my children! Joseph and Mary look at the bread of my children jump! There it goes the bread of my children! He'll never stop the bread the bread the bread of my children!"

This striped marlin jumped, in a straight line to the northwest, fifty-three times, and every time he went out it was a sight to make your heart stand still. Then he sounded and I said to Carlos, "Get me the harness. Now I've got to pull him up the bread of your children."

"I couldn't stand to see it," he says. "Like a filled pocketbook jumping. He can't go down deep now. He's caught too much air jumping."

"Like a race horse over obstacles," Julio says. "Is the harness all right? Do you want water?"

"No." Then kidding Carlos, "What's this about the bread of your children?"

"He always says that," says Julio. "You should hear him curse me when we would lose one in the skiff."

"What will the bread of your children weigh?" I ask with mouth dry, the harness taut across shoulders, the rod a flexible prolongation of the sinew pulling ache of arms, the sweat salty in my eyes.

"Four hundred and fifty," says Carlos.

"Never," says Julio.

"Thou and thy never," says Carlos. "The fish of another always weighs nothing to thee."

"Three seventy-five," Julio raises his estimate. "Not a pound more."

Carlos says something unprintable and Julio comes up to four hundred.

The fish is nearly whipped now and the dead ache is out of raising him, and then, while lifting, I feel something slip. It holds for an instant and then the line is slack.

"He's gone," I say and unbuckle the harness.

"The bread of your children," Julio says to Carlos.

"Yes," Carlos says. "Yes. Joke and no joke yes. *El pan de mis hijos.* Three hundred and fifty pounds at ten cents a pound. How many days does a man work for that in the winter? How cold is it at three o'clock in the morning on all those days? And the fog and the rain in a norther. Every time he jumps the hook cutting the hole a little bigger in his jaw. Ay how he could jump. How he could jump!"

"The bread of your children," says Julio.

"Don't talk about that any more," said Carlos.

No it is not elephant hunting. But we get a kick out of it. When you have a family and children, your family, or my family, or the family of Carlos, you do not have to look for danger. There is always plenty of danger when you have a family.

And after a while the danger of others is the only danger and there is no end to it nor any pleasure in it nor does it help to think about it.

But there is great pleasure in being on the sea, in the unknown wild suddenness of a great fish; in his life and death which he lives for you in an hour while your strength is harnessed to his; and there is satisfaction in conquering this thing which rules the sea it lives in.

Then in the morning of the day after you have caught a good fish, when the man who carried him to the market in a handcart brings the long roll of heavy silver dollars wrapped in a newspaper on board it is very satisfactory money. It really feels like money.

"There's the bread of your children," you say to Carlos.

"In the time of the dance of the millions," he says, "a fish like that was worth two hundred dollars. Now it is thirty. On the other hand a fisherman never starves. The sea is very rich."

"And the fisherman always poor."

"No. Look at you. You are rich."

"Like hell," you say. "And the longer I fish the poorer I'll be. I'll end up fishing with you for the market in a dinghy."

"That I never believe," says Carlos devoutly. "But look. That fishing in a dinghy is very interesting. You would like it."

"I'll look forward to it," you say.

"What we need for prosperity is a war," Carlos says. "In the time of the war with Spain and in the last war the fishermen were actually rich."

"All right," you say. "If we have a war you get the dinghy ready."

APPENDIX E

HANDOUT
SEMINAR EVALUATION

1. When you first began this course, what did you think it would be about?

2. Now that you have finished this course, how would you describe it to students who are interested in taking it?

3. This course has been described as a *process* course, not just a course about one author. Do you agree with this statement? If you do, explain what this means for students beginning the course.

4. What did you enjoy *most* in this course?

5. What did you enjoy *least* in this course?

6. Write any suggestions or comments that would be useful to the instructor and to students who may take a course of this nature in the future.

APPENDIX F
TWELVE WEEK TRIMESTER/
SIXTY DAY SCHEDULE

TENTATIVE SCHEDULE FOR SEMINAR IN AMERICAN LITERATURE: ERNEST HEMINGWAY

Orientation to the Seminar

Day 1. Getting acquainted with the course and each other

Day 2. Introducing Hemingway and the Position Paper

Paper I: "Indian Camp" (1925)

Day 3. Reading aloud and discussion of "Up in Michigan" (1923) and "The Doctor and the Doctor's Wife" (1925)
ASSIGNMENT: Position Paper on "Indian Camp"
Due: _____

Day 4. Reading aloud and discussion of "The End of Something" (1925)

Day 5. Reading aloud and discussion of "Three Day Blow" (1925)

Day 6. Suggestions for Position Paper on "Indian Camp" and in-class writing

Day 7. Reading aloud and discussion of "Ten Indians" (1927)

Day 8. In-class writing or reading aloud and discussion of "The Battler" (1925)

Day 9. Film: *My Old Man* (story published 1923)
Position Paper on "Indian Camp" due

Paper II: *The Sun Also Rises* (1926)

Day 10. Introduction to *The Sun Also Rises;* begin reading
ASSIGNMENT: Position Paper on *The Sun Also Rises*
Due: _____

Day 11. Reading

Day 12. Discussion: Life in Paris in the 1920s

Day 13. Reading and/or distribution of Defense Day papers

Day 14. Defense Day: "Indian Camp"

Day 15. Film: *Hemingway's Spain: "The Sun Also Rises"*

Day 16. Suggestions for Position Paper on *The Sun Also Rises* and reading
Skill: Introductions and Conclusions; using direct quotations

Day 17. Reading or writing

Day 18. Reading aloud and discussion of "The Big Two-Hearted River" (1925)

Day 19. Reading aloud and discussion of "The Big Two-Hearted River"

Day 20. In-class writing and proofreading
Position Paper on *The Sun Also Rises* due

Paper III: *A Farewell to Arms* (1929)

Day 21. Introduction to *A Farewell to Arms;* begin reading
ASSIGNMENT: Position Paper on *A Farewell to Arms*
Due: _____

Day 22.   Reading

Day 23.   Reading aloud and discussion of "In Another Country" (1927), "Now I Lay Me" (1927) and/or "A Very Short Story" (1927)

Day 24.   Reading and skill discussion: transitions, sentence combining, *Roget's Thesaurus*

Day 25.   Suggestions for Position Paper on *A Farewell to Arms*
Discussion of World War I and Hemingway, Dr. Hemingway's suicide, Key West

Day 26.   Reading; distribution of papers for Defense Day

Day 27.   Defense Day: *The Sun Also Rises*

Day 28.   Reading aloud and discussion of "Soldier's Home" (1925) or film of that story

Day 29.   Reading and writing

Day 30.   Writing and proofreading

Day 31.   Reading aloud and discussion of "Fathers and Sons" (1933)
Position Paper on *A Farewell to Arms* due

Paper IV: A Profile of Ernest Hemingway

Day 32.   Review of the Hemingway biography and introduction to Profile Paper
ASSIGNMENT: Profile Paper developed from reading Hemingway biography and autobiography
Due: _____

Day 33.   Film: *Hemingway* or *Ernest Hemingway: Rough Diamond;* suggestions for Paper

Day 34.   Research, reading, and skill discussion (documentation)

Day 35.   Reading; distribution of papers for Defense Day

Day 36.   Defense Day: *A Farewell to Arms*

Day 37.   Reading, research, and writing

Day 38.   Writing or sharing Hemingway anecdotes

Day 39.   Writing and proofreading

Day 40.   Reading aloud and discussion of "A Day's Wait" (1933) and "The Old Man at the Bridge" (1938)
Profile Paper on Ernest Hemingway due

Paper V: Your Choice

Day 41.   Consideration of reading choices for Paper V.
Skill: Plot clarity; relating choice to previous readings
ASSIGNMENT: Position Paper on Hemingway's work of student's choice
Due: _____

Day 42.   Reading; suggestions for position papers

Day 43.   Reading

Day 44.   Reading; distribution of papers for Defense Day

Day 45.   Defense Day: Profile Paper

Day 46.   Reading and writing

Day 47.   Writing

Day 48.   Writing and proofreading

Day 49.   Reading aloud and discussion of "On the Blue Water" (1936)
Your Choice Paper due

Paper VI: *The Old Man and the Sea* (1952)

Day 50.   Introduction to *The Old Man and the Sea;* begin reading
ASSIGNMENT: Position Paper on *The Old Man and the Sea*
Due: _____

Day 51.   Reading and suggestions for Position Paper

Day 52. Discussion: Hemingway and the Prizes—Pulitzer and Nobel

Day 53. Reading, writing, distribution of papers for Defense Day

Day 54. Defense Day: Your Choice Papers

Day 55. Writing and proofreading

Paper VII: The Summing Up

Day 56. Position Paper on *The Old Man and the Sea* due
ASSIGNMENT: Summation Paper and/or Humorous Paper on Hemingway and his work. Suggestions for final paper.
Due: _____

Day 57. Reading, re-reading, research, and writing

Day 58. Writing and distribution of papers for Defense Day

Day 59. Defense Day: *The Old Man and the Sea*

Day 60. Reading aloud of final papers; evaluation of seminar

BIBLIOGRAPHY

BASIC MATERIALS FOR STARTING A SEMINAR

Of course, the school budget determines the quantity of materials. If there is no budget, materials can be obtained from many sources: school and public libraries; student, teacher, or classroom copies; American literature textbooks.

Class sets of paperbacks do provide smoother instruction. In addition to the handouts suggested in this book, the following materials are recommended for starting a Hemingway seminar:

Hemingway, Ernest. *A Farewell to Arms.* New York: Scribner's, 1929. Cloth and paper.

The Old Man and the Sea. New York: Scribner's, 1961. Cloth and paper.

The Short Stories of Ernest Hemingway. New York: Scribner's, 1938. Cloth and paper.

Three Novels: The Sun Also Rises, A Farewell to Arms, The Old Man and the Sea. New York: Scribner's, 1962.

The Sun Also Rises. New York: Scribner's, 1926. Cloth and paper.

Besides the class sets, the instructor may wish to build up a room library of biographical and autobiographical works. Some of these may be secured through libraries. Here is a list of fourteen useful titles:

Baker, Carlos. *Ernest Hemingway: A Life Story.* New York: Scribner's, 1969.

Baker, Carlos, ed. *Ernest Hemingway: Selected Letters, 1917–1961.* New York: Scribner's, 1981.

Buckley, Peter. *Ernest.* New York: Dial Press, 1978.

Callaghan, Morley. *That Summer in Paris: Memories of Tangled Friendships with Hemingway, Fitzgerald, and Some Others.* New York: Coward, 1963.

Cowley, Malcolm. "A Portrait of Mister Papa." *Life,* 10 January 1949, pp. 86–90, 93–94, 96–98, 100–101. This article is reprinted in McCaffery, *Ernest Hemingway,* pp. 34–56; see below for full reference.

Hemingway, Gregory. *Papa: A Personal Memoir.* Boston: Houghton Mifflin, 1976; paper, Pocket Books, 1977.

Hemingway, Leicester. *My Brother, Ernest Hemingway.* [1962] New York: Fawcett World, 1972. Paper.

Hemingway, Mary. *How It Was.* New York: Knopf, 1976.

Hotchner, A. E. *Papa Hemingway: A Personal Memoir.* New York: Random House, 1966.

McLendon, James. *Papa: Hemingway in Key West, 1928–1940.* Miami: E. A. Seeman, n.d.; paper, Popular Library, 1974.

McCaffery, John K. M., ed. *Ernest Hemingway: The Man and His Work.* 1950. Reprint. New York: Cooper Square Publishers, 1969.

Miller, Madelaine Hemingway. *Ernie: Hemingway's Sister Sunny Remembers.* New York: Crown, 1975.

Montgomery, Constance Cappel. *Hemingway in Michigan.* New York: Fleet Publishing Corp., 1966.

Sanford, Marcelline Hemingway. *At the Hemingways: A Family Portrait.* Boston: Little, Brown and Company, 1962.

Audio-visual materials can be obtained from loan libraries, but at least two should be considered for purchase:

Ernest Hemingway Reading. [Record or cassette]. Caedmon, CDL 51185, 45 minutes, 10 seconds, with background notes by A. E. Hotchner and Mary Hemingway. The Nobel Prize address is especially useful. For information, write Caedmon Records, Inc., 505 Eighth Avenue, New York, New York 10018.

Ernest Hemingway. [Filmstrip]. The American Experience in Literature: Five Modern Novelists. Series No. 6911K. Encyclopaedia Britannica Educational Corporation, 1975, with cassette.

VALUABLE BOOKS: BIOGRAPHY AND CRITICISM

Baker, Carlos. *Hemingway: The Writer as Artist.* [1952] 4th rev. ed. Princeton, N.J.: Princeton University Press, 1972. Cloth and paper.

Baker, Sheridan. *Ernest Hemingway: An Introduction and Interpretation.* New York: Holt, Rinehart and Winston, 1967.

Bradbury, Ray. *I Sing the Body Electric.* New York: Alfred A. Knopf, 1969.

Bruccoli, Matthew J. *Scott and Ernest.* New York: Random House, 1978.

Burgess, Anthony. *Ernest Hemingway and His World.* New York: Scribner's, 1978.

Cowley, Malcolm. *A Second Flowering: Works and Days of the Lost Generation.* New York: Viking, 1973; paper, Penguin, 1974.

DeFalco, Joseph. *The Hero in Hemingway's Short Stories.* 1963. Reprint. Darby, Pa.: Arden Library, 1977.

Falk, R. P., ed. *American Literature in Parody.* New York: Twayne, 1955.

Fenton, Charles A. *The Apprenticeship of Ernest Hemingway: The Early Years.* 1954. Reprint. New York: Octagon Books, 1975.

French, Warren C., and Kidd, Walter E., eds. *American Winners of the Nobel Literary Prize.* Norman: University of Oklahoma Press, 1968.

Frenz, Horst, ed., *Nobel Lectures: Literature, 1901–1967.* Amsterdam: Elsevier Publishing, 1969.

Gajdusek, Robert E. *Hemingway's Paris.* New York: Scribner's, 1978.

Hovey, Richard B. *Hemingway: The Inward Terrain.* Seattle: University of Washington Press, 1968.

Kiley, John. *Hemingway: An Old Friend Remembers.* New York: Hawthorn, 1965.

Klimo, Vernon (Jake), and Oursler, Will. *Hemingway and Jake.* [1972] New York: Popular Library, 1973. Paper.

Leggett, John. *Ross and Tom: Two American Tragedies.* New York: Simon and Schuster, 1974.

Loeb, Harold. *The Way It Was.* New York: Criterion Books, 1959.

McCaffery, John K. M., ed. *Ernest Hemingway: The Man and His Work.* 1950. Reprint. New York: Cooper Square Publishers, n.d.

Ross, Lillian. *Portrait of Hemingway.* New York: Simon and Schuster, 1961. (Originally, *New Yorker,* May 13, 1950, Profile)

Rovit, Earl H. *Ernest Hemingway.* New York: Twayne, 1963; paper, College and University Press, 1963.

Sarason, Bertram D. *Hemingway and the Sun Set.* Washington, D.C.: National Cash Register Company/ Microcard Editions, 1972.

Stephens, Robert O., ed. *Ernest Hemingway: The Critical Reception.* New York: Burt Franklin, 1977.

Stuckey, W. J. *The Pulitzer Prize Novels.* Norman: University of Oklahoma Press, 1966.

Waldhorn, Arthur. *A Reader's Guide to Ernest Hemingway.* New York: Farrar, Straus, and Giroux, 1972. Cloth and paper.

Watts, Emily S. *Ernest Hemingway and the Arts.* Urbana: University of Illinois Press, 1971.

Weeks, Robert P., ed. *Hemingway: A Collection of Critical Essays.* Englewood Cliffs, N.J.: Prentice-Hall, 1962.

Young, Philip. *Ernest Hemingway: A Reconsideration.* 2nd ed. University Park: Pennsylvania State University Press, 1966.

ARTICLES AND ESSAYS: BIOGRAPHY AND CRITICISM

Baker, Carlos. "The Boy and the Lions." In *20th Century Interpretations of "The Old Man and the Sea,"* edited by Katherine T. Jobes, pp. 27–33. Englewood Cliffs, N.J.: Prentice-Hall, 1968.

Burgum, Edwin Berry. "Ernest Hemingway and the Psychology of the Lost Generation." In his *The Novel and the World's Dilemma,* pp. 184–204. New York: Oxford University Press, 1947.

Cowley, Malcolm. "Hemingway and the Hero." *New Republic,* 4 December 1944, pp. 754–58.

Eastman, Max. "Bull in the Afternoon." *New Republic,* 7 June 1933, pp. 94–97.

Fiedler, Leslie. *Love and Death in the American Novel,* pp. 304–9, 350–52. New York: Criterion, 1960.

Fuchs, Daniel. "Ernest Hemingway, Literary Critic." *American Literature* 36 (1965):431–51.

Kazin, Alfred. *On Native Grounds.* New York: Harcourt, Brace, 1942; paper, 1972, pp. 393–99.

Lewis, Wyndam. "The Dumb Ox: A Study of Ernest Hemingway." *The American Review* 3 (1934):289–312.

Plimpton, George. "The Art of Fiction, XXI: Hemingway." *Paris Review,* no. 18 (1958), pp. 61–89. Also in *Writers at Work: The Paris Interviews,* Second series, pp. 215–39. New York: Viking, 1963.

Van Gelder, Robert. "Ernest Hemingway Talks of Work and War." In *Writers and Writing,* pp. 95–98. New York: Scribner's, 1946.

Warren, Robert Penn. "Ernest Hemingway." *Kenyon Review* 9 (1947):52–60. Also in *Literary Opinion in America,* edited by Morton D. Zabel, vol. 2, pp. 444–63. 1951. Reprint. Magnolia, Mass.: Peter Smith, 1968.

Wilson, Edmund. "Hemingway: Bourbon Gauge of Morale." In his *The Wound and the Bow: Seven Studies in Literature,* pp. 214–42. New York: Oxford University Press, 1947.

Young, Philip. "Loser Take Nothing." In *20th Century Interpretations of "A Farewell to Arms,"* edited by Jay Gellens, pp. 28–32. Englewood Cliffs, N.J.: Prentice-Hall, 1970.

Young, Philip. "Our Hemingway Man." *Kenyon Review* 26 (1964):676-707.

BOOKS: CHECKLIST OF PRIMARY SOURCES

Three Stories and Ten Poems. [1923] Bloomfield Hills, Mich.: Bruccoli Clark Books, 1977.

In Our Time. [1924, 1925] New York: Scribner's, 1930. Cloth and paper.

The Torrents of Spring. [1926] New York: Scribner's, 1972. Cloth and paper.

The Sun Also Rises. New York: Scribner's, 1926. Cloth and paper.

Men Without Women. New York: Scribner's, 1927. Paper.

A Farewell to Arms. New York: Scribner's, 1929. Cloth and paper.

Death in the Afternoon. New York: Scribner's, 1932. Cloth and paper.

Winner Take Nothing. New York: Scribner's, 1933. Paper.

Green Hills of Africa. New York: Scribner's, 1935. Cloth and paper.

To Have and Have Not. New York: Scribner's, 1937. Cloth and paper.

The Fifth Column and the First Forty-Nine Stories. New York: Scribner's, 1938.

For Whom the Bell Tolls. New York: Scribner's, 1940. Cloth and paper.

Across the River and into the Trees. New York: Scribner's, 1950. Cloth and paper.

The Old Man and the Sea. [1952] New York: Scribner's, 1961. Cloth and paper.

Posthumous Publications

The Wild Years, edited by Gene Z. Hanrahan. New York: Dell, 1962. Seventy-three articles from the Toronto *Star.*

A Moveable Feast. New York: Scribner's, 1964. Cloth and paper.

By-Line: Ernest Hemingway, Selected Articles and Dispatches of Four Decades, edited by William White. New York: Scribner's, 1967. Cloth and paper.

The Fifth Column and Four Stories of the Spanish Civil War. New York: Scribner's, 1969. Cloth and paper.

Islands in the Stream. New York: Scribner's, 1970. Cloth and paper.

Ernest Hemingway, Cub Reporter: Kansas City Star Stories, edited by M. Bruccoli. Pittsburgh: University of Pittsburgh Press, 1970.

Ernest Hemingway's Apprenticeship, Oak Park, 1916-1917, edited by M. Bruccoli. Washington, D.C.: Microcard Editions, 1971. Uncollected early writings, Oak Park, Illinois, High School *Tabula* and *Trapeze.*

EDUCATIONAL FILMS

Ernest Hemingway: Rough Diamond. Centron, 1978. 30 min., color.

Hemingway. NBC: McGraw-Hill. 54 min., b/w.

Hemingway's Spain: "Death in the Afternoon." ABC: McGraw-Hill, 1969. 15 min., color.

Hemingway's Spain: "For Whom the Bell Tolls." ABC: McGraw-Hill, 1969. 19 min., color.

Hemingway's Spain: "The Sun Also Rises." ABC: McGraw-Hill, 1969. 17 min., color.

My Old Man. Encyclopaedia Britannica Educational Corp. 27 min., color.

Soldier's Home. Learning in Focus, Inc.-Coronet Instructional Films, 1977. 41 min., color.

FILMSTRIP-RECORD/CASSETTES

Ernest Hemingway [Filmstrip]. Listening Library, NOOCFX, and cassette. Covers his life from World War I to his suicide. For information, write Listening Library, Inc., 1 Park Avenue, Old Greenwich, Connecticut 06870.

Ernest Hemingway [Filmstrip]. 2 rolls. Educational Dimensions Corp., no. 708, and 2 12-min. discs or 2 cassettes, 15 min. each. For information, write Educational Dimensions Corp., Box 488, Great Neck, New York 11022.

Ernest Hemingway: The Man—A Biographical Interpretation with Carlos Baker [Filmstrip]. 2 rolls. Guidance Associates, 7F-508 307 (LPs) or 7F-508 299 (cassettes), and 2 12-in. discs or 2 cassettes, 16 or 17 min. For information, write Guidance Associates, Pleasantville, New York 10570.

RECORDS AND CASSETTES

Grebstein, Sheldon. *For Whom the Bell Tolls.* Listening Library, N96CX, cassette. Lecture.

Hemingway. Listening Library, N98R, 2 12-in. discs. Memories of the writer from his friends, about his public and private life.

Hemingway, Ernest. *The Old Man and the Sea.* Charlton Heston, reader. Caedmon, TC 2084, 2 12-in. discs or 2 cassettes.

Hotchner, A. E. *Hotchner on Hemingway.* Listening Library, N100CX, cassette.

Hotling, Charles K. *Ernest Hemingway: "The Old Man and the Sea."* Listening Library, N94CX, cassette.

Wylder, Delbert. *The Early Short Stories of Ernest Hemingway.* Listening Library, N101CX, cassette.

——. *The Middle Short Stories of Ernest Hemingway.* Listening Library, N102CX, cassette.

——. *The Late Short Stories of Ernest Hemingway.* Listening Library, N103CX, cassette.

Young, Philip. *A Farewell to Arms.* Listening Library, N97CX, cassette.

——. *The Sun Also Rises.* Listening Library, N95CX, cassette.

For information on the above listings, write Listening Library, Inc., 1 Park Avenue, Old Greenwich, Connecticut 06870.

PICTURES AND POSTERS

Ernest Hemingway [Poster]. Eight Masters of Modern Fiction series. Includes Fitzgerald, Hemingway, Wolfe, Baldwin, Salinger, McCullers, Faulkner, and Steinbeck. Scholastic Book Services, set of 8 pictures, 15 x 20 in. For information, write Scholastic Book Services, 50 West 44th Street, New York, New York 10036.

Ernest Hemingway [Picture]. Perfection Form Co., KJ95948, color, 8 1/2 x 11 in.

A Farewell to Arms [Pictures]. Hemingway series. Perfection Form Co., KJ3012, set of 5 pictures, 10 x 13 in.

For Whom the Bell Tolls [Pictures]. Hemingway series. Perfection Form Co., KJ3072, set of 2 pictures, 8 1/2 x 11 in.

The Old Man and the Sea [Pictures]. Hemingway series. Perfection Form Co., KJ6132, set of 10 pictures.

The Sun Also Rises [Pictures]. Hemingway series. Perfection Form Co., KJ7692, set of 10 pictures, 10 x 13 in.

For information on the above listings, with the exception of the first, write Perfection Form Company, 1000 North Second Avenue, Logan, Iowa 51546.

Note: The instructor should try to secure a copy of *Life,* 14 July 1961, pp. 51-72, for a cover story-photo essay on Hemingway.

HOLLYWOOD FILMS

Most of the Hollywood films based on Hemingway writings are still available through loan libraries. Check with your A-V director for catalogs and prices.

Adventures of a Young Man. Based on the book *In Our Time.* 1962, Twentieth Century-Fox. The script was prepared from a TV series adaptation of ten Nick Adams stories done by A. E. Hotchner. Parts of *A Farewell to Arms* were added to the film. Producer: Jerry Wald. Richard Beymer (Nick); Jessica Tandy (Mrs. Adams); Arthur Kennedy (Dr. Adams); Paul Newman ("The Battler"). Director: Martin Ritt. Color, 145 minutes.

A Farewell to Arms. 1932, Paramount. Gary Cooper (Frederic); Helen Hayes (Catherine); Adolphe Menjou (Rinaldi). Director: Henry King, B/W, 78 minutes. Also, 1957, Twentieth Century-Fox. Rock Hudson (Frederic); Jennifer Jones (Catherine); Vittorio de Sica (Rinaldi). Director: Charles Vidor. Color, 151 minutes.

For Whom the Bell Tolls. 1943, Paramount. Gary Cooper (Jordan); Ingrid Bergman (Maria); Katina Paxinou (Pilar); Akim Tamiroff (Pablo). Director: Sam Wood. Color, 156 minutes.

Islands in the Stream. 1977, Paramount. George C. Scott (Thomas Hudson) with David Hemmings (Eddy), Clare Bloom (Audrey). Director: Franklin J. Schaffner. Color, 110 minutes.

The Killers. 1946, Universal. Burt Lancaster (Ole Andreson). Director: Robert Siedmak. B/W, 102 minutes. Also, 1964, Universal. Lee Marvin (Charlie), Angie Dickinson (Sheila Farr), Ronald Reagan (Browning), John Cassavetes (Johnny North). Director: Don Siegel. Color, 95 minutes.

The Macomber Affair. 1947, United Artists. Gregory Peck (Macomber); Joan Bennett (Margot); Robert Preston (Wilson). Director: Z. Korda. B/W, 89 minutes.

The Old Man and the Sea. 1958, Warner Brothers. Spencer Tracy (Santiago). Director: John Sturges. Color, 86 minutes.

The Sun Also Rises. 1957, Twentieth Century-Fox. Tyrone Power (Jake); Ava Gardner (Brett); Mel Ferrer (Robert Cohn); Errol Flynn (Mike Campbell); Eddie Albert (Bill Gorton). Director: Henry King. Color, 129 minutes.

The Snows of Kilimanjaro. 1952, Twentieth Century-Fox. Gregory Peck (Harry) with Susan Hayward (Helen) and Ava Gardner (Cynthia). Director: Henry King. Color, 117 minutes.

To Have and Have Not. 1944, Warner Brothers. Humphrey Bogart (Harry); Lauren Bacall (Mrs. Morgan). Director: Howard Hawks. B/W, 100 minutes.

Under My Skin. Based on the short story "My Old Man." 1950, Twentieth Century-Fox. John Garfield (Dan Butler) and Luther Adler (Louis Bark). Director: Jean Negulesco. B/W, 68 minutes.

II. IN SEARCH OF J. D. SALINGER

ORIENTATION TO THE SEMINAR
DAYS 1-2

DAY 1: GETTING ACQUAINTED WITH THE COURSE AND EACH OTHER

Goals

1. To acquaint students with the nature of the seminar and to introduce them to its method and content.
2. To help students get to know each other.

Materials

1. Handout 1: Seminar in American Literature.
2. Handout 2: Tentative Schedule.
3. After you have taught in-depth seminars, use evaluations from former students (see Day 90) to interest beginning students.

Procedure

1. Use Handout 1 as a brief introduction to the idea of an in-depth seminar.
2. Using Handout 2 as a guide, offer an overview of the course, noting particularly how writing and reading activities are correlated. Point out the variety of the course, the value of individual exploration and group discussion, the chronological approach, the assignments and due dates, the alloted time for in-class reading and writing, and Defense Day—which will be explained later.
3. Stress that you genuinely want to know the students and to have them know each other. Everyone will be working together in the course.
4. Pair off students who do not know each other or who know each other only slightly. Find a partner for yourself. Ask each student to interview his or her partner without taking notes, asking questions that each partner would like answered—family, job, favorite food, pets, sports, music, travel, plans for the future.

5. After five or ten minutes, ask each student to introduce his or her partner to the seminar by summarizing the answers to the interview questions. Now the class has taken the first step toward becoming a genuine seminar. These introductions may lead to friendships, and they certainly will help to establish the understanding and cooperation needed in later discussions, especially the evaluations on Defense Day.

Additional Suggestion

A classroom bulletin board on J. D. Salinger helps to develop interest: photocopies of pictures in magazines cited in the bibliography, a map of New York City and Vermont/New Hampshire, a sample position paper (one from this handbook or from a previous seminar). Copies of Salinger works should also be displayed in the room.

DAY 2: INTRODUCING SALINGER AND THE POSITION PAPER

Goals

1. To preview Salinger's life and work.
2. To introduce the Position Paper.

Materials

1. Handout 3: The Salinger Chronology. You also may refer to the materials on Salinger's life and times in the Appendix.
2. Handout 4: The Position Paper.

Procedure

1. Referring to Handout 3: The Salinger Chronology, discuss the idea that the seminar will be one of discovery, of learning how

Salinger's ideas and writing developed. The first of the seven position papers focuses on a 1948 *The New Yorker* short story, which begins what some critics call Salinger's "Classic Period." This story, "A Perfect Day for Bananafish," would later appear in his first book of collected stories *(Nine Stories)* in 1953.

2. Note that Salinger's life begins in New York City, the son of Jewish/Catholic middle class parents. Jerome did not appear to be the precocious child that he likes to write about. In fact, except for a diploma at a military school in 1936, he had little success in schools. But he did get interested in becoming a writer there and was publishing by age twenty-one in a national magazine. World War II interrupted his life but not his writing. Many of his key ideas and characters were molded in these days before 1948. In the 1950s, he became famous for *The Catcher in the Rye*. He deserted the city for the quiet of New Hampshire; he married and began a family. From 1948 to 1965, he developed most of his material around the brilliant children of two former vaudevillian actors named Les and Bessie Glass. Salinger also became a serious student of Zen Buddhism. Avoiding the public and interviewers, Salinger stopped publishing in 1965. His marriage collapsed, and he remains steadfast in silence and in popularity.

3. Distribute Handout 4: The Position Paper and discuss the nature of a position paper. Stress the requirements of length and format (typed, double-spaced, one side, unlined paper), since clear, complete copies must be distributed on Defense Day. At this point, do not dwell on evaluation procedures since a positive attitude toward writing does not begin with apprehension about grades. Remind students that typing is required by most college teachers and that it is wise to improve their typing now. Tell them that you will provide position papers written by former seminar students for them to examine; assure them that they will be given considerable class time for reading and writing. Useful background material and even suggestions for topics will be given as specific papers are assigned. Each position paper will stress specific skills. Again, there will be class time for review and instruction of these skills.

HANDOUT 1
SEMINAR IN AMERICAN LITERATURE

Have you ever read an author in depth? If you have, you probably made a number of discoveries:

1. You became acquainted with the writer, his or her basic themes and style.

2. You felt the deliciousness of expertise which includes a sense of chronology, favorite characters, a knowledge of major and minor works, a delight in quotable lines.

3. It was as if the writer became your friend. You may have wanted to learn more about the person, his or her life. You may even have hungered to find other writings or eagerly awaited new books to be published.

So the seminar will go in depth, while the survey course that you just took has skimmed the surface. And as a small group, you will share your discoveries with the seminar—in discussion, in your papers, on Defense Day, informally.

One thing must be kept in focus: This seminar is not concerned with making you an expert on one author (though you may be). Our concern is with the *process* of studying any author. In fact, this is really a Basic Skills (sound familiar?) course: Reading, Writing, Speaking, and Listening.

Reading: Your reading will involve two novels, thirteen short stories, many pages of autobiography or biography. You also will read at least twenty-eight position papers.

Writing: You will write seven position papers—three to five typed (skill) pages. You will be studying other people's writing; the seminar will discuss good writing.

Speaking: You will defend two of your position papers before the seminar. You will also be reading aloud and discussing what you have read—short stories, position papers.

Listening: You will have to listen carefully because Defense Day requires that everyone listen carefully to what is said and read. You will be involved in Defense Day grading.

HANDOUT 2
TENTATIVE SCHEDULE FOR SEMINAR IN AMERICAN LITERATURE:
J. D. SALINGER

Orientation to the Seminar

Day 1.   Getting acquainted with the course and each other
Day 2.   Introducing Salinger and the Position Paper

Paper I: "A Perfect Day for Bananafish" (1948)

Day 3.   Reading aloud and discussion of "The Young Folks" (1940)
ASSIGNMENT: Position Paper on "A Perfect Day for Bananafish" (1948)
Due: _____

Day 4.   Reading aloud and discussion of "Uncle Wiggily in Connecticut" (1948)

Day 5.   Reading aloud and comparison of "The Young Folks" and "Uncle Wiggily in Connecticut"

Day 6.   Suggestions for Position Paper on "A Perfect Day for Bananafish"

Day 7.   Discussion of the prewriting process

Day 8.   In-class writing

Day 9.   In-class writing

Day 10.   Reading additional Salinger stories

Day 11.   In-class writing

Day 12.   Reading aloud and discussion of "Just before the War with the Eskimos" (1948)

Paper II: *The Catcher in the Rye* (1951)

Day 13.   Position Paper on "A Perfect Day for Bananafish" due
Introduction to *The Catcher in the Rye*
ASSIGNMENT: Position Paper on *The Catcher in the Rye*
Due: _____

Day 14.   Reading

Day 15.   Reading

Day 16.   Reading aloud and discussion of "I'm Crazy" (1945) and "Slight Rebellion off Madison" (1946)

Day 17.   Reading

Day 18.   Reading: distribution of papers for Defense Day

Day 19.   Defense Day: "A Perfect Day for Bananafish"

Day 20.   Defense Day

Day 21.   Follow-up discussion: students and critics

Day 22.   Suggestions for Position Paper on *The Catcher in the Rye* and in-class reading

Day 23.   Reading

Day 24.   Discussing skills for Paper II

Day 25. Writing
Day 26. Reading aloud and discussion of "The Laughing Man" (1949)
Day 27. Reading aloud and discussion of "Down at the Dinghy" (1949)
Day 28. Writing and proofreading

Paper III: "Teddy" (1953)

Day 29. Position Paper on *The Catcher in the Rye* due
         Introduction to "Teddy"
         ASSIGNMENT: Position Paper on "Teddy"
         Due: _____
Day 30. Reading
Day 31. Reading aloud and discussion of "For Esme—with Love and Squalor" (1950)
Day 32. Reading aloud
Day 33. Discussion: Zen Buddhism
Day 34. Resource Person or film on Zen Buddhism
Day 35. Suggestions for Position Paper on "Teddy"
Day 36. Distribution of papers for Defense Day
Day 37. Defense Day: *The Catcher in the Rye*
Day 38. Defense Day
Day 39. Follow-up discussion: students and critics
Day 40. Discussing skills for Paper III
Day 41. Writing
Day 42. Writing
Day 43. Writing and proofreading
Day 44. Reading aloud and discussion of "Pretty Mouth and Green My Eyes" (1951)

Paper IV: *Franny and Zooey* (1957)

Day 45. Position Paper on "Teddy" due; introduction to *Franny and Zooey*
         ASSIGNMENT: Position Paper on *Franny and Zooey*
         Due: _____
Day 46. Reading
Day 47. Reading
Day 48. Zen and *Franny and Zooey* and reading
Day 49. Suggestions for position on *Franny and Zooey*
Day 50. Distribution of papers for Defense Days
Day 51. Defense Day: "Teddy"
Day 52. Defense Day
Day 53. Follow-up discussion: students and critics
Day 54. Discussing skills for Paper IV
Day 55. Reading aloud and discussion of "De Daumier-Smith's Blue Period" (1953)

Day 56.   Reading aloud
Day 57.   Writing
Day 58.   Writing
Day 59.   Writing and proofreading

Paper V: A Profile of J. D. Salinger

Day 60.   Position Paper on *Franny and Zooey* due
Review of Salinger biography and introduction to Profile Paper
ASSIGNMENT: Profile Paper based on biography and fiction of
Salinger
Due: _____

Day 61.   Reading and research; suggestions for Profile Paper
Day 62.   Reading and research
Day 63.   Discussion: documentation skills
Day 64.   Reading; distribution of papers for Defense Days
Day 65.   Defense Day
Day 66.   Defense Day
Day 67.   Follow-up discussion: students and critics
Day 68.   Writing
Day 69.   Writing

Paper VI: *Raise High the Roof Beam, Carpenters* (1963)

Day 70.   Position Paper on Profile of J. D. Salinger due
Introduction to *Raise High the Roof Beam, Carpenters;* begin reading
ASSIGNMENT: Position Paper on *Raise High the Roof Beam,
Carpenters*
Due: _____

Day 71.   Reading
Day 72.   Reading; suggestions for Paper VI
Day 73.   Discussion: comparison and contrast skill
Day 74.   Distribution of papers for Defense Days
Day 75.   Defense Day
Day 76.   Defense Day
Day 77.   Follow-up discussion: students and critics
Day 78.   Writing
Day 79.   Writing
Day 80.   Writing

Paper VII: The Summing Up

Day 81.   Position Paper on *Raise High the Roof Beam, Carpenters* due
ASSIGNMENT: Summation Paper and/or a Humorous Paper on
Salinger and his work. Suggestions for Paper VII.
Due: _____

Day 82. Writing
Day 83. Writing and distribution of papers for Defense Days
Day 84. Defense Day
Day 85. Defense Day
Day 86. Follow-up discussion: students and critics
Day 87. Reading aloud of final papers
Day 88. Reading aloud of final papers
Day 89. Final discussion
Day 90. Evaluation of seminar

HANDOUT 3
THE SALINGER CHRONOLOGY

1919	Jerome David Salinger is born January 1, 1919 in New York City to Sol and Miriam Jillich Salinger.
1925–1934	Attends New York City elementary school. Voted "most popular actor" in 1930 at Camp Wigwam. Flunks out of the McBurney School, a private school in Manhattan. In 1934, sent to Valley Forge Military Academy, Pennsylvania.
1935	Becomes literary editor of Academy yearbook. Credited with writing song lyrics for school's Last Parade.
1936	Graduates from Valley Forge Military Academy, his only diploma.
1937	Attends summer session at New York University. After expressing interest in writing career, sent to Vienna, Austria, and Poland to become an apprentice in father's import meat business by learning the trade.
1938	Attends Ursinus College, Collegetown, Pennsylvania for half a semester. Writes "The Skipped Diploma" for *Ursinus Weekly,* a column.
1939	Takes a short-story writing course at Columbia University taught by writer/editor Whit Burnett.
1940	Publishes first story, "The Young Folks" in March–April issue of Burnett's *Story* magazine. "Go See Eddie" appears in December issue of *University of Kansas City Review.*
1941	Publishes stories in *Collier's* and *Esquire.* Lives with parents. Early Holden Caulfield story "Slight Rebellion off Madison" bought by *The New Yorker* but not published until 1946.
1942	Publishes stories in *Story* and *Collier's.* Drafted into U.S. Army. Attends Officers, First Sergeants, and Instructors School in Signal Corps.
1943	Stationed in Nashville, Tennessee. Staff sergeant. Applies to Officer's Candidate School and transferred to Army Counter-Intelligence Corps. Publishes July 17 *Saturday Evening Post* story, "The Varioni Brothers."
1944	Training in Tiverton, Devonshire, England. Writes *Post* stories. On June 6, lands in Normandy, Utah Beach, with 4th Army. Involved in five campaigns, meets Ernest Hemingway, interviews captured Germans; Battle of the Bulge.
1945	Allegedly marries a French physician (divorce 1947). Publishes first Holden Caulfield story, "I'm Crazy," December 22, *Collier's.* Stories in *Esquire, Story,* and *Post.*
1946	Brief hospitalization in Nürnberg. Ninety-nine page novella about Holden Caulfield written but not published. In 1941, Holden Caulfield story published in December 21 *The New Yorker.*

1947–1950   Returns to U.S.; lives in Greenwich Village; Tarrytown, New York; Westport, Connecticut. Stories published in *Mademoiselle, Cosmopolitan, The New Yorker.* 1950, *My Foolish Heart,* film version of "Uncle Wiggily in Connecticut." "For Esme—with Love and Squalor," 1950, *The New Yorker;* story later chosen as one of most distinguished stories of the year.

1951   *The Catcher in the Rye.*

1953   Buys cottage and ninety acres in Cornish, New Hampshire. *Nine Stories.* Interview by Shirlie Blaney, a high school journalist for Windsor, Vermont, *Daily Eagle.* "Teddy," January 31, *The New Yorker.*

1955   Marries Claire Douglas. "Franny," January 29, *The New Yorker.* "Raise High the Roof Beam, Carpenters," November 19, *The New Yorker.* Birth of daughter, Margaret Ann.

1957   "Zooey," May 4, *The New Yorker.*

1959   "Seymour: An Introduction," June 6, *The New Yorker.*

1960   Son, Matthew, born.

1961   *Franny and Zooey.* Makes cover of *Time.*

1963   *Raise High the Roof Beam, Carpenters;* and *Seymour: An Introduction.*

1965   "Hapworth 16, 1924," June 19, *The New Yorker.*

1967   Divorce from Claire Douglas Salinger.

1974   Files civil law suit against John Greenberg and seventeen New York bookstores for illegal publication and sale of early Salinger short stories.

1980   Canadian reporter, Michael Clarkson, describes brief interviews with seclusive author in Cornish, who has moved to a second home located in rural environs—protected by dogs, tunnel entrance, and hillside setting.

HANDOUT 4
THE POSITION PAPER

1. The position paper is just that: you adopt a single position about what you have read, a narrowed focus that can be developed by using concrete examples from the reading or from supplements to the reading. The position is *your* position.

2. The position paper must be three to five typed pages. The papers must be typed because at least two papers will be chosen from each assignment, reproduced, and evaluated during Defense Day by members of the seminar.

3. The possibilities for positions are nearly unlimited. You may want to develop an important quotation from a work, an important symbol, a character or a comparison of two characters, the author's style, his or her ideas about love, death, maturity, society, nature, money. You may wish to explore the author's use of names, choice of title, brand of humor. Suggestions for positions will be given with each assignment.

4. The paper must be your best writing. It will always be read by the instructor. At least two of your papers will be discussed and evaluated by the entire seminar.

5. Do not use the title of the work for your paper. Instead, your title should suggest or reflect your position.

6. Present your position logically and support it with concrete material—quotations and examples from what you have read as well as your own observations about life and literature. Don't neglect the plot or ignore the names of the characters, yet assume that your reader is your seminar classmate, who is also familiar with the work.

7. Writing good papers is hard work. It requires a clear outline. Your paper needs sharp first and last sentences, transitions between solidly developed paragraphs, varied sentences—not all beginning with pronouns, not all simple or compound constructions. It requires your sharpest and most mature language. Good writing is correct writing: don't lose your reader by failing to proofread. Read your paper aloud before typing the final draft. Finally, a good paper uses psychology: work hard on introductions and conclusions —the first and last things that the reader reads.

8. Do not rely on critics. While there will be student position papers for you to examine, take your own position.

9. Do not be afraid to adopt a position that seems "way out," fanciful, outrageous. If you have a strong position, one that may be challenged in the seminar discussion, just be sure that you have the material to defend it.

10. The writing of seven position papers is a cumulative experience. Each paper builds upon its predecessors, so do not hesitate to refer to previous papers or ideas—yours or those of other classmates. Through your own writing and by studying the works of other students, you will make discoveries about your reading and writing. New ideas will come to you. You will become aware of your own style as you consider the writing of others. And, while each paper will not necessarily be better than the last, your final production will speak for itself. You will be impressed!

PAPER I: "A PERFECT DAY FOR BANANAFISH" DAYS 3–12

DAYS 3–5: READING TWO SALINGER STORIES ALOUD

Goals

1. To introduce the Salinger literature by reading aloud and discussing on Day 3 "The Young Folks" (1940) and on Days 4 and 5 "Uncle Wiggily in Connecticut" (1948).
2. To provide background for an independent reading of "A Perfect Day for Bananafish" (1948) and for writing the first Position Paper.

Materials

1. "The Young Folks"; early story appeared March–April 1940 in *Story* magazine.
2. *Nine Stories*.
3. Handout 5: *The Glass Family*.

Assignment

1. Read "A Perfect Day for Bananafish" and write a three-to-five page Position Paper on that story.
2. Insert DUE date for this paper on the Schedule, Day 13. In addition, note the dates of the first Defense Days and explain to students that copies of the position papers for defense will be given out on Days 19 and 20.

Procedure

1. Remind students that Salinger's first stories appeared in magazines, beginning in 1940 when he was attending a writing class at Columbia University. But not until after he served during World War II were they collected in book form, beginning with "A Perfect Day for Bananafish," which was published in *The New Yorker* on 31 January, 1948 and later as the first story in *Nine Stories* (1953). In fact, none of the stories before "Bananafish" have been collected in book form. But the ideas from these stories would blossom into the more famous works. We will be examining some of these 1940–1948 stories in the first two sections of the seminar.
2. Do an oral reading of "The Young Folks." This is the first published story. If you wish to begin with student reading, ask individual students to read sections of two or three paragraphs to the class. They should then summarize what they have read, observing whatever comes to mind about plot development, style, sentence length, dialogue, word choice, characters, names, the title. This March–April 1940 story introduces a basic Salinger concern: innocents and phonies. As the title suggests, young people meet the real world, pathetic and bewildered. This idea, perhaps the product of Salinger's own youth, is expressed with all the vividness of teenage slang and affectation.
3. When you shift to *Nine Stories*, you may wish to stress the dates of all the stories, asking students to write them in the "Contents"—(see dates in Bibliography). Eight years and a dramatic experience of World War II have passed. Salinger's style has matured; he has grown interested in Zen Buddhism. (Ask students to note the book's introductory Zen *koan*. Why is it there? Does it tie the stories together in some way? You may wish to pursue these introductory questions—or wait until the later sections which stress Zen.)

DAY 6: CHOOSING AND LIMITING TOPICS FOR POSITION PAPER I

Goals

1. To discuss appropriate topics for Position Paper I.
2. To demonstrate how to narrow a topic.

Materials

1. Handout 6: Suggestions for Position Paper I.
2. Handout 7: Student Model for Paper I.

Procedure

1. By now students have read "A Perfect Day for Bananafish" and are beginning to understand some basics about Salinger's early life and writing. Do not, however, discuss this story until *after* the position papers are handed in; but the concept of a position paper is probably incomplete and further clarification in class is needed.
2. Distribute Handout 6 and discuss these suggestions for position papers on "A Perfect Day for Bananafish."
3. You may wish to use the model paper, Handout 7, at this point to assist students in their understanding of a position paper—or you may wish to post it on the bulletin board for reference. Note particularly the instructor's comments which follow the student paper.
4. The dedications refer to Dorothy Olding, a New York literary agent, and Gus Lobrano, a magazine editor.
5. Handout 5 is a valuable reference to all the Glass family stories, including "Bananafish" and "Uncle Wiggily." It establishes that Salinger country is largely New York and its environs inhabited by this family and the people they know. The stories, largely from the sophisticated *The New Yorker* magazine (show a copy to the class), concern the problems of urban and suburban East Coast America—though they relate to us all. Note Seymour, who is in "Bananafish," and Walt, who is referred to in "Uncle Wiggily."
6. As the class reads aloud and pieces together "Uncle Wiggily," there should be some recognition of the similarities between this 1948 story with "Young Folks" of 1940.

While the title, like "Bananafish," is more dramatic and perhaps vague (Uncle Wiggily was the kind old rabbit in the Howard Garis children's stories), compare the introductions, the dialogue, the italicized words (Why?), the slang ("Edna baby" vs. "Merritt Parkway, baby"), the world of suburbia—of liquor, cigarettes, college, of people confused and lonely in a world of the young and adult. Note reference to World War II where Seymour and Walt and Jerome Salinger served time.

7. Ask students to think of one possible position over each story, as if they were to write their papers on "Young Folks" or "Uncle Wiggily."

Additional Suggestion

You may wish to make a copy of a New York/Connecticut map for reference with these and later stories. Also ask students to check to see if bananafish exist. At age thirteen, Salinger professed a love of tropical fish.

DAYS 7–10: PREWRITING DISCUSSION, WRITING, AND READING

Goals

1. To provide in-class time for prewriting discussion, as well as time for student writing.
2. To read and discuss at least one early uncollected short story.

Materials

A teacher copy of one of the early stories: (1) "The Hang of It," *Collier's* 108 (12 July 1941):22. (2) "Once a Week Won't Kill You," *Story* 25 (November–December 1944):23–27.

Procedure

1. Day 7 should be a time for prewriting discussion. Students will find it valuable to share their approaches to writing a paper. Do they just pick a suggestion from the handout and begin writing or typing? Do they have a basic outline approach: Introduction, Body, Conclusion? Discuss prewriting concerns:

(1) brainstorming—making notes on ideas that come to you; (2) examining your written ideas, as well as those on the suggestion sheet, and seeing which has the strongest appeal; and (3) seeing if the ideas are related, as well as which ones can be developed.

2. Also discuss the setting and mechanics of writing. When do you write the best, at school, at home? Do you write continuously or stop when things go well—then pick them up later? How many rough drafts do you need? What techniques do you use to get into a paper? Out of a paper? Do you have a reward system to make yourself finish the paper? What are the hazards of last day writing—or the delights? Can you describe a paper that you have written which proved to be among your very best? What made it go so well? How do you pick titles? Do you use others for sounding-boards?

3. Days 8 and 9 should be given for writing.

4. On Day 10, you can continue to give students an understanding of Salinger's early work and development by reading to them one or both stories suggested above. "The Hang of It" is something of a formula surprise ending piece about an Army sergeant just before World War II, humorous with some Salinger touches in dialogue. "Once a Week Won't Kill You" was written while Salinger was in the European Theatre of Operations. Part of a series of three "husband vs. wife in wartime" group, this story does have a two-part structure like "Bananafish" and a familiar Salinger concern with the worlds of reality and illusion.

DAYS 11–12: COMPLETING PAPER I AND READING "JUST BEFORE THE WAR WITH THE ESKIMOS"

Goals

1. To complete writing and proofreading of Paper I.
2. To read aloud and discuss "Just before the War with the Eskimos" (1948).

Materials

Copies of *Nine Stories.*

Procedure

1. Day 11 should be given over to writing and proofreading. Remind students of the skill goals for the first paper: one clear position and a paper which follows directions for typewriting, 3–5 pages in length, double spaced.

2. Remind students that the position paper will be due at the beginning of Day 13.

3. On Day 12, the class should again read aloud and discuss another story from *The New Yorker* written in 1948, one that does not involve the Glass family. "Just before the War with the Eskimos" has another intriguing title which the class can discuss even before reading the story. Again there is the familiar New York setting with a familiar strong character, Eric, who talks in italics. This story may connect for students who see it in terms of Salinger's concern with war, of the strong language of the lonely characters (soon to be seen in *The Catcher in the Rye*), of symbolism (the chicken sandwich will reappear in *Franny and Zooey*), of seeing oneself through another (as in "Uncle Wiggily"), of the absurdity that people see in life (as did Seymour).

Additional Suggestion

In 1949, Hollywood made a ninety-eight minute film entitled *My Foolish Heart.* This version of "Uncle Wiggily in Connecticut," starring Dana Andrews and Susan Hayward, so infuriated J. D. Salinger that he would have nothing to do with filmmakers again. If time and budget allow, a class showing of this film would be valuable in not only comparing the film to the story but also in discussing whether Salinger's ire was justified. Certainly Salinger's continual references to Hollywood and films deserve classroom discussion.

HANDOUT 5
THE GLASS FAMILY

Parents:

Les Glass (Jewish) and *Bessie Gallagher Glass* (called a fat Irish Rose by son Zooey). They were successful Pantages Circuit vaudevillians in the 1920s. By the 1940s, Les was hustling talent for motion picture studio in Los Angeles. In the 1950s, they live in an old but not unfashionable apartment house in the East Seventies in New York with their two youngest children.

Seven Children:

1. *Seymour,* the oldest, born in February, 1917. Entered Columbia at age 15, Ph.D. in English. Shared room with brother Buddy until 1940 at home; then both got apartment near 79th and Madison. Taught English. Married Muriel Fedder, 4 June 1942. World War II soldier. Suicide, 18 March 1948, while on vacation in Florida.

2. *Buddy,* born in 1919 (as was Salinger), the writer of the family. Never finished college; 1942, World War II soldier; a writer in residence and, 1955, teacher at a girl's junior college in upper New York state, who lived alone in a small unelectrified house near a ski run.

3. *Boo Boo,* "a stunning and final girl," a World War II Wave in Brooklyn, married a "resolute-looking man" named *Tannenbaum,* lives in Tuckahoe, has a New England summer place. By 1955, has three children, the oldest named *Lionel.*

4 and 5.   The Twins: *Waker* and *Walt.* Waker by 1955 was a Catholic priest after being a World War II conscientious objector. Walt spent World War II in Pacific; in autumn of 1945, he was killed when a Japanese stove exploded while he was packing it as a souvenir for his commanding officer.

6. *Zachary Martin Glass,* or *Zooey.* Born 1929, "a wholly beautiful face," who became a TV actor after college, though his mother wanted him to get a Ph.D. in mathematics or Greek. By 1952 was playing leads.

7. *Frances* or *Franny.* Born 1934, extraordinarily beautiful. In summer of 1954, played summer stock between junior and senior college years. In her junior year interested in *Lane Coutell.* But by November of 1955 had a spiritual crisis. Helped by Zooey from spiritual collapse.

Over a period of eighteen years, beginning in 1927, one or more of the Glass children performed under the name of Black on a famous radio quiz show, "It's a Wise Child." Their educations were paid for by these performances.

KEEP THIS FAMILY DESCRIPTION AS WE STUDY THE VARIOUS WRITINGS THAT INVOLVE THE GLASS PARENTS AND CHILDREN.

HANDOUT 6
SUGGESTIONS FOR PAPER I: "A Perfect Day for Bananafish" (1948)

1. Examine the title closely. Do any of the words suggest a position?

2. This story has two separate scenes. Are these divisions organic? Do they fit together compactly?

3. Examine the characters' names. Are they symbolic? Focus on one character such as Sybil. What is a "sybil"?

4. Try comparing characters for a position. Note that in "Uncle Wiggily in Connecticut" Walt is contrasted with Lew, Eloise with Ramona.

5. Muriel refers to German poetry by a man that Seymour calls "the only great poet of the century." This man is probably Rainer Maria Rilke. Look up Rilke. How are Seymour and Rilke alike?

6. Why does Seymour kiss Sybil's foot?

7. Salinger is noted for his dialogue. How would you describe it in this story? Be sure to illustrate.

8. Is this story about sex? Does it contain sexual symbolism?

9. Try comparing this story with "Uncle Wiggily in Connecticut."

10. Why is the Florida setting so important to this story?

11. The telephone call is important to this story. Why?

12. Just why does Seymour shoot himself?

13. Salinger is noted for his humor. What kind of humor is found in this story?

14. Examine Seymour and Sybil, Muriel and her mother in terms of their conversations.

15. What is "banana fever"?

16. Can the Zen quotation at the beginning of the nine stories be used with a position about this story?

HANDOUT 7
STUDENT MODEL FOR PAPER I

PLEASURE IN PURSUIT OF PAIN

by Janet Holm

Is humanity such that the inevitable end of pleasure must be pain, that happiness must be followed by destruction, as ultimately, life must be followed by death? If this is indeed the case, then the question must be asked as to what purpose life is led, and what possible worth of satisfaction can be derived from it. How futile life becomes when looked at in this manner, and yet how much greater the experience of joy to know that it is but transient.

J. D. Salinger's story, "A Perfect Day for Bananafish," can be seen as a rather heightened example of the impermanence of any exultation, and the unavoidable loss that ensues. This sentiment is expressed in two different, although parallel, ways within the story. Both center around Seymour Glass, an intellectual and disturbed young man. One is the story he tells, whether actual or imaginary is not know, and the other is the very real circumstances of his life. In each, there is a somewhat fanciful sense of delight and well-being experienced by the reader immediately before the indisputable finality of each incident. This lulling into a false sense of security is rather emphasized by the unexpected quality of innocence that survives in spite of the aura of evil contained in the closing.

In the first instance, Seymour Glass tells Sybil the story of the bananafish. He first stresses the tragic nature of their lives, then explains to Sybil the cycle that they follow. Literally, these ordinary fish swim into a hole that is full of bananas. Once inside, the fish are overcome by greed

1

2

and eat far more bananas than they can hold. They are then trapped within
the hole, unable to exit through the door they entered due to their tremen-
dous size. The fish are then seized by a disease known as "banana fever"--a
disease fatal to bananafish. Thus as the fish seek a satisfaction of desire
and experience a brief period of pleasure, they also feel death as the cul-
mination of their cupidity.

Here the parallel is drawn to the example of Seymour Glass. He is a man
who has suffered in the war, and upon returning has attempted suicide. His
basic despair must be realized before attempting to rationalize the depth of
his emotions that give rise to his actions.

Seymour is sitting on the beach, enjoying the sun, when the little girl,
Sybil, appears. The following encounter with Sybil is, for Seymour, filled
with extreme pleasure and awakening desire. As they talk, Sybil asks Seymour
about another child, Sharon Lipshutz, with whom she has seen Seymour sitting.
Seymour tells her that she had nothing to worry about, although he does like
Sharon because she is so kind. Sybil is obviously jealous of his attentions
to Sharon, and Seymour himself admits to some interest when Sybil once again
mentions Sharon, by saying, "Mixing memory and desire." He is pleased by
Sybil's interest in him, adding to his overall feeling of longing for her.

As Seymour and Sybil begin walking toward the ocean, he tells her the
bananafish story. She takes him seriously, neither of their manners suggesting anything nonsensical in the story. All the while they have been talking,
Seymour has been putting his hand on Sybil's ankles, casually, as if it were
a natural thing, yet this alludes to his awakening desire. Once in the water,
Seymour sits Sybil in the rubber raft, and holding her by the ankles, propels
her over the waves. When a big wave crashes over their heads, Sybil emerges,
claiming that she has seen a bananafish. Seymour then grabs her foot and
kisses it. It is at this point that his climax is reached in fulfilling his

3

desire. Seymour then decides abruptly that there has been enough, and they
return to shore. Sybil is at first reluctant, then as they reach the sand,
runs eagerly away.

This day at the beach approaches perfection in Seymour's mind. He is
in awe of the experience he has had, and yet he is unwilling to allow anyone
else into his momentary paradise, or even to let anyone be aware of what he
has experienced. However, at the same time, he feels very close to Sybil as
the result of his contact with her and wishes to feel even more personal affection for her. This is why he tells Sybil the story of the bananafish: he
sees himself as one of them. In this way, he explains what the time with
Sybil has been for him, for it parallels the life of the bananafish. Thus he
alludes to the fact that following the satisfaction that he has found, there
must be pain, and, in his case, death. When Sybil claims to have seen bananafish, Seymour reaches the peak of his excitement but also begins to know fear.
He feels that she may have seen through the illusion he has created by becoming totally involved in it, and thus may have seen into him. He is unwilling
to reveal himself any further to her for fear of exposing his satisfaction
and also his plan of death.

Within Seymour's desire, within the instinctive actions of the bananafish, as well as within the human mind, there lies a subconscious need for
punishment, for whatever time of ecstasy is sustained. Unknowingly, an end
is sought that will terminate, perhaps permanently, whatever lust, whatever
sensuous pleasure, whatever greed that has been experienced.

The examples within the story are extremes, of course. The sensations
felt do not warrant the ultimate banishment of death, and yet they serve to
represent this quirk of human nature. As with anything absolute, the realization that as warmth and yearning fade, pain must follow, must be accepted, and
rather than endured, must be enjoyed. It comes as a greater willingness to

4

do everything to the fullest, to derive what ever possible value from every instant of joy, whether it be a glimpse of beauty, a bodily sensation, a moment of reverence, or the day-to-day act of living. For always the end must come, and with it suffering, and in time the height of torture, that must also be the height of joy, for it is the final release.

Instructor's Comments

1. <u>Strengths</u>: This first paper has its success because it has a strong position, one stated in the introduction, dissected in a key and symbolic scene, and restated in the conclusion. It is also almost an Old Testament position that should generate seminar discussion. And it is a promising start because the writer is experimenting with a complex style and, best of all, relates fiction to life as she sees it.

2. <u>Weaknesses</u>: At times the sentence complexity and occasional use of passive voice stand in the way of clarity. Her convolutions, such as with the next-to-last paragraph, invite too many re-readings. For example, in that paragraph lie questions of definition, documentation, and generalization: What is "ecstasy"--just lust, greed, sensuality? Do fish really feel a subconscious need for punishment? Can everyone's psyche be equated with that of the war-battered Seymour? The writer also only uses one direct quotation to support her observations. This is a skill in convincing the reader, one that should be stressed in Defense Day and required for Paper II.

PAPER II: *THE CATCHER IN THE RYE* DAYS 13–28

DAYS 13–14: BEGINNING SALINGER'S MOST SUCCESSFUL NOVEL

Goals

1. To orient students to *The Catcher in the Rye*.
2. To begin reading the novel in class.

Materials

Class set of *The Catcher in the Rye*.

Assignment

Note the DUE date of Paper II on the Schedule, Day 29.

Procedure

1. Give students a few minutes for a final proofreading of their first position papers. Then collect them. Choose the papers for Defense Day as soon as possible and make multiple copies. Review the Defense Day procedures in the introduction, in preparation for this discussion/evaluation period. The schedule allows time for you to grade the remaining papers before Defense Day.
2. Remind students that the first Defense Days will be Days 19 and 20. Copies of the papers for defense will be handed out before each day; the first two will be given to all students on Day 18. All corrected papers will be returned at the end of Day 20.
3. Ask students to review The Salinger Chronology (Handout 3) or Appendix A, Life and Times of J. D. Salinger. This first novel has its literary origins as early as 1941 when he began to write about Holden Caulfield in the short story "Slight Rebellion off Madi-

son," which was eventually published by *The New Yorker* in 1946. The story, of course, has its biographical parallels: Salinger was an unconventional adolescent who had flunked out of McBurney School in Manhattan. Then his parents shipped him off to Valley Forge Military Academy in the Pennsylvania hills. Perhaps he felt a misfit by being sent to this model for Pencey Prep. He, like Holden, managed the fencing team. His fellow cadets included one who jumped out of a window, as did James Castle in *Catcher,* and one who was expelled like Holden and ended up at a mental institution on the West Coast. But, beyond that, Salinger and Holden part company; Salinger graduated and even wrote the song for the school's Last Parade.

4. Note the dedication to Salinger's mother, Miriam Salinger. This dedication might be the basis for speculation if one is to force parallels between the author and Holden.
5. Note the title. Ask students if they are acquainted with "Comin' through the Rye" by Robert Burns (1759–1796), a Scottish poet. The poem was set to music.
6. Students should also be aware that this book was very controversial, even banned in the 1950s and 1960s. It appeared during the Korean War, in an era of gray-flannel suits, fear of the A-bomb, rise of corporations, fear of Communism, Dr. Spock's baby book, affluence, and conformity.
7. Day 14 should be an in-class reading day.

Additional Suggestion

You may wish to begin this section by class reading the first few pages of *Catcher*. Not only can the class discusss familiar Salinger trademarks (immediate involvement in the character, italicized words, references to fish and films, autobiographical material), but also there should be mention of why critics compare this book to Mark Twain's *Huckleberry Finn*. Here we see first person flashback, the colloquial and teenage language, and the story of a boy who could not stand civilization.

DAYS 15–17: READING AND BACKGROUNDS OF THE NOVEL

Goals

1. To provide time for in-class reading.
2. To trace the backgrounds of *The Catcher in the Rye* by examining earlier magazine fiction.

Materials

At least one copy of a background short story: (1) "Slight Rebellion off Madison." *The New Yorker* (22 December 1946):82–86. This story was actually written in 1941. (2) "Last Day of the Last Furlough." *Saturday Evening Post* 217 (15 July 1944):61–62, 64. (3) "A Boy in France." *Saturday Evening Post* 217 (31 March 1945):21, 92. (4) "This Sandwich Has No Mayonnaise." *Esquire* 24 (October 1945):54–56, 147–149. (5) "The Stranger." *Collier's* 116 (1 December 1945):18, 77. (6) "I'm Crazy." *Collier's* 116 (22 December 1945):36, 48, 51.

Procedure

1. Day 15 should be a reading day so that students get far enough into the novel that the background information will have impact.
2. On Day 16, the instructor should note that *Catcher* has a ten year history or evolution:
   a. In 1941, Salinger sold "Slight Rebellion off Madison" to *The New Yorker,* but the story was only set into type and not published until 1946. War had broken out and the subject matter apparently was not felt to be right at the time of Pearl Harbor. Holden Caulfield and Sally Hayes interact at Rockefeller Center; the story is told in the third person. (See chapter 17 in *Catcher*.)
   b. The 1944 World War II story, "Last Day of the Last Furlough," concerns Sergeant Babe Gladwaller and his little sister Mattie (a relationship much like Holden and Phoebe), as well as references to his friend Vincent Caulfield, son of an actor and a soap opera writer, whose brother Holden has run away from school again.
   c. The 1945 story "A Boy in France" is about Babe digging a foxhole and reading a letter from his sister about a girl named Frances, a young haughty woman that Babe loves. He enjoys the letter and falls asleep. Some critics see this story as relating to "For Esme—with Love and Squalor" with its letter and to *Franny and Zooey* with the central character finding peace in the communication.
   d. "This Sandwich Has No Mayonnaise" is is a 1945 tale about Vincent Caulfield.
   e. Vincent, who is training for the Air Corps in Georgia, learns that his nineteen year old brother Holden is missing in action in the Pacific.
   f. The final Babe Gladwaller story of 1945, "The Stranger," involves Babe and Mattie going to New York to tell Vincent Caulfield's girl about Vincent's death in Europe during the war. We also learn that the girl did not marry Vincent because he had become so cynical (after his little brother Kenneth died).
   g. "I'm Crazy" is another direct link with *Catcher,* though the language is tamed down. Holden talks with his history teacher before leaving the prep school, and he later talks with sister Phoebe in her bedroom. This 1945 story is especially interesting because Salinger has chosen the first person viewpoint which intrigued so many *Catcher* readers in 1951 and after.
3. "Slight Rebellion off Madison" and "I'm Crazy" provide good material for discussion and are short. "Last Day of the Last Furlough" is especially good for class purposes because of Salinger's interest in children (as students have already noted) and because Babe's advice to Mattie about life and growing up ties to much of Salinger's fiction.
4. Day 17 should be a reading day.

DAYS 18–21: PREPARING FOR AND PARTICIPATING IN DEFENSE DAY AND FOLLOW-UP

Goals

1. To prepare students for the first Defense Days.
2. To conduct the first Defense Days that will provide useful models for the remaining six.
3. To provide a follow-up that offers students the opportunity to express their positions.
4. To help students examine the position of critics.

Materials

1. Copies of the position papers on "A Perfect Day for Bananafish" that you have chosen for the first Defense Days. Make extra copies for students who may have lost or forgotten them on Defense Days.
2. Handout 8: Defense Day: Criteria for Grading Position Papers.
3. The corrected copies of the remaining position papers ready to give out at the end of Day 20.

Procedure

1. On Day 18, hand out copies of the first two papers that you have chosen for Defense Day. Remind students that the second two papers will be given out on Day 19.
2. Give each student a copy of Handout 8: Defense Day: Criteria for Grading Position Papers. This handout can be instructive for the oral grading after each paper has been evaluated by the seminar. (Prior to class, review the discussion of how to conduct a successful Defense Day in the introduction. There are three criteria, with special emphasis on this paper's skill goals of following directions and having a clear single position. Students can use this handout during Day 18 as they read and annotate their copies of these papers so that they will be able to remember their initial reactions.
3. Some instructors may wish to develop a system of anonymous grading, using this handout with each Defense Day paper.
4. Remind students that Defense Day is not Destruction Day. It is a time to learn about the positions of others, to clarify what is not clear, to agree and disagree, to study organization and supporting evidence, to work on mechanics, and to defend what one has written. The word "criticism" implies two responsibilities, for critics to try to understand what a writer has written as well as to react to the writing.
5. Students whose papers have been chosen for Defense Day should prepare to read them aloud.
6. Days 20 and 21 are Defense Days. It is important that you choose good models for these days and that you allot the discussion time equally. Remember, the students, not you, are to do the evaluating. Too much direction on your part will destroy the spirit of Defense Day; instead, encourage discussion, restate or clarify student positions, work for a balanced discussion (call on everyone, ask students who suggest grades to justify their choices), and conclude the defense with positive summation. Always the goal is the next paper.
7. Return the other position papers on Day 21 without comment. The next class period will be given over to these papers.
8. Follow-up Day 21 will allow others in class to state their positions. There are a number of options for this day:
   a. Review the positions taken by the papers defended on the previous days. You may have taken notes on the positions of the remaining students and can, therefore, call on students who have similar or contrasting positions. Or each student can be called upon to state his or her position. Or you may ask other students to read all or selected portions of their papers—again, choose excellent models but ones not chosen for Defense Day.
   b. You may wish to discuss the successes (and failures) of the first Defense Days. Clear the air. Ask students how Defense Days can be improved. If some students argue that the grading was too high or too low, ask them to formulate a fair standard, taking into consideration the pressures of such close examination. Remind them that learning to write is more than just earning a letter grade.

c. You may wish to use the Student Model, Handout 7, for follow-up discussion.

d. You may wish to read aloud a critic's evaluation of "A Perfect Day for Bananafish." Suggestions: (1) pages 19–21 of chapter 3 in *The Fiction of J. D. Salinger* by Frederick L. Gwynn and Joseph L. Blotner; (2) pages 79–87 in chapter 3, "Zen Art and Nine Stories," in *J. D. Salinger* by James Lundquist.

DAYS 22–25: READING, CHOOSING TOPICS FOR PAPER II, DISCUSSING SKILLS, AND WRITING

Goals

1. To provide time for in-class reading and writing.
2. To suggest topics for Paper II.
3. To review and instruct the skills which will be stressed for Paper II.

Materials

1. Handout 9: Suggestions for Paper II.
2. Handout 10: Student Model for Paper II.

Procedure

1. Time to complete the novel may be provided in class if necessary.
2. Handout 9 will give students potential suggestions for their positions on *The Catcher in the Rye*.
3. Handout 10, the Student Model, may be posted on the bulletin board for individual reference or copies may be made for distribution and discussion. You may wish to use the model for follow-up day only.
4. For at least one period, such as Day 24, there should be review of the skills which will be stressed in Paper II evaluation: use of concrete examples, especially *at least one direct quotation,* and focus on the introduction and conclusion. Points to consider:
   a. A position paper is convincing if the ideas are supported not just by logic but also by concrete examples. This means using the facts of the plot, the specific characters and scenes, the direct lines found in the narration or in the dialogue. Students should begin to take notes on key lines and key pages which will help prove their point, as well as give flavor and documented authenticity. The writer does not have to shout that he or she is right; the concrete support does the convincing. Discuss when to use short quotations within the text of the paragraphs and when to use long quotations of four or more typed lines and single space and indent. Warn them, however, that long quotations can be tiring to the eye; and a paper must not just be a series of long quotations tied together with a few student-written sentences. You may wish to discuss how to build a natural transition between text and quotation— or leave this for the next paper after the problems with this skill are observed in the second paper. Also you may wish to discuss editing quotations.
   b. An instructor cannot stress enough how important introductions and conclusions are to a paper. They get the reader interested and they impress the reader at the end—or they don't! Certainly introductions need to mention such details as author and title, but the rest is left to the creative talents of the writer. There can be a general discussion of what student writers have learned from other instructors and what they have learned from experience. Examples: (1) Some have learned to state their position in brief in the first or second sentences; then they summarize this idea, or the ideas of the entire paper, in the conclusion. This method can have the benefit of clarity, but it can have a hazard of dullness. (2) Some have learned stylistic devices: tying titles to introductions and conclusions; repeating lines; using direct quotations as lead-ins and lead-outs; making sure that neither introduction nor conclusion is too long

or too complex to hold impact; starting from a general idea, narrowing it to particulars in the paper, and returning to the general idea at the end; opening with a concrete scene from the book to interest the reader and relate to the position; working hard on sharp prose—clever words, varied sentences—especially long ones followed by very short ones.

5. At least one day, such as Day 25, should be given for in-class writing. Remind students that Paper II is due on Day 29.

DAYS 26-28: READING ALOUD TWO SALINGER STORIES

Goals

1. To read aloud "The Laughing Man" (1949) and "Down at the Dinghy" (1949) and relate them to the Salinger material which has already been discussed, as well as to "Teddy" (1953)—the subject of the next paper.
2. To complete the writing and proofreading of Paper II, if necessary.

Materials

Copies of *Nine Stories.*

Procedure

1. If necessary, give in-class time for any final writing or proofreading.
2. The fourth and fifth stories of *Nine Stories* continue to tie the Salinger opus together. "The Laughing Man," which appeared 19 March 1949 in *The New Yorker,* is an enjoyable story to read aloud. Its male narrator uses the familiar *Catcher* flashback and, like the author, was born in 1919 and attended a public school in New York's upper West Side. Here again is the story of childhood as distinct from the adult world. Here again is the wild imagination. It is also a disturbing story, one with Zen overtones (Is the Chief, a law student, trying too hard to understand existence?), one with symbols (the names, the mask). "Down at the Dinghy," which appeared in the April, 1949 issue of *Harper's,* takes us back to the Glass family and another precocious child. Ask students to examine Handout 5, the Glass Family, again. We meet Boo Boo Glass—and will meet her again in *Raise High the Roof Beam, Carpenters.* There is the tie-up with the sea in "Bananafish" and "Teddy," as well as reference to Seymour. The world of adults and prejudice, which the young soon learn about, is a key to this story.

HANDOUT 8
DEFENSE DAY: CRITERIA FOR GRADING POSITION PAPERS

____ **Clarity of Position**

1. Does the paper pursue *one* position?
2. Can you state this position? If so, write it below:

   _____

   _____

   _____

____ **Organization and Support**

1. Is the position clear because it is logical?
2. Is it clear because it is supported by concrete material, such as direct references and quotations?
3. Is it clear because it pursues an obvious, even minor, position? Consider if the position is complex or original.
4. Is the position supported by the proper language, for example, a humorous position uses humorous images and words?
5. Is there coherence in the paper: transitions between sentences and paragraphs to enhance the organization?
6. Are the introduction and conclusion effective in clarifying the position?
7. Does the paper suffer from irrelevancies or over-emphasis of a minor point?

____ **Mechanics**

1. Do many proofreading errors detract from the paper's position?
2. Are there over ten basic mechanical errors—spelling, punctuation, capitalization, fragments, run-on sentences, usage, misplaced modifiers, parallel structure, words often confused, pronoun forms, verb forms?
3. Is the paper smooth reading? What about awkward sentences, imprecise or redundant word choice?

_____ Grade

USE THIS SHEET AS YOU EXAMINE EACH POSITION PAPER.

HANDOUT 9
SUGGESTIONS FOR PAPER II: *THE CATCHER IN THE RYE* (1951)

1. What does the word "phony" mean? Does Holden use it so loosely that it lacks meaning?
2. What do the women who appeal to Holden have in common?
3. Is this novel optimistic or pessimistic?
4. Children and Adults. Is this a possible position?
5. Is Pencey a symbol of twentieth-century American culture?
6. Does the title suggest a position? Review its origin and Holden's dream.
7. Why does Holden swear so much? Analyze his profanity.
8. Holden and liquor. Is Holden an alcoholic or his drinking symptomatic of a problem that faces many young people?
9. What is Holden's attitude toward religion?
10. The novel contains a good deal about Holden and clothing. What is the function of clothing, especially in this book?
11. What is Holden's attitude about change in the world? Note what he says about museums.
12. Holden fails many of his classes, yet he passes in English and he reads a lot. Meaning?
13. Some readers compare this book to *Huckleberry Finn* by Mark Twain. Is Holden a twentieth-century Huck Finn? Is he too on a journey?
14. Holden lies. Why?
15. Holden and the movies?
16. Could this novel be made into a good film?
17. Is this book about sex and the American teenager?

HANDOUT 10
STUDENT MODEL FOR PAPER II

EGYPTIAN TOMBS, CENTRAL PARK DUCKS, AND OTHER SYMBOLS

by Barb Blodi

Both the consistent reference to death and a symbolic falling or dropping off are means of portraying depression and despair. Holden Caulfield, the teenage narrator of J. D. Salinger's The Catcher in the Rye, reveals this idea in thought and action. This novel, written over two decades ago, seems universally applicable. Throughout the story, Salinger uses the aspect of death and an endless fall as effective representation of Holden's alienation. Certainly, dying is not a new angle to Salinger's stories, for he uses suicide and accidental death in "A Perfect Day for Bananafish."

Using the past tense, Holden tells his story in retrospect, and at the end we realize that Holden is in a mental clinic or institution, where the story is being told. Thus, Holden is looking back, telling of his period of alienation, but he has already rejoined society or is at least making an attempt. Because of this, Holden portrays a different point of view from a story set in the present. Holden has seen his collapse, and through his narration he presents the theme of a symbolic fall from which he has had to climb.

Along with symbols of death, there are the many things which physically repulse Holden. For example, he feels so sick about all the "phonies" in the world, so nauseous, that he wants to vomit. Disgusted at the people he is forced to see, Holden is trying to regurgitate the world around him.

1

2

   The first reference to death comes when Holden, still a student at
Pencey, reflects back on his dead brother, Allie. Holden likes Allie, and
during this period in his life he finds his brother to be one of the few
people that he can respect.

   When Holden leaves school, he journeys to New York City. It is nearly
Christmas, and it is very cold. In a taxi cab, Holden is curious about the
fate of the ducks in Central Park. He asks the driver: "You know those
ducks in that lagoon right near Central Park South? That little lake? By
any chance, do you happen to know where they go, the ducks, when it gets all
frozen over? Do you happen to know, by any chance?" Then Holden tells the
reader, "He turned around and looked at me like I was a madman."

   There is a comparison to make here between the forlorn ducks and Holden,
both in flight, both looking for somewhere to go. Notice here that the
weather is bleak, similar to that of Holden's outlook on life, yet the season
of Christmas, a time of rebirth, is at hand.

   The first evening in New York is spent in the hotel bar, which eventually
leads to his buying a "throw" with a cheap prostitute. Holden does not feel
like having any sexual contact and becomes more and more depressed. At the
end of the chapter, Holden wants to commit suicide--the only thing he can
think of to end his depression: "What I really felt like, though, was com-
mitting suicide. I felt like jumping out the window. I probably would've
done it, too, if I'd been sure somebody'd cover me up as soon as I landed."

   The escapades of the next day follow, and Holden (after visiting Central
Park and actually looking for the ducks) winds up at his home, hoping to
"shoot the breeze" with Phoebe, his little sister. Sneaking in late at
night, Holden wakes up Phoebe, and she enthusiastically greets him. At one
point during the conversation, Phoebe demands Holden to name something he
likes a lot. Holden at first can think of only two things--his brother Allie

3

and an acquaintance at one of his schools who was "accidentally" killed because of an unretracted insult. Both people he likes are dead.

Then Holden divulges an ambition. He wants to be a catcher in the rye.
He says,

> What I have to do, I have to catch everybody (kids) if they
> start to go over the cliff--I mean if they're running and they
> don't look where they're going I have to come out from somewhere
> and <u>catch</u> them. That's all I'd do all day. I'd just be a
> catcher in the rye and all.

Here we see Holden trying to be a savior, rescuing children from a cliff of
terrible fate. This is his only desire at the moment. Holden wants to protect these kids from the same "fall" that he is experiencing.

Holden's fall is foreshadowed in the scene with Mr. Antolini. Holden
has gone to the former English teacher for companionship and shelter in New
York, but he also receives a lot of paternal advice.

> "Frankly, I don't know what the hell to say to you, Holden."
> "I know. I'm very hard to talk to. I realize that."
> "I have the feeling that you're riding for some kind of a
> terrible, terrible fall. But I don't honestly know what
> kind . . ."

Again, the reoccurring theme of a fall or crash towards which Holden
seems to be heading. Holden, perhaps influenced by Mr. Antolini, has this
feeling of falling himself. Later, while walking along Fifth Avenue, he
finds the end of each street block becoming a huge chasm to cross. Holden
comes close to panic.

> Every time I came to the end of a block and stepped off the
> goddam curb, I had this feeling that I'd never get to the other
> side of the street. I thought I'd just go down, down, down,
> and nobody'd ever see me again.

The fear of not being seen again is an indication of Holden's preference
for being a visible part of society. If he had rejected society completely,
he would not have had to worry about being seen.

4

Holden then goes to his sister's school to tell her of his planned departure. With time to kill, he decides to wait at the museum. Annoyed by
the obscenities etched on the bathrooms, stairwell, and other public places,
Holden foresees his own tomb.

> I think, even, if I ever die, and they stick me in a cemetery,
> and I have a tombstone and all, it'll say 'Holden Caulfield'
> on it, and then what year I was born and what year I died, and
> then right under that it'll say 'Fuck you.' I'm positive, in
> fact.

The setting shifts from Holden's imaginary tombstone to the Egyptian
tombs in the basement of the museum. Tombs, of course, represent death again.
Here the physical climax of the book takes place. Holden, down among the
dead, so to speak, passes out--now at the most intense point of isolation,
the farthest from society. But as soon as he recovers from fainting, Holden
immediately feels better. He realizes that he must go meet Phoebe and walks
up from the tombs, leaving the dead behind. Meeting Phoebe and deciding to
remain is clearly Holden's renewed acceptance of his environment.

Yet the story does not end there. Holden continues to tell us about his
afternoon with his sister. They walk to a park where Phoebe rides the
carousel. She reaches for the gold ring as she flies 'round and 'round, and
Holden, although a little worried, realizes that he should not try and stop
her.

> The thing with kids is, if they want to grab for the gold ring,
> you have to let them do it, and not say anything. If they fall
> off, they fall off, but it's bad if you say anything to them.
> —Holden

Here is the final turning point of the story, for Holden has changed his
philosophy. He no longer wants to be a catcher in the rye. Instead, he desires for each individual to be on their own, to be able to grab for the gold
ring. Accepting the fact that all of must face a "fall" of some sort, Holden
is ready to start out fresh. Purified by the falling rain, Holden, once at
the very bottom, is climbing his way back up.

5

Instructor's Comments

1. <u>Strengths</u>: The writer has a solid position, triggered by a clever, Salinger-styled title. She defines the position right away, nicely relating it to the first paper. She obviously had organizational structure and support. Picking key scenes and a number of direct quotations, she convinces the reader. Her concluding sentence is strong and poetic, too.

2. <u>Weaknesses</u>: At times, tighter unity and more plot explanation could clarify the position. Examples: The third paragraph begins noting symbols of death, yet actual examples don't come until later; <u>symbols</u> and <u>references</u> need to be clarified. Clarity comes with more support about why he left school, why park ducks should be in flight literally, why being in the bar led to visiting a prostitute.

PAPER III: "TEDDY"
DAYS 29–44

DAYS 29-30: INTRODUCTION TO "TEDDY"

Goals

1. To orient students to "Teddy" (1953).
2. To provide in-class time to begin the short story.

Materials

Class copies of *Nine Stories*.

Assignment

1. Ask students to note the DUE date for the third paper on the Schedule, Day 45.
2. Remind students that the Defense Days for Paper II (*The Catcher in the Rye*) are Days 37 and 38. Copies of the papers chosen for defense will be handed out on Days 36 and 37.

Procedure

1. Give students the first five to ten minutes for a final proofreading of Paper II. Then collect these papers. Be sure to select the four for the Defense Days and make class copies. Check to see that they have concrete examples/direct quotations.
2. Ask students to review The Salinger Chronology (Handout 3), noting that the next Salinger work for consideration is "Teddy"—the last of the *Nine Stories*. 1953 is a big year for Salinger. He publishes "Teddy" and later the collected nine stories; he buys his retreat in New Hampshire; he allows his only interview to a high school journalist; then he is angered over the printed interview and cuts off contact with future interviewers; and, of course, his book continues to be a best seller.

3. Discuss the title. Again, it suggests a story about another of Salinger's favorite subjects, children. Teddy, not Theodore. The name also suggests a Teddy Bear (or perhaps Teddy Roosevelt). "Teddy" is the only one of the nine stories to focus just on a character—without some suggestion of other implications, as with "The Laughing Man" or Esme or De Daumier-Smith. Indeed, Teddy is another precocious child, the most precocious child of all. However, he is not a member of the Glass family. During this section, we also will read stories six ("For Esme—with Love and Squalor") and seven ("Pretty Mouth and Green My Eyes"); "De Daumier-Smith's Blue Period" will be analyzed in the next section. While the stories are collected in chronological order, remind students that this last story has been seen by some critics as a kind of conclusion of an idea initiated in "A Perfect Day for Bananafish." One idea that is especially interesting is that these stories may relate to Salinger's fascination with Zen Buddhism. Remember that when he published the book he also included a Zen *koan*. More will be said about this on Days 33–34.
4. Ask students to begin reading the story during the remainder of the class period and to finish it on Day 30.

DAYS 31-32: READING ALOUD AND DISCUSSING "FOR ESME—WITH LOVE AND SQUALOR"

Goals

1. To read aloud "For Esme—with Love and Squalor" (1950).
2. To relate this story to previously discussed material.

Materials

Copies of *Nine Stories*.

Procedure

1. This is one of Salinger's finest stories; it has been included in short story anthologies. It obviously has biographical parallels: Salinger also was stationed in Tiverton, Devonshire, in 1944, training with counter-intelligence; he, too, listened to choir practice at a Methodist church in Tiverton; and later, he saw the bloddy battles of World War II. Even the reference to his roommate Clay shooting a cat may relate to Salinger's dramatic meeting with Ernest Hemingway, who shot off the head of a chicken with a Luger.

2. During these two days, the class should give careful consideration to this story as it is read aloud, analyzed, and related to earlier stories. The title has three parts: (1) a dedication to a girl with an unusual name, suggesting another precocious child; (2) a concern with love; and (3) a concern with squalor. Ask students to define "squalor." The title also suggests that the story may have a structure like "A Perfect Day for Bananafish." Suggestions for in-class discussion: Wny doesn't the narrator have a name other than X? What is the function of Esme's vocabulary? (Ask students to deal with various words, e.g., "gregarious," "compassionate," "an extremely gifted genius," and "prolific." Ask information questions: What do the German and French words mean? Who were Goebbels and Dostoevski? What is the function of Charles? How does this story relate to earlier writings: structure ("Bananafish"), war-worn characters (Seymour) and a wife/mother-in-law ("Bananafish"), interaction of child and adult ("Uncle Wiggily"), first person flashback, symbols, riddles, and koans (Charles's question about walls), the problems of pseudo-sophistication (*Catcher*)?

3. Since Day 33 begins a more serious discussion of Zen Buddhism, you may wish to refer to a critic's analysis of Zen in this story. See pages 98–101 in James Lundquist's *J. D. Salinger*.

DAYS 33–34: SALINGER AND ZEN BUDDHISM

Goals

1. To teach or review basic tenets of Zen Buddhism that provide a background to all of Salinger's writing.
2. To suggest that Zen is basic in understanding "Teddy"—which, in turn, should be valuable for writing Paper III.

Materials

1. Handout 11: J. D. Salinger, "Teddy," and Zen Buddhism.
2. Resource persons or films. On Day 34, the Zen instruction can be reinforced by inviting resource persons to class or by showing films. Suggested films: *The Mood of Zen,* Hartley Productions, 1968, (14 min., color); *The Long Search 9: The Land of the Disappearing Buddha,* BBC TV: Time-Life Film, 1978, (52 min., color). You may also wish to build a Zen class library.

Procedure

1. By now the students have read the story and should be aware that Teddy's precocity includes a knowledge of Oriental religion, since he refers to Brahma. Many will be puzzled by this story, especially its ending. Day 33 will be spent trying to clarify some basic tenets and background about Zen.
2. After giving each student a copy of Handout 11, remind them that Salinger became interested in Zen Buddhism in the mid-1940s. With his Catholic-Jewish background, as well as the trauma of world war, he appears to have been seeking a way of life that allowed him to deal with the world that Seymour could not handle. Some critics even note that Holden Caulfield's story begins when he is sixteen years old, the age when the Buddha (Gautama) began to confront the facts of adulthood in North India in the sixth century B.C. Both Holden and Gautama find themselves compelled to set out on a journey.
3. In 1953, the year of "Teddy," Salinger met his wife-to-be Claire Douglas at a

Vermont party. She later told her parents that Salinger lived with his mother, sister, fifteen Buddhist monks, and a yogi who stood on his head—a fanciful tale that dates to the author's earlier days in Greenwich Village when he was giving reading lists about Zen to his dates.

4. Stress the following background concerns:

   a. Western religion is especially interested in words, symbols, and notations, which provide social communication and rules to explain the world. Zen, by contrast, moves away from scripture and dependence on written words to a direct "pointing" to the human mind in order to see into one's true nature and thus attain Buddhahood. It relies heavily on thinking, meditation, contemplation. Zen is not a religion; it is a way of liberation.

   b. How do we know the universe? Zen says we already know it; we are what we are doing now. Children are especially enlightened because they are so natural (note Salinger's interest in children), but their special qualities are eliminated by conventional education.

   c. Thus, it is a mistake to try to understand life by analyzing its facts and events; this only leads to misery and confusion. The goal is spontaneity.

   d. The student thus begins with the assumption that *satori* is within oneself, not outside. The process of Zen begins with the master asking riddles, or *koans,* to the student, such as "What is the sound of one hand clapping?" or "What was your original face?" We must resist trying to answer these questions with our Western minds; when a student tries to use philosophy or wordy answers, the master reprimands him. With increased use of koans, the student feels stupid; he knows nothing—and thus is liberated. The total Zen art includes koans, tea ceremonies, rock garden, archery, calligraphy painting, Haiku paintings—all forms of meditation, a search for silence.

   e. Salinger's fiction reveals lonely, often highly intellectual people and spontaneous children being corrupted by Western sophistication. "Teddy" is a

final comment on the introductory koan. He and Seymour see the absurdity of the Western world, of logic. Unlike Sergeant X, who seems to be saved by the yount girl Esme, Teddy is ready to leave the squalor for good.

   f. Ask students if they see any of these Zen ideas in the first six stories. You may wish to use pp. 69–114, "Zen Art and *Nine Stories,*" in James Lundquist's *J. D. Salinger.*

5. You also may wish to use the rest of the period to let students examine various library books on Zen Buddhism, such as Alan W. Watts's *The Way of Zen.*

6. Day 34 should reinforce this discussion. Resource persons can provide expertise and interaction. These persons can be drawn from the community, the social studies department, professors of religion in nearby colleges or universities. The seminar may wish to contact resource persons through a leased phone service, an inexpensive way of having a speaker from outside the community. The suggested films also are valuable resources.

DAYS 35–38: PREPARING FOR AND PARTICIPATING IN DEFENSE DAY AND FOLLOW-UP

Goals

1. To suggest topics for Paper III.
2. To conduct two Defense Day discussions and follow-up that offer students an opportunity to express and defend their positions.

Materials

1. Handout 12: Suggestions for Paper III.
2. Handout 13: Student Model for Paper III.
3. Copies of papers on *The Catcher in the Rye* for Defense Days.
4. Corrected papers on *The Catcher in the Rye* to be returned on Day 37.

Procedure

1. On Day 35, use Handout 12 to suggest positions for Paper III. You also may wish

to introduce Handout 13 as a model—or simply post it on the bulletin board. Or you may prefer to use it on follow-up day.

2. On Days 35 and 36, hand out the four position papers that you have chosen for Defense Days. Begin Day 35 by reviewing Defense Day procedures, although the seminar should now be familiar with the system. Be sure to return all position papers at the end of Day 37.

3. During the follow-up discussion (Day 38), you might ask other students to read their papers for class comment, discuss the student model (Handout 13), or present the viewpoint of a critic, e.g., any of the thirty-nine essays in *If You Really Want to Know: A Catcher Casebook,* edited by Malcolm M. Marsden; "Raise High the Barriers, Censors" by Edward P. J. Corbett in *J. D. Salinger and the Critics,* edited by William F. Belcher and James W. Lee, pp. 54–59.

DAYS 39–40: REVIEW AND PRACTICING SKILLS FOR PAPER III: TRANSITIONS AND SENTENCE VARIETY

Goals

1. To review the writing skills of transitions and sentence variety.
2. To practice and encourage these skills in preparation for Paper III.

Materials

1. A writing sample, such as a copy of an earlier position paper or a student model paper.
2. A book on sentence combining, such as William Strong's *Sentence Combining: A Composing Book.* New York: Random House, 1973.

Procedure

1. Begin by examining a writing sample, such as a student model, preferably with a copy for each student. Describe how a paper has unity and smoothness in reading if the lines and paragraphs relate. Ask students to circle or underline words or lines or phrases that provide transitions between sentences and paragraphs. Ask them to check their previous two position papers and identify such transitions.

2. Work on sentence combining to encourage students to become more aware of sentence variety. First check the writing sample papers to see what variety exists. How many begin with subject-verb or the same words? How many are just simple sentences? Check for length. Check to see if any can be combined.

3. Try a sentence combining experiment. For example, ask students to study William Strong's "explorations" and then make their own "transforms." See Strong, pp. 157–205.

4. Note: Some teachers may wish to extend this skill review and instruction to more than one class period.

DAYS 41–44: COMPLETING PAPER III AND READING "PRETTY MOUTH AND GREEN MY EYES"

Goals

1. To complete the writing and proofreading of Paper III.
2. To give brief review and instruction with *Roget's Thesaurus.*
3. To read "Pretty Mouth and Green My Eyes" (1951) and relate it to previous Salinger material.

Materials

1. Class copies of *Nine Stories.*
2. A teacher copy or class copies of *Roget's Thesaurus.*

Procedure

1. Days 41–43 should be used for writing and proofreading. Paper III is due Day 45. Remind students that the skills of transitions and sentence variety are important in this paper.

2. During one of the writing days, remind students that variety includes word choice. Ask students if they own a copy of *Roget's Thesaurus,* preferably in dictionary form. You may wish to have students buy a copy

for the seminar. Instruct them on its uses. For example, take an overused word like "interesting" and refer to *Roget's* alternatives. Ask students to name other overused words and then find synonyms.

3. During Day 44, read aloud and discuss "Pretty Mouth and Green My Eyes." This 14 July 1951 *The New Yorker* story seems like a departure from the other eight stories since it deals with just adults. Its use of the telephone reminds us of earlier works, such as *Catcher*, and provides a link to *Franny and Zooey*. While the plot is about a marriage triangle, there also is a familar story of unhappy people trapped in suburbia. Critic James Lundquist sees it as a contrast to "For Esme—with Love and Squalor" because the characters find no Zen transcendence as did Sergeant X; they are the dark side of Charles's koan because they are trapped by their individual walls and will never meet at the corner.

HANDOUT 11
J. D. SALINGER, "TEDDY," AND ZEN BUDDHISM*

I. Background: Mahayana Buddhism entered China during the first two centuries A.D. Then it blended with native Chinese Taoism (a religion of simple spontaneity and natural mysticism) and was forged into a unique form of Buddhism known now by its Japanese name, Zen.

II. Basis: Zen says "Let go." Stop trying to grasp the ungraspable and instead just look—and see the amazing unfolding of the present moment where everything is every instant new. Forget worthy purposes and future goals. Realize the now (below are the key ideas of Zen which influenced Salinger, who read Professor Daisetz Suzuki's [of Columbia] interpretations of Zen for the West):

　　1. "The basic idea of Zen is to come in touch with the inner workings of our being, and to do this in the most direct way possible, without resorting to anything external or superadded."

　　2. "Zen is the ultimate fact of all philosophy and religion . . . Therefore Zen is not necessarily the fountain of Buddhist thought or life alone; it is very much alive also in Christianity, Muhammedanism, in Taoism, and even in . . . Confucianism . . . Zen is what makes the religious feeling run through its legitimate channel and what gives life to the intellect."

III. Practice: Zen is practiced in two ways, by meditation and by sharp question and answer exchange between master and pupil. Dr. Suzuki's Western interpretations advised people to disentangle themselves from the ways of conventional thought and stop trying to justify themselves. Live life as it comes along. To many Americans it was a protest against plastic America.

IV. Key Terms

　　1. "A special transmission outside the Scriptures": Zen is self-reliant and has no patience with one spiritual authority. Let nothing come between you and direct experience.

　　2. "No dependence on words and letters": One must look after oneself. Zen has a lack of dogma and ritual. "What is Zen?" "A bag of rice." Existence.

　　3. "Direct pointing to the mind of man; seeing into one's own nature." Actual experience, first-hand, concrete knowing.

　　4. "Satori": Enlightenment, the moment of waking up to the world as it is in itself where subject-object vanishes, a new birth, the barriers and weight of mental processes—judgments on the state of the world and neighbors, friends, fears—all fall away.

　　5. "The Koan": A question that must be answered but has no logical answer. The master's effort to draw the student's attention to the present moment and to his no-mind.

---

*This material is adapted from *The Way of Zen* (New York: Pantheon, 1957) by Alan W. Watts, and *The Fiction of J. D. Salinger* (University of Pittsburgh Press, 1967) by Frederick L. Gwynn and Joseph L. Blotner, pp. 42–45.

HANDOUT 12
SUGGESTIONS FOR PAPER III: "TEDDY" (1953)

1. Why does Salinger seem to be so fascinated with precocious children?
2. Is the title more than just a character's name? Develop the title as a theme.
3. Take a key quotation, such as the one about the arm symbol, and develop it into a position.
4. Compare Holden of *The Catcher in the Rye* with Teddy.
5. Just what is Teddy's religion all about?
6. Examine the idea of education as discussed in this story. See *Nine Stories*, p. 195.
7. Is this story about death?
8. Compare Teddy and Nicholson.
9. What is the meaning of orange peels, both literally and figuratively?
10. Compare Seymour of "A Perfect Day for Bananafish" with Teddy.
11. Colors. What is the meaning of color in this story—and others that we have read?
12. What does the word "mystic" mean? How could this be a position about "Teddy"?
13. Does some aspect of Zen apply to this story?
14. Just what is the meaning of the ending? Reread it carefully.
15. What does Teddy say about our world today—not just the world around 1953?
16. Is this story about the American family, parents and children?

HANDOUT 13
STUDENT MODEL FOR PAPER III

LOGIC, EMOTION, OR DEATH

by Janice Weiner

At the end of the story, it was Teddy who died. The entire plot led up
to it. From the very beginning, references were made to death, emotionalism,
logic, and conventionalism. The latter three were what drove Teddy to his
death--he found it difficult to meditate and lead a spiritual life in an
American society that not only frowned upon what he believed, but practiced
everything contrary to his beliefs.

Teddy did not believe that there was any use for emotion. When asked
if he had any emotions, he replied, "If I do, I don't remember when I ever
used them. I don't see what they're good for." To him, emotions were a
waste of time and energy. And several times in the story, this "theory" of
his was proven. The first example was at the beginning, when Mr. McArdle
was yelling at Teddy to get down off his Gladstone. Teddy was using it as
a booster so that he could see out of the porthole. All of Mr. McArdle's
yelling and carrying on was really of no avail. Teddy just stayed there,
unperturbed, making observations about orange peels floating on the water,
until he was good and ready to step down. His father's emotional display
proved absolutely nothing. In fact, Teddy might have been inclined to get
off the suitcase sooner had has father not pushed the issue.

Teddy's first encounter with Booper was another case in which his belief
was justified. When Teddy finally managed to locate her, everything she said
or did displayed a negative attitude. "What's she want to see me for? I

1

2

don't want to see <u>her</u>" and "I hate you! I hate everybody in this ocean" are
examples of her hostile attitude. It did not do her any good, though. She
eventually did what Teddy asked, and all her ranting and raving was in vain.

Poetry also bothered Teddy because of the emotionalism involved. The
first indication of this was in one of his journal entries, where he expressed
a distaste for "conventional" poetry. The second was during his conversation
with Nicholson, in answer to Nicholson's query of "Aren't emotions what poets
are primarily concerned with?" His answer was, "Nothing in the voice of the
cicada intimates how soon it will die. Along this road goes no one, this
autumn eve." Two Japanese poems--poetry without a lot of emotionalism.

The second thing about society that did not mesh with Teddy's outlook
on life was logic. He was interested in making spiritual advancements, and
logic proved to be a hindrance. With logic, everything had a designated size
and shape--a given name. Without it, he could get out of the finite dimen-
sions--lose consciousness, and reobtain knowledge that he had retained un-
consciously for eons, and return it to the form of conscious knowledge. When
Teddy was attempting to assist Nicholson in getting out of the finite dimensions, he asked Nicholson what his arm was. Nicholson replied that it was
an arm--that the name was given to distinguish it from other objects. To
that, Teddy replied,

> You're just giving me a regular, intelligent answer. I was
> trying to help you. You asked me how I get out of the finite
> dimensions when I feel like it. I certainly don't use logic
> when I do it. Logic's the first thing you have to get rid of.

There it is--plain and clear. The second part of the American society
that Teddy could not abide was logic. The third was an offshoot of the second,
yet a very important one in itself. It had to do with conventions. This was
also brought up in Salinger's "A Perfect Day for Bananafish," with the conformities that everyone made: Sybil, wearing two pieces of a bathing suit,

3

of which she obviously only needed one, for example. But the one in that
story which really ties into "Teddy" was when Seymour called Sybil's bathing
suit blue, when by society's standards it was yellow. Teddy brought up
almost the exact idea when he told Nicholson what he would do to change the
educational system.

> The same thing with grass, and other things. I wouldn't even
> tell them (children) grass is green. Colors are only names.
> I mean if you tell them the grass is green, it makes them start
> expecting the grass to look a certain way--your way--instead of
> some other way that may be just as good, and maybe better. . . .

Teddy stated it much better than I could have. He believed that a person
needs to get to know himself through meditation and contemplation before any
of society's conformities are forced upon him. Then, being content in the
knowledge of himself, the individual would be free to choose whether or not
he wanted to accept what society had to offer.

Teddy obviously was not overwhelmed with society's offerings. His very
appearance offered proof of that. He wore seersucker shorts that were too
large for him, a T-shirt with a hole in the shoulder, and quite dirty,
ankle-high tennis shoes. That is not what someone wears who is overly
conscious of what people will think of his appearance. He also was in need
of a haircut. This was mentioned several times in the course of the story:
first, in his description, then by his father, and finally by a woman whom
he passed in the corridor. However, Teddy never seemed to pay much attention.
It was just another one of society's bothersome conventions.

Death was also referred to several times before the end. These references helped to piece together the puzzle of why it was Teddy who died at
the end of the story. His second journal entry had what could have been a
foreshadowing of his own death. It contained two sentences which were
seemingly incongruous with the rest of his entry. They read: "It will
either happen today or February 14, 1958 when I am sixteen. It is ridiculous

4

to mention even." This entry was written not long after his morning meditation. It could be that Teddy had foreseen two times that his death could
occur. The possibility of that was strengthened when Teddy was talking to
Nicholson, and Nicholson brought up the subject of Teddy predicting when some
of the professors in the Leidekker experiment group would die. Teddy denied
having told the professors when they would die but said that he could have.
He just felt that no matter how spiritually advanced the professors believed
themselves to be, they would still be emotional when it came to the question
of death--especially their own. Teddy, of course, would not be bothered
since he believed that when one dies one simply is rid of the restrictions
of the body.

Near the end of the story, Teddy made a remark which may also have had
to do with foreseeing his death.

> For example, I have a swimming lesson in about five minutes.
> I could go downstairs to the pool, and there might not be any
> water in it. This might be the day they change the water or
> something. What might happen, though, I might walk up to the
> edge of it, just to have a look at the bottom, for instance,
> and my sister might come up and sort of push me in. I could
> fracture my skull and die instantaneously. . . . My sister's
> only six, and she hasn't been a human being for very many
> lives, and she doesn't like me very much. That could happen,
> all right. . . .

Finally, in the last couple of paragraphs of the story, Nicholson made
his way toward the pool, where Teddy and his sister already were, supposedly
taking a swimming lesson, when he heard "an all-piercing, sustained scream--
clearly coming from a small, female child." Booper had pushed Teddy into the
emptied pool. He, of course, would not scream or show any emotion at such a
time, but she would. And therefore the scream was her reaction to his fall
and his death. I do not know if he was spiritually advanced enough to have
then permanently escaped the world, but he at least escaped American society,
which was what he aimed to do throughout the story.

5

Instructor's Comments

1. Strengths: The first line is a "grabber." It does what an introduction

    must do--creates interest, sets up the rest of the introduction and the

    logical development of the paper. The writer has also worked on another

    skill, that of concrete support, especially direct quotations. Finally,

    the paper relates the book to American society as well as to further

    discussions of Zen.

2. Weaknesses: Introductions also need titles and author's names. The

    problem of "I" appears in this paper, which should trigger a discussion

    of how the first person can put too much focus on the writer and detract

    from the position. The paper also suggests the problem of nonsexist

    language, of when to avoid "he" when referring to either sex.

PAPER IV: *FRANNY AND ZOOEY*
DAYS 45–59

DAY 45: BEGINNING TO READ *FRANNY AND ZOOEY*

Goals

1. To orient students to *Franny and Zooey* (1961).
2. To provide in-class time to begin the novel.

Materials

Class copies of *Franny and Zooey*.

Assignment

1. Ask students to note the DUE date for the fourth paper on the Schedule, Day 60.
2. Remind students that the Defense Days for Paper III ("Teddy") will be Days 51 and 52. Copies of the papers chosen for defense will be handed out on Days 50 and 51.

Procedure

1. Allow students the first five to ten minutes to make a final proofreading of Paper III. Then collect. Be sure to make four copies for the Defense Days.
2. Ask students to review The Salinger Chronology (Handout 3), noting that the next book for consideration is actually a combining of two *The New Yorker* stories, "Franny" in the 29 January 1955 issue and "Zooey" in the 4 May 1957 issue. This combination caused mixed critical reviews, some critics feeling the two make a unified novel and some, like John Updike, feeling that the stories are quite different and don't form a whole.
3. As students examine the class copies, they should note how long each of the two sections are for magazine readers, especially "Zooey." Ask them to note Salinger's quasi-dedication to William Shawn, editor of *The New Yorker,* and to comment on Salinger's language and humor (e.g., "a cool lima bean ") and son Matthew, who is one year old in 1961.
4. The year of "Franny" was the year of Salinger's marriage to Claire Douglas, an English-born Radcliffe student, and the story was Salinger's wedding present to his bride. Claire, who had been previously married to a graduate of the Harvard Business School, was extraordinarily pretty; indeed, her looks, mannerism, and even her blue suitcase became part of the story's central figure, Franny Glass. The Salinger's daughter Margaret Ann was also born in 1955.
5. An amusing sidelight to "Franny": When the story first appeared, many readers thought that Franny's problem was that she was pregnant!
6. "Zooey"—which came two years later—reminds us that Franny's last name is Glass (not mentioned in "Franny"), which, in turn, reminds us of the entire Glass family—many of whom we have already met. On Day 48, we will pursue the Glass family—and Zen—even further.
7. Ask students to begin reading the novel during the remainder of the period.

DAYS 46–48: READING AND REVIEWING THE GLASS FAMILY AND ZEN BUDDHISM

Goals

1. To provide in-class time for reading the novel.
2. To relate the novel to previous material about the Glass family and Zen Buddhism.

Materials

1. Handout 5: The Glass Family.
2. Handout 11: J. D. Salinger, "Teddy," and Zen Buddhism.

Procedure

1. Days 46 and 47 should give students enough in-class reading time to complete "Franny" and to begin "Zooey." Most students understand "Franny" and enjoy reading it, but "Zooey" is more challenging. "Zooey" shifts to first person with Buddy as narrator for fourteen pages and then seemingly back to third person. "Zooey" includes three scenes (the family bathroom, the living room, the parents' bedroom), Salinger's now familiar use of letters, quotations, telephones, italicized words, and religious or Zen images, *plus footnotes*.
2. Using Handout 5, review the entire Glass family.
   a. We met Seymour, the head guru of the other six brothers and sisters, in "A Perfect Day for Bananafish" (1948).
   b. We now meet Buddy narrating the "Zooey" section, and we will see more of him in *Raise High the Roof Beam, Carpenters* (1963), which appeared first in 1955 in *The New Yorker* about eight months after "Franny."
   c. Boo Boo first appeared in "Down at the Dinghy" in a 1949 issue of *Harper's*.
   d. While we meet Waker in a "Zooey" footnote, we have learned about Walt in "Uncle Wiggily in Connecticut" (1948)— he had been Eloise's former boyfriend. We will read more of Walt in *Raise High the Roof Beam, Carpenters*.
   e. Franny and Zooey, of course, become vivid to the students now.
3. Thus it would seem that the Glass children are bright and disturbed characters. Once masters of information for a radio quiz show, they love each other but are unhappy —as was Holden Caulfield. The writer of the family, Buddy, was born in the same year as J. D. Salinger. Seymour, Franny, and Zooey are especially interested in discovering their inner beings; Waker had been a Catholic priest.

4. Then, using Handout 11, review Zen Buddhism, which we have studied in connection with "Teddy"—and referred to in connection with "Bananafish," "The Laughing Man," "For Esme—with Love and Squalor," and *The Catcher in the Rye*.
5. While you do not want to belabor the Zen element in Salinger's writing or to analyze *Franny and Zooey*, students should be encouraged to see Franny's squalor in terms of her trying to use a Western culture approach to solving her problems, especially with her obsession with the Jesus Prayer. (Note: Claire Salinger was also obsessed with this prayer.) Her misery is much like a Zen student trying to make sense out of a koan. Zooey can be seen as a Zen master with Franny on the road to enlightenment, struggling with her ego and the phonies of the world. Encourage students to study the pages about Seymour's Fat Lady. Is this a Christian or a Zen idea?

DAYS 49–53: PREPARING FOR AND PARTICIPATING IN DEFENSE DAY AND THE FOLLOW-UP DISCUSSION

Goals

1. To provide additional in-class time for reading *Franny and Zooey*.
2. To suggest topics for Paper IV.
3. To conduct Defense Days and follow-up discussion that offers students additional opportunity to express their positions about "Teddy."

Materials

1. Handout 14: Suggestions for Paper IV.
2. Handout 15: Student Model for Paper IV.
3. Copies of papers that you have chosen for Defense Days.
4. Correct papers on "Teddy" to return at the end of Day 52.

Procedure

1. On Day 49 suggest positions for Paper IV, using Handout 14 as a point of departure. You may also wish to introduce the Student Model for all students to examine or simply

post it on the bulletin board. Handout 15 can also be used on follow-up day, Day 53.

2. On Day 50 hand out the first two position papers for Defense Day 51. Remind the seminar that on Day 51 they will receive the final two papers and on Day 52 the remaining corrected papers will be returned.

3. Days 49 and 50 can also be used for reading or prewriting.

4. Days 51 and 52 are the Defense Days.

5. During the follow-up discussion (Day 53), you might ask other students to read their papers for class comment, discuss the student paper (Handout 12), or present the viewpoint of a critic, e.g., "Teddy" in *The Fiction of J. D. Salinger* by Frederick L. Gwynn and Joseph L. Blotner, pp. 40-42; or pp. 106-109 in *J. D. Salinger* by James Lundquist.

DAYS 54-56: DISCUSSING WRITING AND READING A FINAL STORY FROM *NINE STORIES*

Goals

1. To discuss various writing concerns of students.

2. To read aloud and discuss "De Daumier-Smith's Blue Period" (1953).

Materials

Copies of *Nine Stories.*

Procedure

1. Day 54 should be an open period for discussing writing. At this point, students should be encouraged to discuss any of their concerns about writing that they have met in this seminar. The Student Model for Paper III, for example, raises the problem of using "I" in a paper. Other suggestions:
   a. Clever titles which are not discussed in the paper.
   b. The function of special punctuation: semicolons, colons, elipses, dashes.
   c. The use of *etc.*
   d. Beginning a paper with a standard dictionary definition.
   e. Beginning a sentence with *But* or *And.*
   f. Use of student slang in a formal paper.

   g. Proofreading techniques.
   h. Building a natural lead-in to a direct quotation.

2. On Days 55-56, the students should read aloud and discuss "De Daumier-Smith's Blue Period." Again, employ the method of dividing the story into sections: begin by discussing the connotations and denotations of the title; then stop after each section and discuss content and style; finally, relate the story to what has already been read and suggest positions for papers.

3. This story, which first appeared in the *Nine Stories* in 1953, will take two class periods to discuss because it is long and fairly complex. The title suggests a new Salinger slant: art. Honore Daumier (1808-79), of course, was a famous French satirical cartoonist and painter; but Salinger has given the name a plebian addition of Smith and then alluded to the modern Pablo Picasso, who also had his Blue Period in painting. Or is "blue period" more squalor? The story has a special craziness with its Canadian setting, Japanese art school proprietor, the narrator's pupil—Sister Irma, the wild-improbable names, and the obvious sexual and religious overtones. Critic James Lundquist finds this story to be the most vivid Zen experience of any Salinger creation. The confused narrator discovers awareness and happiness, drops his phony image and goes home, when he makes his own koan ("Everybody is a nun."). He has reached the "letting go" of Zen, much like Teddy did, but he finds it while observing a girl in a display window putting a new truss on a dummy. Again, mystical experience triumphs.

DAYS 57-59: COMPLETING PAPER IV

Goal

To give students in-class time for writing and proofreading.

Procedure

1. The final three days should be spent with writing and final proofreading.

2. Remind students that Paper IV is due on Day 60.

HANDOUT 14
SUGGESTIONS FOR PAPER IV: *FRANNY AND ZOOEY* (1961)

1. What is really wrong with Franny—and the world?

2. Are the "Franny" and "Zooey" sections unified? Do they fit together as a single "novel"?

3. Compare Franny and Lane with Holden and Sally.

4. The Glass family. Examine the family names, as well as the individual names.

5. Compare the chicken sandwich symbol of "Just before the War with the Eskimos" with Franny.

6. Why are the Glass children created as former radio quiz kids with such high intelligence?

7. Why does Zooey taunt and yet love Bessie? What is her meaning in the book?

8. What is the meaning of Franny reading in the ladies' room and Zooey reading in the bathroom?

9. What is the meaning of the Fat Lady?

10. Compare Zooey on the phone with Franny with Esme and the soldier.

11. Examine the pages in "Zooey" where the reader is confronted with three pages of quotations. Why did Salinger do this?

12. What does Buddy mean when he says his story is a "compound or multiple love story"? Is this also *Franny and Zooey?*

13. Discuss the structure of the book. Is the first person introduction by Buddy Glass necessary? Is his endless letter necessary?

14. One critic said the book is a self-help book—a Power of Positive Thinking book for the upper middle class in America. Is it?

15. John Updike, another famous American writer, said that the Franny of "Franny" and the Franny of "Zooey" are not the same girl. Do you agree?

16. Is this another Zen book about our world which is a place where we must learn to feel, not just think?

17. Do you agree with the critic who said that no matter how inspirational, Salinger persists in his low opinion of mankind in this book?

18. Many critics called this a bad book. What one major fault can be found with it?

HANDOUT 15
STUDENT MODEL FOR PAPER IV

THE QUEST

by Paul Milkman

Franny and Zooey, by J. D. Salinger, is the story of a quest. This story is the epitome of the relationship between a Zen teacher and his student, in which the student is looking for relief from normal life and finds the answer with the help of the teacher. Franny Glass, who needs the satisfaction of truth and beauty, is the student; her brother Zooey is the Zen master. Together, she reaches the final stage of Zen learning.

The story begins with an episode at a college. Lane Coutell, Franny's boyfriend, meets her at the train station. She is obviously disturbed and on the edge of a nervous breakdown. She complains about the lack of beauty in the poetry and drama at her college. She spends a great deal of time telling Lane about a book, one that has noticeable Zen overtones. Then she faints, and "Franny" ends. "Zooey" begins with Zooey in the bathtub and proceeds to dump an awful lot of family history on the reader without much action. The crux of "Zooey," however, is the telephone conversation between Franny and Zooey. Through a long, hard explanation, Zooey teaches Franny to see what is beautiful. The story ends. What does it mean?

First, we must examine what Zen means. Zen is an escape from the rational and an acceptance of creation and beauty. This story centers on beauty. A Zenist is taught by a master that everything that exists has beauty and must be accepted despite any faults it might appear to have. A Zenist is taught by a master to attach his mind to the "whole" to reach

1

2

total satisfaction. This "whole" is eventually described by Zooey as the "fat lady."

Franny and Zooey are Zenists and, as such, take specific roles in the Zen world. Franny is the student; Zooey is the master. A good example of this relationship occurs during the telephone conversation. A Zen teacher must punish or paddle the student for not learning. Zooey does this:

> ". . . I've seen a couple of real breakdowns, and the people
> who had them didn't bother to pick the time and the place
> they--"
> "Just stop it Zooey! Just stop it," Franny said, sobbing.

But Zooey doesn't stop; he goes right on paddling. In fact, he punishes her to tears for two more pages. He says that there are breakdowns now and then, but he objects to her taking the logical form of breakdown. Instead of breaking down thoughtless, she was semi-rational about it. For a Zenist, this won't do.

Knowing the central characters' Zen roles, we can see how the book is also structured. "Franny" has a rising or building action. At first Franny needs advice; she is unable to see beauty--and will need more than one Zen lesson. She has a need for satisfaction. Thus "Franny" is the definition of the problem and the beginning of Franny's quest. In "Zooey," the bathroom scene establishes Zooey as Franny's savior because he seems to understand beauty. He says: "To me everything is beautiful." Zooey understands happiness and Zen completeness. And thus the long conversation between Franny and Zooey in the second story is the end of Franny's quest. The subsequent joy that she achieves with the final dial tone shows her success. It is clear that she has found what she desires:

> For some minutes, before she fell into a deep, dreamless
> sleep, she just lay quiet, smiling at the ceiling.

"Zooey" is the end of the quest and the establishment of a new self for Franny.

3

The total story or novel is one that has its roots in Zen, and it broadcasts its foundations throughout the two parts. The main characters symbolize the Zen master and student. This allows us to see Franny Glass searching for beauty. Clearly, we can see that J. D. Salinger has combined these two <u>New Yorker</u> stories into a whole, the story of a search and the fulfillment, the story of a quest.

Instructor's Comments

1. <u>Strengths</u>: The writer concentrates on a key position in understanding Salinger's development, the influence of Zen. And he narrows the focus to a concern that relates to both theme and structure, to why these two stories were combined. In a few pages, he clarifies his own question: "What does it mean?"

2. <u>Weaknesses</u>: There seems to be a certain vagueness with both plot and structure. For example, the second paragraph could clarify the particular scenes at the railroad station, the restaurant, the New York apartment. References should be made to the Jesus prayer (the Ohm chant?). The "fat lady" deserves more explanation in context of Zen. Even the use of the telephone within an apartment deserves comment. In short, the paper is too short.

PAPER V: A PROFILE OF J. D. SALINGER DAYS 60–69

DAY 60: REVIEWING THE SALINGER BIOGRAPHY AND INTRODUCING THE PROFILE PAPER

Goals

1. To review the Salinger biography, especially the critical stages.
2. To orient students to Paper V, a profile of J. D. Salinger.

Materials

1. Assemble a class library of biographical and autobiographical materials (see Bibliography).
2. Handout 16: J. D. Salinger: Critical Stages.
3. Handout 17: Suggestions for Paper V.
4. Handout 18: Student Model for Paper V.

Assignment

1. Ask students to note the DUE date for Paper V on the Schedule, Day 70.
2. Paper V should be based on reviewing the Salinger fiction and reading biography and autobiography. A bibliography and footnotes are required as the basic skill of this paper.

Procedure

1. Allow the first five to ten minutes for proofreading Paper IV on *Raise High the Roof Beam, Carpenters.* Then collect the papers, noting that the next Defense Days are Days 65 and 66. Be sure to select the next four papers as soon as possible and begin to correct the others.
2. Using The Salinger Chronology (Handout 3) or the Appendix, Life and Times of J. D. Salinger, and Handout 16, review the life of the author. Handout 16 stresses five critical stages or divisions in Salinger's life and writing career.
3. In explaining the assignment, remind students that they may have to lean heavily on the fictional writings of Salinger previously read in class since the biographical and autobiographical material is so sparse. You should review the major sources of information about Salinger's life:
   a. Magazine articles: *Time* (15 September 1961); *Life* (3 November 1961); *People* (25 February 1980); *Newsweek* (30 May 1960; 18 November 1974; 30 July 1979); *Harper's* (February 1959).
   b. Collage biographies: chapter 1, "The American Brainscape and The Disappearing Man" in James Lundquist's *J. D. Salinger;* chapter 1, "The Invisible Man: A Biographical Collage" in *Salinger* edited by Henry Grunwald; "John Skow and The Editors of *Time,*" pp. 1–7 in *J. D. Salinger and the Critics,* edited by William Belcher and James Lee.
   c. Difficult-to-find newspaper articles: high school student, Shirlie Blaney's 1953 interview; the 3 November 1974 *New York Times* article on the Salinger lawsuit against unauthorized publication of early stories in a collected edition; *New York Times* and Des Moines *Register* (2 December 1979) articles by Michael Clarkson, who forced two late 1970s interviews.
4. You may wish to circulate these materials, as well as the West High School interview with Clarkson (see Appendix).
5. You may wish to hold off Handout 17 (Suggestions for Paper V: Profile) until Day 61 so that students can complete

discussion of their initial reactions to Salinger's fiction and his avoidance of interviewers and the public. You may wish to discuss the Shirlie Blaney interview (see Appendix anecdote).

6. Handout 18 (Student Model for Paper V) may be discussed at any time during this section—for references to documentation on Day 63 or for the follow-up of Defense Days.

7. One final note: Remind students that Holden asked Sally to flee New York and to go to New England to escape. (See *Catcher,* Bantam edition, p. 132.) According to an army friend from World War II, David Wright of Rockville, Maryland, Salinger said in 1945: "Davey, ol' buddy, this is to say goodbye. I plan to get a cabin somewhere in New England and pursue my writing. I don't want a telephone and I don't want anybody to bother me. . . . Just forget you ever met me, ol' buddy, because we will never meet again" (Des Moines *Register,* 4 January 1979).

DAYS 61–63: READING AND RESEARCH; REVIEWING DOCUMENTATION SKILLS

Goals

1. To provide in-class time for students to study Salinger materials.
2. To review the skills of footnoting and bibliography.

Materials

1. Class library of Salinger materials.
2. Documentation materials, such as the school stylebook, chosen by the instructor. This could include Handout 18 (Student Model for Paper V).

Procedure

1. Days 61 and 62 should be used for reading and research. Encourage students to take notes, locate direct quotations with page numbers, and review the suggestion handout.

2. On Day 63 (or 61 or 62), review the basic requirements for documentation since Paper V requires weaving information and direct quotations from various sources. Encourage at least three different sources. Suggestions:

a. Begin with a discussion of plagiarism. Stress that plagiarism is often not intended but merely forgetting to cite sources. In previous papers where students have largely used one source, there had been no stress on documentation. Now there must be. Direct quotations must be footnoted; information not common knowledge but reworded should be footnoted. All materials consulted for this paper and, of course, footnoted must be identified in a bibliography.

b. Use a class stylebook or stylesheet with common footnote and bibliographical form. Use actual Salinger books or biographical materials for chalkboard examples. While instructors may differ on the location of footnotes, placing footnotes at the paper's end seems to assist students who have enough trouble with typing and does not detract from reading the text of the paper.

c. This also is a time for reviewing editing of quotations, the use of *Ibid.* and items that are repeated in the footnotes but not in sequence, the insertion of elipses (. . .) and (*sic*) for errors in the source itself, as well as the difference between parentheses and brackets.

d. You may even want to send the students to the chalkboard to practice—make a kind of game out of documentation.

e. While the Salinger material is scanty, it is possible that the *Reader's Guide* may include recent material. This may be a time to review the use of this valuable tool for researchers.

Additional Suggestion

Salinger's 1948 story in *Good Housekeeping,* "A Girl I Knew," seems very autobiographical and could be valuable for an in-class reading.

DAYS 64–67: PREPARING FOR AND PARTICIPATING IN DEFENSE DAY AND FOLLOW-UP

Goal

To help students refine their understanding of the Salinger materials.

Materials

1. Copies of the papers that you have chosen for the two Defense Days.
2. Corrected papers of *Franny and Zooey* to return at the end of Day 66.

Procedure

1. Use Day 64 for research and reading of Paper V and for study and annotation of the position papers for Defense Day 65.
2. Follow the Defense Day procedures outlined earlier. Be sure to give the class the second set of position papers on Day 65; return all papers at the end of Day 66.
3. Use the follow-up day to discuss the papers of other students, to evaluate the student model (Handout 15), or to consider a critic's point of view (for example, see pp. 121–129 in Belcher and Lee, *J. D. Salinger,* for critic Maxwell Geismar's observations).

DAYS 68–69: COMPLETING PAPER V

Goal

To give students in-class time to complete the writing and proofreading of Paper V.

Procedure

1. The final two days should be spent with in-class writing and proofreading.
2. Remind students that Paper V is due on Day 70.

HANDOUT 16
J. D. SALINGER: CRITICAL STAGES

I. Growing Up: Prewriting Period, 1919–1939
   A. Middle class New York family (Sol and Miriam Salinger): grandfather a rabbi, father a businessman; mother Scotch-Irish Catholic
   B. Formal Education
      1. Poor grades in elementary school and flunking out of private school
      2. Interest in drama, tropical fish
      3. 1934: Valley Forge Military Academy, a successful student, first attempts at writing, short stories
      4. Brief college career at New York University
      5. Unsuccessful attempt of father to interest Jerome in ham importing business, in Vienna, Austria
II. The Apprenticeship Period, 1940–1947
   A. Short story class at Columbia University; 1st publication
   B. Lived with parents 1940–1942, until drafted
   C. World War II experience in England, D-Day, Europe, 1942–1946
   D. Subject matter–themes
      1. Sympathetic characters influenced by war
      2. Four stories of lonely teenage girls
      3. Stories of destroyed artists, e.g., a novelist who ends up writing lyrics for pop songs
      4. Marriage in war-time
      5. The Caulfield Stories (6)—from Vincent Caulfield, Babe Gladwaller, and little sister Mattie to Holden ("I'm Crazy") and Phoebe
   E. Brief marriage to a French doctor (1946)
   F. Return to New York, Greenwich Village
III. The Classic or Major Works Period, 1948–1951
   A. Salinger's major successes: A world of psychically underprivileged persons occasionally saved by love
      1. Seymour Glass and "A Perfect Day for Bananafish" (1948)
      2. "Uncle Wiggily in Connecticut" (1948); "Just before the War with the Eskimos" (1948)
      3. "The Laughing Man" (1949); "Down at the Dinghy" (1949)
      4. "For Esme—with Love and Squalor" (1950); "Pretty Mouth and Green My Eyes" (1950)
      5. *The Catcher in the Rye* (1951)
   B. Interest in Zen Buddhism begins; moves outside of New York City
IV. Salinger and the Glass Family Spiritual Period, 1952–1965
   A. Two years of silence (1951–1952), then "De Daumier-Smith's Blue Period" (1953) and "Teddy" (1953)
   B. Zen Buddhism: meets wife Claire Douglas (hung up on Jesus Prayer), wedding present "Franny" (1955); *Raise High the Roof Beam, Carpenters* (1955); "Zooey" (1957); two children, 1955, 1960
   C. Combining stories (*Franny and Zooey*, 1961); *Raise High the Roof Beam, Carpenters* and *Seymour, an Introduction* (1963)
   D. Moves to Cornish, New Hampshire and seclusion; last short story published, 1965
V. Silence, 1966–
   A. Divorce, 1967
   B. Still writing but no publications; address still Cornish

HANDOUT 17
SUGGESTIONS FOR PAPER V: PROFILE

1. Check on Salinger's dedications with each book. A position?

2. J. D. Salinger was voted the most popular actor at Camp Wigwam at Harrison, Maine, in the summer of 1930. Is he an actor, playing roles?

3. What key autobiographical event may have shaped his life and writing?

4. Ambivalence. Salinger was both Jewish and Catholic. What burden might this give to his life and prose?

5. Why does Salinger refuse to allow his writings to be made into films?

6. Is Salinger a "romantic" who refuses to face the real world?

7. Was Salinger a victim of World War II?

8. Why does Salinger use his initials for his writing name? What is wrong with Jerome or Jerome David?

9. Salinger's life and work suggest the making of a satirist. What is the making of a satirist?

10. One critic called him a "successful failure." Position?

11. Authors and Houses. Find information about his residences, especially his present home.

12. What kind of father do you think he is/was?

13. Salinger writes about young people. Is he a self-appointed guru of the young?

14. Is Salinger a man seeking compensation for a low I.Q. score?

15. Why did he stop publishing? Did his writing change during his career? Did new themes appear that might explain his ceasing to publish?

16. Review the incident of Salinger and Shirlie Blaney. What did the story say about the writer?

17. What is Salinger's religion?

18. What does Salinger love? What does he hate?

19. Why is Salinger a "recluse in the Rye"? Why does he refuse interviews? Is his isolation symbolic, real, egotistical?

HANDOUT 18
STUDENT MODEL FOR PAPER V

THE SMART DUMMY

by John Corrigan

What is intelligence? For centuries man has been trying to devise a method of measuring this component in each one of us. In 1905, the I.Q. (Intelligence Quotient) was introduced in the United States to determine just how "smart" a person is. According to this standardized test, which became the foremost measurement of mental capacity, average intelligence hovers around 100 while high intelligence does not begin to appear until about 130. When J. D. Salinger was in elementary school, he scored 108 (Salinger Chronology). But he proved himself to be a very smart dummy, who would attack the system.

At first glance, his record in formal schooling might suggest that the test was accurate. An average elementary school student, he left public education for the McBurney School in Manhattan but then flunked out. His only diploma would come from the Valley Forge Military Academy; his work at Ursinus College and Columbia University produced no degrees. In 1942 he was drafted into the U.S. Army (Salinger Chronology).

However, during Salinger's stay in the army, he worked in Intelligence. He was trained and served as a security agent for the Counter-Intelligence of the 12th Infantry Regiment (Salinger Chronology). When he returned to the United States, he would launch a series of stories that dealt with intelligence and the problems of the educational system, if not the society itself.

1

2

For example, there is Holden Caulfield, the main character of Salinger's novel, <u>The Catcher in the Rye</u>. Holden, like Salinger, had trouble staying in school. Through Caulfield, Salinger attacked the "phonies," the so-called educated people who love to flaunt their sophistication. For instance, at one point in the book, Holden goes to a play with a girl named Sally. At the play, they meet an acquaintance of Sally's, a sophisticated, well-educated young man. Holden says,

> His name was George something--I don't even remember--and he went to Andover. Big, big deal. You should've seen him when old Sally asked him how he liked the play. . . . He said the play <u>itself</u> was no masterpiece, but that the Lunts, of course, were absolute angels. Angels. For Chrissake. <u>Angels</u>. That killed me. . . . It was the phoniest conversation you ever heard. (Salinger, 1972, p. 127)

Salinger is obviously criticizing the superficial methods of deciding just who can and cannot be considered intellectual.

Salinger also condemns the educational process in the story "Franny," the first half of the book <u>Franny and Zooey</u>. The central character Franny belongs to the Glass family, whose children are incredibly gifted people. But Franny is disappointed with herself as well as with everyone else involved in the college rat race of sophistication. She says, "It's just that if I'd had guts at all, I wouldn't have gone back to college at all this year. I don't know. I mean it's all the most incredible farce." Then she cuts down the system when she tells Lane Coutell, her boyfriend, that he is acting just like "a section man":

> . . . a section man's a person that takes over a class when the professor isn't there or is busy having a nervous breakdown or is at the dentist or something. . . . Anyway, if it's a course in Russian Literature, say, he comes in, in his little button-down-collar shirt . . . and starts knocking Turgenev, for about a half hour. Then, when he's finished, when he's completely <u>ruined</u> Turgenev for you, he starts talking about Stendhal or somebody he wrote his thesis for his M.A. on. . . . They're all so brilliant they can hardly open their mouths-- (Salinger, 1961, p. 14)

3

This is an open assault on education; no reading behind the lines is necessary.

A good example of the alternate weapons in Salinger's arsenal is his use of precocious children. In addition to the Glass children, he uses such youngsters as Teddy of "Teddy," Esme of "For Esme--with Love and Squalor," and Phoebe of The Catcher in the Rye. Salinger scoffs at the adult world by manipulating these kids who have a talent for showing up the adults in the stories.

In "Teddy" the nine-year-old boy embarrasses his parents and adult friends by turning his conversations with them to his liking. His Zen-like wisdom, his interpretations of mystical and complex poems, his recitations-- all place his comprehension not only beyond most children but also most adults. Esme is also incredibly smart. She is different because she tries to be sophisticated. During her conversation with the narrator, a soldier who also is a writer, Esme tells him that he must create a story for her. Showing off her vocabulary, she responds to his reply that he would try al- though he "wasn't terribly prolific": "It doesn't have to be terribly pro- lific. Just so it isn't childish and silly" (Salinger, 1971, p. 100). Salinger has caught her in the game of proving that she knows more than she does, a game he feels is taught to young people. Even little Phoebe has not yet been corrupted; she can tell the good movies from the "lousy" ones (Salinger, 1972, p. 67).

J. D. Salinger was a smart dummy. Considered to be a poor student with a low I.Q., he reacted with anger at the world of intellectuals and sophis- tication. His characters react to the phoney world that ruins its children, and his children have insight where the adults do not. Even as a writer, he could parody the scholars:

4

The facts at hand presumably speak for themselves, but a trifle
more vulgarly, I suspect, than facts even usually do. As a
counterbalance, then, we begin with that everfresh and exciting
odium: the author's formal introduction. (Salinger, 1961, p. 47)

Was this the language of an intellectual inferior?

Bibliography

Salinger Chronology. American Literature Seminar, West High School, Iowa
    City, Iowa, 1980.

Salinger, J. D. Franny and Zooey. New York: Bantam, 1961.

Salinger, J. D. Nine Stories. New York: Bantam, 1971.

Salinger, J. D. The Catcher in the Rye. New York: Bantam, 1972.

Instructor's Comments

1. Strengths: Certainly this paper establishes a thought-provoking position.
    Could Salinger have been offended by schools and his I.Q. test? The
    writer's evidence that is drawn from fiction certainly supports this
    theory. The focus on Salinger's use of precocious children and a large
    vocabulary makes this position open to a lively Defense Day discussion.

2. Weaknesses: One problem with the paper is with the word "dummy"--clever
    as it might be in the title. 108 is an average I.Q., subject to much
    scrutiny by a test-maker before drawing any conclusions. Then too,
    Salinger did well at Valley Forge, and his Columbia class led to his
    first publication, if not his career. Of course, all this does not deny
    that Salinger may have had a grudge against formal education, as well as
    a concern for what it does to the young.

PAPER VI: *RAISE HIGH THE ROOF BEAM, CARPENTERS*
DAYS 70–80

DAY 70: READING *RAISE HIGH THE ROOF BEAM, CARPENTERS*

Goals

1. To orient students to *Raise High the Roof Beam, Carpenters* (1963).
2. To provide in-class time to begin reading the story.

Materials

Class copies of *Raise High the Roof Beam, Carpenters* and *Seymour, an Introduction*.

Assignment

1. Ask students to note the DUE date for the sixth paper on the Schedule, Day 81.
2. Remind students that the Defense Days for Paper V (Profile) will be Days 75 and 76. Copies of the papers chosen for defense will be handed out on Days 74 and 75.

Procedure

1. Allow students the first five or ten minutes to make a final proofreading of Paper V. Then collect. Since the first Defense Day is only five days from now, be sure to select the papers immediately and begin to read the others during this period.
2. Ask students to review The Salinger Chronology (Handout 3), as well as The Glass Family (Handout 5). While this is Salinger's final book, printed in 1963, *Raise High the Roof Beam, Carpenters* is really a 1955 *New Yorker* story about the Glass family. Note that it appeared after "Franny" and before the 1957 magazine story "Zooey." "Seymour, an Introduction" is a long, complex 1959 *New Yorker* piece, a sort of dialogue between Buddy and Seymour's ghost.

3. Also ask students to note Salinger's introduction or dedication: the reader, Claire Douglas Salinger, Margaret and Matthew Salinger, all "split the dedication."
4. Before the students begin silent reading, remind them that Buddy Glass begins the narration, much as he did with "Zooey." The story deals with Seymour's wedding to Muriel, whom we have met in "A Perfect Day for Bananafish." The setting is 1942 New York City, World War II.
5. Salinger's concern with Zen is obvious from the beginning; the story's title is drawn from the sixth century B.C. Greek poet Sappho—another obscure Salinger title that carries a message about the heroic Seymour, who, like the Greek god of war Ares, cannot find his way among mere mortals. You may want to have students review what they have learned about Seymour and Buddy and Boo Boo before they begin reading.

DAYS 71–73: READING, SUGGESTIONS, AND SKILL DISCUSSION

Goals

1. To provide in-class reading time.
2. To suggest possible positions for the Defense Days.
3. To discuss a writing skill goal for this paper, comparison and contrast.

Materials

1. Handout 19: Suggestions for Paper VI.
2. Handout 20: Student Model for Paper VI.

Procedure

1. Day 71 should be devoted to in-class silent reading.

2. On Day 72, distribute Handout 19, which suggests a number of positions for Paper VI. You also may wish to give students copies of the Student Model paper—or simply post one copy on the bulletin board. Some instructors may prefer to use it on Day 77, the follow-up discussion period.

3. Day 73 can be used for discussion of a skill goal, such as comparison and contrast, or for in-class oral reading of Salinger's final published writings:

   a. While comparison and contrast, or at least references to stories previously read aloud or assigned, have already been encouraged, some instructors may wish to require that in this paper students compare *Raise High the Roof Beam, Carpenters* with a previous story—such as "A Perfect Day for Bananafish" or *Franny and Zooey*. A comparison paper will stress similarities; a contrast paper will stress differences. Suggestions for possible structures: (1) Introduction, asserting that both stories deal with a similar concern such as the use of colors as symbols; Body, citing examples in one story and then the other which document this position; Conclusion, tying your position and examples together. (2) Introduction, asserting that one story has a basic difference from another—a difference which reveals something about Salinger's development (For example, Salinger switches from third person in "Bananafish" to first in *Raise High* . . . , a shift from 1948 to 1955. Why did he do this?); Body, discussing the meaning and examples of the more impersonal third person in the earlier work to the personal "I" of Buddy (Salinger?) in later writing; Conclusion, a final speculation, as well as a summary.

   b. Salinger's final published works offer ponderous, heavy-handed sentences and symbolism that may suggest his farewell to his readers, especially those so delighted with *Catcher*. *Seymour, an Introduction* (1959) and "Hapworth 16, 1924" (1965) are probably too long for a complete in-class reading. But instructors may wish to spend at least one period on one of these works—in part-

so students can both see the final publications and speculate on just what has happened to the J. D. Salinger who wrote the early stories, *Catcher,* and the Glass family stories. Is he rejecting his reader, preparing for his Zen-like isolation in Cornish, New Hampshire? Is he beginning to write just for himself?

DAYS 74–77: PREPARING FOR AND PARTICIPATING IN DEFENSE DAYS AND FOLLOW-UP

Goal

To encourage a full discussion of student concerns with J. D. Salinger, the man and the writer.

Materials

1. Copies of the Profile Papers for the two Defense Days.
2. Corrected copies of the remaining papers to be returned on Day 76.

Procedure

1. On Day 74, distribute the first two Defense Day papers for student reading and annotation; be sure to distribute the remaining two papers at the end of Day 75.
2. Conduct the Defense Days 75 and 76 with the familiar seminar method. Return all corrected papers on Day 76.
3. On Day 77, you may wish to use the Student Model paper (Handout 20), other students' papers, or the ideas of critics. Since Salinger has resisted interviewers and biographers so vigorously, perhaps there should be even more discussion of the American writer and his right of privacy. You may wish to use Appendix C, "The Telephone Connection: Stalking the Mysterious Mr. J. D. Salinger," for this discussion.

DAYS 78–80: WRITING PAPER VI

Goal

To provide in-class time for writing and proofreading.

Procedure

1. These three days can be used for writing and proofreading.
2. Remind students that Paper VI is due on Day 81.

Additional Suggestions

1. Some instructors may wish to use one of these days for further in-class reading of "Seymour: An Introduction."

2. "The Inverted Forest" (December, 1947 *Cosmopolitan*) is another seemingly autobiographical story which could be valuable for a reading by the instructor. A rather complicated story about a psychotic poet, it suggests Salinger's concern with how people treat each other, how sex can be destructive, and just how moral a writer Salinger is—an author often accused of writing a "dirty" book, *The Catcher in the Rye*.

HANDOUT 19
SUGGESTIONS FOR PAPER VI: *RAISE HIGH THE ROOF BEAM,*
CARPENTERS (1963)

1. Until now, Seymour has been a rather shadowy figure. What do we learn about him in this story?

2. What is the function of the deaf-mute? Is he a Zen figure?

3. Here is another unusual Salinger title. Is there a position in it?

4. Critics often discuss the language of Holden Caulfield. What about the slang of adults in this story—and earlier ones?

5. This story first appeared in *The New Yorker* in 1955. Check the other stories that we have examined from this sophisticate magazine. Just what is a *"New Yorker"* story?

6. Concentrate on one scene, such as the taxi scene. Why did Salinger spend so much time on this section?

7. Is Salinger's use of the diary-and-letter method of narration successful or unsuccessful in holding the reader's interest?

8. Focus on the Matron of Honor. What is her purpose?

9. Buddy seems to be a detached narrator. Why does Salinger give him this air of detachment?

10. Does this story suggest that Salinger is at a new stage of thematic development, or is this more of the same thing?

11. At times this is a very humorous story. Try to think of one word that defines the type of humor.

12. Salinger dwells on colors as symbols, such as yellow in "A Perfect Day for Bananafish." Yellow is in this story, too. Discuss yellow in both stories.

13. Buddy slams shut Seymour's diary at the line: "I suspect people of plotting to make me happy." What does the word "happy" mean?

14. Compromise. Critic James Lundquist believes that Seymour taught Buddy, Zooey, and Franny to move toward compromise if they want to have a philosophy they can live by. Do you see this, too?

15. Some critics found this book to be a failure because there is too much Salinger technique in it and not enough character interacting with character. What techniques weaken the novel?

16. Examine the last paragraph of the story. Can its symbolism be dissected into a position in terms of how conclusions can summarize an entire work?

HANDOUT 20
STUDENT MODEL FOR PAPER VI

SEYMOUR AND HIS SHADOW

by Debbie Fedge

Like a bashful child hiding behind a curtain, the unsociable Seymour
Glass is hidden behind a screen of unanswered questions. In J. D. Salinger's
<u>Raise High the Roof Beam, Carpenters</u> his presence is alluded to only by his
shadow. Through character parallels, Salinger reminds the reader of Seymour's
presence, and it is the supporting actor--the deaf, mute old man--that is the
shadow.

Just like a mid-morning or afternoon sun, Seymour's shadow is short
"without being either a midget or a dwarf." He is a small, tiny man whose
feet don't "quite touch the floor" of the taxi cab. Seymour's mental abilities, like the little man's physical size, are unusual. Seymour was a precocious child, who starred on the radio quiz show "It's a Wise Child." He
is a highly intelligent man, caught up in a combination of Eastern and Western
philosophies. Both Seymour and the old man attract attention and interest
because of their unique characteristics.

The narrator of the book, Buddy Glass, describes the old man in the
second person:

> You must have sat very erect, maintaining a clearance of four or
> five inches between your top hat and the roof, and you stared
> ferociously ahead at the windshield. If Death--who was out there
> all the time, possibly sitting on the hood--if Death stepped
> miraculously through the glass and came in after you, in all
> probability you just got up and went along with him, ferociously
> but quietly.

1

2

Seymour's father-in-law's uncle (the deaf-mute old man) would face "Death"
with quiet defiance. Similarly, Seymour greeted his own type of death in
the same manner. Buddy, his brother, states that he went to each broadcast
of "It's a Wise Child" as though "he were going to his own funeral. He didn't
even talk to you, for God's sake, the whole way down on the bus or subway."

Their similar responses to death follow in their respective responses
to society. Due to physical limitations, the uncle is unable to hear or
verbally communicate with his neighbors. His senses prevent him from re-
sponding normally to the hearing world. In comparison, Seymour won't respond
to society. From reading "A Perfect Day for Bananafish" and Raise High the
Roof Beam, Carpenters, even the casual reader realizes that Seymour prefers
to evade analysts and the "real" world. His inner senses prevent him from
doing so. He doesn't respond normally to society.

The limits set by Seymour's and the uncle's abilities to communicate
force them to write. Traveling to the wedding reception with a number of
other guests, the uncle uses language for the first and last time. Accepting
the invitation to "quit" the temporarily stalled and crowded cab with the
rest of the guests, he writes:

> The single word "Delighted." The Matron of Honor, reading
> over my (Buddy's) shoulder, gave a sound faintly like a
> snort, but I quickly looked over at the great writer and tried
> to show by my expression that all of us in the car knew a poem
> when we saw one, and were grateful.

Curiously, Buddy describes his brother, Seymour, in the same way. Seymour,
says Buddy, is "A poet, for God sakes. And I mean a poet."

Like the uncle, this poet expressed his "delight" through writing. In
Raise High the Roof Beam, Carpenters, Seymour expressed his thoughts and
feeling through his diary. He refers to himself as a "happy man" experiencing
the "joy of responsibility for the first time." Seymour's happiness and his
desire to marry Muriel and make her happy are clearly stated in his diary.

3

It is this happiness that leads to the Matron of Honor's conclusion that Seymour is crazy. She presents her argument to Mrs. Silsburn, one of the wedding guests, in the cab:

> But what man in his right mind, the night before he's supposed
> to get married, keeps his fiancee up all night blabbing to her
> all about how he's too <u>happy</u> to get married and that she'll
> have to <u>postpone</u> the wedding till he feels <u>steadier</u> or he won't
> be able to come to it? . . . Use your head, now, if you don't
> mind. Does that sound like somebody <u>normal</u>? Does that sound
> like somebody in their right mind?

It is the general consensus of Muriel's family and friends that Seymour is insane. In his diary, Seymour records his future in-law's opinion:

> Her mother thinks I'm a schizoid personality. Apparently she's
> spoken to her psychoanalyst about me, and he agrees with her.
> Mrs. Fedder has asked Muriel to find out discreetly if there's
> any insanity in the family.

Seymour's conversation with the family results in claims of his eccentricity. Likewise, the uncle's actions affect people's impressions of him:

> His face was in the ferocious repose that had fooled me during
> most of the car ride, but as he came closer to us in the hall,
> the mask reversed itself; he pantomimed to us both the very
> highest salutations and greeting . . . "What is he? Crazy?"
> the Matron of Honor said.

According to some people, anyone unconventional is "crazy." Buddy answers to the Matron of Honor by saying "I hope so"--expressing his wish that, like his brother, the uncle is different.

Both Seymour and the uncle provide a unique freshness to the story. Their shared, unusual characteristics constitute the basis of their comparison. They both seem to be crazy. They both communicate best in writing. Like a real object and its shadow, the uncle and Seymour can be considered one. The parallels between these two characters, Seymour and his shadow, are why Buddy wishes to send Seymour "a blank sheet of paper" with the uncle's wedding gift "by way of explanation."

4

Instructor's Comments

1. <u>Strengths</u>: The writer gives an original interpretation to a strong and puzzling character. Through clear and concrete organization and support, she reveals sharp parallels to her shadow thesis. While some readers see the Zen influence again, she provides an intriguing alternative.

2. <u>Weaknesses</u>: It is no easy task to unify direct quotations with the rest of the paper. Examples: In the quotation about Buddy and the radio show, the reference to "he" within the single sentence is confusing, as is the use of two complete sentences directly quoted and then built into a single sentence. The direct quotation using "Delighted" is more than just the writing of the deaf-mute; it included Buddy's comments. "Buddy's" should be in brackets since it is not part of a direct quotation.

PAPER VII: THE SUMMING UP
DAYS 81–90

DAYS 81–83: BEGINNING THE FINAL PAPER AND PREPARING FOR DEFENSE DAY

Goals

1. To help students select a topic for Paper VII.
2. To provide class time to begin the final paper.
3. To prepare for Defense Days.

Materials

1. Handout 21: Suggestions for Paper VII.
2. Handout 22: Student Model for Paper VII.
3. Instructors may also wish to make use of the discussion of parody writing and another student model, Appendix D, "Parody: A Student's Response to J. D. Salinger."
4. Copies of Paper VI *(Raise High the Roof Beam, Carpenters)*.

Assignment

Ask students to insert DUE dates for Paper VII on the Schedule.

Procedure

1. On Day 81, give students five or ten minutes at the beginning to make a final proofreading of their position papers on *Raise High the Roof Beam, Carpenters*. Then collect.
2. As soon as possible select the Paper VI Defense Day papers and reproduce them for final seminar evaluations.
3. Orient students to the final paper by suggesting that it offers a number of alternatives:

a. If time allows, you may wish to assign both a serious summation and a creative paper.
b. Most likely, you may wish to be more flexible, rewarding students for their work in the seminar by letting them select either type of paper.
c. A technique that has worked very well: Agree to give *A* grades to all students who read their final paper aloud to the seminar. These readings may take two days. They release final tensions about grades and yet encourage valuable writing experiences. Review various options by using Handout 21. You also may wish to use Handout 22 or the Appendix student models. (Also see the hilarious parody, "Catcher in the Oatmeal," by Dan Greenburg in *Esquire*, February, 1958.)

4. Day 82 is a research and writing day.
5. Day 83 should allow both writing and reading/annotating of the first two Defense Day papers, VI. The second two papers will be handed out on Day 84.
6. Note: Parodies can be of any length, not restricted to the three to five page requirement of position papers.

DAYS 84–86: PARTICIPATING IN DEFENSE DAYS AND FOLLOW-UP DISCUSSION

Goal

To complete the Defense Days and follow-up discussion.

Materials

Extra copies of position papers for students who have forgotten them.

Procedure

1. Follow the established procedures for Defense Day. Return all papers at the end of the period on Day 85.
2. The follow-up discussion Day 86 can be spent by discussing other papers, the student model, or the insight of critics. Suggestion: pp. 137–142 of chapter 4, "A Cloister of Reality: The Glass Family," in *J. D. Salinger* by James Lundquist.

DAYS 87–88: SHARING THE FINAL PAPERS

Goal

To encourage students to share their final paper with the class in an atmosphere no longer involving formal evaluation.

Procedure

1. Since these are not Defense Days, the atmosphere should be more relaxed as each student reads his or her paper aloud. However, there is still a concern for quality among peers, especially at the end.
2. Encourage positive responses to each paper. If you have required that these papers should be typed, be alert to papers which

might be copied for models for future seminars.

DAYS 89–90: FINAL DISCUSSION AND EVALUATION

Goals

1. To encourage students to evaluate the seminar.
2. To share final discussion about Salinger and the seminar.

Materials

Handout: Seminar Evaluation (see Appendix F).

Procedure

1. The last two days offer a number of concluding possibilities: formal evaluation, discussion, final summation, an examination, or amusing games.
2. Be sure to ask the students to complete the course evaluation anonymously.
3. You may wish to share your final impression of the seminar with the students and try to synthesize what has been learned about Salinger, about his writing, and about the writing process.
4. Some instructors may enjoy a final interaction that involves group activities such as charades, Twenty Questions, or even a Salinger party with students dressed to suggest characters or titles.

HANDOUT 21
SUGGESTIONS FOR PAPER VII

The Summing Up

1. Do Salinger's stories and novels so evolve that it was inevitable that he would cease publication?
2. What is Salinger's special kind of religion?
3. Is Salinger an author restricted to analyzing only Americans of Eastern cities and suburbs?
4. Is Salinger ultimately a satirist?
5. Is Salinger's infatuation with precocious children symbolic of his rejection of the adult world?
6. What is the ultimate purpose of the humor in his writing?
7. Which work was your favorite?
8. Consider his titles. Can you develop a theory about his choices?
9. Salinger first made impact in the 1950s. Then came the civil rights movement, the Viet Nam War, and a back-to-the-basics swing to the right. Has Salinger, unpublished since the mid-1960s, still something to say about America?

Creative Suggestions

1. Try a parody of a work by Salinger. Take a short story or a passage from a novel and distort his style and plot.
2. Try a parody of Salinger by taking a simple plot and writing it in the famous Salinger style. For example, take a children's story such as "Little Red Riding Hood."
3. Write an imaginary interview with Salinger.
4. Write a first person account of one of Salinger's characters meeting the author.
5. Write a story, written under a pen name, which has been declared to be a Salinger creation.
6. Write a personal essay on "How to Write a Salinger Profile with No Material."
7. Write a Salinger story that he has finally allowed to be published, revealing the latest phase of his thinking.
8. Write a news account of a university professor who has discovered a piece of information about Salinger that could change everything we have learned.

HANDOUT 22
STUDENT MODEL FOR PAPER VII

TEDHARTHA

by Jennifer Gardner

"Teddy" is about Zen Buddhism, which is about nothing and going no-
where, so this paper doesn't exist now, and I shouldn't think about it or
I'll get somewhere, which wouldn't be anywhere good because traveling is
where it's at, so forget this paper and draw a blank. (But don't be blank.)

For that matter, if I close my eyes, I can't prove that I'm even here.
And if you're not watching me write this, then who's to know that I'm not
eating ravioli instead of writing? And furthermore, if I don't believe I'm
here, then I'm not really enrolled in this class. So why bother writing a
paper on a nonexistent class? Does any typewriter exist? (Gosh, I hope not.)
Should I be hit over the head with a paddle for asking? To contradict my
first statement, "Teddy" isn't. The story doesn't exist.

Instructor's Comments

O.K.! The writer, with a little help from Hesse and an overdose of Zen,
makes a delightful point.

APPENDIXES

APPENDIXES

APPENDIX A
THE LIFE AND TIMES
OF J. D. SALINGER

J. D. Salinger	The Times
GROWING UP: THE PREWRITING PERIOD, 1919–1939	
1919	
Jerome David Salinger is born January 1, in New York City to Sol and Miriam Jillich Salinger, the second of two children and only son.	Treaty of Versailles after World War I ends. Volstead Prohibition Act. Sherwood Anderson, *Winesburg, Ohio.*
1920–1929	
Attends Manhattan's Upper West Side elementary schools. *B* grades, IQ 104, difficulty with arithmetic.	U.S. population: 105,710,620, in 1920. Prosperity under Harding, Coolidge, and then 1929 Stock Market Crash.
1930	
Voted "most popular actor" at Camp Wigwam, Harrison, Maine.	Sinclair Lewis wins Nobel Prize.
1932	
Enrolled at McBurney School, a private school in Manhattan. Develops interest in dramatics and tropical fish. Flunks out in 1933.	13 million unemployed. Roosevelt elected President.
1934	
Sent to Valley Forge Military Academy, Pennsylvania.	Mao's Long March in China.
1935	
Becomes literary editor of Academy yearbook. Credited with writing lyrics for school song for Last Parade. Writes first short stories.	WPA. Italy invades Ethiopia.
1936	
Graduates from Valley Forge Military Academy, his only diploma.	Spanish Civil War, Franco vs. Loyalists. *Gone with the Wind,* by Margaret Mitchell.
1937	
Attends summer session at New York University. Sent by father to Vienna, Austria and Poland to learn import meat business but returns.	Violence and strikes in General Motors factories.
1938	
Attends Ursinus College, Collegetown, Pennsylvania, for half a semester. Writes "The Skipped Diploma" for *Ursinus Weekly,* a column.	Pearl Buck wins Nobel Prize. Hitler and Chamberlain meet in Munich.

1939

Takes a Columbia University short-story writing course taught by writer/editor Whit Burnett.

THE APPRENTICESHIP PERIOD, 1940–1947

1940

Publishes first story "The Young Folks" in March–April issue of Burnett's *Story* magazine. "Go See Eddie" appears in December issue of *University of Kansas City Review*.

1941

Works as an entertainer on Swedish Liner *M.S. Kungsholm* in Caribbean.* Publishes stories in *Collier's* and *Esquire*. Lives with parents. Early Holden Caulfield story "Slight Rebellion off Madison" bought by *The New Yorker* but not published until 1946.

1942

Publishes stories in *Story* and *Collier's*. Drafted into U.S. Army. Attends Officers, First Sergeants, and Instructors School in Signal Corps.

1943

Stationed in Nashville, Tennessee. Staff Sergeant. Applies to Officer's Candidate School and transferred to Army Counter-Intelligence Corps. Publishes July 17 *Saturday Evening Post* story, "The Varioni Brothers."

1944

Training for counter-intelligence in Tiverton, Devonshire, England. Three *Post* stories. Involved in five campaigns, from June 6 Normandy with 4th Army to Battle of the Bulge. Awarded five battle medals. Meets Ernest Hemingway; Interviews captured Germans as Security Agent for 12th Infantry Regiment.

1945

Allegedly marries a French physician (divorce, 1947). [Critics such as James Lundquist believe this is one of Salinger's biographical fabrications.] Publishes first Holden Caulfield story, "I'm Crazy" in December 22 *Collier's*. Stories in *Esquire, Story*, and *Post*.

1946

Brief hospitalization in Nürnberg. Ninety-nine page novel about Holden Caulfield written but not published. "Slight Rebellion off Madison" in December 21 *The New Yorker*.

1947

Returns to New York City, publishes in *Mademoiselle* and *Cosmopolitan*. Spends time in Greenwich Village, studies Zen, moves to Tarrytown.

For Whom the Bell Tolls, Ernest Hemingway. *Grapes of Wrath,* John Steinbeck.

Nazi bombing of Britain. New York World's Fair closes. U.S. population 131 million.

December 7, Japanese bomb Pearl Harbor, U.S. enters World War II. *Watch on the Rhine,* Lillian Hellman.

U.S. Air Force bombs Europe. Naval battles in the Pacific. *Skin of Our Teeth,* Thornton Wilder.

Invasion of Italy by Allies. 75 percent of Hamburg destroyed by fire bombs. *Oklahoma,* Rodgers and Hammerstein.

D-Day, 156,000 Allied soldiers reach Normandy. Milestone battles: Leyte Gulf in Pacific, Ardennes in Luxembourg. *A Bell for Adano,* John Hersey.

V-E, V-J Days. UN Charter. Death of Roosevelt. Truman administration (1945–1952).

Atomic bomb tests in Pacific. *All the King's Men,* Robert Penn Warren. Churchill delivers "Cold War" speech.

U.S. government asks for loyalty oaths from workers.

THE CLASSIC OR MAJOR WORKS PERIOD, 1948–1951

1948

"A Perfect Day for Bananafish" in January 31 *The New Yorker.*

Berlin Airlift. Marshall Plan. Pulitzer to James Michener, *Tales of the South Pacific.*

1949

"The Laughing Man" in March 19 *The New Yorker;* "Down in the Dinghy" in April issue of *Harper's.* Moves to Westport, Connecticut.

NATO. *Guard of Honor,* James Gould Cozzens.

1950

"My Foolish Heart," a Hollywood film starting Susan Hayward and Dana Andrews and made from "Uncle Wiggly in Connecticut." Salinger upset and allows no more film versions. "For Esme—with Love and Squalor" in April 8 *The New Yorker* and later chosen by Martha Foley as one of distinguished short stories in 1950 American magazines.

U.S. population over 150 million. Korean War begins. McCarthy hunts communists.

1951

The Catcher in the Rye. Salinger goes to Europe to avoid publicity. The novel is a product of ten years of work.

The King and I, Broadway smash. Mickey Spillane's *One Lonely Night* sells 3 million copies.

SALINGER AND THE GLASS FAMILY SPIRITUAL PERIOD, 1952–1965

1952

Travels to Mexico. Honored by Valley Forge Military Academy as a Distinguished Alumnus of the Year.

Ralph Ellison, *Invisible Man.* Eisenhower administration (1952–60).

1953

Buys cottage and 90 acres in Cornish, New Hampshire. *Nine Stories.* Interviewed by Shirlie Blaney, a high school journalist for Windsor, Vermont *Daily Eagle.* Offended by November 13 editorial page interview.

Korean War armistice. Pulitzer to Hemingway's *Old Man and the Sea.*

1955

Marries Claire Douglas. "Franny" in January 29 *The New Yorker.* Birth of daughter, Margaret Ann, December 10. Salinger said "Franny" was a wedding present to Claire.

"Rock Around the Clock"—a popular song in rock 'n' roll era. Montgomery, Alabama bus boycott.

1957

"Zooey" in May 4 *The New Yorker.*

Sputnik I launched by Russians.

1959

"Seymour: An Introduction" in June 6 *The New Yorker.*

Cuban Revolution.

1960

Son, Matthew, born February 13.

Kennedy administration (1960–63).

1961

Franny and Zooey. Makes cover of *Time,* September 15, but avoids interviewers.

Berlin Wall erected. Hemingway commits suicide.

1963

Raise High the Roof Beam, Carpenters; and *Seymour: An Introduction.*

Assassination of Kennedy.

1965

"Hapworth 16, 1924" in June 19 *The New Yorker.*

U.S. bombs North Viet Nam.

SILENCE

1967

Divorce from Claire Douglas Salinger.

Emergence of the "hippies" in San Francisco.

1974

Files civil law suit against John Greenberg and 17 New York bookstores for illegal publication and sale of early Salinger stories.

Patty Hearst is kidnapped. Nixon resigns as President of the U.S.

1980

Canadian reporter, Michael Clarkson, describes brief interviews with seclusive author in Cornish, who has moved to a second home located in rural environs—protected by dogs, tunnel entrance, and hillside setting.

THE SALINGER FAMILY

Since Salinger has resisted interviewers and biographers, the biographical information is both scant and subject to question as to its accuracy.

Born January 1, 1919 in New York City, Jerome David Salinger is the second child and only son of Sol and Miriam Jillich Salinger. His father was the son of a Jewish rabbi and his mother was Scotch-Irish (but changed her first name, Marie, to Miriam to please her in-laws). Sol was a prosperous importer of hams and cheeses. Sister Doris was eight years older than Jerome. Salinger allegedly married a French physician when he was twenty-six and divorced her in 1947. On 17 February 1955, he married Claire Douglas. He had met Claire at a Manchester, Vermont party in 1953. She was English-born, a Radcliffe student, who told her parents that Salinger lived "with his mother, sister, fifteen Buddhist monks, and a yogi who stood on his head" (Lundquist, *J. D. Salinger,* p. 30). This was Claire's second marriage. They had two children: Margaret Ann (Peggy), born 13 November 1953; Matthew, born 13 February 1960. The marriage of Jerome and Claire ended in divorce in October 1967.

APPENDIX B
SALINGER ANECDOTE

Jerome David Salinger has been called "the most inaccessible, mysterious and fascinating recluse in all U.S. literary history." He has refused to allow his biography in *Who's Who in America*. He has warned his friends, such as William Shawn, editor of the *The New Yorker* who was recognized in the dedication of *Franny and Zooey*, not to discuss his private life. And he has built two "moated" castles, a first house near Cornish, New Hampshire, with a high wooden fence and an unlisted telephone number, and a second cliffside home nearby with access by a concrete tunnel guarded by dogs.

Few reporters have been able to penetrate this mystery, though like his fans they have been curious why the author of *The Catcher in the Rye* has not published since 1965. His friends, fellow authors, and relatives have revealed almost nothing. In fact, much of what was last heard from Salinger was gathered in an interview by a high school student.

One fall day in 1953, Shirlie Blaney (Class of '54) was having trouble finding news for the high school page in the Claremont, New Hampshire *Daily Eagle*. As she and her fellow journalist were wracking their brains, Shirlie saw "Jerry" walking across the street. Unlike her friends, she knew a little about the newcomer to the area. She had met Salinger at his home when she and some friends had dropped by for Cokes, potato chips, and records. Salinger "was just one of the gang, except that he never did anything silly the way the rest of us did"—said Shirlie. Salinger had even encouraged her to write.

So Shirlie Blaney asked J. D. Salinger for an interview and got it. They went to a local hangout and talked. The interview didn't appear in the next Monday's issue, as Shirlie had expected, and Salinger called to ask why. Four days later, she was relieved to see her story. But Salinger never called again. In fact, he never even talked with Shirlie or any other local student again. Instead, he built a high wooden fence around his home. [Source: Ernest Havemann, "The Recluse in Rye," *Life,* 3 November 1961, pp. 129–144.]

APPENDIX C
THE TELEPHONE CONNECTION: STALKING THE MYSTERIOUS MR. J. D. SALINGER

What really knocks me out is a book that, when you're all done reading it, you wish the author that wrote it was a terrific friend of yours and you could call him up on the phone whenever you felt like it. That doesn't happen much, though.

Holden Caulfield, *The Catcher in the Rye*

If you really want to hear about it, the first thing you should know is that you just don't call "Jerry" on the telephone. Even if you have loved *Catcher* (like me) since it first appeared in 1951, even if you have been one of the eight million buyers of this high school best-seller (second only to John Steinbeck's *Of Mice and Men*), he'll never be a terrific friend of yours. You can enjoy his writing, but he won't talk to you.

That's what I told my fifteen juniors and seniors in our Salinger seminar at West High School in Iowa City last spring. "Don't think I haven't tried," I said. I told them about the first time I taught the seminar: "I did all the things that got us interviews with Mary Hemingway and Gregory Hemingway—a letter of inquiry, a stamped return envelope. But Salinger didn't even send a refusal." Then I told them about the 1976 seminar when I wrote Salinger again (again, no answer), as well as his son Matt (no answer), and *The New Yorker* editor, William Shawn.

"Mr. Shawn was very gracious," I said. "He even called me at school. But he would not grant a conference interview with the class because he said that Salinger had warned all of his friends never to discuss his private life."

The students were naturally disappointed. After all, they had spent over six weeks building their enthusiasm for the author. They had written and defended four position papers on "A Perfect Day for Bananafish" (1948), *The Catcher in the Rye* (1951), "Teddy" (1953), and *Franny and Zooey* (1961); they had read aloud and discussed much of Salinger's fiction that had appeared in magazines such as *Story, Esquire, Collier's,* and *The New Yorker*. (And they also knew that my Steinbeck seminar had just been granted a telephone interview with the Nobel Prize winner's former lawyer.)

Kim, a junior whose enthusiasm had multiplied when she brought a resource speaker on Zen Buddhism, was the first to voice the general disappointment. "It's not fair!" she said. "There are so many questions that I'd love to ask him about Zen. I mean, it's in nearly everything he wrote."

"Until 1965," said Joel, a senior. "He hasn't published a thing since then. And maybe that's the point. Salinger is living the life of a Zen monk up in New Hampshire!" The class laughed.

"Or maybe he just enjoys being mysterious," said Kim.

"Well, if we can't call him and we can't call his friends or relatives, we're stuck. We're really stuck," said Joel.

Joel was referring to their next paper, a thematic profile of the author based on the reading of biographical and autobiographical materials. And I knew, as did the students, that everything we had was in a folder: two 1961 *Life* and *Time* magazine articles; a chapter-length "collage" biography from a book of literary analysis—one that leaned heavily on the two articles and on Salinger's fiction; a 1974 *New York Times* telephone interview with the headline "J. D. Salinger Speaks about His Silence", and a 30 July 1979 "update" from *Newsweek*.

From the 1961 *Life* article ("The Recluse in the Rye") to the 1979 *Newsweek* update ("The Dodger in the Rye"), the message is the same: Stalking the mysterious J. D. Salinger is hard work with meager results, even for professional journalists. Twenty-eight years of profile produced a sketchy, if intriguing, outline: Salinger, now in his 60s, was raised by middle class, Jewish-Catholic parents in New York City. After poor grades in elementary school and flunking out of a private school, Jerome received his only diploma from Valley Forge Military Academy where he wrote the school song and his first stories. Not interested in his father's ham importing business, Salinger briefly attended two colleges, published his first short story, and then left for World War II in Europe where he was a Staff Sergeant for Army Intelligence.

Then the outline gets fuzzy. Did he really get married to a European doctor after the war? Could he have paid the rent and the grocery bill in Greenwich Village from the sale of eleven short stories from 1946 to 1951 when *Catcher* was published? Then come the tougher questions. Why did he—a city boy—move to the rural environs

200

of Cornish, New Hampshire? Why did he become close friends with the locals and then suddenly build a huge fence around his house? Why would a recluse marry, start a family of two children, and then divorce himself from them in 1967? And finally, why would he stop publishing over fifteen years ago, move up the unpaved road to a second retreat which can only be reached through a fifty foot cement tunnel from his garage which is patrolled by dogs?

"Can't we at least talk to Shirlie Blaney?" asked John, who was well acquainted with the folder. I knew that someone would ask about Shirlie since I had told the class that a member of our music department had been on the 1953 Windsor, Vermont High School newspaper staff when they decided to print an interview with Salinger from nearby Cornish.

"I'm afraid that's out, too," I said. "Dr. Comstock doesn't remember her married name. Then too, that was a long time ago, and she may have moved."

So that was that. Protected by his physical environment and the silence of those who know him best, J. D. Salinger would not give my seminar students any further insight into his special world.

Or so we thought.

Just before the profile papers were due, we discovered Michael Clarkson. Thanks to Becky, a senior who had done some research, we read aloud the 25 February 1980 issue of *People* magazine, which described how a thirty-one year old police reporter for the Niagara Falls (Ontario) *Review* had confronted his own teenage idol, first in 1978 and again in June of 1979. Here at last was someone who had scaled the wall! We wrote him.

Our May interview was held in the conference room of the West library. As Mr. Clarkson had requested, we sent him fifteen questions that covered the territory that interested us. Each student was in charge of one question, and Mr. Clarkson agreed to our taping of the entire interview which lasted about forty minutes.

Whether intentional or not, Melanie's first question revealed something about all of us who stalk J. D. Salinger. She asked, "What made you so interested in him that you would go to such extremes to get an interview?" By "extremes" she was referring to the fact that Clarkson had twice driven over 450 miles to Cornish, the first time convincing a local variety store clerk to hand Salinger a cryptic note which read: "A man is in Cornish. Amateur, perhaps, but sentimentally connected. The saddest—a tragic figure without a background. Needing a future as much as your past. Let me." Then he drove to the author's country driveway to wait for him and eventually to force a five minute conversation. The second trip Clarkson climbed the steep backside hill to the house, passed barking dogs, peeked into a window—and startled Salinger into a fifteen minute talk. (While all of this seems impulsive, my

students had suggested—before they heard of Clarkson—that they would resort to similar tactics.)

Clarkson told Melanie that he had been strongly influenced by Salinger's writings when he was in high school, though he had never studied them in a classroom. But when Caroline asked him what he had expected to get from his trips to Cornish and why he had resorted to the cryptic note, Clarkson became very candid. He said, "I never went with the intention of asking questions about his career or even publishing a story. I wanted to be around a man who thought like I thought, perhaps was on the same wave length that I was. I was in a depressed frame of mind, and I felt like nobody understood me. The cryptic note was used because I felt it was the only way to get through to him. I think if it wasn't for that note he wouldn't have seen me."

At this point, I could see that this was more than an informational interview, a collecting of facts to fill in empty spaces. Actually, he told much of what we already knew or felt. He told Joel that Salinger's house is much like Holden's dream cabin in *Catcher,* remote, with a thirty-five mile view which is both beautiful and protective against intruders. He told Karen that he saw no physical evidence that Salinger is still writing, though he has been told by others that the author is working on a long novel about the Glass family. He told Leanne that he had doubts about any first wife, and he told Diane that Salinger's family has left the Cornish area—his former wife Claire to California, the daughter Peggy and the son Matt to higher education and parts unknown. The first house with its high fence and concrete bunker writing room has been sold. And he told Lisa that Salinger looks quite different from the 1951 photos—"tall, thin, very gray, about six feet two, serious, bold and confident at home, timid in town." Clarkson said, "When he came at me, I said, 'My god, he looks like my grandfather!'" But he also conceded that Salinger is no saffron-robed monk; instead he dresses in everything from relaxed blue jeans, work shirt, and sneakers to more formal black turtleneck and jacket.

Clarkson admitted to Paul that he wasn't sure what role Zen Buddhism still played in Salinger's life. "It might be a way of relaxing for him," he said. "He is obviously very intense." He described Salinger as a man alone, without a secretary, not shy but sensitive, introspective, and perhaps best revealed by his fictional alter-egos such as Buddy Glass who was terrified by mobs. Yet, he also confirmed that a writer who lives in a modern cliffside chalet, watches television and 1930s films on his home projector, and drives a BMW to town to pick up his *"Times"* is hardly living the Way of Zen.

"Why is it, then, that he shuns the public?" asked Kim. This was a key question, a frustrating one not only to the seminar but also to Clarkson. Jennifer had earlier asked him if Salinger had been "sarcastic, sincere, conceited, or remote"; and he replied that Salinger was "throwing logic in my face like a pie—sincere like he had said the same things over and over again to the same people." When Clarkson told him he was a reporter, Salinger "looked daggers at me, almost like he hated me." And he told Becky that even the people in the Cornish community, especially the teenagers, largely knew him as a "legend," only visible when he picks up the mail.

"I got the feeling he couldn't handle the requests of people," said Michael Clarkson, his voice rising. He obviously felt involved with this question since he admitted writing five letters and sending a tape to J. D. Salinger—and receiving no answer. "Salinger mentioned that he didn't know what to say when people came to him with deep questions about life," he said. "He claims he is not a philosopher, just a fiction writer, although I disagree with him. I think he writes about love and loneliness and moral standards. I think if these things are fiction, then for me at least, life is really not worth anything."

Clarkson had raised a sensitive question: "What is the obligation of an author to his public?" While this may seem like an academic question about an author who has not released any material for publication since 1965 and told Clarkson "I write for myself!", the young Canadian reporter felt that an author who makes money and touches people deeply should respond to his readers. He said that Salinger should have hired a secretary and, at the very least, sent a form letter to his public. Yet, it was obvious that Michael Clarkson would never have been satisfied with such a letter. When he had read *The Catcher in the Rye* back in the 1960s, he had been "really knocked out," as Holden might say. He never forgot that experience. Like Holden, he wished that Salinger was a "terrific friend"; like my students, he wanted some form of direct, personal contact. And like Holden, and my students too, he found "that doesn't happen much."

Debbie asked the last question: "Has your impression of Salinger and his literature changed since you have talked to him?"

"Surprisingly, no," he said. "I still feel the fan in me is a one-to-one relationship with Salinger. At the time, as I sat in my car, I was worried that I was destroying this and it would never be the same. But I think I still can relate with his alter-egos. I still read *The Catcher in the Rye* before I go to bed." Clarkson paused, almost reflectively.

"As a person, he is different than I thought. I had expected a charismatic person," he said. "I still think he thinks like I do, but I don't think I'll ever be as strongly influenced by one person again. I think I feel more confident in my own abilities after seeing him. He made me feel as important as he was. Certainly my opinion of him as a writer hasn't altered. He is still a great writer."

Perhaps Michael Clarkson, the ultimate stalker of the mysterious Mr. J. D. Salinger, had given us more than we had telephoned for. As a group, we were curious, we wanted more facts, and we were willing to compromise for secondary material—the kind of information that high school students seem to live with. After all, Michael Clarkson was no friend, no relative; his total time with Salinger was less than ours with him. But when our telephone interview ended and the students stood around in the conference room talking excitedly, I could see that this had been one of the most successful classroom experiences that I had ever conducted.

Michael Clarkson was us. We had been knocked out by Salinger, too, by what Clarkson called a literature "that touches people as human beings." And since we are well over 1000 miles from Cornish, at the end of our folder of information, a bit angry that our friend wouldn't even send us a form letter, we were glad to have Michael Clarkson do our work. It was almost like a movie script, a Poe plot, a mystery novel.

But as with good literature, especially that of J. D. Salinger, we were left with basic questions and a high level of ambiguity. Do we really have the right to demand that every writer should come to the phone, return the stamped, self-addressed envelope? Why should we expect charisma in those writers who shape our dreams with words on a piece of paper? Michael Clarkson told us that J. D. Salinger was very human, like Holden and Buddy and Franny and Zooey and Seymour. Isn't that what we really expected?

APPENDIX D
PARODY: A STUDENT'S RESPONSE
TO J. D. SALINGER

Brooke Workman

When my fifteen juniors and seniors handed in their position papers on *Raise High the Roof Beam, Carpenters,* I could see that they were tired and puzzled. And they had good reason. After all, they had written their sixth position paper in eleven weeks; and now with barely a week left in our spring trimester, I was asking them to write another (typed) masterpiece on something called "The Summing Up."

Paul raised his voice.

"Have you noticed it's spring, Dr. Workman? And we only have five class days to write and defend our last paper?" he said, smiling.

"I'm a wreck, a burn-out," shouted Joel, a senior.

I nodded. "I know, I know," I said. "I'm going to make it easy on you. First, you have no reading this time. Second, if you write the paper and read the paper to class, you get an automatic A."

"You mean there's no Defense Day? I don't get to tear Joel's miserable prose apart?" said Paul.

I nodded.

Leanne raised her hand. "But what is a 'Summing Up'?" she asked.

Then I told them that it meant almost anything, not just a final summary position about Jerome David Salinger's fiction. However, I did review what we had accomplished in the course: our chronological pursuit of the emerging writer who began with the lonely girl stories such as "The Young Folks," first introduced Holden Caulfield in "I'm Crazy" (1945) and the Glass family in "A Perfect Day for Bananafish" (1948), then fleshed out these characters in *The Catcher in the Rye* (1951), *Franny and Zooey* (1961), and our most recent selection, written in 1963. I reminded them of their positions on "Bananafish," *Catcher,* "Teddy," and *Franny and Zooey*—as well as struggles for a profile of

an author who has resisted interviewers since 1953, when he talked to a high school student from Windsor, Vermont.

"Don't forget the cryptic note!" said John, the humorist of the seminar. "Or my speaker and the Koans!" shouted Kim, who was our expert on Zen Buddhism after she brought a resource speaker from the university's school of religion.

"Ah yes, the cryptic note. We must give credit to Michael Clarkson," I said. Indeed, we had tried everything to piece together the latest information on an author who has not published since 1965. Then Becky brought in the February 25, 1980, issue of *People* magazine. She read to us how Clarkson, a Canadian reporter, had gone to Salinger's Cornish, N.H. retreat and handed the author an unusual note as he was emerging from a local drugstore. And the author paused long enough to talk with Clarkson. Then we wrote Clarkson, and he paused long enough to talk with us on our conference telephone.

"So . . . we have read most of the works, chewed over the *Nine Stories,* dissected over fifteen position papers, and tried to understand the mind and world of J. D. Salinger," I said. Then I discussed other possibilities beside summation—an imaginary interview with Salinger, a series of letters between them and the author, a "recently discovered" work of Salinger, even an essay on the agonies of studying an author or of writing position papers. I also mentioned a parody.

"Parody? You mean like what we did in the regular American Lit course?" asked Leanne. Before I could nod, Joel said, "I liked what somebody did with Sandburg's 'Prayers of Steel'—you know, 'Prayers of Pizza'."

"Me, too," I said. "And now you can tackle Salinger's style if you like."

Reprinted from *English Journal* 70 (January 1981).

We discussed how close reading and discussion of an author makes for understanding style. We went around the circle, identifying Salinger trademarks—an immediate contact with the reader, though sometimes the story line is confusing; the italicized words for stress; the colloquial language, often too strong for thin-skinned censors—though not for most high school students; the symbolic names of characters and titles of stories; the Zen images; and, best of all, the honesty of feeling that attracts readers who, like Holden or Seymour or Franny or Buddy, are searching for meaning in an often crazy world.

Then the students went to work. On that last day, June 3, they read their papers—good, oh so good, that they applauded each other while I prepared to grab them and run to the office xerox machine.

Nearly everyone wrote a parody. Why? I didn't ask, but I think their response is instructive. They did it because it is fun both to exaggerate and criticize the literature of the course. Besides they felt comfortable with the parody because they knew Salinger's style. The result was a marvelous safety valve—and a chance to show off what they had learned.

What had they learned? The parodies reveal as much as any final examination about content, theme, style, and student response. They present the most gratifying summation of a demanding literature course. But enough. Here's an example:

A Close Encounter of the Phony Kind

If you really want to hear about it, the first thing you'll probably want to know is why I went, and what my lousy trip was like, and all that kind of crap, but I don't feel like going into it, if you want to know the truth. In the first place, that kind of stuff bores me, and in the second place Salinger would probably have some kind of fit. No kidding. I'm not going to tell you my whole autobiography or anything. I'll just tell you about this madman stuff that happened to me last March.

Where I want to start telling is the day I left West High in Iowa City. I decided to take some madman class called Seminar in American Literature, or some phony thing. Anyway there was this teacher who said we should study some author in depth. That killed me. You take teachers in high school, and they're always asking you to study some madman author in *depth* or something. I don't know. I really don't. Anyway we chose this guy J. D. Salinger who wrote some crazy books about one hundred years ago. This Salinger guy went into seclusion about fifty years ago and he won't talk to the press and all. For all we know, he doesn't even exist. Or if he does, he makes about as much noise as one hand clapping. No kidding. I mean it.

I guess I kind of got off the subject. I was telling you about the day I left school. Since I would have to spend about twelve centuries studying this phony author I didn't even know, I decided I better try to get to know him. I wrote a letter to him full of crap about how I wanted to get to know him and all. I would include the letter here verbatim, if I thought it was important, but I just don't think it is that significant. I know it should be, but I don't know.

Surprisingly enough, he wrote me back some madman letter about how he loved children, and how he'd love to talk to *me*. That killed me. I mean, you take a guy like Salinger and he doesn't talk to anyone. Then one day he gets a letter from someone who is practically an adult, like me, and he says all this crap about liking *children* and he agrees to talk to *me*. I think what he really needs is a doctor—or maybe some chicken soup. I don't know.

Well, I had nothing else to do last March, so I took off a few days from school and went to Cornish, New Hampshire, where this guy is supposed to be. He didn't give me any specifics, so I went and asked some guy that worked at the town drug store, who must have been about five hundred years old, where I could find Salinger. He said to try the rye field because Salinger sometimes went down there to be with all the little kids and all, and he'd keep them from falling off some madman cliff. No kidding.

When I got there I found him saving all these little kids from falling off this cliff. Anyway, I went over to him and he said he'd talk to me for about five lousy seconds or something. He said it didn't matter anyway because nothing is *real* in the *first* place. He mumbled something about orange peels, for Christsakes, and then he went on to say some madman thing about some Glass family, while he took a pack of cigarettes to smoke. I don't know.

Then, the interesting part. He said his secret of success was repetition. He said he liked using the same phony ideas over and over to get them through to the reader. (I personally felt he just couldn't think of any new ideas, the phony jerk.) *He* said he had to pound his madman ideas into the readers' thick skulls. So, I decided that Salinger repeats these phony ideas for fame. No kidding. I mean it.

That's all I'm going to tell about. I could probably tell you what I did when I went back to school and all, but I don't feel like it. I really don't. That stuff doesn't interest me too much right now. A lot of people, especially this one teacher they have here, keeps asking me if I'm going to write some madman article or book or something. It's such a stupid question, in my opinion. I mean how do you know what you're going to do till you do it? The answer is you *don't*. No kidding, I mean it.

Diane Scott

APPENDIX E
CATCHER COMES OF AGE

Adam Moss

This year, the book that changed the lives of generations of young rebels reaches maturity; on its thirtieth birthday, its own life passes before it, ready for reappraisal.

If you really want to hear about it, *The Catcher in the Rye* was a literary event even before it rolled off the press that summer of '51. A small but sophisticated sect had already begun to honor its shy thirty-two-year-old author—and on no more evidence than a couple of dozen short stories, mostly published in *The New Yorker.* A few years earlier, in the pages of Esquire, J. D. Salinger had said that he was a "dash man and not a miler, and it is probable that I will never write a novel," but there it was on Little, Brown's list—277 pages at three dollars—and people were so curious that the Book-of-the-Month Club took the unusual step of making this first novel its midsummer selection. Few could have expected what was to happen. From the book's opening sentence, it was clear the world had had thrust upon it a rudely original, highly unlikely new hero: a tall, skinny, prematurely gray-haired kid from West Seventy-first Street, a self-proclaimed pacifist and sex maniac with a fondness for profanity, Thomas Hardy, red hunting caps, and his sister, Phoebe, and an obsessive aversion to phonies. That Holden Caulfield, he was all right.

The literary establishment didn't quite know how to respond to this boy, described alternately as "a very normal specimen of his age," "a disturbed adolescent," and "a sorry little worm." Called "a brilliant tour de force" by *The Atlantic* and "remarkable" by *Saturday Review,* the book also had its detractors, among them Riley Hughes of *Catholic World,* who proclaimed Holden "a latter-day. . .Huck Finn. . .made monotonous and phony by the formidably excessive use of amateur swearing and coarse language." Amateur swearing indeed—237 *goddamns,* 58 *bastards,* 31 *Chrissakes,* and one fart were enough to earn the book its place as a major target of righteous school boards and legions of decency everywhere. After all, this was a book to be read by *children,* and read it they did, along with everyone else. Teenagers learned to perfect the nuances of Holden's speech; one review of the book, in *The New York Times Book Review,* was written entirely in Holdenese. Young writers took to their typewriters with renewed conviction, reveling in their perception that there was an audience for the fresh use of everyday language, that American literature lived.

It might have been a fad, but it was not. *The Catcher in the Rye* became one of those rare books that influence one generation after another, causing each to claim it as its own. Today, in its fifty-third edition in the Bantam paperback alone, it sells almost as many copies as it did the first year it was published. It is taught in countless high schools in the country; there are more than ten million copies in print. It has endured. Now it is thirty and shows no signs of fatigue. Holden, Phoebe, pimply old Ackley boy, we celebrate you. *Happy birthday, ya morons!*

NUMBERS

It is said that Little, Brown was not the first publisher to see the book, that Salinger brought it to another house first but withdrew it because his editor there thought Holden was "crazy." We do know that the manuscript eventually found its way into editor Ray Everett's hands at Little, Brown, which set the book's publication for the spring of 1951. The Book-of-the-Month Club's choice of the novel as its midsummer selection pushed the publication date to July, and on the sixteenth, *The Catcher in the Rye* was officially unleashed. By the end of the month, it had been reprinted five times and had climbed to fourteenth place on *The New York Times*'s best-seller list. Reprinted three times in August, and twice more in September,

Catcher claimed the fourth spot on the list five weeks after its publication. By the third edition, the photo of J. D. Salinger had been discreetly removed from the jacket.

Grosset & Dunlap published an edition in June of the following year, and in 1953 Signet issued the first paperback edition, priced at fifty cents. Ten years later, when Signet discontinued its edition, the book had sold 3,364,000 copies. Modern Library published the book in 1958; Franklin Watts put out a "special edition for libraries" in 1967. The book has been translated into at least a dozen languages, incuding French, Finnish, Hebrew, and Polish.

Bantam brought out the current paperback edition in 1964, at seventy-five cents. Today, orders for the book, now priced at $2.50 a copy, are close to the 1964 level—twenty to thirty thousand copies a month. *Catcher* is second only to *Of Mice and Men* as the most frequently taught novel in public schools.

More than ten million copies of the book have been issued. The current Little, Brown edition, in its thirty-fifth printing, sells for $10.95. A mint copy of the first edition is worth about $200.

THE COMPLETE J. D. SALINGER

Jerome David Salinger was born on the first day of the year 1919 to a Scotch-Irish woman named Miriam, who had changed her name from Marie when she married his father, Sol, a Jewish importer of hams. His grandfather was a rabbi.

He has an IQ of 111. He flunked out of high school in New York and was sent to Valley Forge Military Academy, where he received his only diploma.

He likes to lie. He is known to have told women at parties in Greenwich Village that he was a goalie for the Montreal Canadiens and the son of an umbrella salesman. On the jacket biography of *Franny and Zooey,* he wrote, "I live in Westport with my dog" long after he had moved away from Westport, Connecticut, with his dog, Benny, a Schnauzer.

He was a staff sergeant with counterintelligence in the 12th Infantry of the 4th Division of the Armed Forces.

He has been married twice, first to a doctor, possibly French and almost surely a psychiatrist, and then to a Radcliffe student named Claire Douglas, who divorced him in 1967. They have two children.

He wears dark sunglasses in town, picks up his mail at about ten A.M., and occasionally buys books: light fiction, detective stories, and philosophical tomes.

He works from the very early morning until at least noon every day in a concrete bunker near his house.

Just after he moved to Cornish, New Hampshire, in 1953, he befriended a group of local high school students. Jerry, as he was known to the students, fre- quented their hangout, a luncheonette called Nap's Lunch, and hosted parties at which he served Coke and potato chips and played classics and show tunes on his hi-fi. One day he erected a six-and-a-half-foot fence around his house and is not known to have talked to any of the students again.

He recently built a fifty-foot cement tunnel from his garage to his house, which he keeps patrolled by dogs. It is the only entrance to his home.

"I pay for this kind of attitude," he has said. "I'm known as an aloof kind of man."

CATCHER IN THE NEWS

July 1951: *The Catcher in the Rye* is published by Little, Brown and Company of Boston, Massachusetts.

November 1953: J. D. Salinger grants his first interview—to a sixteen-year-old high school student named Shirlie Blaney. "He is a tall and foreign-looking man," writes Blaney of Salinger in the Claremont, New Hampshire, *Daily Eagle.* Asked if *The Catcher in the Rye* is autobiographical, Salinger replies, "Sort of. . . .My boyhood was very much the same as that of the boy in the book, and it was a great relief telling people about it."

July 1956: The manager of the book department of a Reno, Nevada, department store refuses to remove the book from his shelves after it is declared objectionable by the National Organization for Decent Literature.

November 1960: A Baptist minister in Marin County, California, decries the use of the book in public schools. It brings "reproach upon the name of God," he declares, with its "profanity, lewd words, and poor English."

March 1961: In Tulsa, Oklahoma, a teacher assigns the book to her eleventh-grade English class. Eight parents protest and demand that she be fired. The teacher is permitted to stay, but the book is banned. The same month, a San Jose high school removes the book from its twelfth-grade supplementary reading list. The teacher who compiled the list is transferred.

February 1965: *The Catcher in the Rye* is banned in a Brentwood, Pennsylvania, school as "risqué, pretty sexy." "The question," says the school superintendent, "is whether the fifteen-year-old can take it."

July 1970: In Camden, South Carolina, *The Catcher in the Rye* is stricken from Kershaw County's list of acceptable books after the local sheriff pronounces parts of the book obscene.

November 1974: J. D. Salinger grants his first interview since 1953, to denounce the publication of a pirated anthology of his previously uncollected short stories, including two early sketches of Holden Caulfield.

November 1977: In Olivet, New Jersey, parents of a sixteen-year-old girl who brought the book home as required reading for an English class fight unsuccessfully to have it banned. The book is "filthy," says the girl's father; "sex education," says the mother.

July 1980: J. D. Salinger grants his third interview. "There's no more to Holden Caulfield," he tells a reporter from *The Boston Globe*. "Read the book again. It's all there. Holden Caulfield is only a frozen moment in time."

December 1980: With a copy of *The Catcher in the Rye* in his pocket, Mark David Chapman shoots John Lennon outside the rock star's apartment house in New York. Before the police arrive, Chapman begins to read the book. Later, at his sentencing he reads aloud this passage:

> Anyway, I keep picturing all these little kids playing some game in this big field of rye and all. Thousands of little kids, and nobody's around—nobody big, I mean—except me. And, I'm standing on the edge of some crazy cliff. What I have to do, I have to catch everybody if they start to go over the cliff—I mean if they're running and they don't look where they're going I have to come out from somewhere and catch them. That's all I'd do all day. I'd just be the catcher in the rye and all.

THE WIT AND WISDOM OF HOLDEN CAULFIELD

On life: If you get on the side where all the hot-shots are, then [life is] a game, all right. . . . But if you get on the *other* side, where there aren't any hot-shots, then what's a game about it?

On religion: I like Jesus and all, but I don't care too much for most of the other stuff in the Bible. Take the Disciples, for instance. . . . They were all right after Jesus was dead and all, but while He was alive, they were about as much use to Him as a hole in the head.

On women: They're always leaving their goddamn bags out in the middle of the aisle.

On mothers: Mothers are all slightly insane.

On books: What really knocks me out is a book that, when you're all done reading it, you wish the author that wrote it was a terrific friend of yours and you could call him up on the phone whenever you felt like it.

On courtship: I think if you don't really like a girl, you shouldn't horse around with her at all, and if you *do* like her, then you're supposed to like her face, and if you like her face, you ought to be careful about doing crumby stuff to it, like squirting water all over it.

On sex: Sex is something I really don't understand too hot. You never know *where* the hell you are. I keep making up these sex rules for myself, and then I break them right away.

On girls: The trouble with girls is, if they like a boy, no matter how big a bastard he is, they'll say he has an inferiority complex, and if they *don't* like him, no matter how nice a guy he is, or how big an inferiority complex he has, they'll say he's conceited.

On courage: It's no fun to be yellow. . . . If you're supposed to sock somebody in the jaw, and you sort of feel like doing it, you should do it.

On conversation: Lots of times you don't *know* what interests you most till you start talking about something that *doesn't* interest you most.

On New York: New York's terrible when somebody laughs on the street late at night. You can hear it for miles.

On kids: You take adults, they look lousy when they're asleep and they have their mouths way open, but kids don't. Kids look all right. They can even have spit all over the pillow and they still look all right.

On peace: You can't ever find a place that's nice and peaceful, because there isn't any. You may *think* there is, but once you get there, when you're not looking, somebody'll sneak up and write "Fuck you" right under your nose.

HOLDEN REARS HIS HEAD

Holden Caulfield first surfaced in a 1944 *Saturday Evening Post* story called "Last Day of the Last Furlough," about two young soldiers on the eve of their assignment overseas. One of the soldiers is Vincent Caulfield, who "has a kid brother in the Army who flunked out of a lot of schools." The kid brother, simply "missing," is named Holden.

The following year Esquire published "This Sandwich Has No Mayonnaise," in which Holden figures heavily, although, as in "Furlough," he does not in fact appear (and may even be dead). The story concerns Vincent's obsession with Holden's disappearance: "He's only nineteen years old, my brother is, and the dope. . .can't do anything but listen hectically to the maladjusted little apparatus he wears for a heart."

That same year, 1945, Salinger killed off Vincent Caulfield in a story called "The Stranger" and finally introduced the Holden we know, a neurotic postwar teenager, in another story, "I'm Crazy." Both stories appeared in *Collier's*. The next year, Holden turned up in a *New Yorker* story, "Slight Rebellion off Madison." Both "I'm Crazy" and "Slight Rebellion off Madison" are early workings-out of scenes that later appear in the book. "Slight Rebellion off Madison" is a third-person account of Holden's rendezvous with Sally and Carl during a legitimate vacation from Pencey. Holden has a middle name, "Morrisey." Sally and he skate at Radio City and attend a Broadway matinee in which the Lunts star, though the play is *O Mistress Mine,* not *I Know My Love* as it is in the book. Other incidental details show up differently in *Catcher,* but the heart of the chapter in the book and this story is the same: Holden's confession of disrepair and his plea to Sally to join him in a cabin by a brook in the woods.

LASTING IMPRESSIONS

The first time I heard of *The Catcher in the Rye* was from my roommate at Harvard around 1952. He read passages aloud with great animation. I didn't read the book myself until 1955; maybe I was already too old. I found it admirable—funny, poignant, vivid, actual—yet somehow less useful to my burgeoning sense of what writing was about than Salinger's short stories, which I *had* read in college. You could see in *Catcher* the seeds of that cloyingness that the later Salinger developed luxuriantly. I was a little disturbed by Holden's fastidiousness, his snobbishness, his sense that the world was something to shelter yourself from.

Salinger was most magical for me in a story like "Just before the War with the Eskimos." *Nine Stories* showed me a way to write about life *now,* in the Fifties —that open-ended Zen quality they have, the way they don't snap shut in that wired-up way of a story by John O'Hara, say, or Dorothy Parker. For me, they're as revolutionary as Hemingway's stories or, later, Barthelme's. Recently I read the pirated edition of Salinger's early stories. They were interesting, the mix of slickness and tenderness, but I finished them thinking he had been right to leave them uncollected.

As to his problems with fame, I fear he brought trouble on himself with that line about wishing the author of a book you liked was a friend, someone you could call when you felt like it. I remember thinking how unlike it was to my own reaction. I've always assumed a writer is giving you his best self on the page, and we should let him alone otherwise.

I'm glad that *The Catcher in the Rye* has an enduring adolescent readership. That's a fine fate for it and makes it a very rare book. I hear Salinger is writing, and yes, I'd be curious to read whatever it is he's produced. The literary world misses him. He was the closest thing we've seen to a saint, at least since Marianne Moore.

—John Updike

During Salinger's brief stay in Westport, we became fast friends. I knew at the time that he was writing the book, and I was enormously interested in the idea, without ever dreaming that I was being made privy to the early workings-out of a classic. I remember saying that it all sounded very wonderful, but couldn't he think up a more catchy title?

Of course, later I read the book and it *was* wonderful. Rereading it recently I found that I have an even stronger feeling of fondness for the characters than I remembered. It's a literature of character, really. Holden is a wonderful creation. Though he throws himself around as if he disparages the human race, he does not have the misanthropy that you associate with that kind of disparagement. He has a real *feeling* for people, that's the richness of his characterization. My guess is that it will last forever. Now, predicting something's immortality is a tricky thing, but then *The Catcher in the Rye* is a gem of a book.

—Peter DeVries

I had a friend, an aspiring novelist (later quite a successful novelist) named William Hoffman. He was living on West 103rd Street in a rented room papered with rejection slips, and he was *raving* about the book, so I read it. That was 1954. I was twenty-three.

I was completely captivated by the tone, by the seemingly conversational, candid tone. But at the same time, I was baffled by its message. Later, after I had lived in New York, it finally dawned on me. *The Catcher in the Rye* is a completely New York book. The cynicisms about school and parents—that was completely alien to me. But the alien quality was also fascinating, as if someone had pulled back layers and revealed some strange and diseased terrain. Come to think of it, I doubt that I had ever met a real cynic prior to reading the book. Alien or not, though, it's one of the few books that artfully explore the doubts and humiliations that make up 95 percent of the life of an adolescent.

I read *Nine Stories* and loved that as well. I enjoyed *Franny and Zooey,* but after that Salinger's writing seemed to get more and more tedious. He turned out to be a small, precious talent. I think that everything he wrote uses the same material worked over and over again: namely his own early years. It's the same old story. The writer is convinced that the only valid material is his personal life. Pretty soon he has consumed every last shred of it, roots and all. Finally Salinger moved up to New England and sank up to his kneecaps, which is where he exists to this day, I gather. He seems to be the classic burnt-out case.

—Tom Wolfe

APPENDIX F
TWELVE WEEK TRIMESTER/
SIXTY DAY SCHEDULE

HANDOUT
SEMINAR EVALUATION

1. When you first began this course, what did you think it would be about?

2. Now that you have finished this course, how would you describe it to students who are interested in taking it?

3. This course has been described as a *process* course, not just a course about one author. Do you agree with this statement? If you do, explain what this means for students beginning the course.

4. What did you enjoy *most* in this course?

5. What did you enjoy *least* in this course?

6. Write any suggestions or comments that would be useful to the instructor and to students who may take a course of this nature in the future.

APPENDIX G
TWELVE WEEK TRIMESTER/
SIXTY DAY SCHEDULE

TENTATIVE SCHEDULE FOR SEMINAR IN AMERICAN LITERATURE: J.D. SALINGER

Orientation to the Seminar

Day 1.   Getting acquainted with the course and each other

Day 2.   Introducing Salinger and the Position Paper

Paper I: "A Perfect Day for Bananafish" (1948)

Day 3.   Reading aloud and discussion of "The Young Folks" (1940)
ASSIGNMENT: Position Paper on "A Perfect Day for Bananafish" (1948)
Due: _____

Day 4.   Reading aloud and discussion of "Uncle Wiggily in Connecticut" (1948)

Day 5.   Reading aloud and comparison of "The Young Folks" and "Uncle Wiggily in Connecticut"

Day 6.   Suggestions for Position Paper on "A Perfect Day for Bananafish"

Day 7.   Discussion of the prewriting process

Day 8.   In-class writing

Day 9.   Reading aloud and discussion of "Just before the War with the Eskimos" (1948)

Day 10.   Reading aloud and final writing/proofreading

Paper II: *The Catcher in the Rye* (1951)

Day 11.   Position Paper on "A Perfect Day for Bananafish" due
Introduction to *The Catcher in the Rye*
ASSIGNMENT: Position Paper on *The Catcher in the Rye*
Due: _____

Day 12.   Reading

Day 13.   Reading aloud and discussion of "I'm Crazy" (1945) and "Slight Rebellion off Madison" (1946) or Reading

Day 14.   Reading and distribution of papers for Defense Day

Day 15.   Defense Day

Day 16.   Defense Day

Day 17.   Suggestions for Position Paper on *The Catcher in the Rye* and discussion of skills for Paper II

Day 18.   Writing

Day 19.   Writing

Day 20.   Reading aloud and discussion of "The Laughing Man" (1949)

Paper III: "Teddy"

Day 21.   Position Paper on *The Catcher in the Rye* due
Introduction to "Teddy"; ASSIGNMENT: Position Paper on "Teddy"
Due: _____

Day 22.   Reading or discussion of skills for Paper III

Day 23. Reading aloud and discussion of "Down at the Dinghy" (1949)
Day 24. Resource person or film on Zen Buddhism
Day 25. Suggestions for Position Paper on "Teddy" and distribution of papers for Defense Day
Day 26. Defense Day
Day 27. Defense Day
Day 28. Reading aloud "For Esme—with Love and Squalor" (1950)
Day 29. Reading aloud and writing
Day 30. Writing or reading aloud of "Pretty Mouth and Green My Eyes" (1951)

Paper IV: *Franny and Zooey* (1957)

Day 31. Position Paper on "Teddy" due; introduction to *Franny and Zooey*
         ASSIGNMENT: Position Paper on *Franny and Zooey*
         Due: _____
Day 32. Reading
Day 33. Zen and *Franny and Zooey* and reading
Day 34. Reading and suggestions for *Franny and Zooey;* distribution of papers for Defense Day
Day 35. Defense Day
Day 36. Defense Day
Day 37. Discussing writing skills for Paper IV
Day 38. Writing
Day 39. Reading aloud and discussion of "De Daumier-Smith's Blue Period" (1953)
Day 40. Reading aloud; writing and proofreading

Paper V: A Profile of J. D. Salinger

Day 41. Position Paper on *Franny and Zooey* due
         Review of Salinger biography and introduction to Profile Paper
         ASSIGNMENT: Profile Paper based on biography and fiction of Salinger
         Due: _____
Day 42. Reading and research; suggestions for Profile Position Paper
Day 43. Reading and research; distribution of papers for Defense Day
Day 44. Defense Day
Day 45. Defense Day
Day 46. Discussion of documentation skills and writing
Day 47. Writing
Day 48. Writing

Paper VI: *Raise High the Roof Beam, Carpenters* (1963)

Day 49. Position Paper on Profile of J. D. Salinger due
         Introduction to *Raise High the Roof Beam, Carpenters;* begin reading
         ASSIGNMENT: Position Paper on *Raise High the Roof Beam, Carpenters*
         Due: _____
Day 50. Reading
Day 51. Reading; Suggestions for Paper VI
Day 52. Distribution of papers for Defense Days
Day 53. Defense Day
Day 54. Defense Day
Day 55. Writing and proofreading

Paper VII: The Summing Up

Day 56.   Position Paper on *Raise High the Roof Beam, Carpenters* due
ASSIGNMENT: Summation Paper or a Humorous Paper on Salinger and the
seminar. Suggestions for Paper VII
Due: _____

Day 57.   Writing and distribution of papers for Defense Day

Day 58.   Defense Day

Day 59.   Reading aloud of final papers

Day 60.   Reading aloud of final papers. Final discussion and evaluation.

BIBLIOGRAPHY

BASIC MATERIALS FOR STARTING A SEMINAR

A Salinger seminar should be inexpensive. Besides the materials in this handbook, the basic requirements largely involve paperbacks. Class sets of these paperbacks provide smooth instruction. However, if the budget is slim, materials can be obtained from other sources: school and public libraries, used book stores, and student, teacher, or classroom copies. The following are recommended for starting a Salinger seminar:

Nine Stories. Bantam, 1971.

The Catcher in the Rye. Bantam, 1971.

Franny and Zooey. Bantam, 1971.

Raise High the Roof Beam, Carpenters and *Seymour: An Introduction.* Bantam, 1971.

Besides class sets, the instructor may wish to make available individual uncollected stories (See bibliography entry: "Checklist of Major Primary Sources"), as well as the collage biographies in *Time,* 15 September 1961, and *Salinger* by Henry Anatole Grunwald (New York: Harper and Brothers, 1962), pp. 1-22. "The Search for the Mysterious J. D. Salinger: The Recluse in the Rye" in *Life* 51 (November 1961), and "A Young Writer Brings the World a Message from J. D. Salinger: 'Go Away'," in 25 February 1980 *People* would also be useful.

Since there are few biographical sources, you also may wish more than one copy of the following titles. They are also valuable critical sources for the instructor and for follow-up days:

Belcher, William F., and Lee, James W., eds. *J. D. Salinger and the Critics.* Belmont, Calif.: Wadsworth Publishing Company, 1964. This includes the *Time* biography, critical essays on *Catcher,* and essays on Salinger stories as well as general criticism.

Grunwald, Henry Anatole, ed. *Salinger: A Critical and Personal Portrait.* New York: Harper and Brothers, 1962. This includes the collage biography, ten essays on various stories and books, and a Postscripts section with plot summaries of early stories and discussion of Holden's language in *Catcher.*

Gwynn, Frederick L. and Blotner, Joseph I. *The Fiction of J. D. Salinger.* Critical Essays in Modern Literature series. Pittsburgh, Pa.: University of Pittsburgh Press, 1958. This divides and discusses periods in Salinger's fiction, up to 1957.

Lundquist, James. *J. D. Salinger.* New York: Frederick Ungar, 1979. This is an excellent source, especially on Zen influences and themes. Over twenty-two pages of bibliography make it especially useful. It covers all of Salinger's work.

Audio-visual materials are as scarce as biography. Suggestion:

The Catcher in the Rye (cassette). N 136 CX. Listening Library, Inc., 1 Park Avenue, Old Greenwich, CT 06870. A lecture by critic James E. Miller.

VALUABLE BOOKS: BIOGRAPHY AND CRITICISM

French, Warren. *J. D. Salinger.* New York: Twayne, 1963.

Hamilton. *J. D. Salinger: A Critical Essay.* Grand Rapids: William B. Eerdmans, 1967.

Laser, Marvin, and Fruman, Norman, eds. *Studies in J. D. Salinger: Reviews, Essays, and Critiques of the Catcher in the Rye and Other Fiction.* New York: Odyssey Press, 1963.

Marsden, Malcolm M., ed. *If You Really Want to Know: A Catcher Casebook.* Chicago: Scott, Foresman, 1963.

Miller, James E., Jr. *J. D. Salinger.* Minneapolis: University of Minnesota Press, 1965.

Simonson, Harold P., and Hager, Philip E., eds. *Salinger's 'Catcher in the Rye': Clamor vs. Criticism.* Boston: D. C. Heath, 1963.

VALUABLE ARTICLES AND ESSAYS

"A Young Writer Brings the World a Message from J. D. Salinger: 'Go Away'." *People,* 25 February 1980, pp. 43-44.

Blaney, Shirlie. "An Interview with an Author." *Daily Eagle* (Claremont, New Hampshire), 13 November 1953.

Carpenter, Frederic. "The Adolescent in American Fiction." *The English Journal* 46 (September 1957): 313-319.

Elfin, Mel. "The Mysterious J. D. Salinger. . .His Woodsy Secluded Life." *Newsweek* 50 (30 May 1960):92-94.

Fosburgh, Lacey. "J. D. Salinger Speaks about His Silence." *New York Times,* 3 November 1974, pp. 1, 69.

Geismar, Maxwell. "J. D. Salinger: The Wise Child and the *New Yorker* School of Fiction." in *American Moderns: From Rebellion to Conformity.* New York: Hill and Wang, 1958.

Greenburg, Dan. "Catcher in the Oatmeal." *Esquire* (February 1958):46-47. This parody of Salinger appears under the title "3 Bears in Search of an Author." Parodies of James Joyce and Ernest Hemingway accompany the piece.

Havemann, Ernest. "The Search for the Mysterious J. D. Salinger: The Recluse in the Rye." *Life* 50 (3 November 1961):129-144.

Hicks, Granville. "J. D. Salinger: Search for Wisdom." *Saturday Review* 42 (25 July 1959):13, 30.

Kaplan, Charles. "Holden and Huck: The Odysseys of Youth." *College English* 27 (November 1956):76-80.

Kazin, Alfred. "J. D. Salinger: 'Everybody's Favorite!' " *Atlantic* 207 (August 1961):27-31.

McCarthy, Mary. "J. D. Salinger's Closed Circuit." *Harpers* 225 (October 1962):46-48.

Mizener, Arthur. "The Love Song of J. D. Salinger." *Harpers* 218 (February 1959):83-90.

"The No-Nonsense Kids." *Time* 70 (18 November 1957): 51-54.

Skow, John. "Sonny: An Introduction." *Time* 68 (15 September 1961):84-90.

Steiner, George. "The Salinger Industry." *Nation* 189 (14 November 1959):360-363.

"The Catcher on the Hill." *Newsweek* (18 November 1974):17.

"The Dodger in the Rye." *Newsweek* (30 July 1979):28.

THE PUBLISHED WORKS OF J. D. SALINGER

"The Young Folks." *Story* 16 (March-April 1940): 26-30.

"Go See Eddie." *University of Kansas City Review,* December, 1940, pp. 121-124.

"The Hang of It." *Collier's* 108 (12 July 1941):22.

"The Heart of a Broken Story." *Esquire* 16 (September-October 1941):32, 131-133.

"The Long Debut of Lois Taggett." *Story* 21 (September-October 1942):28-34.

"Personal Notes on an Infantryman." *Collier's* 110 (12 December 1942):96.

"The Varioni Brothers." *Saturday Evening Post* 216 (17 July 1943):12-13, 76-77.

"Both Parties Concerned." *Saturday Evening Post* 216 (26 February 1944):14, 47-48.

"Soft-Boiled Sergeant." *Saturday Evening Post* 216 (15 April 1944):18, 82, 84-85.

"Once a Week Won't Kill You." *Story* 25 (November-December 1944):23-27.

"Elaine." *Story* 26 (March-April 1945):38-47.

"A Boy in France." *Saturday Evening Post* 217 (31 March 1945):21, 92.

"This Sandwich Has No Mayonnaise." *Esquire* 24 (October 1945):54-56, 147-149.

"The Stranger." *Collier's* 116 (1 December 1945): 18, 77.

"I'm Crazy." *Collier's* 116 (22 December 1945):36, 48, 51.

"Slight Rebellion off Madison." *The New Yorker* 22 (21 December 1946): 76-79.

"A Young Girl in 1941 with No Waist at All." *Mademoiselle* 25 (May 1947):222-223, 292-302.

"The Inverted Forest." *Cosmopolitan* 123 (December 1947):73-80, 85-86, 88, 90, 92, 95-96, 98, 100, 102, 107, 109.

"A Perfect Day for Bananafish." *The New Yorker* 23 (31 January 1949):21-25.

"A Girl I Knew." *Good Housekeeping* 126 (February 1948):37, 186, 188, 191-196.

"Uncle Wiggily in Connecticut." *The New Yorker* 29 (20 March 1948):30-36.

"Just before the War with the Eskimos." *The New Yorker* 24 (5 June 1948):37-40, 42, 44, 46.

"Blue Melody." *Cosmopolitan* 125 (September 1948): 51, 112-119.

"The Laughing Man." *The New Yorker* 25 (19 March 1949):27-32.

"Down at the Dinghy." *Harper's* 197 (April 1949): 87-91.

"For Esme—with Love and Squalor." *The New Yorker* 26 (8 April 1950):28-36.

The Catcher in the Rye. Boston: Little, Brown, 1951.

"Pretty Mouth and Green My Eyes." *The New Yorker* 27 (14 July 1951):20-24.

"De Daumier-Smith's Blue Period." *World Review* (London) (May 1952):33-48.

"Teddy." *The New Yorker* 28 (31 January 1953): 26-36, 38.

Nine Stories. Boston: Little, Brown, 1953.

"Franny." *The New Yorker* 30 (29 January 1955): 24-32, 35-43.

"Raise High the Roof Beam, Carpenters." *The New Yorker* 31 (19 November 1955):51-58, 60-116.

"Zooey." *The New Yorker* 33 (4 May 1957):32-42, 44-139.

"Seymour: An Introduction." *The New Yorker* 35 (6 June 1959):42-52.

Franny and Zooey. Boston: Little, Brown, 1961.

Raise High the Roof Beam, Carpenters; and *Seymour: An Introduction.* Boston: Little, Brown, 1963.

"Hapworth 16, 1924." *The New Yorker* 41 (19 June 1965):32-40.

EDUCATIONAL FILMS

The Mood of Zen. Hartley Productions, 1968. 14 min., color.

The Long Search 9: The Land of the Disappearing Buddha. BBC TV: Time-Life Film, 1978. 52 min., color.

FILMSTRIPS/RECORDS/CASSETTES

The Modern Novel: The Catcher in the Rye [Filmstrip]. 19 min., color/sound, with either LP record or cassette. No. 722. Educational Dimensions Corporation, P. O. Box 488, Great Neck, NY 11022.

PICTURES AND POSTERS

J. D. Salinger [Poster]. Eight Masters of Modern Fiction series. Includes Fitzgerald, Hemingway, Wolfe, Baldwin, Salinger, McCullers, Faulkner, and Steinbeck. Scholastic Book Services, set of 8 pictures, 15 x 20 in. For information, write Scholastic Book Services, 50 West 44th Street, New York, NY 10036.

J. D. Salinger [Poster]. Famous Author Super Posters, 23 x 29 in., SN00918.

J. D. Salinger [Picture]. United States Authors, 8½ x 11 in., SN95777. For information, write The Perfection Form Company, 1000 North Second Avenue, Logan, IA 51546.

EDUCATIONAL REPRINTS

Salinger and Updike. Reprint 8. *Life* Educational Reprints. For information, write Primary Communications Inc., P. O. Box 480, Southern Pines, NC 28387. Multiple copies of this inexpensive 1961 *Life* article would be valuable for the profile paper.

HOLLYWOOD FILMS

Despite the numerous references to Holywood and films, only one movie was made of a Salinger work. Salinger was so dissatisfied with film that he refused further Hollywood versions of his stories. This film is available through commercial loan libraries. Consult your library or A-V director.

My Foolish Heart. 1949, RKO. Dana Andrews (Walt Dreiser); Susan Hayward (Eloise Winters); Gigi Perreau (Romona). Director: Mark Robson, B/W, 98 minutes. This version of "Uncle Wiggily in Connecticut" not only altered the names (Walt Glass, Eloise Wegler) but also turned the plot into a sentimental romance. Bosley Crowther, reviewing the film for the *New York Times* early in 1950, described it as "a wartime romance and the consequent despairs of the young lady when she finds herself with child and her unwed lover killed." [*The New York Times Film Reviews,* 1913-1968. New York: *New York Times* and Arno Press, 1970, p. 2394.]

III. IN SEARCH
OF JOHN STEINBECK

ORIENTATION TO THE SEMINAR
DAYS 1–2

DAY 1: GETTING ACQUAINTED WITH THE COURSE AND EACH OTHER

Goals

1. To acquaint students with the nature of the seminar and to introduce them to its method and content.
2. To help students get to know each other.

Materials

1. Handout 1: Seminar in American Literature.
2. Handout 2: Tentative Schedule.
3. After you have taught in-depth seminars, use evaluations from former students (see Day 90) to interest beginning students.

Procedure

1. Use Handout 1 as a brief introduction to the idea of an in-depth seminar.
2. Using Handout 2 as a guide, offer an overview of the course, noting particularly how writing and reading activities are correlated. Point out the variety of the course, the value of individual exploration and group discussion, the chronological approach, the assignments and due dates, the allotted time for in-class reading and writing, and Defense Day—which will be explained later.
3. Stress that you genuinely want to know the students and to have them know each other. Everyone will be working together in the course.
4. Pair off students who do not know each other or who know each other only slightly. Find a partner for yourself. Ask each student to interview his or her partner without taking notes, asking questions that each partner would like answered—family, job, favorite food, pets, sports, music, travel, plans for the future.
5. After five or ten minutes, ask each student to introduce his or her partner to the seminar by summarizing the answers to the interview questions. Now the class has taken the first step toward becoming a genuine seminar. These introductions may lead to friendships, and they certainly will help to establish the understanding and cooperation needed in later discussions, especially the evaluations on Defense Day.

Additional Suggestion

A classroom bulletin board on John Steinbeck helps to develop interest: photographs, magazine clippings, material from books about or by Steinbeck, a sample position paper (one from this handbook or from a previous seminar), maps (California, the Joad route from Oklahoma to California [see Paper IV], Long Island, New York). Perhaps some students have visited geographical settings of Steinbeck's life and literature and have materials to contribute to an evolving bulletin board.

DAY 2: INTRODUCING STEINBECK AND THE POSITION PAPER

Goals

1. To preview Steinbeck's life and work.
2. To introduce the Position Paper.

Materials

1. Handout 3: The Steinbeck Chronology. You may also refer to the materials on Steinbeck's life and times in the Appendix.
2. Handout 4: The Position Paper.

Procedure

1. Referring to Handout 3: The Steinbeck Chronology, discuss the idea that the seminar will be one of discovery, of learning how Steinbeck's ideas and writing developed. The first of the seven position papers focuses on the early short stories, from 1933 to 1938, from *The Red Pony* to *The Long Valley*. In particular, the paper will formulate a position about "The Harness," which appeared in *The Long Valley*. Around this time, Steinbeck had been living in Los Gatos, California, trying desperately to succeed as a published author and developing the basic themes and style that would make him famous.

2. Note that Steinbeck's life is divided into two parts: West Coast and East Coast, California and New York. His distinctive boyhood home in Salinas, California, molds and nurtures his love of the land and the people who lived and worked on it. He observed nature, the animals, and the problems of human beings in his home state. He wanted to be a writer; he could not wait for a college diploma at Stanford. He went to the East Coast to find literary success—and failed. He returned to California and then published his first novel—which was a failure. Undaunted, even by the Great Depression, he worked at his craft in his California environment. Despite near-poverty and family tragedy, he found success with *Tortilla Flat* and *Of Mice and Men*. But the controversial nature of his social comment during the 1930s led to strong criticism even in his home town of Salinas. The crisis came with the 1939 publication of *The Grapes of Wrath*. This, plus a shattered marriage, led

him to flee to New York. With a New York base, Steinbeck's life would take him to Europe (especially as a World War II correspondent), the Middle East, Russia, and Asia. He would travel across the American landscape with his poodle; he was always in pursuit of the past, especially the travels of King Arthur. He would continue to write of California, but he also shifted his locale to France and New York. And when he died, his ashes were buried in the California soil of Salinas.

3. Distribute Handout 4: The Position Paper and discuss the nature of a position paper. Stress the requirements of length and format (typed, double-spaced, one side, unlined paper), since clear, complete copies must be distributed on Defense Day. At this point, do not dwell on evaluation procedures since a positive attitude toward writing does not begin with apprehension about grades. Remind students that typing is required by most college teachers and that it is wise to improve their typing now. Tell them that you will provide position papers written by high school juniors and seniors for them to examine; assure them that they will be given considerable class time for reading and writing. Useful background material and even suggestions for topics will be given as specific papers are assigned.

Additional Suggestion

Some students may already have read books by or about Steinbeck. Encourage them to share their initial impressions. If they have seen television or film versions of his works, this should also be shared. (See Bibliography for description of film versions.)

HANDOUT 1
SEMINAR IN AMERICAN LITERATURE

Have you ever read an author in depth? If you have, you probably made a number of discoveries:

1. You became acquainted with the writer, his or her basic themes and style.

2. You felt the deliciousness of expertise which includes a sense of chronology, favorite characters, a knowledge of major and minor works, a delight in quotable lines.

3. It was as if the writer became your friend. You may have wanted to learn more about the person, his or her life. You may even have hungered to find other writings or eagerly awaited new books to be published.

So the seminar will go in depth, while the survey course that you just took has skimmed the surface. And as a small group, you will share your discoveries with the seminar—in discussion, in your papers, on Defense Day, informally.

One thing must be kept in focus: This seminar is not concerned with making you an expert on one author (though you may be). Our concern is with the *process* of studying any author. In fact, this is really a Basic Skills (sound familiar?) course: Reading, Writing, Speaking, and Listening.

> Reading: Your reading will involve four novels, at least eight short stories, over 100 pages of autobiography or biography. You also will read at least 28 position papers.
>
> Writing: You will write seven position papers—three to five typed (skill) pages. You will be studying other people's writing; the seminar will discuss good writing.
>
> Speaking: You will defend two of your position papers before the seminar. You will also be reading aloud and discussing what you have read—short stories, position papers.
>
> Listening: You will have to listen carefully because Defense Day requires that everyone listen carefully to what is said and read. You will be involved in Defense Day grading.

HANDOUT 2
TENTATIVE SCHEDULE FOR SEMINAR IN AMERICAN LITERATURE:
JOHN STEINBECK

Orientation to the Seminar

Day 1.   Getting acquainted with the course and each other

Day 2.   Introducing Steinbeck and the Position Paper

Paper 1: "The Harness" (1938)

Day 3.   Reading aloud and discussion of "The Chrysanthemums"
ASSIGNMENT: Position Paper on "The Harness"
Due: _____

Day 4.   Teacher Reading of "The White Quail" (1935)

Day 5.   Reading aloud and discussion of "The Snake" (1935)

Day 6.   Suggestions for Position Paper on "The Harness" and in-class writing

Day 7.   In-class writing

Day 8.   Reading aloud and discussion of *The Red Pony* (1933)

Day 9.   Reading aloud and discussion of *The Red Pony*

Day 10.   Reading aloud or film

Paper II: *Tortilla Flat* (1935)

Day 11.   Position Paper on "The Harness" due
Introduction to *Tortilla Flat;* begin reading
ASSIGNMENT: Position Paper on *Tortilla Flat*
Due: _____

Day 12.   Reading

Day 13.   Discussion: Thomas Malory and Ed Ricketts

Day 14.   Reading

Day 15.   Reading

Day 16.   Reading and/or distribution of Defense Day papers

Day 17.   Defense Day: "The Harness"

Day 18.   Follow-up discussion: students and critics

Day 19.   Suggestions for Position Paper on *Tortilla Flat* and reading/writing

Day 20.   Discussion of the prewriting process

Day 21.   Reading aloud and discussion: "Tularecito" (1932)

Day 22.   In-class writing and proofreading

Day 23.   Teacher reading and discussion of "Johnny Bear" (1937)

Paper III: *Of Mice and Men* (1937)

Day 24.   Position Paper on *Tortilla Flat* due
Introduction to *Of Mice and Men;* begin reading
ASSIGNMENT: Position Paper on *Of Mice and Men*
Due: _____

Day 25.   Reading

Day 26.   Reading

Day 27.   Suggestions for Position Paper on *Of Mice and Men*

Day 28.   Reading aloud and discussion of play version of *Of Mice and Men*

Day 29.   In-class reading and discussion of play

Day 30.   In-class reading and discussion of play and/or distribution of first Defense Day papers

Day 31.   Defense Day: *Tortilla Flat;* distribution of second Defense Day papers

Day 32.   Defense Day

Day 33.   Follow-up discussion: students and critics

Day 34.   Review and instruction: transitions and sentence variety

Day 35.   Writing; discussion of *Roget's Thesaurus*

Day 36.   Writing and discussion/in-class reading of "Breakfast" (1938)

Paper IV: *The Grapes of Wrath* (1939)

Day 37.   Position Paper on *Of Mice and Men* due
          Introduction to *The Grapes of Wrath;* begin reading
          ASSIGNMENT: Position Paper on *The Grapes of Wrath*
          Due: _____

Day 38.   Reading

Day 39.   Examining the geography of the novel

Day 40.   Review of the Great Depression

Day 41.   Audio-visual material about the 1930s

Day 42.   Reading

Day 43.   Historical perspectives of the Great Depression and the Dust Bowl

Day 44.   Reading

Day 45.   Reading and/or distribution of Defense Day papers

Day 46.   Defense Day

Day 47.   Defense Day

Day 48.   Follow-up discussion: students and critics

Day 49.   Reading and suggestions for Position Paper on *The Grapes of Wrath*

Day 50.   Discussing the Pulitzer Prize and the Theory of the Phalanx

Day 51.   Film: *The Great American Novel: The Grapes of Wrath*

Day 52.   Writing

Day 53.   Writing

Paper V: A Profile of John Steinbeck

Day 54.   Position Paper on *The Grapes of Wrath* due
          Review of Steinbeck biography and introduction to Profile Paper
          ASSIGNMENT: Profile Paper on reading of biography and autobiography
          Due: _____

Day 55.   Reviewing Steinbeck biography with A-V materials

Day 56.   Reading and research
Day 57.   Reading and research
Day 58.   Anecdote Day
Day 59.   Anecdote Day
Day 60.   Discussion of documentation skills; distribution of Defense Day papers
Day 61.   Defense Day
Day 62.   Defense Day
Day 63.   Follow-up discussion: students and critics
Day 64.   Writing
Day 65.   Writing
Day 66.   Film: *America and Americans*

Paper VI: Paper of Choice

Day 67.   Position Paper on Profile due
Consideration of reading choices for Paper VI
ASSIGNMENT: Position Paper on Steinbeck work of a student's choice
Due: _____
Day 68.   Reading
Day 69.   Reading
Day 70.   Reading
Day 71.   Reading and/or distribution of Defense Day papers
Day 72.   Defense Day
Day 73.   Defense Day
Day 74.   Follow-up discussion: students and critics
Day 75.   John Steinbeck and the Nobel Prize
Day 76.   Reading
Day 77.   Writing and discussion of clarity and comparison/contrast skills
Day 78.   Writing
Day 79.   Writing
Day 80.   Writing

Paper VII: The Summing Up

Day 81.   Position Paper of Choice due
Reading, re-reading, research, and writing; Suggestions
ASSIGNMENT: Summation Paper and/or a Humorous Paper on Steinbeck and his work
Due: _____
Day 82.   Writing
Day 83.   Writing and distribution of papers for Defense Days
Day 84.   Defense Day
Day 85.   Defense Day
Day 86.   Follow-up discussion: students and critics

Day 87.   Writing and proofreading

Day 88.   Reading aloud of final papers

Day 89.   Reading aloud of final papers

Day 90.   Final discussion; evaluation of seminar; reading aloud by instructor

HANDOUT 3
THE STEINBECK CHRONOLOGY

1902   Born in Salinas, California, the third child and only son of John Ernst Steinbeck and Olive Hamilton Steinbeck.

1919   Graduates from Salinas High School and begins irregular attendance at Stanford University.

1924   Publishes stories in Stanford *Spectator*.

1925   Leaves Stanford without a degree. Visits sister in New York and works as an assistant bricklayer on Madison Square Garden. Works as cub reporter for N.Y. *American*. Fails to find a publisher for stories.

1926   Returns to California. Finishes first novel while being a winter caretaker of a Lake Tahoe estate.

1929   Publishes first novel, *Cup of Gold,* about a pirate.

1930   Marries Carol Henning and moves to family cottage at Pacific Grove. Meets Ed Ricketts, a marine biologist and friend for life. Acquires New York literary agent: McIntosh and Otis.

1932   *Pastures of Heaven,* a short story collection built around one family. Moves to Los Angeles.

1933   *To a God Unknown* and first two parts of *The Red Pony*.

1934   His mother, Olive Hamilton Steinbeck, dies. Short story "The Murder" wins O. Henry prize.

1935   His father, John Ernst Steinbeck, dies. Steinbeck's first commercial success, *Tortilla Flat*.

1936   *In Dubious Battle*. Moves to Los Gatos.

1937   *Of Mice and Men* (novel) published, while play version wins New York Drama Critics' Circle Award. Travels with Okies from Oklahoma to California.

1938   *The Long Valley* and fourth part of *The Red Pony* published.

1939   *The Grapes of Wrath*. Elected to National Institute for Arts and Letters.

1940   Steinbeck and Ed Ricketts visit Gulf of California. *The Grapes of Wrath* wins Pulitzer Prize.

1941   *Sea of Cortez*. Separates from Carol Steinbeck and moves to New York City.

1942   *The Moon Is Down,* novel published, play produced. Divorced from Carol.

1943   Marries Gwyndolyn (Gwen) Conger. Visits war zone in Africa and Italy for New York *Herald Tribune*.

1944   Film *(Lifeboat)*. Son Thom born. Moves back to California.

1945   *Cannery Row, The Red Pony* in four parts published. Returns to New York and buys a home.

1946   Son John born.

1947   *The Wayward Bus* and *The Pearl* (book and film). Travels to Russia.

1948   *A Russian Journal.* Separates from Gwen and goes back to California. Divorce.

1949   Film of *The Red Pony* released. Steinbeck returns to East Coast.

1950   Marries Elaine Scott. *Burning Bright,* novel and play. *Viva Zapata!,* film.

1951   *The Log from the Sea of Cortez.*

1952   *East of Eden.* Correspondent in Europe for *Colliers'.*

1954   Lives in Paris for nine months. *Sweet Thursday.*

1955   Broadway musical *Pipe Dream* flops. Buys cottage at Sag Harbor, Long Island, New York.

1957   *The Short Reign of Pippin IV* published. Steinbeck begins research on Malory and *Morte d'Arthur.*

1958–1960   Travels to England and lives there eleven months. *Once There Was a War.* Back to Sag Harbor and then off with poodle traveling across America.

1961   Last novel, *Winter of Our Discontent.* First heart attack, in Europe.

1962   *Travels with Charley.* Wins Nobel Prize for Literature.

1963   Takes cultural exchange trip behind Iron Curtain with Edward Albee.

1964–1965   Death of editor and good friend, Pascal Covici. Trips to Ireland, Israel, and Southeast Asia. *America and Americans.*

1968   Dies of heart attack, December 20.

1969   *Journal of a Novel: The East of Eden Letters.*

1975   Wife Elaine and Robert Wallsten edit *Steinbeck: A Life in Letters.*

1976   *The Acts of King Arthur and His Noble Knights.*

HANDOUT 4
THE POSITION PAPER

1. The position paper is just that: you adopt a single position about what you have read, a narrowed focus that can be developed by using concrete examples from the reading or from supplements to the reading. The position is *your* position.

2. The position paper must be three to five typed pages. The papers must be typed because at least two papers will be chosen from each assignment, reproduced, and evaluated during Defense Day by members of the seminar.

3. The possibilities for positions are nearly unlimited. You may want to develop an important quotation from a work, an important symbol, a character or a comparison of two characters, the author's style, his or her ideas about love, death, maturity, society, nature, money. You may wish to explore the author's use of names, choice of title, brand of humor. Suggestions for positions will be given with each assignment.

4. The paper must be your best writing. It will always be read by the instructor. At least two of your papers will be discussed and evaluated by the entire seminar.

5. Do not use the title of the work for your paper. Instead, your title should suggest or reflect your position.

6. Present your position logically and support it with concrete material— quotations and examples from what you have read as well as your own observations about life and literature. Don't neglect the plot or ignore the names of the characters, yet assume that your reader is your seminar classmate, who is also familiar with the work.

7. Writing good papers is hard work. It requires a clear outline. Your paper needs sharp first and last sentences, transitions between solidly developed paragraphs, varied sentences—not all beginning with pronouns, not all simple or compound constructions. It requires your sharpest and most mature language. Good writing is correct writing: don't lose your reader by failing to proofread. Read your paper aloud before typing the final draft. Finally, a good paper uses psychology: work hard on introductions and conclusions —the first and last things that the reader reads.

8. Do not rely on critics. While there will be student position papers for you to examine, take your own position.

9. Do not be afraid to adopt a position that seems "way out," fanciful, outrageous. If you have a strong position, one that may be challenged in the seminar discussion, just be sure that you have the material to defend it.

10. The writing of seven position papers is a cumulative experience. Each paper builds upon its predecessors, so do not hesitate to refer to previous papers or ideas—yours or those of other classmates. Through your own writing and by studying the works of other students, you will make discoveries about your reading and writing. New ideas will come to you. You will become aware of your own style as you consider the writing of others. And, while each paper will not necessarily be better than the last, your final production will speak for itself. You will be impressed!

PAPER I: "THE HARNESS"
DAYS 3–10

DAYS 3–5: READING THREE *THE LONG VALLEY* STORIES ALOUD

Goals

1. To introduce the Long Valley stories by reading aloud and discussing on Day 3 "The Chrysanthemums" (1937); on Day 4, the instructor reading of "The White Quail" (1935) to the class; on Day 5, class reading and discussion of "The Snake" (1935).
2. To provide a background for an independent reading of "The Harness" (1938) and for writing the first Position Paper.

Materials

1. *The Portable Steinbeck*, which includes "The Chrysanthemums," "The Snake," and "The Harness."
2. A teacher copy of *The Long Valley* for reading "The White Quail."
3. Handout 5: John Steinbeck: California.

Assignment

1. Read "The Harness" and write a three-to-five-page Position Paper on that story.
2. Insert DUE date for this paper on the Schedule. In addition, note the date of the first Defense Day and explain to students that copies of the position papers chosen for defense on that day will be given out on Day 16.

Procedure

1. Distribute Handout 5, asking students to locate Salinas, California—the author's home town. Remind students that Steinbeck was born and raised in the fertile Salinas River valley, beautiful country between the Gabilan Mountains and the Santa Lucia Mountains that bordered the Pacific Ocean. This is the setting for many of his stories and novels, including those to be examined in the first section. They come from *The Long Valley* (1938). Steinbeck attended Salinas High School, spent summers with his family at their Pacific Grove cottage, went fishing, worked as a laborer for a canal dredging company, spent a summer with a surveyor's crew near Big Sur, and was a hired hand at a huge sugar-beet ranch in the long valley.

2. Read "The Chrysanthemums" aloud for immediate reaction. If the implied sexual content of "The Snake" is too strong for your choosing, use "Flight" (1938)—or you may wish students to read it overnight and then hold only classroom discussion. Ask individual students to read a section aloud to the seminar; then summarize what they have read, observing whatever comes to mind about plot development, style, sentence length, dialogue, word choice, characters, names, the title, and the theme.

3. As students read aloud, hear, and discuss these three stories on three consecutive days, they should make some discoveries that will relate to "The Harness" and future writing: (1) Steinbeck often opens a story with a description of the locale, detail, and poetic images that place the characters in their California settings. (2) Though the characters might seem ordinary and unremarkable in their social setting, they have human emotions that relate to important ideas that concern us all. (3) Steinbeck enjoys symbols. What figurative meanings have the titles, the images of flowers and birds and snakes?

4. Do the stories relate to your students? If not, what can you do to help them "connect"? A final question for the class: Suggest for

each story at least one position that might be established in a three-to-five-page paper. "The Chrysanthemums": Do others exploit you by playing with what they perceive to be your secret sensitivities? "The White Quail": Do we exploit others to foolishly get our own way? "The Snake": Who is really weird in our weird world—the so-called snake woman or the objective Dr. Phillips? "Flight": How does a teenager achieve maturity?

DAY 6: CHOOSING AND LIMITING TOPICS FOR POSITION PAPER I

Goals

1. To discuss appropriate topics for Position Paper I.
2. To demonstrate how to narrow a topic.

Materials

1. Handout 6: Suggestions for Position Paper I.
2. Handout 7: Student Model Paper I.

Procedure

1. By now students have read "The Harness" and are beginning to understand Steinbeck's early life and writing. Do not, however, discuss this story until *after* the position papers are handed in; but the concept of a position paper is probably incomplete and further clarification in class is needed.
2. Before suggesting suitable topics and how to narrow them, you may want to provide more background for the students. Useful sources:
   a. Chapter 8, pp. 71-76, in Thomas Kiernan's *The Intricate Music: A Biography of John Steinbeck.*
   b. Nelson Valjean, *John Steinbeck: The Errant Knight,* pp. 59-61, 152.
   c. *Steinbeck: A Life in Letters,* edited by Elaine Steinbeck and Robert Wallsten, pp. 85-86 (letter dated 25 February 1934).
3. Distribute Handout 6 and discuss these suggestions for position papers on "The Harness." Since suggestion 9 focuses on animals, an important concern throughout

the seminar, you may want to remind the students of Steinbeck's lifelong love of dogs, of the animals in the three stories now discussed, and of his interest in natural science that began in high school. See chapter 5 in Kiernan's biography.
4. You may wish to use the model paper for "The Harness" at this point. You might post it on the bulletin board for student reference or make multiple copies for individual study. Note particularly the instructor's comments which follow the student paper.
5. Stress: The goal for this paper is following directions and proofreading. Students must have a single position. If time remains, students should attempt to define individual positions, review the short story, and begin writing. Encourage them to see that the prewriting stage includes talking to others, jotting down broad ideas and then narrowing, trying to state a position in a single sentence.

DAYS 7–10: COMPLETING PAPER I, READING AND VIEWING A FILM

Goals

1. To provide in-class writing time for the completion of Paper I.
2. To read and discuss stories in *The Red Pony* (1933).
3. To view a film version of *The Red Pony.*

Materials

1. *The Portable Steinbeck.*
2. Film: *The Red Pony* (101 min., color).

Procedure

1. Day 7 should be used for in-class writing. Proofreading, a concept that must be developed throughout the semester, can be handled on the day before the papers are collected—or at the beginning of Day 11.
2. *The Red Pony,* based in part on Steinbeck's small chestnut named Jill which he received in the summer of 1912, is probably too long for in-class reading in its entirety. The book defines a basic Steinbeck concern: human beings with unique minds caught in what

seems a mindless natural order, often helpless, and victims of fate. It also is a familiar story of growth from innocence to knowledge and disillusionment. Jody survives four personal experiences: human fallibility, the wearing out of human beings, nature as unreliable, and the exhaustion of nature. Jody learns compassion.

3. Read and discuss at least "The Gift"—though, if time allows, you may wish to extend oral analysis beyond Day 10.

4. There are various versions of *The Red Pony* available in film. The 1973 film has serious flaws and departures from the Steinbeck text, though the sense of the California land is its major asset for classroom use. However, even this film can have value when its obvious changes are considered in terms of what Steinbeck might have thought of it, given his major themes at this point.

Suggestion

See *Steinbeck: A Life in Letters*, p. 70, for Steinbeck's 1933 letter to friend George Albee about *The Red Pony*.

HANDOUT 5
JOHN STEINBECK: CALIFORNIA

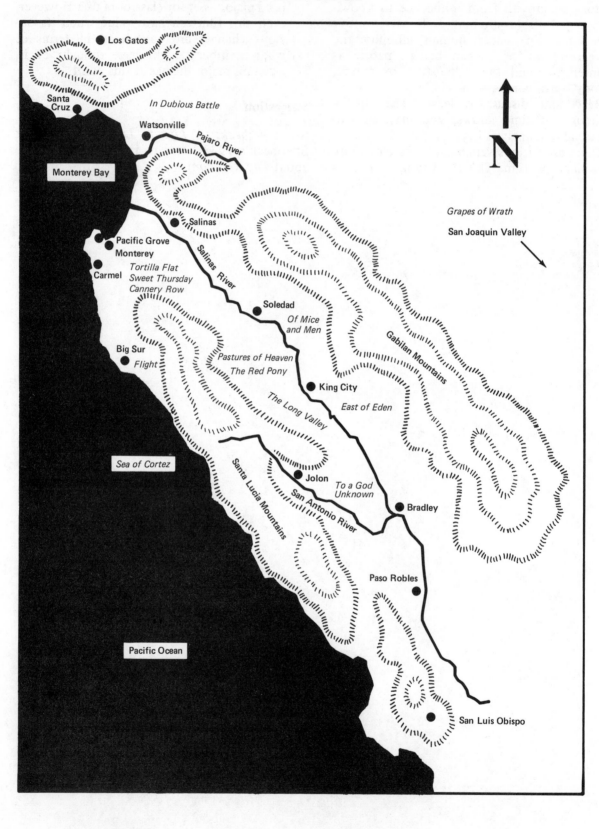

HANDOUT 6
SUGGESTIONS FOR PAPER I:
"THE HARNESS" (1938)

1. We have seen that "The Chrysanthemums" is a title open to a position that can be traced in that story. Can this story's title also be symbolic?

2. Some critics say all the stories in *The Long Valley* are *ironic*. Is "The Harness"? Check the definition of "irony."

3. Study the names of the characters. Develop a theory about how Steinbeck chose these names—or concentrate on one character.

4. What is the meaning of the sweet peas?

5. What is the function of the minor character Ed Chappell?

6. "The Chrysanthemums" concerned a husband and a wife. So does this story. Do these stories have a common theme?

7. Study the ending of the story. Does a position lie there?

8. Find a key quotation in the story for a focus.

9. Steinbeck sees animal in man. Does he see it in this story?

10. Find a key word, such as "frustration," which is a central concern in this story. Then develop and illustrate it in your paper.

11. Was the wife really so bad? Is Steinbeck a male chauvinist?

12. Is this just a story about 1938 California? Does it apply to our world today?

13. One critic believes that Steinbeck's stories are concerned with ignorance which leads to bondage. Does this apply to "The Harness"?

14. Examine the beginning of this story. Why did Steinbeck begin it that way? Is it similar to other stories that we have examined? Develop a theory about how he begins stories.

15. Define "love" and then discuss your definition in terms of this story. Is there any love in this story?

HANDOUT 7
STUDENT MODEL FOR PAPER I

RANDALL'S REVOLT

by David Barker

In "The Harness," by John Steinbeck, it is apparent that a strong force
is acting upon Peter Randall, molding his actions. Peter's inner desires
would have him taking wild chances, spending his money on drink and whore-
houses, and generally neglecting his own welfare. These desires are held in
check by his wife Emma, representing his conscience and mores. After Emma's
death, however, the same conscience bombards him through the medium of
neighbors and friends. He cannot escape this domination.

In the beginning of the story Peter seems the strong marriage partner,
responsible for the good life that he and Emma have achieved. He is respected in the community.

> Peter Randall was one of the most highly respected farmers
> in Monterey county. Once, before he was to make a little
> speech at a Masonic convention, the brother who introduced
> him referred to him as an example for young Masons of Cali-
> fornia to emulate.

No one in the community would have suspected that Emma wielded as much power
as she did, for to them she seemed weak.

> Concerning Peter's wife, Emma, people generally agreed that
> it was hard to see how such a little skin-and-bones woman could
> go on living, particularly when she was sick most of the time.

Emma is later found to be quite different from what her appearance would suggest. She is described as having a "feverish determination to live." Her
father had been a high-ranking member of the Masons, of which she is proud.

1

2

Much of what Peter does is the result of prodding by Emma. He keeps
an immaculate yard and flower garden.

>   In the garden, under Emma's direction, Peter raised button
>   dahlias and immortelles, carnations and pinks.

This arrangement is especially significant, considering the role of this type
of work in other stories in <u>The Long Valley</u>. In other stories the women
generally tend to flowers and decorative things, while the men prefer more
practical occupations.   Peter does this work for Emma, suggesting that she
has control over him. After Emma's death Peter says, "I don't know how she
got me to do things, but she did."

The full extent of Emma's domination over Peter is revealed after her
death, when Peter tells Ed Chappel that she made him wear a harness to keep
his back straight and an elastic belt to keep in his stomach. This harness,
the title of the story, is Steinbeck's symbol for society's inflexible control over our lives. Emma is part of the same symbolism. She kept the house
clean and made sure that Peter made no foolish ventures. Her absolute
authority is explained when Peter says, "When she was alive, even when she
was sick, I had to do things she wanted."

Peter did not enjoy his situation. Once a year he took a trip to San
Francisco, where he crammed as much sin as he could into a week of drunken
happiness. Upon his return, however, he paid pennance for his indulgence.
He says, "God, how she worked my conscience when I came back."

Peter's revolutionary attitude is revealed in his name. Randall is an
adaptation of the word "rand," which means to rant and rave about. Peter's
first name has Biblical origins, suggesting a conflict between Peter's true
nature and the moral forces which bind him.

Peter finally revolts after Emma's death. He decides to burn his harness and belt, track dirt into the house, and hire a voluptuous maid. Emma

3

had never let Peter plant the crop he wanted (sweet peas), because of the
risk involved. After her death Peter is sure that the ecstatic sensual
pleasures of a crop of sweet peas would justify the risk. He says,

> Think how it'd be to sit on the front porch and see all those
> acres of blue and pink, just solid. And when the wind came
> up over them, think of the big smell. A big smell that would
> almost knock you over.

Randall's revolt is never realized, however. He never allows his house to
degenerate; he succumbs to the wishes of the community. When discussing the
matter with Ed Chappel, he becomes sheepish and ashamed. By disapproving of
Peter's intentions, Ed brings back Emma and all that she meant to Peter.
Earlier in the story Emma was referred to several times as "bird-like." While
working the fire during the conversation, Ed symbolically reminds Peter of
his duties.

> Chappell went to the grate and stirred the glowing wood until
> lots of sparks flew up the chimney like little shining birds.

The sweet pea crop is looked upon among the townspeople in a different
way than by Peter. Their opinion of the crop depends on its ability to succeed, while Peter enjoys the wanton excess of pleasure and beauty.

Even Peter cannot resist the values by which he has been dominated for
so long. Although his crop is a success, he worries about it a great deal.
He says,

> Sure I made money--but it wasn't a bit better than gambling.
> It was just like straight gambling.

Emma, through the community or through Ed Chappel, still rules him.

> She didn't die dead. She won't let me do things. She's worried
> me all year about those peas. I don't know how she does it.

If Peter is typical of those of us who read "The Harness," it seems impossible to break out of the conformity of life in society. Society's goals
and ideals are ingrained into us, even if we must be bribed with cakes and
pies or drugged into submission.

4

Instructor's Comments

1. <u>Strengths</u>: This first paper has strengths that make it a good model for
beginning students. It takes a strong position about Peter Randall's
failure to revolt against Emma and the community which, in turn, relates
to all of us who seek to rebel. The writer sees Steinbeck in terms of
himself. To prove his point, he organizes fact and quotation (an important success for a first paper) in chronological fashion. He even
relates this story to <u>The Long Valley</u> stories which were discussed in
class. And finally, he reminds the seminar that Steinbeck uses symbols--
names, key words, sensitive scenes.

2. <u>Weaknesses</u>: While the position is largely clear, the first Defense Day
readers can profit by discussing ambiguities and mechanical considerations. What is the difference between <u>conscience</u> and <u>mores</u>? Is Emma
really a representation of the entire society or a particular individual
of our society? Shouldn't the writer make clear which particular <u>Long
Valley</u> stories relate to "The Harness"? Do all of them? Has the writer
read all of them? What particular "biblical origins" relate to the name
of <u>Peter</u>? When does a writer single space a direct quotation and not
include it within flowing text of a paragraph?

PAPER II: *TORTILLA FLAT*
DAYS 11–23

DAYS 11–12: BEGINNING A STEINBECK NOVEL

Goals

1. To orient students to *Tortilla Flat* (1935).
2. To begin reading the novel in class.

Materials

Class set of *Tortilla Flat.*

Assignment

Note the DUE date of Paper II on the Schedule, Day 24.

Procedure

1. Remind students that the first Defense Day will be coming up in about five days. Copies of the papers for defense will be handed out the day prior to Defense Day. All papers will be returned at the end of Defense Day.
2. Ask students to review The Steinbeck Chronology (Handout 3), noting that we will be analyzing Steinbeck's first successful novel. His 1929 fictionalized biography of the pirate Henry Morgan and his 1933 mystical novel of Joseph Wayne and California were commercial failures. While living in Pacific Grove, Steinbeck met Susan Gregory, a young Monterey high school teacher, who told him about her town's poor Mexican *paisano* population that lived in shanties in the hills above Monterey. Gregory had found these people to have humor and dignity; she wrote poems about them. She took Steinbeck to "Tortilla Flat," as it was called locally, and told him stories about the people there. Steinbeck began to write stories about the *paisanos,* partly to escape his problems such as the serious illnesses of his parents. Then he began to unify them under a specific theme that he had discussed with his friend Ed Ricketts. More will be discussed about these ideas later.
3. Pass out copies of *Tortilla Flat.* Note the dedication and the above background.
4. *Tortilla Flat* is an episodic novel of the *paisanos* of Monterey. The seventeen stories revolve around their leader Danny who is at first blessed and then burdened by the ownership of some old shacks, by property. However, the preface announces that this 1920s California story is somehow related to King Arthur and the Knights of the Round Table. While the book is wild, even bawdy, and funny, students should be reminded that it is serious too. You may wish to begin this section by oral reading and discussion of the preface.
5. Use the rest of Day 11 and all of Day 12 for in-class reading.

Additional Suggestions

1. Refer to Handout 5 (and other California maps) for the setting of the novel.
2. To introduce the King Arthur influence: Chapter 2, pp. 14–18, about Steinbeck's childhood interest in King Arthur, in Kiernan, *The Intricate Music: A Biography of John Steinbeck.*

DAY 13: INFLUENCES: THOMAS MALORY AND ED RICKETTS

Goal

To provide biographical and philosophical/thematic background to *Tortilla Flat.*

Materials

During John Steinbeck's Salinas childhood, he came under the influence of *Morte d'Arthur* by Thomas Malory (d. 1471). This book was a gift from his favorite Aunt Molly (Mrs. Edward Martin). He especially loved the old spellings of this Caxton version in archaic English. His obsession with these stories of King Arthur and the Round Table led him in a life-long pursuit of research and writing to make a modern version. His unfinished version, in fact, was published after his death. To familiarize your students with Steinbeck and Malory, you may wish to do the following:

1. Secure a copy of Malory's book or a children's version, as well as the 1976 Steinbeck book, *The Acts of King Arthur and His Noble Knights.*
2. *Steinbeck: A Life in Letters,* pp. 96–97, 552–554.
3. Appendix B: Letter to John Murphy/ King Arthur.

In 1930, Steinbeck met Monterey biologist, Ed Ricketts, who later encouraged John to write *Tortilla Flat.* Ricketts and Steinbeck became close friends; they worked together on *The Log from the Sea of Cortez.* Later, Steinbeck would write a beautiful tribute preface to this book, "About Ed Ricketts." Ricketts is also the model for Dr. Phillips in "The Snake." Much has been made by critics about Ricketts's influence on Steinbeck's fiction. On this day, you can begin to suggest this influence. More can be done on this subject with Papers III, IV. Suggested materials:

1. *The Log from the Sea of Cortez.*
2. *The Intricate Music:* pp. 159–161, 177.
3. *John Steinbeck: The Errant Knight* by Nelson Valjean.

Procedure

1. Using photographs in *John Steinbeck: The Errant Knight* reminds students that Tortilla Flat was a real place. Also show pictures of Steinbeck and Ed Ricketts. Note how *Tortilla Flat* is a blend of real people and places, of Steinbeck's childhood reading and his adult concerns.
2. Begin by discussing the Malory influence. Read from the Malory and Steinbeck ver-

sions. Review the basic concern of these books: the reign of King Arthur ending in catastrophe and the end of the Round Table; the quest for the Holy Grail, in which Lancelot fails because of his sin with King Arthur's wife; and Galahad's success. In other words, a legend of the search for perfection in an imperfect world.
3. Remind students of the preface. Use Appendix B letter of 1961 to show how this concern never ceased for our author. Refer to other Steinbeck letters.
4. Then note that the book was somewhat influenced by Steinbeck's friend Ed Ricketts. You may wish to read the pages from *The Intricate Music* and then brief cuttings (such as the first pages) from "About Ed Ricketts."

Additional Suggestion

Slides concerning Tortilla Flat, Malory and King Arthur, and Ed Ricketts could be made to reinforce or introduce this discussion. These slides could be made from the suggested sources, as well as others.

DAYS 14–16: READING *TORTILLA FLAT* AND PREPARING FOR DEFENSE DAY

Goals

1. To provide time for students to continue reading *Tortilla Flat.*
2. To prepare students for the first Defense Day.

Materials

1. Copies of the position papers on "The Harness" that you have chosen for the first Defense Day.
2. Handout 8: Evaluation Criteria.

Procedure

1. Two full days, 14 and 15, will give students time to read most of this medium-sized novel. Hopefully, the previous discussions of King Arthur and Ricketts will motivate this reading.
2. On Day 16, hand out copies of the papers

you have chosen for the first Defense Day, Day 17.

3. Encourage students to annotate their copies of these papers so that they will be able to remember their initial reactions to clarity, organization and support, and mechanics. Remind them that Defense Day is not Destruction Day. It is a time to learn about the positions of others, to clarify what is not clear, to agree and disagree, to study organization and supporting evidence, to work on mechanics, and to defend what one has written. The word "criticism" implies two responsibilities, for critics try to understand what a writer has written as well as to react to the writing.

4. Remind students that the skill goals for this paper were: following directions, one clear position, and proofreading.

5. Give each student Handout 8. Note: This handout is to help students understand the nature of evaluation on Defense Day. Some instructors may wish to use this vehicle for anonymous Defense Day evaluation; others may see it only as a point of reference on the Defense Day which stresses oral grading.

6. Students whose papers have been chosen for Defense Day should prepare to read them aloud.

DAYS 17–18: PARTICIPATING IN DEFENSE DAY AND FOLLOW-UP

Goals

1. To conduct a first Defense Day that will provide a useful model for the remaining six.
2. To provide a follow-up that offers other students the opportunity to express their positions.
3. To help students examine the position of critics.

Materials

1. Extra copies of the position papers for students who may have lost or forgotten them.
2. Prior to class, review the discussion of how to conduct a successful Defense Day in the introduction. Write the three criteria on the board: Clarity of Position; Organization and Support; Mechanics. Or use Handout 8.

3. The corrected copies of the remaining position papers ready to give out at the end of the period.

Procedure

1. It is important to choose good models for the first Defense Day and to allot the discussion time equally. Remember, the students, not you, are to do the evaluating. Too much direction on your part will destroy the spirit of Defense Day; instead, encourage discussion, restate or clarify student positions, work for a balanced discussion (call on everyone, ask students who suggest grades to justify their choices), and conclude the defenses with a positive summation. Always the goal is the next paper.

2. If oral grading ever proves too stressful during the seminar, you may wish to use anonymous grading with Handout 8 as the basis. During the clarity discussion, be sure to ask all students to write a one sentence description of the position on the handout. Collect all handouts at the end of the period, arrive at a consensus grade, and return all evaluations with consensus grade to the writer the next class period.

3. Return the other position papers at the end of the period without comment. The next class period can be given over to these papers.

4. Follow-up, Day 18, will allow others in the class to state their positions. Note: Some instructors may prefer to have two Defense Days; others may wish to substitute discussions on writing skills or other Steinbeck material. For example, the *Tortilla Flat* paper skills include using direct quotations and ideas about introductions and conclusions. Here the instructor may wish to deal with selecting and editing quotations, building short ones of under four lines of text into a paragraph while single spacing and indenting longer ones. Also appropriate is discussion on the psychological importance of introduction and conclusions, on the varieties of approaches, and on the idea of a key line which defines the position in either the introduction or conclusion. Even

the idea of a title built from the introduction or conclusion might be discussed.
5. Other options:
    a. Review the positions taken by the papers defended on the previous day. You may have taken notes on the positions of the remaining students and can, therefore, call on students who have similar or contrasting positions. Or each student can be called upon to state his or her position. Or you may ask other students to read all or selected portions of their papers—again, excellent models but ones not chosen for Defense Day.
    b. You may wish to discuss the successes (and failures) of the first Defense Day. Clear the air. Ask students how Defense Days can be improved. If some students argue that the grading was too high or too low, ask them to formulate a fair standard, taking into consideration the pressures of such close examination. Remind them that learning to write is more than just a letter grade.
    c. You may wish to read aloud some critic's evaluations of "The Harness." It should be noted that this story, unlike others in the seminar, has had little in-depth critical response. However, Warren French's discussion of *The Long Valley* stories in chapter 8 of *John Steinbeck*, pp. 80–84, examines this story in contrast with the others.

DAYS 19–20: CHOOSING TOPICS FOR PAPER II AND THE PREWRITING PROCESS

Goals

1. To suggest topics for Paper II.
2. To complete reading and encourage prewriting processing.

Materials

Handout 9: Suggestions for Paper II.
Handout 10: Student Model for Paper II.

Procedure

1. Handout 9 may be used in identifying positions for the second paper. The student paper for this assignment may be posted on the bulletin board for individual reference or copies may be made for distribution and discussion.
2. Time to complete the novel may be provided in class if necessary.
3. Students should be encouraged to find direct quotations that will support their positions—a goal of this paper.
4. A discussion of the prewriting process can be valuable at this point. Ask students to share with the class the way they found their position on Paper I. Discuss such prewriting concerns: (1) Brainstorm—make notes on ideas that come to you. (2) Examine your written ideas and see which one has the strongest appeal. (3) See if the ideas are related, as well as which ones can be developed. What would be concrete material, scenes, characters, direct quotations that would support your idea?
5. Also discuss the setting and mechanics of writing: When do you write best? Must you write or type to get results? What rewards do you give yourself? Do you write continuously—or do you stop when things are going good, a time when you can easily return to the manuscript? How do you get into a paper, into the introduction? Do you have special devices for introductions, such as beginning with a prefatory or thematic quotation?

DAY 21: READING ALOUD ANOTHER STEINBECK STORY

Goals

1. To read aloud "Tularecito" from *The Pastures of Heaven* (1932) and to relate it to *Tortilla Flat*.
2. To suggest how this story will relate to our next reading, *Of Mice and Men*.

Materials

Class copies of *The Portable Steinbeck*.

Procedure

1. Remind students that this story comes from a 1932 anthology of short stories, *The Pastures of Heaven*, which relates incidents in the lives of people living in a secluded

valley in California, Las Pastureas del Cielo. See Handout 5. It is the story of a cursed valley. Tularecito, like Danny and his paisanos, has great difficulty surviving and adapting in his environment. Like Lennie in *Of Mice and Men,* he is a freak of nature.

2. Ask students to read the story aloud, section by section, summarizing and reflecting on Steinbeck's style and themes. How is this story similar to what has been studied? What would be a position about this story?

3. Repeat a concern of both Ed Ricketts and Steinbeck: One of man's greatest deficiencies as a species is an inability to adapt to an environment of continual change. Animals adapt, but humans with their intellects resist adaptation and change. This is a curse. Danny was happy when he lived for each day but cursed when he began to worry.

DAYS 22–23: COMPLETING PAPER II AND READING A BACKGROUND STORY FOR *OF MICE AND MEN*

Goals

1. To complete the writing and proofreading of Paper II.
2. To read "Johnny Bear" (1937) in preparation for *Of Mice and Men.*

Materials

A teacher copy of *The Long Valley.*

Procedure

1. Day 22 should be given over to writing and proofreading. Since students saw that proofreading errors detracted from the papers read on the first Defense Day, they will be more concerned about careful proofreading.

2. Remind students that Paper II is due at the beginning of the period on Day 24.

3. Day 23 should provide students with an introduction to *Of Mice and Men,* as well as remind them of "Tularecito." "Johnny Bear" is another story of a freak of nature, a physical monster who does not think when he reproduces the conversations of the "good" people of the Long Valley. But Steinbeck is not just interested in freaks; like Ricketts, he sees these characters in terms of the balance between the human and the animal in nature. In this story, we see the animal behind the facade of the "good" people; the freaks are vehicles for revealing the truth.

4. This is a gripping story. It should help to pull together ideas already discovered and help students prepare for Lennie and the so-called normal people of *Of Mice and Men.*

HANDOUT 8
DEFENSE DAY: CRITERIA FOR GRADING POSITION PAPERS

____ **Clarity of Position**

1. Does the paper pursue *one* position?
2. Can you state this position? If so, write it below:

    _____

    _____

    _____

____ **Organization and Support**

1. Is the position clear because it is logical?
2. It it clear because it is supported by concrete material, such as direct references and quotations?
3. Is it clear because it pursues an obvious, even minor, position? Consider if the position is complex or original.
4. Is the position supported by the proper language, for example, a humorous position uses humorous images and words?
5. Is there coherence in the paper: transitions between sentences and paragraphs to enhance the organization?
6. Are the introduction and conclusion effective in clarifying the position?
7. Does the paper suffer from irrelevancies or over-emphasis of a minor point?

____ **Mechanics**

1. Do many proofreading errors detract from the paper's position?
2. Are there over ten basic mechanical errors—spelling, punctuation, capitalization, fragments, run-on sentences, usage, misplaced modifiers, parallel structure, words often confused, pronoun forms, verb forms?
3. Is the paper smooth reading? What about awkward sentences, imprecise or redundant word choice?

_____ Grade

USE THIS SHEET AS YOU EXAMINE EACH POSITION PAPER.

HANDOUT 9
SUGGESTIONS FOR PAPER II: *TORTILLA FLAT* (1935)

1. Why would this novel become a best seller in the Great Depression?
2. You have heard that this book somehow relates to King Arthur and the Round Table. How?
3. Some critics feel this book is a satire. Is it? If so, focus on one concern that is being satirized.
4. Relate two episodes in terms of a single position.
5. This book is an example of Steinbeck humor. What is the essential humorous device?
6. What single episode symbolizes the entire novel?
7. Is this a racist novel?
8. What view of women emerges in this novel which appears to be about men?
9. There is a great deal of drinking in this book. Why?
10. Look closely at the names of the characters. Is there a position?
11. How is Joe Portagee's finding love related to the novel and life?
12. Again we meet animals and animal language. What does this mean?
13. What does this book say about sex? About love?
14. Is this a social protest novel?
15. Some readers feel that some of Steinbeck's books should be banned from high school classes and libraries. What is a position why this book should or should not be banned at your school?

HANDOUT 10
STUDENT MODEL FOR PAPER II

THE GOOD LIFE

by Eugene Barth

As John Steinbeck states in the preface, <u>Tortilla Flat</u> is the story of
Danny and his friends, the story of a Paisano community in the small coastal
town of Monterey. Steinbeck's approach, as always, is naturalistic, but the
grim atmosphere frequently associated with this technique is absent. His
treatment of the daily thoughts and actions of the Paisanos falls in a very
entertaining and humorous vein. However, despite the lightness of the book,
Steinbeck presents certain truths, or at least ideas, which transcend the
momentary laugh. In Tortilla Flat he is again exploring the question of
individual contentment in society, and it becomes apparent that his idea of
a good life is not to be found in twentieth-century industrialized America,
but rather in the Paisanos of Monterey.

The Paisano way of life contains several elements which Steinbeck considers necessary to a good life. One of these, both obvious and at the same
time important, is animalism. This facet of Paisano life is seen throughout
the book. During Danny's party and in big Joe Portagee's love affair, the
reader clearly sees that the Paisanos engage in sex when and where they want
it with no moral qualms. Likewise, the reader sees that fighting has no
social stigma attached. It is something that is accepted and enjoyed by the
Paisanos. Friends engage in it and are drawn closer by it. That Steinbeck
considers this release of sexual tension and aggression a healthy thing is
reflected in his portrayal of the Paisanos as a content and mentally stable

1

2

people. Steinbeck's belief in the necessity of animalistic behavior for a
healthy life can also be seen in "Johnny Bear" and "The Harness." Both of
these stories deal, to a certain extent, with the fate of people living in
a society where animalism is forbidden. In "The Harness" the result is a
guilt-stricken automaton, a man totally subdued and living only out of habit.
In "Johnny Bear" the result is a suicide. Clearly Steinbeck feels the expression of certain aspects of the animal in man is necessary to a good life,
as seen in the tragic results of repression.

The Paisano closeness to nature, an aspect perhaps related to and en-
compassing animalism, is yet another feature of their way of life which
Steinbeck finds appealing. The Paisanos do not live by nature in the sense
of being totally dependent on it for food, clothing, or wine. They obtain
the necessities from an "unwilling world." Outside of this, however, they
are not connected with the typical American way of life. They are, as
Steinbeck says, "clean of commercialism, free of the complicated systems of
American business." Their alarm clock is the sun, and frequently a ditch or
matting of pine needles serves as a bed. The Paisanos love the wind and the
ocean. They love and appreciate all beauties and truths which nature, and
life in general, have to offer. Their life, free of typical American responsibilities, is ideally suited to the contemplation of these beauties and
truths.

To Steinbeck, this closeness to nature also contributes to a better
life. In the first place, it provides the Paisano with the means of isolat-
ing himself totally. By the beach, on the docks, or in the woods the Paisano
can think about his own fate and the fate of those around him. He can enjoy
a feeling of total control over himself, or at least an understanding of his
destiny; he can enjoy the feeling of freedom that accompanies this knowledge.
He can, in short, escape society completely. That Steinbeck considers this

3

healthy is again reflected in the contentment and stability of the Paisanos and again in the stories "Johnny Bear" and "The Harness." Both Peter of "The Harness" and Amy of "Johnny Bear" were unable to feel free of society's scrutiny, and the result was anything but a good life. Steinbeck, then, admires the Paisano's closeness to nature, for out of it comes fundamentally strengthened and secure people--individuals containing an element of the good life.

The unity with nature achieved by the Paisanos also gives rise to mysticism. The Paisano, alone with the earth, feels close to something much bigger than himself, something he calls God. And while feeling very small, he at the same time feels very large. The Paisano experiences an overwhelming love for all things affiliated with his world and an overwhelming desire to do good. Pilon brings this out clearly when he thinks to himself:

> Our Father is in the evening . . . these birds are flying
> across the forehead of the Father. Dear birds, dear sea
> gulls, how I love you all. Your slow wings stroke my heart
> as the hand of the gentle master strokes the full stomach of
> a sleeping dog, as the hand of Christ stroked the heads of
> little children. Dear birds fly to our Lady of Sweet Sorrows
> with my open heart.

This spiritual desire to do good, coupled with the security of knowing one's destiny and perhaps with the brotherhood which persons in the same circumstances feel, results in a people possessing the moral of humanitarianism, a people capable of great kindness. The Paisano's capacity for kindness and understanding is seen throughout the book. It is visible in the beating and healing of big Joe Portagee in the episode with the soldier, in the protection of Pirate's hoard, and in the individual deeds and thoughts of the Paisanos. In fact, it can be described as lightly permeating their way of life. That Steinbeck feels this humanitarianism is an element of the good life goes without saying.

4

With the addition of humanitarianism, Steinbeck's exploration of the individual's contentment in society is complete. Together, animalism, closeness to nature, and humanitarianism comprise the major aspects of Paisano life which Steinbeck considers elements of a good life. They are, of course, interrelated. A closeness in nature is perhaps the most important in that the other two are, in part, reflections of it. It should be noted, however, that although these aspects are present in Paisano life they are not the only ones. Survival, greed, social status, and a myriad of other factors, many of them a result of twentieth-century encroachment, frequently override the above features of Paisano life, especially humanitarianism. Pilon is a classic example of this. More often than not, his use of logic and moralism is designed to facilitate a crime such as the proposed theft of Pirate's hoard, or to obtain wine and avoid work as in the case of the St. Andrew's Eve adventure with big Joe Portagee.

The Paisano life is a life of physical hardship, hardship which most Americans don't know and would just as soon remain ignorant of. And of course, it is not a lifestyle on which a large society can be founded. However, Steinbeck definitely feels that in many ways it is superior to the industrialized and urbanized mode of American life. This fact is best seen in the contentment of the Paisanos, a content which is clearly demonstrated when Pilon asks, "Pablo, dost thou never get tired of sleeping in ditches, wet and homeless, friendless and alone?" Pablo simply answers, "No."

Instructor's Comments

1. Strengths: This is a complex paper, obviously the product of much thought, organization, and search for concrete support. The position becomes clear as the introduction suggests it, the next paragraphs

5

define the four sub-topics, and the conclusion restates Steinbeck's (and the student's?) concern with modern America. The last quotation is a sharp conclusion, chosen for both documentation and impact. And even better, the student has gone beyond the skills of support and introduction/conclusion; he has summarized the key material of the seminar thus far.

2. <u>Weaknesses</u>: This is obviously a student who is developing a mature writing style. He is concerned with transitions, with complex sentences. While the paper may be flawed with wordiness, with self-consciousness (the introductory <u>that</u> clauses), with strange word choice ("lightly permeating their way of life"), it also is ambitious. It is difficult to attack such ambition.

PAPER III: *OF MICE AND MEN*
DAYS 24–36

DAY 24: INTRODUCTION TO STEINBECK'S CLASSIC NOVEL AND SUCCESSFUL PLAY

Goals

1. To orient students to *Of Mice and Men* (1937).
2. To provide in-class time to begin the novel.

Materials

Class copies of *The Portable Steinbeck*.

Assignment

1. Ask students to note the DUE date for the third paper on the Schedule, Day 37.
2. Remind students that Defense Days for Paper II *(Tortilla Flat)* will be Days 31 and 32. Copies of the papers chosen for defense will be handed out on Day 30.

Procedure

1. Give students time at the beginning of the period to proofread position papers and then collect Paper II.
2. Ask students to review The Steinbeck Chronology (Handout 3), noting that the next book for consideration is the very successful, almost classic American novel *Of Mice and Men*. Also note the Handout 5 map. The setting of this story is about four miles below Soledad, on the Salinas River, which also is the approximate location of a ranch where Steinbeck had worked in 1920 after he briefly left Stanford. It should be noted that Steinbeck had first-hand knowledge of agricultural laborers, common

people; he was always sympathetic, never bored, with simple, illiterate people.
3. In 1936, while living in Pacific Grove, Steinbeck began to work on a story he called "Something That Happened." Encouraged by author John O'Hara and friends like Ed Ricketts, he continued to pursue his interest in his themes of the shattering of illusions, the tragic-comic Arthurian striving for a dream, the loneliness of individuals. He began to experiment with the material of a novel in the form of a play.
4. Steinbeck chose a new title based on a line from the Scottish poet Robert Burns: "The best laid scheme o' mice an' men gang aft a-gley." See full poem in Appendix F. The title, suggested by Ed Ricketts, related to their mutual concern that humans are enslaved to forces they cannot control and that destroy their illusions. The book opens with two humans in contact with the calm and order of nature, a conflict that sets the mood and theme.
5. An amusing background note: Steinbeck wrote the small book in just over two months—and, in fact, rewrote a good part of it after his dog Toby had chewed up much of the original. See *Steinbeck: A Life in Letters,* 27 May 1936.
6. Steinbeck did not expect this new book to make much money, calling it "such a simple little thing." But his editor Pascal Covici was enthusiastic, as was the public. It became a Book-of-the-Month Club selection and a best-seller. Soon it would be dramatized and later made into a film. In February, 1937, the book sales approached 100,000.
7. Ask students to begin reading.

DAYS 25–27: CONTINUING TO READ *OF MICE AND MEN*; CHOOSING TOPICS FOR PAPER III

Goals

1. To provide in-class time for reading *Of Mice and Men*.
2. To suggest topics for Paper III.

Materials

1. *The Portable Steinbeck.*
2. Handout 11: Suggestions for Paper III.
3. Handout 12: Student Model for Paper III.

Procedure

1. Use Days 25–26 for in-class reading of *Of Mice and Men*.
2. During Day 27 suggest positions for Paper III, using Handout 11 as a point of departure.
3. You also may wish to introduce the student model (Handout 12) at this point.

DAYS 28–30: READING ALOUD AND DISCUSSING THE PLAY VERSION; PREPARING FOR PAPER III

Goals

1. To relate the novel to the play.
2. To reinforce student reading of the novel.
3. To show how Steinbeck fitted his novel to a dramatic form with considerable public appeal.
4. To preview first position papers for Defense Day.

Materials

1. Class copies of *Of Mice and Men*. One source: Clurman, Harold, editor. *Famous American Plays of the 1930s.* New York: Dell Publishing, 1970.
2. Two position papers *(Tortilla Flat)* for Day 31.

Procedure

1. Remind students of the first Defense Day, Day 31. Give them the two copies on Day 30.

2. The oral reading of the play can be handled by assigning parts. Discussion can come at the end of each act. Encourage students to compare play with novel.
3. Background notes: The play was first staged in the spring of 1937 in San Francisco, almost repeating the novel, by a labor-theater group. Steinbeck decided it needed more dramatic adaptation before it reached New York. With the help of playwright/director George S. Kaufman, he took about 85 percent of the lines of the novel, juggled a few incidents, introduced a few new ones, and omitted some such as Lennie's imaginary speech to his Aunt Clara at the end of the novel. Steinbeck hated the publicity that he received in New York; he left before opening night, 23 November 1937. The play opened at the Music Box Theatre, starring Wallace Ford as George, Broderick Crawford as Lennie, and Clare Luce as Curley's wife. It was a smash hit, running 207 performances and winning the Drama Critics' Circle Award for best play of the year. Around this time, Steinbeck and his wife were visiting the Dust Bowl area in Oklahoma.

DAYS 31–33: PARTICIPATING IN THE DEFENSE DAYS AND THE FOLLOW-UP DISCUSSION

Goals

1. To conduct two Defense Days and a follow-up that offer students an opportunity to express and defend their positions.
2. To encourage students to look ahead to the third paper, accepting again the challenge of how best to present a well-documented position.

Materials

1. Copies of the papers you have chosen for both Defense Days.
2. Corrected papers of *Tortilla Flat* to return at the end of the second Defense Day.

Procedure

1. Begin Day 31 by reviewing the Defense Day procedures, although the seminar should now be familiar with the system.

2. Hand out the second set of two papers for Day 32 at the end of the period. Remind students that all corrected papers will be returned at the end of Day 32.

3. Return all corrected papers at the end of Day 32.

4. During follow-up discussion (Day 33), you might ask other students to read their papers for class comment, discuss the student paper (Handout 12), or present the viewpoint of a critic, for example, chapter 5, "Morte d'Malory" in Warren French's *John Steinbeck.*

DAY 34: REVIEW AND PRACTICING SKILLS FOR PAPER III: TRANSITIONS AND SENTENCE VARIETY

Goals

1. To review the writing skills of transitions and sentence variety.

2. To practice and encourage these skills in preparation for Paper III.

Materials

1. A writing sample, such as a copy of an earlier position paper or a student model paper.

2. A book on sentence combining, such as William Strong's *Sentence Combining: A Composing Book.* New York: Random House, 1973.

Procedure

1. Begin by examining a writing sample, such as a student model, preferably with a copy for each student. Describe how a paper has unity and smoothness in reading if the lines and paragraphs relate. Ask students to circle or underline words or lines or phrases that provide transitions between sentences and paragraphs. Ask them to check their previous two position papers and identify such transitions.

2. Work on sentence combining to encourage students to become more aware of sentence variety. First check the writing sample papers to see what variety exists. How many begin with subject-verb or the same words? How many are just simple sentences? Check

for length. Check to see if any can be combined.

3. Try a sentence combining experiment. For example, make copies of William Strong's "explorations" and ask students to study the models and then make their own "transforms." See Strong, pp. 157–205.

4. Note: Some teachers may wish to extend this skill review and instruction to more than one class period.

DAYS 35–36: COMPLETING PAPER III AND READING A BACKGROUND STORY FOR *THE GRAPES OF WRATH*

Goals

1. To complete the writing and proofreading of Paper III.

2. To give brief review and instruction with *Roget's Thesaurus.*

3. To read "Breakfast" (1938) in preparation for *The Grapes of Wrath.*

Materials

1. Class copies of *The Portable Steinbeck.*

2. A teacher copy or class copies of *Roget's Thesaurus.*

Procedure

1. Day 35 should be given over to writing and proofreading. The position paper is due on Day 37. Remind students that the skills of transitions and sentence variety are important for this paper.

2. Remind students that variety, as well as precision, in word choice is important in a mature paper. Ask how many students own a *Roget's Thesaurus,* preferably one in dictionary form. You may wish to have students buy a copy for the seminar; you may wish to gather school copies for brief review and instruction. Take a commonly repeated word like "interesting" and refer to Roget's options. Ask students to name an overused word and then find alternatives.

3. During Day 36, ask students to read aloud "Breakfast" (1938) which appeared first in *The Long Valley* and then in an altered form in *The Grapes of Wrath.* Also note p. *xx* of the introduction to *The Portable Steinbeck.*

This sketch of sharing a meal with a stranger will help define Steinbeck's concern for humanity that is developed in the next section.

Final Suggestion

If the budget allows or you can secure a free copy through a library, be sure to show the 1939 film of *Of Mice and Men* (107 minutes). This excellent film, starring Burgess Meredith as George and Lon Chaney, Jr. as Lennie, with music by Aaron Copland, retains the sensitivity and content of the novel. Also see Bibliography for other film suggestions.

HANDOUT 11
SUGGESTIONS FOR PAPER III: *OF MICE AND MEN* **(1937)**

1. Check the origin of the title. Is it better than Steinbeck's original choice, *Something That Happened?*

2. Trace the meaning of a symbol: the river, caves, animals.

3. Relate this novel to another story or book of Steinbeck's in terms of his concern about the impossibility of the quest for perfection.

4. Pick a character that you think Steinbeck likes or dislikes.

5. What do the dreams of the characters mean? Concentrate on one character, such as George.

6. Who is the developing character in this novel?

7. Discuss the power of Steinbeck's language, such as his use of swearing.

8. What is the meaning of Candy and his dog?

9. What do Candy, Crooks, and Curly's wife all have in common?

10. Discuss the nature of the dialogue of any one character.

11. Strength vs. Skill. Is this a possible position?

12. Curly's wife. What is Steinbeck suggesting about sex?

13. Note how violence builds in the novel, especially toward the end. Develop a position on violence.

14. Compare Lennie with Johnny Bear.

15. Is Lennie responsible for George's bad luck? What is responsibility?

16. What does the incident of the shooting of the dog mean?

17. Is this a universal novel or a topical novel about the 1930s?

HANDOUT 12
STUDENT MODEL FOR PAPER III

THE ANIMALS THAT DREAM

by Mark Workman

Animals don't dream, or if they do they can't convey their dreams.
People dream. John Steinbeck has shown that he believes that we are all
animals, but the fact that we can dream sets us apart from other animals.
In <u>Of Mice and Men</u>, as in many other of his stories, he has utilized different writing techniques to define the human animal who dreams.

One interesting Steinbeck technique is his selection of symbolic names
for his characters. These names seem to give reference to the dreams that
the characters may have had at one time but were hopelessly unreachable.
For example, poor Crooks was doomed by the abnormality of his body structure,
not to mention the problems of a social caste system which is imposed upon
him because of his black skin color. The pitiful futility of his situation
is conveyed to Lennie one night in the harness room of the ranch while all
the so-called "men" are in town. Crooks says,

> You got George. You know he's goin' to come back. S'pose
> you didn't have nobody. S'pose you couldn't go into the bunk
> house and play rummy 'cause you was black. How'd you like
> that? S'pose you had to sit out here an' read books. Sure
> you could play horseshoes till it got dark, but then you got
> to read books. Books ain't no good. A guy needs somebody--
> to be near him.

Crooks has realized what it is like to go without friends in an isolated
existence. A black man in a white world, he lives life secondhand by watching others live it and by retreating into a world of books.

1

2

Steinbeck seems to deprive his characters of their dreams by giving them ironic titles for names. It appears almost as though he is making a satirical comment about people and their dreams. Consider the main characters, George Milton and Lennie Small. George's last name is Milton, which is also the last name of a famous English writer--John Milton who wrote Paradise Lost. George's last name is a solid Steinbeck clue that the best laid plans of George are going to go astray, that George will never realize his dreams of a ranch and freedom and his own paradise. And then there's Lennie Small. Small is a strange name for Lennie because he is so large. Maybe John Steinbeck was not just referring to body size. Perhaps the name Small is a reference to Lennie's meager mental capacity, which like Crooks' deformity, denies him any hope of sharing George's dream.

Finally there is Candy, an old man physically deformed. His name, like that of Small, seems just the opposite of his situation. He is a man obviously soured on life, molded by a harsh environment; Candy is in need of a hand in the masculine ranch world. Reduced to taking care of the bunkhouse, he is left with an old dog and $250 dollars--what his hand was worth. When he learns of the dreams of Lennie, George, and Crooks, he sees a way out. He wants a share of paradise, too.

But the story of Candy and his dog is Steinbeck's warning that no one will get their dream in this story. Candy has an old dog that smells, and the ranch hands, such as Carlson, want him destroyed. Finally Carlson has his way; Candy's only defense is silence. He, like the dog, is treated like an animal. Candy says,

> You seen what they done to my dog tonight? They says he wasn't
> no good to himself nor nobody else. When they can me here I
> wisht somebody'd shoot me. But they won't do nothing like
> that. I won't have no place to go, an' I can't get no more
> jobs.

George, Lennie, and Crooks listen to Candy's complaint, but they don't understand that he is warning them all.

3

Steinbeck's names are symbols: George in search of paradise; Lennie, the huge man with small hope; Crooks, bent out of shape by nature and prejudice; and Candy, who finds nothing sweet in his past or future. As Steinbeck's title suggests, man and animal don't always get what they want. But at least animals don't have to follow dreams that never can be. Perhaps Crooks explains the Steinbeck theme best when he says, "Nobody ever gets to heaven, and nobody gets no land. It's just in their head. They're all the time talkin' about it, but it's jus' in their head."

Instructor's Comments

1. <u>Strengths</u>: This is an important position because it not only reveals Steinbeck's use of symbols, especially in his characters' names, but also because it focuses on Steinbeck's and Rickett's ideas about human beings in a natural world. The structure is logical, the quotations well chosen, and the goals of sentence variety and transitions obviously achieved.

2. <u>Weaknesses</u>: The writer might have used Curley's wife and her dreams. Steinbeck didn't even bless her with a name. Some students will challenge whether these characters represent all of life; they seem to be failures and freaks, not humanity in general. Perhaps more quotations on the nature of each character's particular dream would have been valuable; perhaps quotations about their animal natures might also have value.

PAPER IV: *THE GRAPES OF WRATH*
DAYS 37-53

DAY 37: BEGINNING TO READ STEINBECK'S PULITZER PRIZE NOVEL

Goals

1. To orient students to *The Grapes of Wrath* (1939).
2. To provide in-class time to begin the novel.

Materials

Class copies of *The Grapes of Wrath.*

Assignment

1. Ask students to note the DUE date for the fourth paper on the Schedule, Day 53.
2. Remind students that Defense Days for Paper III *(Of Mice and Men)* will be Days 46–47. Copies of the papers will be given out on Days 45 and 46.

Procedure

1. Allow the first few minutes of the period for a final proofreading of the Paper III positions. Collect Paper III.
2. Ask students to review the Steinbeck Chronology (Handout 3), noting that *The Grapes of Wrath* was both a best-seller and winner of the Pulitzer Prize.
3. Ask students to open their copies to the dedication: "To Carol who willed this book" and "To TOM who lived it." Carol is Steinbeck's wife who not only typed the manuscript but also suggested the title. Tom is Tom Collins, a friend and psychologist who had managed a government camp for migrants near Weedpatch in the Bakersfield,

California area—a camp similar to the one in the novel. Ask students about the origin of the title—a Civil War song.

4. Backgrounds: In 1936, Steinbeck wrote a series of articles called "The Harvest Gypsies" for the San Francisco *News,* an exposé of California migrant workers, primarily from Oklahoma and Arkansas. His 1937 tour of the Oklahoma Dust Bowl and the 1938 tour of California migrant camps for *Life* magazine, as well as visits to model government camps run by compassionate people like Tom Collins, who worked for the Farm Security Administration, gave him the mood and material for his new novel. Steinbeck was outraged. (It might also be worth noting that Steinbeck's marriage to Carol is beginning to fall apart as he labors over this long book at Los Gatos.)
5. It might be worth noting that Steinbeck will now be published by Viking Press under the editor and friend Pascal (Pat) Covici.
6. Two final suggestions to students: (1) The book has the Joad family plot—the move from Dust Bowl Oklahoma to California (probably around 1938 when there were torrential rains)—but it also has interchapters dividing this plot and conveying Steinbeck's anger, philosophy, and compassion for the Okies. (2) This book would cause Steinbeck all sorts of trouble with Californians, who were already offended by *In Dubious Battle* and *Tortilla Flat,* and with Oklahomans; both felt that much of the book was slanted, an ugly picture of their states, inaccurate, and even socialistic or communistic. This trouble eventually would lead to Steinbeck's moving to New York.

7. Ask students to begin reading the novel during the remainder of the class period.

DAYS 38–39: CONTINUING TO READ *THE GRAPES OF WRATH;* GEOGRAPHY OF THE NOVEL

Goals

1. To provide in-class time for reading of *The Grapes of Wrath.*
2. To orient students to the geography of the novel.

Materials

1. Class copies of *The Grapes of Wrath.*
2. Handout 13: *The Grapes of Wrath:* From Sallisaw, Oklahoma to Bakersfield, California.

Procedure

1. Use Day 38 for in-class reading of *The Grapes of Wrath.*
2. On Day 39, discuss Handout 13, noting the approximate route of the Joads on Highway 66 from the Dust Bowl of Oklahoma to the rich fields of California. Note McAlester, Oklahoma, where Tom Joad spent his prison days. Note: For some reason, Steinbeck's characters actually did not live in the Dust Bowl section of Oklahoma. Bakersfield, California, is near the camp of Tom Collins, who had been mentioned in the dedication.

Suggestion

At this point or at various critical points in this section, you may wish to increase student interest by noting the violent reaction to the book. Examples: "The Reception of *The Grapes of Wrath* in Oklahoma" by Martin Staples Shockley in *Steinbeck and His Critics; Steinbeck: A Life in Letters,* 23 June 1939 and editor's note about threats upon Steinbeck's life; "Excuse It, Please" by Burton Rascoe in 1 May 1939 *Newsweek,* which points out errors in the novel.

DAYS 40–43: REVIEWING THE GREAT DEPRESSION; READING

Goals

1. To review the historical backgrounds of the novel.
2. To provide in-class time for reading.

Materials

1. Films: (a) *The Okies—Uprooted Farmers,* Films, Inc. (24 min., b/w), includes cuttings from the film version of the novel; (b) *The Dust Bowl,* National Science (23 min., b/w); (c) *Life in the Thirties,* NBC (52 min., b/w).
2. Or filmstrip: *Grapes of Wrath and the 1930s,* Educational Audio-Visual, 1972.

Procedure

1. Day 40 should be a review day of the Great Depression. Using the chalkboard, develop a chronology of the 1930s, beginning with the 1929 stock market crash, 1930 riots in major cities over unemployment insurance, 1931 miners' strikes, 1932 pledge of FDR for a New Deal, 1933 first 100 Days creation of relief organizations like CCC, NRS, TVA, AAA, 1934 shooting of John Dillinger, 1935 CIO labor union formed, 1936 FDR elected again, 1937 sit-down strikes, migrations west from Dust Bowl, 1938 Munich Pact with Hitler, 1939 war begins in Europe.
2. Day 41 should be used for some audio-visual reinforcement of historical and novel backgrounds.
3. Day 42 should allow students to return to in-class reading.
4. Day 43 should continue historical reinforcement. You may wish to use resource persons such as history teachers or members of the community who remember the Great Depression. You may wish to gather library materials, especially those with good photographs of the 1930s, for student inspection, e.g., Time-Life *Fabulous Century* volumes. 1930s artifacts such as old magazines,

newspapers, or yearbooks also are useful. Finally, phonograph records are especially valuable, such as Woody Guthrie's "Dust Bowl Ballads," which includes a song about Tom Joad. Also: *Hard Times: An Oral History of the Great Depression in America* (1970) by Studs Terkel.

DAYS 44–45: READING STEINBECK MATERIAL AND PREPARING FOR DEFENSE DAY

Goals

1. To provide time for students to read this long novel.
2. To prepare for Defense Day on Paper III.

Materials

1. *The Grapes of Wrath.*
2. Copies of the Paper III positions for Defense Day.

Procedure

1. Day 44 should be an in-class reading day.
2. Day 45: Hand out the first two *Of Mice and Men* position papers for student reading and annotation.

DAYS 46–49: PARTICIPATING IN DEFENSE DAYS AND FOLLOW-UP

Goals

1. To allow students to defend the positions taken in Paper III.
2. To discuss follow-up considerations.
3. To suggest topics for Paper IV, *The Grapes of Wrath.*

Materials

1. Copies of papers for Defense Days on Paper III.
2. Handout 14: Suggestions for Paper IV.
3. Handout 15: Student Model for Paper IV.

Procedure

1. Days 46 and 47 are Defense Days, following the procedure outlined in the introduction. Return all corrected papers at the end of Day 47. Be sure to give students the second set of two papers at the end of Day 46.
2. For the follow-up discussion on Day 48, you may use the papers of other students, the Student Model (Handout 12), or the discussion of a critic such as Warren French's chapter, "End of a Dream," pp. 72–79, in *John Steinbeck.*
3. On Day 49, distribute Handout 14 and discuss positions for *The Grapes of Wrath.* Handout 15, the Student Model may also be discussed at this time.

DAY 50: DISCUSSING THE PULITZER PRIZE AND THE THEORY OF THE PHALANX

Goals

1. To provide background information on Steinbeck's winning the Pulitzer Prize.
2. To explain and discuss the "phalanx theory," which many critics feel is crucial in understanding *The Grapes of Wrath*, if not many earlier works.

Materials

1. You may wish to use W. J. Stuckey's *The Pulitzer Prize Novels*, pp. 118–121.
2. Handout 16: John Steinbeck: The Influence of Ed Ricketts. You also may wish to refer to important "phalanx" letters in *Steinbeck: A Life in Letters*, pp. 74–82, written in 1933.

Procedure

1. The public and critical impact of *Tortilla Flat* (1935) and *Of Mice and Men* (1937) in both novel and dramatic forms built a foundation for interest in *The Grapes of Wrath.* It became a best-seller. But it was an angry book, and the Pulitzer Committee and

sponsors were sensitive. Without much fanfare, they announced Steinbeck had won the prize, especially for its epic sweep of social history—not for its strong language or social criticism. Steinbeck was "pleased and flattered" for his 1940 award.

2. At this point review:
   Pulitzer Prize. When Joseph Pulitzer died in 1911, he left a fortune of nearly $19 million amassed through his development of sensational journalism; owner of the St. Louis *Post-Dispatch* and the New York *World,* he nevertheless felt his work to have integrity. So in 1903 he convinced Columbia University to enhance the field of journalism by establishing a school of journalism—and he gave $1 million for the project. Then, he was persuaded to use half of another million-dollar gift for his pet project: annual cash prizes for journalism and letters. Thus the Pulitzer Prizes were established. An advisory board was placed in charge of the $1000 prizes, including the category of the best novel: "Annually, for the American novel published during the year which shall best present the wholesome atmosphere of American life and the highest standard of American manners and manhood, $1000" (Stuckey, *The Pulitzer Prize Novels,* p. 6). The prizes for novels began in 1917.

   Through the years, the advisory board wrestled with the problem of the standards for choosing a winner, especially the problem of "wholesome," since many novels, such as *The Grapes of Wrath,* challenged American life. The president of Columbia University, Nicholas Murray Butler, was unhappy with the Steinbeck novel and apprehensive. But the choice stood.

3. Using Handout 16, review what has been said about the influence of the natural sciences, Ed Ricketts, and Malory's version of King Arthur. Point out how the novel begins discussing a turtle crossing the road in Oklahoma. Some observers note that a turtle is also a tortoise or *testudo,* the same word for the ancient Roman *phalanx*—a close order advance of soldiers with shields locked overhead.

4. Steinbeck was interested in how humans behave as individuals and in groups. Ricketts encouraged Steinbeck to observe his characters in scientific manner, to see life as it is and not how it should be. The Joads' movement westward is a phalanx, as is the movement of the Okies; the Californians who, as a group, oppose the Okies but may relent as individuals, form a phalanx.

5. It should be noted that Steinbeck seemed to depart from strict scientific observation when he suggests that the Okie phalanx or other phalanxes of the poor will revolt against the society that abuses it. His preference for the government camps suggests moralizing, if not political preference. Nevertheless, Ricketts liked Steinbeck's close study of man and nature.

DAYS 51–53: COMPLETING PAPER IV; RELATING THE NOVEL TO CONTEMPORARY AMERICA

Goals

1. To provide time for students to complete Paper IV.
2. To observe how this novel has "classic" qualities which relate to modern America.

Materials

Film: *The Great American Novel: The Grapes of Wrath,* BFA Educational Media (25 min., color).

Procedure

1. Show film, *The Great American Novel: The Grapes of Wrath,* which compares the 1930s Joads with a modern migrant family that travels to Chicago. There is effective use of lines from the Steinbeck novel to relate past and present. The film may be shown any of these three days.
2. At least two class periods should be given for writing and proofreading. Remind students that their papers are due Day 54.

Final Suggestions

1. If the budget allows, or if a free copy is available through local libraries, be sure to view the classic 1940 John Ford film starring Henry Fonda as Tom Joad. 129 minutes.

2. In these final days, the skill goals for this paper (special writing techniques) may be discussed, such as use of the first person, repetitions, and contrasting lengths of sentences in the same paragraph.

HANDOUT 13
FROM SALLISAW, OKLAHOMA, TO BAKERSFIELD, CALIFORNIA

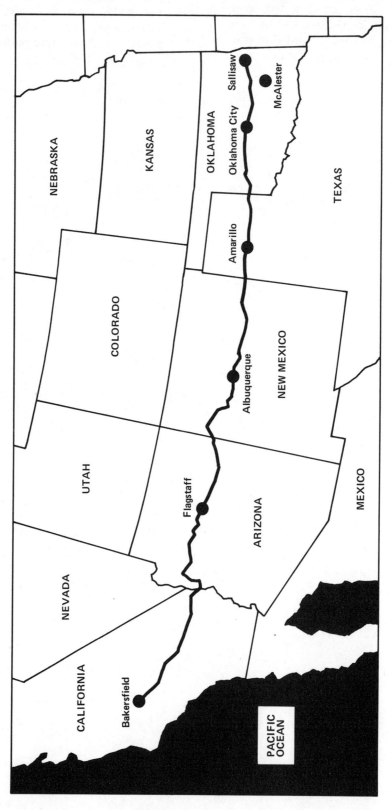

HANDOUT 14
SUGGESTIONS FOR PAPER IV: *THE GRAPES OF WRATH* **(1939)**

1. Why do various members of the Joad family drop out during the novel, especially on the trip to California?
2. John Steinbeck once said, "The Joads pass through a process of the education of the heart." Position?
3. Is this book, a 1930s propaganda novel about Okies, dated?
4. What is the meaning of "family" in this book?
5. Is Steinbeck fair to all parties? Pick a side that you feel he has a bias for or against.
6. What is the origin of the title. Is it a good title?
7. *The Grapes of Wrath:* A biblical novel? Can you illustrate this idea?
8. What is the meaning of Ma? Is Steinbeck a male chauvinist?
9. Develop a symbol: the turtle, Muley, the automobile, character's names.
10. What is the most objectionable aspect of this novel?
11. Why does the author use the interchapters that break up the Joad story?
12. What is the meaning of the weather?
13. What is the meaning of the preacher? Is he a major character?
14. Is this book an attack on America? Is Steinbeck advocating socialism? Is the government camp a symbol?
15. Discuss the ending—so vivid and controversial.
16. One critic said: The book is "a story of the awakening of man's conscience." Is it that? Whose conscience?
17. Answer those critics who want to ban this book from high schools.
18. What is the meaning of the land? Remember that the land, the American "good earth" was so important to Americans in 1939—if not now.

HANDOUT 15
STUDENT MODEL FOR PAPER IV

JIM CASY OF NAZARETH

by Charles Dorsey

If a man who was much the same as Jesus Christ appeared in modern time, few people would recognize him for what he had to offer. John Steinbeck demonstrates this lamentable theme in his Pulitzer Prize novel, The Grapes of Wrath. In this book, Steinbeck presents the character of preacher Jim Casy as a modern-day Jesus of Nazareth, and throughout the novel there are strong parallels to be drawn between the lives of these two holy men.

The first parallel is perhaps the most obvious. Jim Casy and Jesus have the same initials, and moreover, their respective names both have three syllables. It is probable that Steinbeck intended this to call first attention to what the character of Casy represents.

Of greater importance, though, are the similarities between Jim Casy's ideas and actions concerning religion and those of Jesus Christ. This is a vital point because Christ is best known as the founder of the Christian faith, and to seriously compare Casy to Christ requires that Casy share similar views on religion. Therefore, it is important to note that both men thought through the Christian dogma for themselves. Christ had to exemplify his convictions, for he was the one who originally established them. In the case of preacher Casy, he questioned the accepted religious values at a time when it was considered slightly blasphemous to do so. Casy relates this to Tom Joad: "I went off alone, an' I sat and figured. The spirit's strong in me, on'y it ain't the same. I ain't so sure of a lot of things."

1

2

Secondly, both Casy and Christ spent long periods of isolation in the wilderness for the purpose of testing and examining their religious beliefs. In the Bible, it is related that the Holy Spirit commanded Jesus to spend forty days and nights in the wilderness. When Casy says grace for the Joad family, he explains that he did the same as Jesus: "I got tired like Him, an' I got mixed up like Him, an' I went into the wilderness like Him . . . An' I got thinkin' how we was holy when we was one thing, an' mankin' was holy when it was one thing." In this passage, Steinbeck makes the relation-ship between Casy and Christ obvious.

Next, there is a parallel between the two men's religiously based re-lationship with women. After Jesus converted and protected Mary Magdalene, there are suggestions that the pair becomes intimate in a non-sexual fashion. Jim Casy also had relationships with women after introducing them to religion. Casy confesses to Tom: ". . . some I'd baptize to bring 'em to. An' then-- you know what I'd do? I'd take one of them girls out in the grass, an' I'd lay with her." This is one of the more obscure similarities between the two theologians, but it indicates the depth of the Steinbeck symbolism.

Lastly, both Christ and Casy have informal preaching methods. Jesus spread his teaching by telling parables to any crowd, large or small. In The Grapes of Wrath, the reader learns that Casy would baptize people in irrigation ditches during unstructured meetings, preach sermons in a barn, and not take in regular collections.

Another important parallel is that Jim Casy, like Jesus Christ, was an advocate of an oppressed people. In the novel, the land owners can be com-pared to the Romans who occupied Israel during the lifetime of Jesus. Both land owners and Romans were evil oppressers of the Okies and the Jews. Through his religion, Christ offered home and solace to many Jews who were struggling with Roman totalitarianism and heavy taxes. And in his own way,

3

Casy tried to aid the Okies against the land owner totalitarianism with his ideas of worker unity and with his willingness to spread these ideas. Casy describes his role to Tom, "Them cops been sayin' how they gonna beat the hell outa us an' run us outa the country. They figger I'm a leader 'cause I talk so much." Clearly Jim Casy has regard for the welfare of the Okies that goes beyond concern for his personal well being, much like Jesus' altruism for his fellow man.

The character of Tom Joad is significant in this analogy of Christ and Jim Casy because he can be considered a modern Peter Simon. Peter was Jesus' good friend and disciple, once described by Christ as having rock-like solidity. Tom is a good friend of Jim Casy, a solid friend who carefully listens to Casy's ideas. Yet Tom left Casy to face the police alone in the Hooverville, rather than standing up for what he thought was right. This is much like Peter who denied that he knew Christ after he was arrested.

Perhaps the most important parallels between Jim Casy and Jesus Christ are those relating to the circumstances surrounding their deaths. It is here that Steinbeck makes the most conclusive connection between the two men.

First, both Casy and Jesus were martyrs for their causes. Jesus was persecuted by the local Roman government because he was preaching tenets to the common people that were against the interests of the ruling class. It was exactly the same with Casy, who tried to organize the exploited workers against the growers. Both men died trying to further their cause. Jesus did not stop his activities with his disciples to escape arrest; Casy expounded his ideas with his friends just before he was caught and killed.

Secondly, neither man tried to renounce his beliefs in an effort to save himself. Jesus had many opportunities to do so, but instead went to the cross showing his faith in the things he said. Stopped by a grower's guard, Casy could have sworn that he wasn't a labor organizer, but instead

4

he died appealing to the humanity of the guards. He said, "Listen . . .
You're helpin' to starve kids."

Lastly, both Casy and Christ were killed by hired troops of the oppressors. Roman soldiers nailed Christ to a wooden cross and thus killed him.
A hired thug swung a pick handle at Casy, killing the preacher with a blow
to the head. Before each man died, their last words form a final parallel.
As the soldiers nailed Christ to the cross, he cried out, "Father, forgive
them, for they know not what they do." And the last thing Jim Casy said before the pick handle ended his life was: "You don' know what you're a-doin'."

If a man who was much the same as Jesus Christ appeared during the Okie
migration to California in the 1930s, his passing would go unnoticed among
the cruel inhumanity and human suffering that prevailed. This is what John
Steinbeck demonstrated so vividly with the character of Jim Casy in The
Grapes of Wrath.

Instructor's Comments

1. Strengths: This student took the suggestion of Biblical symbolism and
    narrowed it to a convincing position. With a debater's mind, he lays
    out each comparison with fact, quotation, and comparison. The title is
    a good one. The position is refreshing for those of us concerned with
    critics who wish to ban such a sensitive and compassionate novel.

2. Weaknesses: The debater's points, which having logic, also have a cer-
    tain heaviness. In fact, near the middle of the paper ("Lastly, both
    Christ and Casy . . ."), one feels the conclusion is at hand, when in
    fact, more points are to be made. Also, some students of the Bible might
    find such parallels as Jesus/Mary Magdalene and Casy and his sexual en-
    counters to be more than "obscure." Yet, while a certain wordiness and

5

repetition prevails (though the repetition of the first and last lines of the paper is an interesting stylistic device), the paper's success must be seen in comparing a novel of over 600 pages with the Bible.

HANDOUT 16
JOHN STEINBECK: THE INFLUENCE OF ED RICKETTS

Ed Ricketts—biologist, friend of Steinbeck, and "Doc" (in "The Snake" and *Cannery Row*); owned laboratory at Monterey; coauthor of *Sea of Cortez: A Leisurely Journal of Travel and Research* (Pacific Biological Laboratories)

Ideas and Theories of Ricketts

1. Show every reader how thin the line is between one's own animal and human nature. Aspirations grow out of human mental processes, but failures often stem from animalistic reflexes.

2. A good writer must be "a scientist of the imagination"—a good writer must tell lies but only to gain a reader's attention. Once the writer has the reader's attention, he or she must put together evidence—through the thoughts and actions of the characters—that will lead the reader to accept the inescapable truths of the human condition and the truth about him- or herself.

3. One of humanity's greatest deficiencies as a species is the inability to adapt to a changing environment. (Note: Ricketts suggested that Robert Burns poem for the title of *Of Mice and Men*.)

4. Ricketts was opposed to "teleological" or moral approaches to life; he felt they were useless because they concerned themselves with what should be, could be, or might be—instead of with what actually *is*. The teleological outlook—the need to find a purpose and explanation for everything—led to the destructive compulsion to make things in nature conform to society's conceptions of what they ought to be, which in turn led to war, injustice, inequality.
    a. Ricketts thought "nonteleological" thinking more useful.
    b. If people would observe *what is*, they would create a sane and integrated society.
    c. He thought *The Grapes of Wrath* too moral, yet he liked Steinbeck's detached examination of the Joads, as well as his descriptions of the forces of nature.

5. Groups are separate and distinct from the individuals that compose them in the same way as individuals are separate and distinct from the bodily cells of which they are constituted. The group is at once dependent on and independent of its individuals, just as the individual is at once dependent on and independent of the body's cells. The independence of the group evinces itself in its collective nature—that is, the nature of the group is distinct and separate from the nature of any of its members. People do not exercise their own ordinary natures but behave on the basis of the group nature, a separate and distinct mechanism. This separate nature of the group or "the phalanx" gives the group its transcendent power.

PAPER V: A PROFILE OF JOHN STEINBECK DAYS 54–66

DAY 54: REVIEWING THE STEINBECK BIOGRAPHY AND INTRODUCING THE PROFILE PAPER

Goals

1. To review the Steinbeck biography in broad outline and in four divisions.
2. To orient students to Paper V, a profile of John Steinbeck.

Materials

1. Handout 17: Four Divisions of John Steinbeck's Life.
2. Assemble a class library of biographical and autobiographical materials (see Bibliography).
3. Handout 18: Suggestions for Paper V.

Assignment

1. Ask students to note the DUE date for Paper V on the Schedule, Day 67.
2. Paper V should be based on the reading of nonfictional materials about or by Steinbeck. These pages (suggestion: at least fifty pages) may be taken from a single source or from several sources. A bibliography and footnotes are required; these documentation skills will be reviewed or taught during this section.

Procedure

1. Give students time at the beginning of the period to proofread Paper IV *(The Grapes of Wrath)*. Then collect those papers.
2. In explaining the assignment, remind students that they may use the fictional writings of Steinbeck previously read in class but that this material must also reinforce the required nonfictional material for the Profile Paper. Also remind them that this is not a biographical sketch; it is a single position paper.
3. Before considering the suggestions for this paper, review the life of Steinbeck with Handout 17. Note the four divisions. Reference also may be made to Steinbeck chronologies in this handbook. Students should note that we have largely been examining material from the first two divisions. Then Steinbeck left California and his first wife, went to New York, remarried, and became a father of two sons. His reputation was now established. Still interested in California material, he would write books like *East of Eden*. But he also would pursue new subjects —his own King Arthur book, France, New England, Russia. And while he would win the Nobel Prize, some critics would claim that he had lost his touch. His personal problems, especially his marital troubles with Gwen, would resolve themselves in a happy marriage to Elaine. Finally, Steinbeck continued to work on films and plays, write many letters, work with carpentry, travel with his dog, and keep an eye on controversy, such as the Viet Nam War. His son John was involved in that war; some students might wish to pursue this topic and read his son's book, *In Touch* (Knopf, 1969).
4. Distribute Handout 18 (Suggestions for Paper V) for previewing now and for reference later.
5. Encourage students to examine the class collection of Steinbeck materials and to seek out materials in libraries. You may wish to distribute copies of portions of the Bibliography. You also should remind students that there is no scholarly biography

of John Steinbeck, such as the one Carlos Baker wrote of Ernest Hemingway. The three best books: (1) the collected letters *(Steinbeck: A Life in Letters)*, edited by John's third wife Elaine and friend Robert Wallsten; (2) *John Steinbeck, The Errant Knight* by friend Nelson Valjean; (3) *The Intricate Music: A Biography of John Steinbeck* by Thomas Kiernan, an admirer who once met the author.

Additional Suggestions

1. You may wish to make copies (see Appendix E) of Steinbeck's note written to friends on their copy of *Travels with Charley.*
2. The seminar may wish to contact resource persons through, for example, the Bell Telephone leased phone system (see Appendix C). Those who knew Steinbeck or know much about him, such as college English professors or even biographers, may be willing to be interviewed by seminar members.

DAY 55: REVIEWING THE STEINBECK BIOGRAPHY WITH AUDIO-VISUAL MATERIALS

Goals

1. To review Steinbeck's life and works.
2. To stimulate reading and research about Steinbeck.

Materials

Instructors are encouraged to examine bibliography suggestions, noting which ones are available locally. For example, you may wish to use the filmstrip-tape *John Steinbeck* in The American Experience in Literature, Five Modern Novelists, available from the Encyclopaedia Britannica Educational Corporation.

Procedure

Show audio-visual materials and relate them to the chronology/divisions handouts.

Suggestion

You may wish to consider a slide or slide/tape presentation developed locally, by you or the A-V department. Using photographs from books (e.g., Nelson Valjean's biography), magazines (e.g., *National Geographic*s on California), as well as book covers of Steinbeck works, you could produce an inexpensive and permanent resource. Also check if students have any slides of subject matter that might be useful. This program could be a seminar project. Finally, you may wish to make a photocopy of pictures of Steinbeck's final homes at New York and Sag Harbor, Long Island.

DAYS 56–59: READING AND RESEARCH; LOCATING AND SHARING A STEINBECK ANECDOTE

Goals

1. To help students locate interesting biographical information about Steinbeck.
2. To provide a range of anecdotal material that will help students choose a biographical focus for Paper V.

Materials

1. Class library, supplemented by student research.
2. Six anecdotes for the Steinbeck Biography (see Appendix D).

Assignment

1. Ask each student to find one concrete anecdote about John Steinbeck to share with the class. If you have a problem with materials, divide the class into pairs with each pair relating an anecdote. (See six anecdotes in Appendix D.)
2. Anecdote Day or Days, 58 and/or 59, should help trigger a position. A single anecdote may be used to define a position or several anecdotes along a similar line may suggest a tactic. Encourage students to use each other's anecdotes and to share source materials.

Procedure

1. Days 56–57 are reading and research days. Announce the Anecdote assignment on Day 56.
2. On Day 58 (or 58–59) ask students to tell their anecdotes and let the seminar respond to each one. While some students may be capable of independent research in finding these anecdotes, others may require a more directed approach, using the Appendix suggestions. The following suggestions will simplify the assignment and help ensure that all students find interesting "slice-of-life" anecdotes.

   a. A college student and later biographer meets John Steinbeck: Thomas Kiernan, *The Intricate Music: A Biography of John Steinbeck*, pp. ix–xvii.

   b. A black high school classmate remembers John: Kiernan, *Ibid.*, pp. 29–32.

   c. The influence of a college teacher: Kiernan, *Ibid.*, pp. 90–98.

   d. The boy gets a pony: Nelson Valjean, *John Steinbeck: The Errant Knight*, pp. 35–36.

   e. A high school student is "sick": Valjean, *Ibid.*, p. 40.

   f. John pulls a college prank: Valjean, *Ibid.*, pp. 85–86.

   g. John, Ed Ricketts, and the origin of "The Snake": Valjean, *Ibid.*, pp. 152–153.

   h. John meets Ed Ricketts: "About Ed Ricketts" in Steinbeck's *The Log from the Sea of Cortez*, pp. vii–xiii.

   i. His dog eats *Of Mice and Men:* Elaine Steinbeck and Robert Wallsten, eds. *Steinbeck: A Life in Letters*, pp. 124–125 [Penguin edition, here and below].

   j. Steinbeck agonizes over the condition of migrants: *A Life in Letters*, pp. 161–162.

   k. Steinbeck writes an angry letter to a man who wants to know if he is Jewish: *A Life in Letters*, pp. 203–204.

   l. John sees his name in the clouds: *A Life in Letters*, p. 285.

   m. Steinbeck stamps his letters with a flying pig: *A Life in Letters*, p. 296.

   n. Steinbeck and his love of earthy stories: *A Life in Letters*, pp. 514–515.

   o. A letter to son Thom about love: *A Life in Letters*, pp. 600–601.

DAYS 60–63: PREPARING FOR AND PARTICIPATING IN DEFENSE DAY AND FOLLOW-UP

Goal

To help students refine their understanding of how a position becomes warranted through clear argumentation and adequate documentation.

Materials

1. Copies of Handout 19: Student Model for Paper V.
2. Copies of papers chosen for Defense Days.
3. Corrected papers on *The Grapes of Wrath* to return at the end of Defense Days, on Day 63.

Procedure

1. You may wish to use Handout 19, the student model of a Profile, especially to remind students of documentation. During Day 60, there should be a discussion of footnoting and bibliography that covers the stylebook form that you wish for each, as well as the problems of plagiarism and when to footnote indirect and direct quotations.
2. At the end of Day 60, give all students the copies of Paper IV *(The Grapes of Wrath)* for Defense Day. Remind them that the second set will be given out on Day 61 and that all corrected papers will be returned at the end of Day 62.
3. Follow Defense Day procedures outlined earlier. Return all papers on Day 62.
4. Use the follow-up Day 63 to discuss papers of other students, to evaluate the student model (Handout 15), or to consider a critic's point of view, for example, "Christian Symbolism in *The Grapes of Wrath*" by Martin Staples Shockley in *Steinbeck and His Critics*, edited by E. W. Tedlock, Jr. and C. V. Wicker, pp. 266–271.

DAYS 64–66: COMPLETING PAPER V; WATCHING A STEINBECK FILM

Goals

1. To give students time to write, revise, and proofread the Profile Paper.
2. To see a film of a Steinbeck book, narrated by the author.

Materials

Film: *America and Americans,* McGraw-Hill, 1968 (52 min., color).

Procedure

1. Days 64 and 65 are final days for research, writing, revision, and proofreading.
2. Day 66 can be used for showing *America and Americans,* which is based on Steinbeck's 1965 nonfiction book. Steinbeck appears in the film and narrates it. This film makes a nice transition between this profile section and the Paper VI choice paper.
3. Remind students that Paper V is due on Day 67.

HANDOUT 17
FOUR DIVISIONS OF JOHN STEINBECK'S LIFE

I. The Aspiring Californian, 1902–1934
   A. California-born: A big, beautiful land, a last frontier, the new El Dorado
      1. A land of history: Spanish settlers, Gold Rush, migrants, minorities
      2. A land of writers, such as Frank Norris, Upton Sinclair, Robinson Jeffers, Ambrose Bierce
      3. Salinas, a regional agricultural center
   B. Relatives
      1. His Grosssteinbeck grandfather: left Germany, married Massachusetts girl, served in Civil War as Confederate, moved from Florida to Massachusetts, to California in 1874
      2. His maternal Hamilton grandfather: came from Ireland to California in 1851, followed by wife
      3. His father, John Ernst II: managed flour mill, ran grain and feed store, served as treasurer of Monterey County
      4. His mother, Olive: taught school for a time in places like Big Sur
      5. Three sisters, two older, one younger
   C. His Education
      1. Nature: farms, mountains, ranches, horses, birds, fish
      2. Books: Malory's *Morte d'Arthur,* Bible, Milton, George Eliot, Flaubert, Thomas Hardy, Dostoevski
      3. High School: Salinas, president of senior class, editor of class yearbook, drama society and science club; Stanford University, irregular attendance, English club, published in *Spectator,* inspired by writing teachers
      4. Jobs: ranches, railroad gang, sugar beet factory, later New York's Madison Square Garden building as manual laborer
   D. In 1925: trip to New York, works for the *American,* book of short stories rejected, comes back to work on novels, caretaker of lodge near Lake Tahoe
   E. *Cup of Gold,* 1929: 1533 copies sold
   F. Depression folds publishing houses interested in *The Pastures of Heaven,* which sold for $400.
   G. First wife: Carol Hemming, a San Jose girl with whom he elopes to Los Angeles; they settle in Pacific Grove, live in cottage provided by his father, along with $25 a month
   H. Influence: meeting Ed Ricketts, proprietor of a biological supply lab in Monterey
   I. 1933: moves to Los Angeles and back to Monterey
   J. 1934: difficult times, except for money from *The Red Pony* and O. Henry Prize for "The Murder"
II. The California Celebrity, 1935–1943
   A. *Tortilla Flat* and Success: Chicago bookman Ben Abrahamson tells Pascal Covici about Steinbeck's talent; Covici publishes book; Hollywood gives $4000 to Steinbeck, now living on $35 a month
   B. New home in Los Gatos; 1936 a busy year with controversial *In Dubious Battle*
   C. Steinbeck in demand by magazines, like *Esquire;* San Francisco paper commissions a series on migrants

    D. 1937 *Of Mice and Men:* 75,000 copies sold by Book-of-the-Month Club; play a hit, and film rights go for $300,000; dinners in New York, tours abroad

    E. 1939 *Grapes of Wrath:* based on research and living with migrants; another hit—500,000 sold in 1st edition; Pulitzer; film sold

    F. 1942 Divorce: $220,000 settlement; gives $1000 Pulitzer money to help a Monterey writer with career; meets FDR

    G. World War II: works on propaganda war pieces, then shifts to California fiction, *Cannery Row*

III. The New Yorker, 1943–1960

    A. Marries Gwendolyn Conger in New Orleans (1943); 1945 home in New York City, East 78th Street brownstones

    B. Children: John, Jr. and Thom—protected from public eye

    C. 1945—considered for Nobel Prize, as books still popular, book club selections

    D. Travels to Russia, recognized by American Academy of Arts and Letters, Hollywood contacts with *Viva Zapata.*

    E. With failure of plays in 1950s and poor critical reception of *East of Eden,* Steinbeck at low point; divorce, loss of children

    F. Begins research on dream book about King Arthur; moves to Sag Harbor home

    G. Marries third wife, Elaine Scott, former wife of film star Zachery Scott; they go to Somerset, England to pursue Malory book for a year, consulting scholars; happy marriage

IV. The Nobel Winner and Decline, 1961–1968

    A. Travels with poodle Charley through America to rediscover his land

    B. *The Winter of Our Discontent* chosen for Book-of-the-Month Club and starts movement toward Nobel Prize

    C. 1961: ten months traveling abroad with family

    D. 1962: Nobel Prize and fear of what it will do to his career

    E. 1963–1965: "I'm not the young writer of promise any more"; little writing, cultural trips, interest in politics

    F. Illnesses and operations, a final trip to Viet Nam; realizes that his great Malory dream book is not to be accomplished; stays at Sag Harbor, working in his special writing house; a series of heart attacks ends writing: "my fingers have avoided the pencil as though it were an old and poisoned tool"

HANDOUT 18
SUGGESTIONS FOR PAPER V: THE PROFILE PAPER

1. John Steinbeck loved dogs and used them in his fiction. Why?
2. Develop a position about Steinbeck's concern for privacy.
3. Study Steinbeck's relationship with one of his wives, one of his sons.
4. What does his lifelong pursuit of the King Arthur material really mean?
5. What theory can you develop by examining the dedications of his books?
6. Examine Steinbeck's friendship with Ed Ricketts in terms of a position.
7. What was his religion, his philosophy of life?
8. Who were Steinbeck's "teachers"—the ones who molded him?
9. Steinbeck had great sympathy with the working classes, though he came from the middle class. Why?
10. Study Steinbeck's letters. Why did he write so many letters? Select a letter that gives us insight into the man.
11. Who was Pascal Covici? Why was he such a good friend of Steinbeck?
12. Concentrate on one aspect of his life: his family, his home town, high school, college.
13. Is Steinbeck a Californian? What is a Californian?
14. What was his attitude toward America and Americans?
15. Reflect on his interests: the sea, carpentry, biology.
16. Why was Steinbeck so interested in freaks such as Lennie?
17. Do some research on how he reacted to prizes and success. Concentrate on one prize, such as the Nobel or the Pulitzer.
18. Was Steinbeck an autobiographical writer? Use examples of his life and fiction to illustrate your position.

HANDOUT 19
STUDENT MODEL FOR PAPER V

A MAN OF TRUTH

by Cathy Freeman

> Half of the cell units of my mother's body have rebelled.
> Neither has died, but the revolution has changed her functions
> . . . She, as a human unit, is deterred from functioning as
> she ordinarily did by a schism of a number of her cells. (Stein-
> beck and Wallsten, 1975, p. 76)
>   John Steinbeck

John Steinbeck, a scientific man, saw the deteriorating cell units of
his mother as readily as her withering appearance. Steinbeck was a man of
truth and looked for its presence everywhere. As he studied with his good
friend and biologist, Ed Ricketts, he became interested with the non-
teleological approach to life. It was a concept that could not please everyone because it concerns itself with what "is" in contrast to what "could be"
or "might be."

As one can see from the above quotation, Steinbeck's approach to death
was from the realist's viewpoint, thus maintaining his non-teleological state
of mind. He did not allow for the euphemism to ease the pain when illness or
death was imminent. This can be seen not only in his letters but also in
many of his major works.

While attending Stanford University, Steinbeck spent much of his time
studying biology. His interest in science is not surprising to any of his
avid readers, for they almost immediately pick up his awareness and continual
involvement in nature. In his work, Steinbeck stressed that nature is re-
lentless. Nature, especially in the course of dying, maintains its unsym-
pathetic role.

1

2

In The Red Pony, Steinbeck portrayed the brutality of nature. As the
vultures closed in on the dead pony, Steinbeck described in sickening detail
the birds who tore the flesh from the still warm carcass: "The first buzzard
sat on the pony's head and its beak had just risen dripping with dark eye
fluid" (Steinbeck, 1945, p. 34-35). Although this seems gruesome, Steinbeck
was merely revealing a truth: nature has no sympathy for the weak, and the
strong must eat to survive. He was almost as crude when he described his
mother as a mass of dying cells; he was obviously aware that his mother had
become a member of the weak. Nature would eventually win out over medicine,
and death would take its course. The similarities between his mother and the
red pony are striking. It is interesting to note that it was during the time
of his mother's illness that Steinbeck wrote The Red Pony.

As can be seen through The Red Pony, John Steinbeck dealt with death
candidly. But that is not to say he was ignorant to the ways many human
beings handle the situation. He recognized how death is continually a matter
both avoided and denied by most people. The feeling of denial was exempli-
fied by the death of Rose of Sharon's baby in The Grapes of Wrath.

> She pointed to the corner of the car where the apple box was.
> "That ain't doin' no good. Jus' cause trouble and sorra.
> Couldn' you fellas kinda--take it out an' bury it?" (Stein-
> beck, 1939, p. 493)

The baby's death caused much grief for the members of the family. The
disposal of the child was strongly desired, for the sooner it was disposed,
the sooner they could forget it. The death of the child was clearly a subject
avoided in hopes it would seen be erased from their thoughts.

Even Steinbeck, seemingly a man of tough nature, was not immune to this
desire to forget. The illness and eventual death of his mother caused him a
great deal of pain and unhappiness.

3

> "Two things I really want and I can't have either of them and
> they are both negative. I want to forget my mother lying for
> a year with a frightful question in her eyes and I want to
> forget and lose the pain in my heart that is my father."
> (Steinbeck and Wallsten, 1975, p. 93)

One might say that Steinbeck was caught between his desire to forget and

his desire to accept unpleasant and often traumatic occurrences. Although

he felt it best to always concern himself with what "is," his human character-

istics would never free him from at least a trace of longing for what "could

be." Basically, though, Steinbeck was a man of acceptance. In countless

situations he revealed his ability to live mutually with the truth. In fact,

Steinbeck was often so brusque that he almost seemed insensitive. In speak-

ing about his mother, he said:

> "Mother's mind gets farther and farther from its base. She is
> pretty much surrounded by dead relatives now." (Steinbeck and
> Wallsten, 1975, p. 85)

Another interesting example occurred when he spoke about the illnesses of

his mother and father as casually as he did his own work.

> "My father collapsed a week ago under the six month's strain
> and very nearly landed in the same position as my mother. It
> was very close. Paradoxically, I have started another volume
> (Tortilla Flat), and it is going like wildfire." (Steinbeck
> and Wallsten, 1975, p. 88)

Apparently, Steinbeck felt the acceptance of death extremely important. In

The Grapes of Wrath, he again stressed this point through Sairy's acceptance

of her own death.

> "I want to go. I knowed I wouldn' live to the other side,
> but he'd be acrost anyways . . . I'm just pain covered with
> skin. I know what it is, but I won't tell him . . . He
> wouldn' know what to do anyways. Maybe in the night, when
> he's a-sleepin—when he waked up, it won't be so bad." (Stein-
> beck, 1939, p. 240)

Steinbeck described Sairy favorably. She accepted her fate and did not

dwell on self-pity, something that he disliked greatly.

4

So Steinbeck appears to have been a very strong man. Maintaining a scientific outlook, he managed to see only the truth, which is, in the gravest of circumstances, death. But one can't help question the sincerity of this image. Was Steinbeck really that strong? Or, being the independent man he was, was he merely afraid to reveal weakness?

> "Lastly, I do not find illness an eminence, and I do not under-
> stand how people can use it to draw attention to themselves
> since the attention they draw is nearly always reluctantly
> given and unpleasantly carried out. I dislike helplessness in
> other people and in myself, and this is by far my greatest fear
> of illness." (Steinbeck and Wallsten, 1975, p. 857)

Bibliography

Steinbeck, Elaine, and Robert Wallsten, eds. Steinbeck: A Life in Letters.
    New York: The Viking Press, Inc., 1975.

Steinbeck, John. The Grapes of Wrath. New York: The Viking Press, 1939.

Steinbeck, John. The Red Pony. New York: The Viking Press, 1945.

Instructor's Comments

1. Strengths: The writer has tackled a strong position that obviously dis-
   turbs her, if not all of us. She knows her Ricketts and her sources,
   both fictional and nonfictional. While she may not approve of Steinbeck's "truth," she establishes her position with the introductory quotation. The tone of her paper parallels the theme. Her documentation
   is exemplary.

2. Weaknesses: Perhaps the backgrounds on the quotations and the characters
   could be more clarified in context of the stories and biography. One
   wonders if Steinbeck's theory was formed around the time of his mother's
   death. Also the writer needs to reconsider active vs. passive voice in

5

the paragraph about the death of Rose of Sharon's baby. Finally, one
must be cautious about unsupported claims ("In countless situations
. . .).

PAPER VI: PAPER OF CHOICE
DAYS 67–80

DAY 67: CONSIDERING READING CHOICES FOR PAPER VI

Goals

1. To suggest topics for Paper VI, the paper of choice.
2. To note writing problems special to this paper.

Materials

1. A class library of books for Paper VI, including *The Portable Steinbeck.*
2. Handout 20: Suggestions for Paper VI.
3. Handout 21: Student Model for Paper VI.

Assignment

1. Ask students to note the DUE date for the sixth paper on the Schedule, Day 81.
2. Remind students that the defenses of Paper V (The Profile Paper) will begin on Day 72.

Procedure

1. Spend the first few minutes of the period asking students to make a final proofreading of Paper V, The Profile. Then collect these papers.
2. This time students may select any book (or story, if time is pressing) that has not been studied in class. Assess the time remaining and reading skills of individual students in suggesting whether a student should read another book or short selections in *The Portable Steinbeck.*
3. Briefly review the following materials, giving plot summaries. (Note: You may wish to hold to chronology and only allow books after *The Grapes of Wrath*.)

Books: Fiction

Cup of Gold: A Life of Henry Morgan, Buccaneer (1929). A tale which traces the life of Henry Morgan, from his boyhood in Wales to his death as lieutenant governor of Jamaica.

In Dubious Battle (1936). A controversial novel about a strike in the fruit country of California, as seen through the eyes of a radical labor sympathizer.

The Moon Is Down (1942). A short novel, written during World War II to encourage the resistance against the Nazi occupation, which is set in a small unnamed (though suggests Norway) mining town occupied by an unidentified army.

Cannery Row (1945). Steinbeck takes the reader to the row of shacks along the Monterey shoreline in California; the characters and atmosphere remind us of Tortilla Flat and Ed Ricketts.

The Pearl (1947). A short novel about a Mexican fisherman who discovers a large pearl and then pays the price for it—a parable.

The Wayward Bus (1947). A group of strangers are stranded overnight at a roadside gas station and lunchroom in California.

East of Eden (1952). This is a *long* novel, only for the gifted reader. It is the story of two American families (obviously related to Steinbeck). The Trasks and the Hamiltons. The major focus is the Salinas area around the turn of the century and extending through World War II.

Sweet Thursday (1954). This is Cannery Row II, comic and bawdy, after World War II.

The Short Reign of Pippin IV (1957). The critics were not impressed. But you may like this satire, the story of a modern descendent of Charlemagne who tries to revive monarchy in modern France.

The Winter of Our Discontent (1961). A New England setting, the last novel, around the time of the Nobel Prize. Steinbeck's story revolves around his concern that American society corrupts even the most virtuous of men, even one whose roots go deep into the New England past.

Books: Nonfiction

Travels with Charley: In Search of America (1962). Steinbeck and his French poodle travel across America and back in Rocinante (the idealistic Don Quixote's horse), his truck-trailer.

America and Americans (1966). Steinbeck (with photographs of America) considers the beauty and character of his native land.

Stories

"The Murder" (1934). The story of murder, Monterey, a marital triangle—with a twist.

"St. Katy, the Virgin" (1936). The story of a pig who becomes a saint.

"How Mr. Hogan Robbed a Bank" (1956). The genesis of *The Winter of Our Discontent.*

4. Distribute and discuss Handout 20: Suggestions for Paper VI.
5. Stress that this paper should be especially clear about the basic plot and characters since most readers will not have read the material.
6. You may distribute Handout 21: Student Model for Paper VI now or reserve it for discussion later.

DAYS 68–71: READING STEINBECK MATERIAL OF CHOICE AND PREPARING FOR DEFENSE DAYS

Goals

1. To provide time for students to read the Steinbeck material of choice.

2. To prepare for Defense Day on Paper V.

Materials

1. Class library and *The Portable Steinbeck.*
2. Copies of the profile papers chosen for Defense Days.

Procedure

1. Days 68–70 give students time to read the book or story of their choice and the instructor time to correct the profile papers.
2. On Day 71, hand out the profile papers to be used on the first Defense Day, Day 72. Students may continue reading or study the two profile papers.

DAYS 72–74: PARTICIPATING IN DEFENSE DAYS AND FOLLOW-UP

Goals

1. To allow students to defend the positions taken in the Steinbeck Profile Paper.
2. To consider biographical insights of major Steinbeck critics.

Materials

1. Again, extra copies of the papers for Defense Days may be needed.
2. Corrected papers should be returned on Day 73.

Procedure

1. Days 72–73 will follow the usual Defense Day system of evaluation.
2. Day 74 is follow-up, and again you have the options of discussing the papers of other students, the student model paper (Handout 19), or the observations of critics. Suggestions for the latter: "The Man Behind the Books" by Warren French in *John Steinbeck,* pp. 19–30. Or: "Philosophy on Cannery Row" by Joel Hedgpath in *Steinbeck: Man and His Works,* pp. 89–123.

DAY 75: JOHN STEINBECK AND THE NOBEL PRIZE

Goal

To provide background information on Steinbeck's winning of the Nobel Prize.

Materials

1. *The Portable Steinbeck,* which includes the Nobel Acceptance Speech.
2. You may wish to refer to *American Winners of the Nobel Literary Prize* edited by Warren G. French and Walter E. Kidd, specifically to the chapter "John Steinbeck" by Warren G. French, pp. 193–223.

Procedure

1. Ask a student to read Steinbeck's acceptance speech aloud.
2. Then, review *The Nobel Prize.* The Nobel Prize for Literature was one of the five international awards established in the 1895 will of Swedish industrialist Alfred Nobel, the inventor of dynamite. The prize "to the person who shall have produced in the field of Literature the most distinguished work of an idealistic tendency" (French and Kidd, eds., *American Winners of the Nobel Literary Prize,* p. 6) is directed by the Nobel Foundation; the annual award includes a large cash gift (from the accrued interest of Nobel's original gift), a gold medal, and a diploma bearing the winner's name and field of achievement. The winner must be alive and actively writing. The Nobel judges may decide not to give an award for a particular year.

   The first awards were given in 1901, but no American received one until 1930. Steinbeck became the seventh winner on the American list, which has since increased to nine: Sinclair Lewis (1930), Eugene O'Neill (1936), Pearl Buck (1938), T. S. Eliot (1948, then a British citizen), William Faulkner (1949), Ernest Hemingway (1954), John Steinbeck (1962), Saul Bellow (1976), Issac Bashevis Singer (1978).

3. Background stories on Steinbeck's Nobel Prize may be covered during Anecdote Day; nevertheless, review is advisable. Steinbeck had been nominated in 1945, when his career was at a high point with both public and critics. His books of the 1930s and 1940s about California had made their impact. However, by 1962, many critics had lost interest in him and felt his recent work second rate. When the winner was announced, few literary magazines responded and popular magazines such as *Time* were unfavorably impressed with the choice. Steinbeck, who learned of his award while watching television news at his home in Sag Harbor, was surprised and honored; he called it a "kind of fantasy." See *Steinbeck: A Life in Letters,* pp. 742–750. He worried about his acceptance speech, asked advice of friends, went to Stockholm with Elaine, and later became afraid. See *Steinbeck: A Life in Letters,* pp. 757–764.

4. It is interesting to discuss awards at this point, since many writers both want and fear them. Fame, recognition, sudden popularity can be time-consuming, distracting from one's work, the kiss of death. Steinbeck believed that little good material was written by Nobel winners after they received their awards. Some writers have even been driven to suicide after winning the Pulitzer. (See John Leggett, *Ross and Tom: Two American Tragedies.)* Why does a writer write? Why did Steinbeck write? Does the public demand too much of such shy writers as Steinbeck?

Nobel Prize Committee Recognition and Citation:

> His sympathies always go out to the oppressed, the misfits, and the distressed; he likes to contrast the simple joy of life with brutal and cynical craving for money. [Nobel Committee Recognition]

> For his at one and the same realistic and imaginative writings, distinguished as they are by a sympathetic humor and social perception. [Nobel Prize Citation by the Swedish Academy (French and Kidd, *American Winners,* pp. 221–222)]

5. Prior to Steinbeck's acceptance speech, R. Sandler, a member of the Royal Academy of Sciences, said,

> Mr. Steinbeck—In your writings, crowned with popular success in many countries, you have been a bold observer of human behavior in both tragic and comic situations. This you have described to the reading public of the entire world with vigour and realism. [Frenz, Horst (ed.), *Nobel Lectures: Literature, 1901–1967*, New York: Elsevier Publishing Company, 1969, p. 577.]

DAYS 76–80: COMPLETING PAPER VI; REVIEWING SKILLS

Goals

1. To provide time to complete reading and writing.
2. To discuss skills for Paper VI.

Procedure

1. Day 76 should be given to students for final in-class reading time.

2. On Day 77, remind students that their basic plots must be clear. Their classmates may have not read their book or story; if they come up for Defense Day, they should not have to explain their books orally to the class. Encourage comparison/contrast papers, using the familiar in-common readings with the choice selection. Discuss possible structures for such papers: (a) Introduction, establishing position; Body, beginning with in-common reading and discussing both plot and comparison position idea; then moving to choice reading with same procedure; Conclusion, summary of position in both works. (b) Introduction, establishing position; Body, beginning with basic plot summary paragraph or paragraphs of both books; then defining sub-topics of comparison position and discussing examples from both books to support each point; Conclusion, summarizing the sub-topics and position.

3. Days 78–80 should be given over to writing and proofreading Paper VI. Remind students of due date, Day 81.

HANDOUT 20
SUGGESTIONS FOR PAPER VI: PAPER OF CHOICE

Books: Fiction

1. *Cup of Gold* (1929)
   a. Is this a novel advocating the free life of adventure or criticizing civilization which destroys innocence?
   b. Relate how this book fits into Steinbeck's interest in King Arthur.

2. *In Dubious Battle* (1936)
   a. Critic Warren French believes this book is not even primarily about a strike. Do you agree?
   b. Consider the title. Who is "in" battle? What is a "dubious" battle?

3. *The Moon Is Down* (1942)
   a. Is this just a propaganda novel of World War II?
   b. Focus on Mayor Orden. What is his function in the book?

4. *Cannery Row* (1945)
   a. Contrast this book to *Tortilla Flat*. What do they have in common?
   b. Is Doc a Steinbeck hero?

5. *The Pearl* (1947)
   a. There is general agreement that the pearl is a symbol. A symbol of what?
   b. What is a "fable"? Is this novel a fable?

6. *The Wayward Bus* (1947)
   a. Critic Peter Lisca calls this book "a pitiless examination of the world." Do you agree? If so, define one aspect which is studied closely.
   b. Consider the idea of people with various personalities on a wayward bus as an allegory of the journey through life.

7. *East of Eden* (1952)
   a. Steinbeck said this book was what he had been "practicing to write" all his life. What idea, already familiar, is repeated in this long novel?
   b. Study the biblical story of Cain and Abel. How might this apply to this book?

8. *Sweet Thursday* (1954)
   a. What is the function of the inter-chapters in this novel? Does this function differ from their use in *The Grapes of Wrath*?
   b. Concentrate on the character of Joe Elegant. This character was dropped when the book was made into a musical comedy (*Pipe Dream*). Any theories?

9. *The Short Reign of Pippin IV* (1957)
   a. Some critics felt that this book was evidence of Steinbeck's decline. Concentrate on one aspect that you feel supports or contradicts this criticism.
   b. There is much of Steinbeck himself in Pippin. Demonstrate.

10. *The Winter of Our Discontent* (1961)
    a. Dishonesty. What is the meaning of this word in Steinbeck's last novel?
    b. Some readers were disturbed with the setting of the novel, not the typical California landscape. What is the function of this setting?

Books: Nonfiction

Travels with Charley (1962)
    a. Steinbeck loved dogs. What is the meaning of Charley in this book?
    b. Concentrate on one section. Define it in terms of one typical Steinbeck concern.

America and Americans (1966)
    a. One critic finds this book as one largely of disapproval of contemporary America. Do you agree? What one thing does Steinbeck like?
    b. Can you find one definition of "America" in this book?

Stories

"The Murder" (1934): Is this story about a double standard?

"St. Katy, the Virgin" (1936): What is Steinbeck saying about religion?

"How Mr. Hogan Robbed a Bank" (1956): Biographer Thomas Kiernan calls this story "an almost perfect realization of the narrative effectiveness of the Ricketts-Steinbeck theory of nonteleological writing." Can you illustrate this?

HANDOUT 21
STUDENT MODEL FOR PAPER VI

PROMOTING UNDERSTANDING

by Seth Meisel

John Steinbeck once said, "My whole work drive has been aimed at making people understand each other." This motive is clearly evident in The Moon Is Down where Steinbeck details the tragedy of misunderstanding between conquerors and the conquered. He shows in this novel that the conquerors are doomed to fail because they fail to comprehend the inherent need for freedom in man. While this point is revealed in the plot, it is Steinbeck's stylistic devices that make it a universal statement.

The novel begins as a small European town is invaded and half its militia, six men, is killed. The story then follows the inverted situation of the victors and the vanquished. The invaders initially feel proud and victorious, but this feeling quickly changes to anxiety and paranoia. The villagers progress from shock to resentment to finally sensing an inevitable success. The invaders insist that order be maintained in the town and that the mayor remain in his post. However, when a local miner, Alex, kills one of the invading soldiers, the start of a revolt has begun.

The villagers then leave their normal roles and become saboteurs, snipers, and spies. The embattled feeling among the soldiers grows to the point where one of the conquerors remarks that theirs is merely a victory where "the flies have conquered the flypaper." As the resistance continues, with each side making reprisals, thousands of dynamite sticks are parachuted in. Threatening to execute the mayor if any of the dynamite is used, the

1

2

commanding officer, Colonel Lanswer, takes Mayor Orden hostage. Soon after

the arrest, however, explosions are heard and the Mayor is shot.

Apparently written about the German occupation of a Norwegian village

in World War II, the novel achieves universality through Steinbeck's refusal

to be specific. It is this stylistic vagueness that makes the theme of the

"free" spirit in man universal. The setting is in a small, snow-covered town

in the mountains. Unlike his descriptions of his own Salinas Valley, Stein-

beck gives the town none of the usual colloquial flavor, nor does he develop

description of the people, the houses, the land, or the weather. The names

of the villagers--Alexander Morden, Annie, Joseph, Doc Winter, and Mayor

Orden--and of the invaders--Colonel Lanser, Captains Loft and Bentick, Lieu-

tenants Prackle and Tonder and Major Hunter--also do little to suggest the

nationality of either group. Much like the old man in Ernest Hemingway's

"The Old Man and the Sea" who symbolized the displaced in wartime, Steinbeck's

people are not important as individuals, but rather as symbols of the spirit

in man. This stylistic device shows how Steinbeck is not concerned with the

French, Dutch or Norwegian occupation, but rather seeks to demonstrate man's

need to be free, regardless of nationality.

John Steinbeck also uses the character of Alex Morden to show how basic

the need for freedom is in man. When Alex is brought to the mayor to explain

why he killed the Captain, he confesses, "I was mad. I have a pretty bad

temper. He said I must work. I am a free man. I got mad and I hit him.

I guess I hit him pretty hard." Here Steinbeck stylistically shows through

Alex's short and simple prose how simple and basic Alex is. This adept

characterization demonstrates how freedom is not an esoteric idea solely for

an idealistic elite but a basic concept in man.

The last technique is Steinbeck's use of a speech, the one where Mayor

Orden recites before he is executed. Mayor Orden is reminiscing with his

3

friend Doc Winter and begins to deliver the reading he gave on the night of
their high school graduation. The speech is an excerpt from the Apology,
Socrates' final statement before he was given a cup of hemlock. Condemned
to death for practicing and preaching ideas that were not accepted by the
Greeks, Socrates condemned the court for abridging his freedom: "I prophesy
to you who are my murderers that immediately after my departure punishment
far heavier than you have inflicted on me will surely await you." This pro-
nouncement, which parallels Mayor Orden's prediction of the fate for the
town's invaders, also shows the universal nature of freedom--not merely a
modern concept but a need that springs from ancient civilization.

Through these stylistic devices of vagueness of location and time, the
characterization of Alex, and Socrates' speech, John Steinbeck reveals that
man's need for freedom is a need that transcends nationality, mental capacity,
and time. And by doing this, he comments on all those who conquer and deny
freedom, as well as on all those who seek freedom.

Instructor's Comments

1. Strengths: The writer makes a good case, by defining Steinbeck's stylistic devices, that this is not just a World War II propaganda piece.
   His organization is clear, he cites concrete examples, and he largely
   achieves the position paper skill of clarifying the plot.

2. Weaknesses: The first Steinbeck quotation could use a footnote, and the
   book could use a publication date. The point about the villagers' "sensing an inevitable success" needs to be clarified in terms of the plot's
   actual conclusion. The writer needs to be reminded of his overworking
   such verbs as "shows."

PAPER VII: THE SUMMING UP
DAYS 81–90

DAYS 81–83: BEGINNING THE FINAL PAPER AND PREPARING FOR DEFENSE DAY

Goals

1. To help students select a topic for Paper VII.
2. To provide class time to begin final paper.
3. To prepare for Defense Day.

Materials

1. Handout 21: Suggestions for Paper VII.
2. Handout 22: Student Model for Paper VII.
3. Copies of Paper VI (Choice Paper) to be used on Days 84–85.

Assignment

Ask students to insert DUE dates for Paper VII on the Schedule.

Procedure

1. Give students a few minutes at the beginning of Day 81 to proofread. Then collect Paper VI (Paper of Choice).
2. As soon as possible, select and reproduce the papers to be used for the final Defense Day discussions.
3. Orient students to the final paper by suggesting that it offers a number of alternatives:
   a. If time allows, you may wish to assign two papers—a serious summation of John Steinbeck and his work and a parody assignment.
   b. Most likely, you may wish to be more flexible. Students may elect to write either a serious or a humorous paper. Even the length may be shortened to three or fewer pages.
   c. Another possibility that has worked very well: agree to give a grade of A to any final paper that is read aloud to the seminar. These presentations may take two days, but they release final tensions. There is, then, no Defense Day for Paper VII; instead, there is a chance for creativity and an opportunity to summarize. In addition, everyone is justifiably rewarded for having cooperated throughout the course. Note: Still require that Paper VII be typed.
4. Refer to one of the Chronology handouts, such as Handout 3. Note Steinbeck's death and posthumous publications. You also may wish to refer to what has happened to people who knew Steinbeck. See Kiernan, *Intricate Music,* pp. 316–317.
5. Using Handouts 21 and 22, refer to this assignment as a point of departure. Encourage students to review materials by Steinbeck, position papers.
6. Day 82 is for research and writing.
7. Hand out on Day 83 copies of the first papers to be defended. Students may study these papers in class or continue to work on Paper VII.

DAYS 84–86: PARTICIPATING IN DEFENSE DAYS AND FOLLOW-UP

Goal

To complete the Defense Days and follow-up discussion.

Materials

Extra copies of position papers for students who have forgotten them.

Procedure

1. Follow the established procedures for Defense Day. Return all papers at the end of the period on Day 85.
2. The final follow-up day (Day 86) can be spent discussing other papers, the student models, or the insights of critics. Suggestion: *"Cannery Row:* Steinbeck's Pastoral Poem" by Stanley Alexander in *Steinbeck: A Collection of Critical Essays,* edited by Robert Murray Davis, pp. 139–148.

DAYS 87–89: COMPLETING THE FINAL PAPERS AND SHARING THEM IN CLASS

Goals

1. To provide in-class time to complete Paper VII.
2. To encourage students to share their final paper with the class and to respond to the papers of fellow students.

Procedure

1. Day 87 should be given over to completing Paper VII.
2. Days 88–89 can be set aside for all students to read aloud their final papers. If you elect to cut off the final pressure by granting a uniform grade of A on Paper VII, the experience will be even more enjoyable, and the students may elect a humorous approach. Experience has shown that these papers are of high quality. Although these readings do not constitute a Defense Day, the class should attempt to respond to each paper—and so should the instructor.

DAY 90: FINAL DISCUSSION, READINGS, EVALUATION

Goals

1. To encourage students to evaluate the seminar.
2. To share a final Steinbeck experience.

Materials

1. Handout 23: Seminar Evaluation (see Appendix G).
2. You may wish to use a humorous commencement/graduation address written but never spoken by Steinbeck. See *Steinbeck: A Life in Letters,* 16 May 1956, pp. 528–533.

Procedure

1. Without comment, ask students to complete the evaluation anonymously. Collect.
2. You may wish to ask seminar students to give their final impressions of the course, of Steinbeck, of what they have learned. My classes have elected for a kind of fun day, such as a Twenty-Questions Day and a Charades Day based on Steinbeck plots and characters. One seminar even planned a Steinbeck party, and each student dressed as a character from a story or novel.
3. Some instructors may wish to read Steinbeck's humorous graduation speech. This is great fun if the course ends in the spring.
4. Some instructors may wish to give a final examination, as well as make a final summary and personal reflection on the course.

HANDOUT 22
SUGGESTIONS FOR PAPER VII

The Summing Up

1. Did Steinbeck deserve the Nobel Prize?
2. How did Steinbeck treat nature?
3. Examine his Nobel Acceptance Speech. Can this lead to a position?
4. Consider his titles. Can you develop a theory about his choices?
5. How does Steinbeck treat women in his books?
6. Steinbeck was obviously not religious in the conventional sense of the word. How would you describe his "religion"?
7. Why do you think that Salinas has *now* accepted their native son?
8. Which work was your favorite?
9. Is Steinbeck a topical or regional writer, but not a universal writer?

Creative Suggestions

1. Try a parody of a work by Steinbeck. Take a short story or a passage from a novel and distort his style and plot.
2. Try a parody of Steinbeck by taking a simple plot and writing it in the famous Steinbeck style. For example, take a children's story such as "The Three Little Pigs."
3. Write a recently discovered work of John Steinbeck.
4. Write an imaginary interview with Steinbeck.
5. Write a newspaper article about a professor who has found a piece of information that reveals a new side of Steinbeck (for example, he really hated dogs).
6. Write a first draft of Steinbeck's Nobel Prize address which he threw away because Elaine didn't like it.
7. Write a personal essay on the agonies that you experienced while studying John Steinbeck or preparing for Defense Day.
8. Develop a series of letters between Steinbeck and a member of this class.
9. Write a series of so-called samples of Steinbeck's writing, from kindergarten to college—all with teacher comments.

HANDOUT 23
STUDENT MODEL FOR PAPER VII

IN THE BEGINNING, JOHN SAID . . .

by John Corbett

It was late afternoon and the cars buzzed westward down Route 80. The brightly colored vehicles created a sharp contrast to the vivid greenness of the farmland. From the interstate arteries shot capillary ramps, connecting them with veiny rural roads. These were interrupted sporadically with a meshy lung of suburbia. The circulation of traffic flowed in and out of the suburbs and passed identical houses row on row and concluded at their equally similar driveways.

At the end of one of these driveways sat a small boy. Leaning against the garage, he stared dreamily, almost mesmerized.

"Whatcha doin', son?" asked a middle-aged man straining with a large box as he passed the boy. "Ya like the new house?"

"It's okay. Sorta like our second house," said the boy. "I'm gonna go 'round back and look around, okay?"

"Yeah, just be back in about ten minutes. We've gotta get some fried chicken or something."

A thud sounded from within the house, followed by refrained cursing. The boy got up and slowly turned the corner of the garage past a small, un-attended garden. A bright blue bus passed behind him and a steamy sound appeared as its driver applied his air brakes, slowing for a corner. Startled at this new sound, the boy turned and watched the bus drive away. Scanning the dirty red bricks strewn randomly in his path, he resumed his exploration.

1

2

The back yard was small and weed infested. Dandelions had assumed rule over the grass, giving a thicker, more lumpy appearance to the lawn. A muttered "yuck" came from the boy, and he spun around towards the street. . . .

Instructor's Comments

The writer knows Steinbeck beginnings, the careful setting of the scene and mood. He pours on the biological references to parody the writer's naturalistic style, then comes down to earth with a character who speaks a down-home colloquial tongue. The modern Okie has joined suburbia. The short piece, contrasting nature and man-made, actually departs from parody and invites and intrigues us.

APPENDIXES

APPENDIX A
THE LIFE AND TIMES OF
JOHN STEINBECK

John Steinbeck	The Times

THE ASPIRING CALIFORNIAN, 1902-1934

1902

Born February 27 in Salinas, California, the third child of John Ernst and Olive Hamilton Steinbeck. His father was the county treasurer; his mother had been a school teacher.

Theodore Roosevelt's administration (1901-1909).

1911-1912

His Aunt Molly gives him a copy of Thomas Malory's *Morte d'Arthur;* his father gives him a chestnut pony.

U.S. population now around 92 million; *Titanic* disaster.

1919

President of senior class at Salinas High School. Graduates and begins irregular attendance at Stanford University.

Treaty of Versailles. Volstead Amendment. *Winesburg, Ohio* by Sherwood Anderson.

1924

"Adventures in Arcademy"—satirical piece published in Stanford *Spectator.*

How to Write Short Stories, Ring Lardner.

1925

Leaves Stanford without a degree. Visits sister in New York, works as assistant bricklayer on Madison Square Garden. Works as cub reporter for N.Y. *American.* Fails to find publisher for stories.

The Great Gatsby, Fitzgerald. Scopes Monkey Trial.

1926

Returns to California. Finishes first novel while a winter caretaker of a Lake Tahoe estate.

Byrd flies over North Pole. NBC is organized. *The Sun Also Rises,* Hemingway.

1927-1928

Works at Lake Tahoe City Hatchery where he meets Carol Henning. Moves to San Francisco to work on novel.

Charles Lindbergh flies from New York to Paris in *Spirit of St. Louis.*

1929

First novel—*Cup of Gold*—about Henry Morgan, a buccaneer from Wales; father offers John $25 a month so he can be a full-time writer.

Stock Market crash. William Faulkner, *The Sound and the Fury.* Hoover administration (1929-1933).

1930

Marries Carol Henning, moves to family cottage at Pacific Grove. Meets Ed Ricketts, a marine biologist and lifetime friend. Acquires a N.Y. literary agent: McIntosh and Otis.

U.S. population approaches 123 million. Sinclair Lewis, first U.S. writer to win Nobel Prize.

1931

Depressed by rejections, working on a manuscript called "Dissonant Symphony."

Ford's 20 millionth car.

1932

Pastures of Heaven, a short story collection built around one family. Moves to Los Angeles.

War veterans' bonus march on Washington. FDR pledges a "New Deal."

1933

To a God Unknown and first two parts of *The Red Pony.*

FDR's administration (1933–1945). Depression. CCC, TVA, NRA, AAA. Hitler, German Chancellor.

1934

Olive Hamilton Steinbeck dies. Short story "The Murder" wins O. Henry Prize.

Nationwide strikes. Dillinger shot by FBI.

THE CALIFORNIA CELEBRITY, 1935–1943

1935

Tortilla Flat, Steinbeck's first commercial success. After making $870 in seven years of writing, Steinbeck receives $4000 for film rights alone. Father John Ernst Steinbeck dies.

WPA. Wagner Act declares collective bargaining. *Waiting for Lefty,* Odets. WPA. Federal Writers project. Proletarian literature.

1936

In Dubious Battle, published and controversial. Buys new home in Los Gatos, California.

Spanish Civil War, Franco vs. Loyalists. REA. Sandburg's *The People, Yes.*

1937

Of Mice and Men (novel) published, while play version wins N.Y. Drama Critics' Circle Award. Travels with Okies from Oklahoma to California.

CIO sitdown strike. Japan invades China. Golden Gate Bridge dedicated.

1938

The Long Valley and fourth part of *Red Pony* published.

Pearl Buck wins Nobel Prize.

1939

The Grapes of Wrath. 500,000 sold of first edition. Elected to National Institute of Arts and Letters.

Regular transatlantic air service. World War II begins; Germany attacks Poland.

1940

Steinbeck and Ed Ricketts visit Gulf of California. *The Grapes of Wrath* wins Pulitzer. Film of *The Grapes of Wrath* big hit.

U.S. population 131 million. N.Y. World's Fair closes. Nazis bomb Britain.

1941

Sea of Cortez. Separates from Carol Steinbeck and moves to New York.

December 7, Japanese bomb Pearl Harbor. U.S. enters World War II.

1942

The Moon Is Down, novel published, play produced. Divorced from Carol, $200,000 settlement. Meets FDR.

U.S. Air Force bombs Europe, naval battles in Pacific.

THE NEW YORKER, 1943-1960

1943

Marries Gwyndolyn (Gwen) Conger. Visits war zone in Africa and Italy for N.Y. *Herald Tribune.*

General Eisenhower leads forces in Africa and Italy, then made Supreme Allied Commander in Europe.

1944

Film: *Lifeboat.* Son Thom born.

D-Day landing at Normandy.

1945

Cannery Row, The Red Pony in four parts published. Buys two brownstones on East 78th St. in New York City.

V-E, V-J Days. Atomic Age begins. UN Charter. Death of FDR. Truman administration (1945-1952).

1946

Son John born. Travels to Denmark.

Hiroshima, John Hersey. Atomic tests in Pacific.

1947

The Wayward Bus and *The Pearl* (book and film). Travels to Russia.

Marshall Plan, Truman Doctrine.

1948

A Russian Journal. Divorce from Gwen. Elected to American Academy of Arts and Letters. Returns to California. Death of Ed Ricketts.

Norman Mailer, *The Naked and the Dead.* Berlin Airlift.

1949

Film of *The Red Pony.* Steinbeck comes back to East Coast. Meets Elaine Scott.

U.S. signs NATO pact.

1950

Marries Elaine Scott. *Burning Bright*, novel and play. *Viva Zapata!*, film.

Korean War begins. McCarthy era.

1951

The Log from the Sea of Cortez.

J.D. Salinger, *Catcher in the Rye.*

1952

East of Eden. Correspondent in Europe for *Collier's.*

Eisenhower administration (1952-1960). Ralph Ellison, *Invisible Man.*

1953

Rents a cottage in Sag Harbor, Long Island. Works on a manuscript called *Bear Flag*—later to be called *Sweet Thursday.*

Korean War armistice.

1954

Sweet Thursday. Lives in Paris for nine months.

Supreme Court rules racial segregation unconstitutional.

1955

Broadway musical *Pipe Dream* flops. Buys home in Sag Harbor.

Faulkner's *A Fable* wins Pulitzer.

1956

Covers national political conventions for Louisville *Courier-Journal* and syndicate.

Israeli-Egyptian War.

1957

The Short Reign of Pippin IV. Steinbeck begins research on Malory and *Morte d'Arthur.*

Russia launches *Sputnik. On the Road,* Jack Kerouac.

1958

Once There Was a War.

Lolita, Nabokov.

1959

Spends most of a year in Bruton, Somerset, England, working on his version of Malory.

Kruschev visits the U.S. Cuban Revolution and Castro.

1960

Travels throughout the U.S. with his poodle Charley collecting material for a book.

U.S. population over 170 million. Nixon-Kennedy TV debate.

THE NOBEL WINNER AND DECLINE, 1961-1968

1961

Winter of Our Discontent, last novel. First heart attack, in Europe.

Kennedy administration (1961–1963).

1962

Travels with Charley. Wins Nobel Prize for Literature.

John Glenn first American in orbit. 5000 Americans in Viet Nam.

1963

Takes cultural exchange trip behind Iron Curtain with Edward Albee.

Kennedy assassinated in Dallas. Lyndon Johnson administration (1963–1968).

1964

Death of Steinbeck's editor and good friend, Pascal Covici. Trip to Ireland.

Rise of the Beatles.

1965

Trips to Israel and S.E. Asia for *Newsday.*

Malcolm X shot in New York City. *Keepers of the House* by Shirley Ann Grau wins Pulitzer.

1966

America and Americans.

U.S. bombs Hanoi. College protests.

1967

Steinbeck undergoes surgery for a spinal fusion.

Summer riots in 127 cities.

1968

John Steinbeck dies December 20 of a heart attack. His ashes are buried in Garden of Memories, Salinas, California.

1969

Journal of a Novel: The East of Eden Letters.

1975

Wife Elaine and Robert Wallsten edit *Steinbeck: A Life in Letters.*

1976

The Acts of King Arthur and His Noble Knights.

Robert Kennedy and Martin Luther King are assassinated. 550,000 in Viet Nam.

APPENDIX B
LETTER TO JOHN MURPHY/
KING ARTHUR

Sag Harbor
June 12, 1961

Dear John:

All my life has been aimed at one book and I haven't started it yet. The rest has all been practice. Do you remember the Arthurian legend well enough to raise in your mind the symbols of Launcelot and his son Galahad? You see, Launcelot was imperfect and so he never got to see the Holy Grail. So it is with all of us. The Grail is always one generation ahead of us. But it is there and so we can go on bearing sons who will bear sons who may see the Grail. This is a most profound set of symbols.

The setting down of words is only the final process. It is possible, through accident, that the words for my book may never be set down but I have been working and studying toward it for over forty years. Only the last of the process waits to be done—and it scares the hell out of me. Once the words go down—you are alone and committed. It's as final as a plea in court from which there is no retracting. That's the lonely time. Nine tenths of a writer's life do not admit of any companion nor friend nor associate. And until one makes peace with loneliness and accepts it as a part of the profession, as celibacy is a part of priesthood, until then there are times of dreadful dread. I am just as terrified of my next book as I was of my first. It doesn't get easier. It gets harder and more heartbreaking and finally, it must be that one must accept the failure which is the end of every writer's life no matter what stir he may have made. In himself he must fail as Launcelot failed—for the Grail is not a cup. It's a promise that skips ahead—it's a carrot on a stick and it never fails to draw us on. So it is that I would greatly prefer to die in the middle of a sentence in the middle of a book and so leave it as all life must be—unfinished. That's the law, the great law. Principles of notoriety or publicity or even public acceptance do not apply. Greatness is not shared by a man who is great. And by the same token—if he should want it—he can't possibly get near it.

Yours,
John

SOURCE: Steinbeck, Elaine, and Robert Wallsten, eds., *Steinbeck: A Life in Letters* (New York: Viking Press, 1975), p. 802.

APPENDIX C
IN SEARCH OF JOHN STEINBECK

Carmel, California is just a telephone call from Iowa City. But our American literature seminars at West High School knew that this was to be more than just a telephone call. This was an important last link in our search for John Steinbeck.

Actually it all began eight years ago when our English department offered an in-depth spring seminar on F. Scott Fitzgerald. The idea behind this elective for juniors and seniors was simple: we wanted to share with our students the satisfaction of knowing something well. And we knew that chronological exploration of a single author could provide an opening wedge to all of literature.

Of course, we knew that this class would be demanding. Students would be asked to write (and type!) seven position papers in twelve weeks. Every student would have to defend two of these papers before the entire class—papers based on one short story, three novels, 100 pages of biography or autobiography, a story or book of choice, and final summation. All this, plus classroom oral reading, discussion, films, and resource persons was pretty heavy stuff for high school students.

But by last spring, our experiment had grown to three sections. Two of them were on John Steinbeck. By late April, our students had read and discussed much of *The Long Valley* and *The Red Pony*, as well as written papers on "The Harness," *Tortilla Flat*, and *Of Mice and Men*. They knew their California map; they knew about Steinbeck's love of the King Arthur legends; they knew about his good friend Ed Ricketts. And now they were into *The Grapes of Wrath*, reviewing the Great Depression, and examining Steinbeck's letters that were collected by his wife Elaine and Robert Wallsten around 1975.

In fact, many of the seniors were already thinking about the fifth paper, the profile of Steinbeck. They were getting edgy with their research. Knowing how Steinbeck resisted biographers, they weren't satisfied with either Nelson Valjean's *John Steinbeck: The Errant Knight* or the more recent Thomas Kiernan's *The Intricate Music*. One of them expressed their dissatisfaction. "There are so many questions I'd like to ask him," he said. "His letters are really good, and yet I wish we could at least talk to somebody who knew him."

I sympathized. After all, the Hemingway seminar had made good use of our school's telephone interview kit last year when they called Papa's youngest son, Dr.

Gregory Hemingway, in Jordan, Montana. But I also knew how previous Steinbeck seminars had been politely refused by Elaine Steinbeck and Elizabeth Otis, the Nobel Prize winner's New York agent. Nevertheless, I had done some research myself and come up with another address.

"Shall we try Toby Street?" I asked.

So we did. Or rather, we first wrote to his law office in Monterey, California. He answered promptly: "I accept your invitation almost as a matter of course." Then we mailed him fourteen questions suggested by individual students and refined by consensus.

Finally, we reviewed what we knew about Toby Street: Mr. Webster F. Street, first met Steinbeck when they were students at Stanford in the early 1920s. Later, abandoned a literary career for law, even gave one of his plays to Steinbeck who turned it into the 1933 novel *To a God Unknown*. The author's lawyer and lifetime correspondent ("a very nice guy"), he still lived in Steinbeck country, his home in Carmel, his law office of Hudson, Martin, Ferrante & Street not far away. And his letter suggested that he was more than "alert": "Did it ever occur to you that Pepys must have known and talked to dozens of people who knew Shakespeare? And yet in all the thousands of words of his diary he speaks no word of any biographic significance about him."

By the time of our May 16 interview, the students had not only completed *The Grapes of Wrath* but also were in the last stages of their research about the life of Steinbeck. They had just completed Anecdote Day, a sharing of stories about the author. Naturally, they were excited when we gathered in a conference room of the West High library that Friday morning.

The interview began with a question that took Mr. Street back to the 1920s. Mary asked, "What attracted you to John Steinbeck and caused you to become a lifelong friend?" His answer was immediate. "Vitality!" he said. "John Steinbeck was a 'here person'—not wandering around in the woods." Toby Street went on to describe how they had shared similar interests in literature and writing. He said that Steinbeck was not satisfied with just completing a limiting degree program; instead, John was always reading, auditing classes, haunting the library, drawing out people.

When Seth and Pam and Van asked him questions based on their reading of biography and literary criticism, Toby Street sided with those skeptical seniors. Like them, he didn't buy Kiernan's theory about Steinbeck's childhood ugliness influencing his writing, nor was he impressed with biologist Ed Rickett's philosophical influence. He told Pam that he just couldn't see John in any of his fictional characters.

But when Seth asked about Steinbeck's personal tastes, he felt right at home. Cars: "John was always interested in how perfect a car could run, but not in how it looked." Dogs: "He always had a dog, but he had no feeling for fancy dogs." Food: "John was indifferent to food—not a gourmet." Music: "He seemed to like ballads, fifteenth-century music, but there was no definite lure for him." Sports: "Absolutely indifferent, except maybe for polo when he was young." Clothing: "Indifferent. He couldn't pick out clothes."

As Toby Street began to flesh in the man Steinbeck with these bits and pieces, he also was defining what we had discussed in class—the many fictional dogs, his knowledge of cars in *The Grapes of Wrath*, and his descriptive indifference to other subjects so common with authors. And for the next twenty minutes, this tying of life to literature continued:

In *The Grapes of Wrath*, Tom Joad says, "Well, maybe like Casy says, a fella ain't got a soul of his own, but on'y a piece of a big one."
Toby Street: Steinbeck came from devout ancestors, but he was not tied to one church.

In *Tortilla Flat*, the house of Danny and his poor paisano friends is said to be "Not unlike the Round Table."
Toby Street: John's favorite book was Malory's *Morte d'Arthur*. In fact, he never had a favorite of his own; he wouldn't discuss any of his books after they were published.

Why was Steinbeck so interested in subnormal characters like Lennie in *Of Mice and Men*?
Toby Street: Lennie may have been based on a man that John and I saw in a 1920s speakeasy in Castroville, a town near his home. But Lennie isn't so much subnormal as he is part of an idea that people like he and George can get trapped by society.

Near the end of the interview, the discussion shifted to Steinbeck and the public, then and now. Toby Street said, "John was a distinctly private person. He was so shy that he would even blush when he said something clever." Thus Steinbeck avoided public recognition. But when Debbie asked about how John's home town of Salinas felt about him, he laughed. "At first they regarded him as a scourge. They didn't like the publicity of his writing about the life of migrant workers near their town. But now they honor him." He then described how they had recently celebrated the Steinbeck postage stamp.

Though the students knew about Steinbeck's public acclaim—his Pulitzer and Nobel prizes, the plans now for a commemorative gold medal, they also knew about the censorship controversy in Iowa over *The Grapes of Wrath*. When the Iowa situation was described, Toby Street laughed, "Why don't they ban the *Iliad*?" Then he reflected, "I suppose a lot of school boards don't care too much for realism, and that makes it tough for teachers who are trying to give their pupils an overall view of anything."

Toby Street knew our last question. We had framed it just for him, though it posed the burden of reexamining over forty years of friendship with John Steinbeck: "Is there something you think we should know about Steinbeck?"

"Read everything you can. To understand him, read everything, even his 'turkeys'." Then he asked us a question, "Do you know anything in the English language that equals *Of Mice and Men*?"

APPENDIX D
ANECDOTES FROM
THE STEINBECK BIOGRAPHY

The following six anecdotes are included in this handbook to initiate the profile discussion. For those teachers and students who have difficulty locating reference materials in their school or community, these anecdotes are offered as models, resources, alternates for a large group discussion, or whatever seems most useful.

ANECDOTE 1

On June 3, 1928, John Steinbeck arrived for work at the Tahoe City fish hatchery in an ancient Dodge. He carried with him some battered luggage, a typewriter, and some manilla envelopes. The job only lasted for about three months, but his coworkers and associates never forgot him. They remembered that he had a sense of humor, liked girls, and was intent on becoming a successful writer.

His humor was noticed right away. Steinbeck began to joke about being a "midwife to a fish." He called himself "Dr. Steinbeck" and posted a sign: "PISCA-TORIAL OBSTETRICIAN." As for the girls, he worked them into his schedule when he wasn't writing. When he wasn't writing, he invited them up to his bachelor's cottage. One night a co-worker found him holding a young lady by her ankles as she hung downward from outside his upstairs window. Steinbeck just explained that he was trying to get her to be more friendly.

One of his friend's favorite stories is about the night he and a young man named Allan Pollett had gone on a double date. As they drove along, John would engage in some passionate love-making, then stop and write on a memo pad. When his female companion asked him what he was doing, he said, "Some day I'll sort out these memos and write another book." Then the girl asked, "You mean, you get ideas for a book when you're—well, when you're making love?" "That's right," said Steinbeck. [Source: Nelson Valjean, *John Steinbeck: The Errant Knight,* pp. 111–113.]

ANECDOTE 2

When John Steinbeck was nine years old, his Aunt Molly gave him a copy of *Morte d'Arthur* by Sir Thomas Malory. Although the book was written in fifteenth-century Middle English, young Steinbeck was fascinated by the legend of King Arthur and his Round Table. This fascination lasted for a lifetime.

Though Steinbeck's famous novels of the Great Depression in California seem a long way from the tales of Launcelot and Guinevere, *Tortilla Flat* (1935) opens on page one with mention of the Round Table. Steinbeck, the so-called realist, was intrigued by the stories of myth, and pride, and even victory. He felt that the modern world was a world of loss—of heroes, gods, and authority. This affection for the ancient past kept him reading and rereading the Arthurian legends, consulting scholars, and even naming his Sag Harbor, Long Island work-house his "Joyous Garde," a reference to the castle where Launcelot took Guinevere.

In 1959, Steinbeck and his wife Elaine spent nearly a year in Somerset, England, trying to write his version of Malory while living in the middle of Arthurian country. By 1961, he confessed that he might never achieve his goal of a book about King Arthur. In a letter to a friend, Steinbeck summarized his own forty-year quest: "All my life has been aimed at one book . . . The rest is practice. The Grail is always one generation ahead of us . . . the Grail is not a cup. It's a promise that skips ahead —it's a carrot on a stick and it never fails to draw us on. So it is that I would greatly prefer to die in the middle of a sentence in the middle of a book and so leave it as all life must be—unfinished."

John Steinbeck never wrote that book. [Source: Elaine Steinbeck and Robert Wallsten, eds., *Steinbeck: A Life in Letters,* pp. 740–741, 802.]

ANECDOTE 3

After a long dry spell of rejection slips and books that made no financial or literary dent, John Steinbeck and his wife began to have even more troubles. Added to his bleak outlook was the poor health of his parents which troubled him as he was trying to write. Then he got an idea for a short amusing book about some California paisanos. Though he thought the book light, even second-rate, the writing went like wildfire which took his mind from his worries. He wrote a friend about how he felt: "I need something to help me over this last ditch. Our house is crumbling rapidly and when it is gone there will be nothing left. . . ."

When the new book, *Tortilla Flat* was issued in 1935, Steinbeck discovered that his story of Danny and his friends and his two houses pleased both the public and the critics. He was making so much money and the readers were making such a fuss that he became frightened by his sudden popularity. He and his wife Carol decided to escape to Mexico for a vacation around the time they heard that Hollywood was interested in the novel. They piled into their old Ford and headed south.

In September, his agent wired Steinbeck in Mexico that the movie rights for *Tortilla Flat* would earn him $4000, a lot of money in 1935. Steinbeck was delighted with the telegram, especially how it affected the local telegraph operator. He replied to his agent: "It is rather amusing what the Mexican operator must have thought of your wire. '$4000 dollars for Tortilla.' Probably thought it was either a code word or a race horse." [Source: Elaine Steinbeck and Robert Wallsten, eds., *Steinbeck: A Life in Letters*, pp. 83, 104, 105, 108.]

ANECDOTE 4

The Grapes of Wrath (1939), the novel about the Oklahoma Joads who came to California in search of the Promised Land, did not just win Steinbeck the Pulitzer Prize. The best-seller also won him a great deal of controversy. He discovered that the book he thought not too many people would read was literary dynamite.

While he was doing his research in the migrant camps and then searching for a title (later suggested by his first wife Carol), Steinbeck believed that the long novel would not be popular. But when his Viking Press editors read the book, they were emotionally exhausted and wrote him of its greatness. After publication, Steinbeck and his agent received a flow of money, hundreds of telegrams and telephone calls of congratulation (and pleas for money), and an offer to write Hollywood scripts at $5000 a week.

The Grapes of Wrath with its story of economic and social injustice made the California Associated Farmers hopping mad. Then things got rough. The undersheriff of Santa Clara County warned Steinbeck that he should not be alone in a hotel room, that he should keep records of his travels when not on his Los Gatos ranch, and that he must travel with one or two friends.

Steinbeck was curious about why he must not be in a hotel room alone. His friend said, "Maybe I'm sticking my neck out but the boys got a rape case set up for you. You get alone in a hotel and a dame will come in, tear off her clothes, scratch her face and scream and you try to talk yourself out of that one. They won't touch your book but there's easier ways." [Source: Elaine Steinbeck and Robert Wallsten, eds., *Steinbeck: A Life in Letters*, pp. 165, 171, 175.]

ANECDOTE 5

John Steinbeck was a loving father to his two sons, John IV and Thom. He also was a great letter writer. Each morning, he would warm up for the day's writing by sending a letter or two to friends, relatives, or his New York agent. His letters were always personal, concrete, and affectionate. Often they were very amusing, especially when he wrote his boys.

On November 6, 1958, the father wrote John IV, who was in prep school. The letter, which was in response to one sent by his son, illustrates Steinbeck the man, the writer, and especially the father:

Dear Cat,

Of course I was terribly pleased to get your last letter and to hear that you had the second highest mark in 'Bugby.' I didn't even know you were taking it. It sounds fascinating. That and your triumph in mathematics seem to have set your handwriting back a little bit, but we can't have everything. I have often told you that spelling was fairly unimportant, except that sometimes it can be a little confusing. You said, for instance, that the 'wether' up there is cold. A wether is a castrated sheep and I'm sorry he's cold but there is nothing I can do about it from here. I am also sorry that I will not see your crew cut in full flower, but maybe it will be rather pretty when it leafs out. . . . [signed] Fa

[Source: Elaine Steinbeck and Robert Wallsten, eds., *Steinbeck: A Life in Letters*, pp. 563-564.]

ANECDOTE 6

John Steinbeck learned that he had won the 1962 Nobel Prize for literature while he was watching television. He had turned on the set one morning during the tense period of the Cuban missile crisis. His first reaction was disbelief. Then he had a cup of coffee.

Winning the Nobel Prize proved to be "a monster in some ways." Congratulatory messages—from four to five hundred each day—poured in and Steinbeck felt it imperative to answer each one. When he took a short trip to New York City, he was besieged by seventy-five news reporters and photographers. Then too, he began to have fears about writing and giving an acceptance speech. Largely a private man, Steinbeck asked his good friend Adlai Stevenson for advice, confessing that he was "literally scared to death."

However, when Steinbeck reached Stockholm, everything went well, especially his acceptance speech. Yet, the author soon reflected that the Nobel Prize was something like the kiss of death. He noted that Sinclair Lewis, Ernest Hemingway, and William Faulkner had produced little of merit after they won their prizes. He also was aware that many American critics were not excited that he had won the award. *Time* magazine didn't even give him a cover story. Steinbeck knew that now returning to the kind of anonymous life that he preferred as a writer was an immense problem. And indeed his last years were largely unproductive. [Source: *Stars & Stripes*, 8 November 1962, p. 11; Elaine Steinbeck and Robert Wallsten, eds., *Steinbeck: A Life in Letters*, pp. 694-711.]

APPENDIX E
NOTE TO FRIENDS

Travels with Charley

Dear Sylvia and Lennie—
        I have a
great idea. My next book will
be printed on potato pancakes.
You read a page and eat
it. No lending. Dam pen
went dry. This invention
would change the whole
face of publishing. Then
the critics would have a
whole new approach. Time
magazine. "The so called
novel Dorstine by J. Steinbeck
is wordy, stupid flaccid, greasy
and undercooked."
        Love to you both
            John Steinbeck

SOURCE: Signed cover of first edition, now owned by Dr. Robert E. Rakel, Iowa City, Iowa.

APPENDIX F

TO A MOUSE

*On Turning Her Up in Her Nest
With the Plough, November, 1785*

Wee, sleekit, cow'rin', tim'rous beastie,
O what a panic's in thy breastie!
Thou need na start awa sae hasty,
        Wi' bickering brattle!
I wad be laith to rin an' chase thee
        Wi' murd'ring pattle!

I'm truly sorry man's dominion
Has broken Nature's social union,
An' justifies that ill opinion
        Which makes thee startle
At me, thy poor earth-born companion,
        An' fellow-mortal!

I doubt na, whiles, but thou may thieve;
What then? poor beastie, thou maun live!
A daimen-icker in a thrave
        'S a sma' request:
I'll get a blessin' wi' the lave,
        And never miss 't!

Thy wee bit housie, too, in ruin!
Its silly wa's the win's are strewin'!
An' naething, now, to big a new ane,
        O' foggage green!
An' bleak December's winds ensuin'
        Baith snell an' keen!

Thou saw the fields laid bare and waste.
An' weary winter comin' fast,
An' cozie here, beneath the blast,
        Thou thought to dwell,
Till crash! the cruel coulter past
        Out-thro' thy cell.

That wee bit heap o' leaves an' stibble
Has cost thee mony a weary nibble!
Now thou's turn'd out, for a' thy trouble,
        But house or hald,
To thole the winter's sleety dribble,
        An' cranreuch cauld!

But, Mousie, thou art no thy lane,
In proving foresight may be vain:
The best laid schemes o' mice an' men
        Gang aft a-gley,
An' lea'e us nought but grief an' pain
        For promis'd joy.

Still thou art blest compar'd wi' me!
The present only toucheth thee:
But oh! I backward cast my e'e
        On prospects drear!
An' forward tho' I canna see,
        I guess an' fear!

Robert Burns (1759–1796)

314

APPENDIX G

HANDOUT
SEMINAR EVALUATION

1. When you first began this course, what did you think it would be about?

2. Now that you have finished taking this course, how would you describe it to students who are interested in taking it?

3. This course has been described as a *process* course, not just a course about a single author. Do you agree with this statement? If you do, explain what this means for students beginning the course.

4. What did you enjoy *most* in this course?

5. What did you enjoy *least* in this course?

6. Write any suggestions or comments that would be useful to the instructor and to students who may take a course of this nature in the future.

APPENDIX H
TWELVE WEEK TRIMESTER/
SIXTY DAY SCHEDULE

TENTATIVE SCHEDULE FOR SEMINAR IN AMERICAN LITERATURE: JOHN STEINBECK

Orientation to the Seminar
Day 1.   Getting acquainted with the course and each other
Day 2.   Introducing Steinbeck and the Position Paper

Paper I: "The Harness" (1938)
Day 3.   Reading aloud and discussion of "The Chrysanthemums"
         ASSIGNMENT: Position Paper on "The Harness"
         Due: _____
Day 4.   Teacher Reading of "The White Quail" (1935)
Day 5.   Reading aloud and discussion of "The Snake" (1935)
Day 6.   Suggestions for Position Paper and in-class writing
Day 7.   In-class writing
Day 8.   Reading aloud and discussion of *The Red Pony*
Day 9.   Reading aloud and discussion of *The Red Pony*
Day 10. Reading aloud or film

Paper II: *Tortilla Flat* (1935)
Day 11. Position Paper on "The Harness" due; introduction to *Tortilla Flat*
         ASSIGNMENT: Position Paper on *Tortilla Flat*
         Due: _____
Day 12. Reading
Day 13. Discussion: Thomas Malory and Ed Ricketts
Day 14. Reading
Day 15. Reading and/or distribution of Defense Day papers
Day 16. Defense Day
Day 17. The prewriting process
Day 18. Writing
Day 19. Reading aloud of "Tularecito" (1932)
Day 20. Teaching reading and discussion of "Johnny Bear" (1937)

Paper III: *Of Mice and Men* (1937)
Day 21. Position Paper on *Tortilla Flat* due; introduction to *Of Mice and Men*
         ASSIGNMENT: Position Paper on *Of Mice and Men*
         Due: _____
Day 22. Reading
Day 23. Review and instruction: transitions and sentence variety
Day 24. Suggestions for Position Papers and distribution of papers for Defense Day
Day 25. Defense Day

Day 26.   Writing or reading of the play version
Day 27.   Writing; discussion of *Roget's Thesaurus*
Day 28.   Writing and discussion/in-class reading of "Breakfast" (1938)

Paper IV: *The Grapes of Wrath* (1939)

Day 29.   Position Papers on *Of Mice and Men* due; introduction to *The Grapes of Wrath*
ASSIGNMENT: Position Paper on *The Grapes of Wrath*
Due: _____
Day 30.   Reading
Day 31.   Reading
Day 32.   Examining the geography of the novel; review of the Great Depression
Day 33.   Audio-visual material about the 1930s
Day 34.   Reading and distribution of Defense Day papers
Day 35.   Defense Day
Day 36.   Reading
Day 37.   Suggestions for Position Papers; discussion of Pulitzer Prize and Phalanx theory
Day 38.   Reading and writing
Day 39.   Writing
Day 40.   Writing

Paper V: A Profile of John Steinbeck

Day 41.   Position Paper on *The Grapes of Wrath* due; review of Steinbeck biography
Suggestions for paper. ASSIGNMENT: Profile Paper on John Steinbeck
Due: _____
Day 42.   Reading and research; reviewing Steinbeck with A-V materials
Day 43.   Reading and research
Day 44.   Anecdote Day
Day 45.   Discussion of documentation skills; distribution of Defense Day papers
Day 46.   Defense Day
Day 47.   Defense Day
Day 48.   Writing

Paper VI: Paper of Choice

Day 49.   Position Paper on Profile due; consideration of choices and suggestions
ASSIGNMENT: Position Paper on a Steinbeck work of a student's choice
Due: _____
Day 50.   Reading
Day 51.   Discussion of Writing Skill and John Steinbeck and the Nobel Prize
Day 52.   Reading and writing; distribution of Defense Day papers
Day 53.   Defense Day
Day 54.   Writing

Paper VII: The Summing Up

Day 55.   Position Paper of Choice due; suggestions for final paper
ASSIGNMENT: A summation or creative paper on Steinbeck and the seminar
Due: _____
Day 56.   Writing
Day 57.   Writing and distribution of papers for Defense Day
Day 58.   Defense Day
Day 59.   Reading final papers aloud
Day 60.   Reading final papers aloud. Final discussion and evaluation.

BIBLIOGRAPHY

BASIC MATERIALS FOR STARTING A SEMINAR

Of course, the school budget determines the quantity of materials. If there is no budget, materials can be obtained from many sources: school and public libraries; student, teacher, or classroom copies; American literature textbooks.

Class sets of paperbacks do provide smoother instruction. In addition to the handouts suggested in this book, the following materials are recommended for starting a Steinbeck seminar:

The Portable Steinbeck. Penguin, 1971. This paperback, edited for Viking by Pascal Covici, includes "The Harness," "Chrysanthemums," "The Snake," "Flight," "Tularecito," *Of Mice and Men, The Red Pony*, "Breakfast," "Knowing Ed Ricketts," "Nobel Prize Acceptance Speech"—and cuttings from other works.

Tortilla Flat. Penguin, 1977.

The Grapes of Wrath. Penguin, 1976.

Besides class sets, the instructor should build a room library of Steinbeck works (see Bibliography entry: "Checklist of Major Primary Sources"), as well as multiple copies of Elaine Steinbeck and Robert Wallsten, eds., *Steinbeck: A Life in Letters* (Penguin, 1976). Note handout references to that source refer to the hardback edition, Viking, 1975. Since there are scanty biographical and autobiographical resources, you may also wish more than one copy of the following titles:

French, Warren. *John Steinbeck*. New Haven: College and University Press, 1961.

Kiernan, Thomas. *The Intricate Music: A Biography of John Steinbeck*. Boston: Little, Brown, 1979.

Lisca, Peter. *The Wide World of John Steinbeck*. New Brunswick, N.J., 1958.

O'Connor, Richard. *John Steinbeck*. New York: Mc-Graw-Hill, 1970.

Steinbeck, John. *Journey of a Novel: The East of Eden Letters*. New York: Viking, 1969.

Steinbeck, John. *The Log from the Sea of Cortez*. New York: Viking, 1951.

Steinbeck, John. *Travels with Charley*. New York: Viking, 1962.

Tedlock, E. W., Jr., and Wicker, C. V. *Steinbeck and His Critics*. Albuquerque, N.M.: The University of New Mexico Press, 1957.

Valjean, Nelson. *John Steinbeck: The Errant Knight*. San Francisco: Chronicle Books, 1975.

A major resource for Steinbeck scholarship is the John Steinbeck Collection at Stanford University. The Steinbeck Collection *Catalogue*, prepared by Susan Rigg, is available from the Stanford University Libraries.

Audio-visual materials can be obtained from loan libraries, but at least one of the following should be considered for purchase:

Steinbeck's America. [2 filmstrips, 2 cassettes]. Educational Dimensions, P.O. Box 126, Stamford, CT 06094.

Grapes of Wrath and the 1930s. [Filmstrip]. Educational Audio-Visual, Inc., Pleasantville, N.Y. 10570, 1972.

John Steinbeck. [Filmstrip]. The American Experience in Literature: Five Modern Novelists. Series No. 6911K. Encyclopaedia Britannica Educational Corporation, 1975, with cassette.

VALUABLE BOOKS: BIOGRAPHY AND CRITICISM

Allen, Walter. *The Modern Novel*. New York: E.P. Dutton and Co., 1965.

Astro, Richard. *John Steinbeck and Edward F. Ricketts: The Shaping of a Novelist*. Minneapolis: University of Minnesota Press, 1973.

Astro, Richard, and Hayashi, Tetsumaro, eds. *Steinbeck: The Man and His Work*. Corvallis: Oregon State University Press, 1971.

Davis, Robert Murray, ed. *Steinbeck: A Collection of Critical Essays*. Englewood Cliffs, N.J.: Prentice-Hall, Inc., 1972.

Donahue, Agnes, ed. *A Casebook on The Grapes of Wrath*. New York: Viking, 1963.

Fensch, Thomas, ed. *Steinbeck and Covici: The Story of a Friendship*. Middlebury, Vermont: P.S. Eriksson, 1979.

Fontenrose, Joseph Eddy. *John Steinbeck: An Introduction and Interpretation.* New York: Barnes and Noble, 1963.

French, Warren, ed. *A Companion to The Grapes of Wrath.* New York: Viking, 1963.

French, Warren, and Kidd, Walter E. *American Winners of the Nobel Literary Prize.* Norman: University of Oklahoma Press, 1968.

Gray, James. *John Steinbeck.* Minneapolis: University of Minnesota Press, 1971.

Hayashi, Tetsumaro, ed. *John Steinbeck: A Dictionary of His Fictional Characters.* Metuchen, N.J.: Scarecrow Press, 1976.

Hayashi, Tetsumaro, ed. *Steinbeck's Travel Literature: Essays in Criticism.* Muncie, Indiana: Ball State University Press, 1980.

Hayashi, Tetsumaro, ed. *Study Guide to Steinbeck: A Handbook of His Major Works.* Metuchen, N.J.: Scarecrow Press, 1974.

Leggett, John. *Ross and Tom: Two American Tragedies.* New York: Simon and Schuster, 1974.

Levant, Howard. *The Novels of John Steinbeck.* Columbia: University of Missouri Press, 1975.

Moore, Harry T. *The Novels of John Steinbeck: A First Critical Study.* Chicago: Normandie House, 1939.

Schmitz, Anne-Marie. *In Search of Steinbeck.* Los Altos, California: Hermes Publications, 1978.

Steinbeck IV, John. *In Touch.* New York: Knopf, 1961.

Stuckey, W. J. *The Pulitzer Prize Novels.* Norman: University of Oklahoma Press, 1966.

Watt, I. W. *John Steinbeck.* New York: Grove, 1962.

Wilson, Edmund. *The Boys in the Back Room.* San Francisco: Colt Press, 1941.

ARTICLES AND ESSAYS: BIOGRAPHY AND CRITICISM

Carpenter, F. I. "John Steinbeck: American Dreamer." *Southwest Review* 26 (1941):454-467.

Champney, Freeman. "Critics in Search of an Author." *Antioch Review* 18 (Fall 1958):371-375.

"February Is Steinbeck Month in Steinbeck Country," *Sunset* 162 (February 1979):44-45.

Frazier, George. "John Steinbeck! John Steinbeck! How Still We See Thee Lie." *Esquire* (November 1969):150-151.

Frohock, W. M. "John Steinbeck—The Utility of Wrath." In *The Novel of Violence in America,* pp. 124-142. Dallas: Southern Methodist University Press, 1958.

Gannett, Lewis. "John Steinbeck: Novelist at Work." *Atlantic Monthly* (December 1945):55-60.

Geismar, Maxwell. "John Steinbeck: Of Wrath of Joy." In *Writers in Crisis, The American Novel, 1925-1940,* pp. 237-270. Boston: Houghton Mifflin, 1942.

Grommon, Alfred H. "Who Is 'The Leader of the People'?" *English Journal* 48 (November 1959):449-461, 476.

Kazin, Alfred. *On Native Grounds.* New York: Doubleday Anchor Books, 1956, 304-310.

Kennedy, John S. "John Steinbeck: Life Affirmed and Dissolved." In *Fifty Years of the American Novel,* edited by H. C. Gardiner. New York: Scribner's, 1951.

Lewis, R. W. B. "John Steinbeck: The Fitful Daemon." In *The Young Rebel in American Literature,* edited by Carl Bode. New York: Praeger, 1960.

Rascoe, Burton. "Excuse It, Please." *Newsweek,* 1 May 1939, p. 38. [An attack on the inaccuracies of *The Grapes of Wrath.*]

Richards, Edmund C. "The Challenge of John Steinbeck." *North American Review* 243 (Summer 1937): 406-413.

Shaw, Peter. "Steinbeck: The Shape of a Career." *Saturday Review* (8 February 1969):10-4, 50-51.

"Steinbeck: Critical Thorns and a Nobel Laurel." *Time* (5 November 1962):65. [Typical of the negative reactions to Steinbeck's Nobel Prize.]

Steinbeck, John. "Always Something to Do in Salinas." *Holiday* (March 1976):28, 65.

Steinbeck, John. "A Plea to Teachers." *Saturday Review* 37 (30 April 1955):24.

Steinbeck, John. "How to Tell the Good Guys from Bad Guys." *The Reporter* 12 (10 March 1955):42-44.

Steinbeck, John. "I Go Back to Ireland." *Collier's* 131 (21 January 1953):48-50.

Taylor, Walter Fuller. *"The Grapes of Wrath* Reconsidered." *Mississippi Quarterly* 12 (Summer 1959): 136-144. [Discusses shortcoming of the novel from a conservative Christian viewpoint.]

Weeks, Donald. "Steinbeck Against Steinbeck." *Pacific Spectator* 1 (Autumn 1947):447-457. [Critical of Steinbeck's sentimentality.]

Whipple, T. K. "Steinbeck: Through a Glass Brightly." In *Study Out the Land.* Berkeley: University of California Press, 1943.

Wilson, Edmund. "The Boys in the Backroom." In *Classics and Commercials,* pp. 35-45. New York: Farrar, Straus, 1950.

BOOKLIST: CHECKLIST OF MAJOR PRIMARY SOURCES

Cup of Gold: A Life of Henry Morgan, Buccaneer. New York: Robert M. McBride & Co., 1929.

The Pastures of Heaven. New York: Brewer, Warren & Putnam, 1932.

To a God Unknown. New York: Robert O. Ballou, 1933.

Tortilla Flat. New York: Covici, Friede, 1935.

In Dubious Battle. New York: Covici, Friede, 1936.

"St. Katy, the Virgin" (short story). New York: Covici, Friede, 1936.

Of Mice and Men (novel). New York: Covici, Friede, 1937.

Of Mice and Men (play). New York: Covici, Friede, 1937.

The Red Pony. New York: Covici, Friede, 1937.

The Long Valley. New York: Viking Press, 1938.

The Grapes of Wrath. New York: Viking Press, 1939.

The Forgotten Village (with Ed Ricketts). New York: Viking Press, 1941.

Sea of Cortez. New York: Viking Press, 1941. [Reissued in 1951 with "About Ed Ricketts" as *The Log from the Sea of Cortez.*]

Bombs Away: The Story of a Bomber Team. New York: Viking Press, 1942.

The Moon Is Down. New York: Viking Press, 1942.

Cannery Row. New York: Viking Press, 1945.

The Wayward Bus. New York: Viking Press, 1947.

The Pearl. New York: Viking Press, 1947.

A Russian Journal. New York: Viking Press, 1948.

Burning Bright. New York: Viking Press, 1950.

East of Eden. New York: Viking Press, 1952.

Sweet Thursday. New York: Viking Press, 1954.

The Short Reign of Pippin IV. New York: Viking Press, 1957.

Once There Was a War. New York: Viking Press, 1958.

The Winter of Our Discontent. New York: Viking Press, 1961.

Travels with Charley. New York: Viking Press, 1962.

America and Americans. New York: Viking Press, 1966.

Posthumous Publications

Journal of a Novel: The East of Eden Letters. New York: Viking Press, 1969.

Steinbeck: A Life in Letters, edited by Elaine Steinbeck and Robert Wallsten. New York: Viking Press, 1975.

The Acts of King Arthur and His Noble Knights. New York: Viking Press, 1976.

SCRIPTS, PLAYS, MUSICALS

Of Mice and Men: A Play in Three Acts. New York: Covici, Friede, 1937.

The Forgotten Village [film script]. New York: Viking Press, 1941.

The Moon Is Down: A Play in Two Parts. New York: Viking Press, 1943.

"A Medal for Benny" in *Best Film Plays—1945,* edited by John Gassner and Dudley Nichols. New York: Crown, 1946.

Burning Bright [acting edition], Dramatic Play Service, 1951.

Viva Zapata [film script], abridged in *Argosy,* February, 1952.

Pipe Dream. New York: Viking Press, 1954. [Steinbeck worked with director on this 1955 musical version of *Sweet Thursday.*]

EDUCATIONAL FILMS

America and Americans. McGraw-Hill. 52 min., color.

Life in the Thirties. NBC. 52 min., b/w.

The Dust Bowl. National Science. 23 min.

The Great American Novel: The Grapes of Wrath. BFA Educational Media. 25 min., color.

The Land. National Audio Visual Center, 1941. 44 min., b/w. [This film portrays the grim agricultural life of the 1930s, accenting eroded farms, unemployment, migrants.]

The Okies—Uprooted Farmers. Films, Inc. 24 min., b/w. [This film includes cuttings from the 1940 film of *The Grapes of Wrath.*]

The Red Pony. Phoenix. 101 min., color. [This film version, made in 1973, stars an aging Henry Fonda. Teachers should be warned that this film does some interesting distorting of the Steinbeck work.]

FILMSTRIP-RECORD/CASSETTES

John Steinbeck [Filmstrip]. Educational Dimensions Corporation, 707, 1 full color sound filmstrip, 15 minutes, LP or cassette. Reviews his life during the most fruitful period, the 1930s. For information, write Educational Dimensions Corporation, Box 488, Great Neck, NY 11022.

John Steinbeck: Antaeus East of Eden [Filmstrip]. Listening Library, Inc. N 155 CFX, with cassette. Emphasis on Steinbeck country, *Cannery Row* to the *Long Valley,* quotations from letters and speeches.

Of Mice and Men [Filmstrip]. Listening Library, Inc. N 149-1 CFX includes three rolls/cassette/book and uses the Hollywood film. N 150 CFX is one filmstrip with cassette, analyzes the novel.

The Grapes of Wrath [Filmstrip]. Films Incorporated, MovieStrip Division. Three filmstrips with cassettes, 40 minutes, summarizes the plot, discusses Depression, explores Ma Joad. Write: Films Incorporated, 1144 Wilmette Ave., Wilmette, IL 60091.

The Pearl [Filmstrip]. Listening Library, Inc. N 152 CFX includes three rolls and cassettes, using the Hollywood film. N 153 CFX has one roll and cassette and analyzes the novel.

The Red Pony [Filmstrip]. Listening Library, Inc. N 147-1 CFX includes three rolls and cassettes and uses the film version. N 148 CFX has one roll/cassette and analyzes the novel.

RECORDS AND CASSETTES

The only commercial recording of Steinbeck reading is now out of print. On this single Columbia (ML-4756) disc, he reads "The Snake" and "Johnny Bear." Check local libraries or university library for copies.

John Steinbeck: The Grapes of Wrath. A reading by Henry Fonda, Caedmon, 1995 Broadway, New York, NY 10023. LP or cassette.

John Steinbeck: The Red Pony. A reading by Eli Wallach, Caedmon, LP/cassette.

The Twentieth Century American Novel. A Listening Library series with lectures by professors of literature. *The Grapes of Wrath* discussed by Warren French. Cassette. *Of Mice and Men* discussed by Warren French. Cassette.

The Grapes of Wrath. LP (N 145 R) or cassette (N 145 CX). Listening Library, Inc. Henry Fonda reading.

The Red Pony. LP (N 147 R) or cassette (N 147 CX). Listening Library, Inc. Eli Wallach reading.

For information on above listings, write Listening Library, Inc., 1 Park Avenue, Old Greenwich, CT 06870.

PICTURES AND POSTERS

John Steinbeck [Poster]. Eight Masters of Modern Fiction series. Includes Fitzgerald, Hemingway, Wolfe, Baldwin, Salinger, McCullers, Faulkner, and Steinbeck. Scholastic Book Services, set of 8 pictures, 15 x 20 in. For information, write Scholastic Book Services, 50 West 44th Street, New York, NY 10036.

John Steinbeck [Posters, Jumbo Crossword Puzzle Posters, Perma-Notes, Muralettes]. Write Perfection Form Company, 1000 North Second Avenue, Logan, IA 51546.

John Steinbeck [Pictures]. 8½ x 11 in. SN95979. Perfection Form Company.

HOLLYWOOD FILMS

Most of the Hollywood films of Steinbeck's writing are still available through loan libraries. Check with your A-V director for catalogs and prices. Also check with your local city or university libraries.

Of Mice and Men. 1939, United Artists. Lon Chaney, Jr. (Lennie); Burgess Meredith (George); music by Aaron Copland. Director: Frank Ross. B/W, 107 minutes.

Grapes of Wrath. 1940, Twentieth Century-Fox. Henry Fonda (Tom Joad); Jane Darwell (Ma); John Carradine (Casy). Director: John Ford. B/W, 129 minutes.

Forgotten Village. 1941, MGM. Director: Herbert Kline. B/W.

Tortilla Flat. 1942, MGM. Spencer Tracy (Pilon); John Garfield (Danny); Hedy Lamarr (Dolores). Director: Victory Fleming. B/W, 105 minutes.

The Moon Is Down. 1943, Twentieth Century-Fox. Lee J. Cobb (Dr. Winter); Sir Cedric Hardwicke (Col. Lanser); Henry Travers (Mayor Orden). Director: Irving Pichel. B/W, 90 minutes.

Lifeboat. 1944, Twentieth Century-Fox. Tallulah Bankhead (Connie Porter); William Bendix (Gus); Walter Slezák (The German). Director: Alfred Hitchcock. B/W, 96 minutes.

A Medal for Benny. 1945, Paramount. Dorothy Lamour (Lolita Sierra); J. Carrol Nash (Charley Martini). Director: Irving Pichel. B/W.

The Pearl. 1948, RKO. Pedro Armendariz (Kino); Maria Elena Marques (Juana). Director: Emilio Fernandez. B/W, 77 minutes.

The Red Pony. 1949, Republic. Robert Mitchum (Billy Buck); Peter Miles (Tom); Sheppard Strudwick (Fred Tiflin); Myrna Loy (Alice Tiflin). Director: Lewis Mileston. Color, 89 minutes.

Viva Zapata! 1952, Twentieth Century-Fox. Marlon Brando (Zapata); Jean Peters (Josefa); Anthony Quinn (Eufemio). Director: Elia Kazan. B/W, 113 minutes.

East of Eden. 1955, Warner Brothers. James Dean (Cal); Julie Harris (Abra); Raymond Massey (Adam). Director: Elia Kazan. Color, 73 minutes.

The Wayward Bus. 1957, Twentieth Century-Fox. Joan Collins (Alice); Jayne Mansfield (Camille); Dan Dailey (Ernest Horton). Director: Victor Vicas. B/W, 89 minutes.

AUTHOR

Brooke Workman is Instructor of English and Humanities and a supervisor of student teachers at West High School, Iowa City, Iowa. He has had over twenty years of experience in the teaching of English at the junior high and high school levels. His publications include numerous journal articles and book reviews and *Teaching the Decades: A Humanities Approach to American Civilization* (NCTE, 1975). Workman holds a Ph.D. in American Civilization from the University of Iowa.